"This sweeping overview of liturgical history is useful for both the novice and the expert. Every chapter is carefully written, deeply researched, and cogently synthesized. The organization of material provides readers with a useful framework for further expanding their knowledge. A highly recommended resource for those seeking to grasp not only the multiple origins of Christian worship but also the complexity of traditions as they continue to develop today."

—**Gerardo Martí**, Davidson College; author of *Worship across the Racial Divide: Religious Music and the Multiracial Congregation*

"The second volume of this much-needed series is a *lively* historical read. It engages the reader in a manner that leads them to know many new things about the ways in which God works through his gathered assemblies and, by so doing, invites the reader to know even more about their ecclesial neighbors. As we receive the witness of those whom God has been shaping through the ages, we are given the gift to hear and see our Christian sisters and brothers, not in competition, or with disdainful theological critique, but as those who live within the splendor of our Lord's continual prayer that 'all may be one.' *Historical Foundations of Worship* will serve the whole *oikumenē* in the way that rocks in a tumbler bring out each other's radiance, so that in a unity of spirit, we will seek to join together in the psalmist's doxological imperative to 'worship the Lord in the beauty of holiness.'"

—**Amy C. Schifrin**, president emeritus, North American Lutheran Seminary

"This collection offers an admirable and engaging introduction for the student navigating a way into liturgical studies, and it is a comprehensive guide for anyone responsible for overseeing that journey. The contributors have brought scholarly depth as well as a lively sense of the practice of worship to their readers. They write with animation and understand the virtues of conciseness and reading lists that encourage further study rather than inducing dismay. It is particularly good to see chapters on the Anabaptist, Pentecostal, and evangelical traditions joining the 'mainstream' Eastern Orthodox, Roman Catholic, and Protestant families in one volume."

—**Bridget Nichols**, Church of Ireland Theological Institute, Dublin

# Historical
# Foundations
# of Worship

# Worship Foundations

*How Theology, History, and Culture
Inform Our Worship Practice*

**Series Editors:** Melanie C. Ross and Mark A. Lamport

# Historical Foundations of Worship

*Catholic, Orthodox, and Protestant Perspectives*

**Edited by**
**Melanie C. Ross and Mark A. Lamport**

Introductions by
NICHOLAS WOLTERSTORFF and JOHN WITVLIET

Baker Academic
*a division of Baker Publishing Group*
Grand Rapids, Michigan

© 2022 by Melanie C. Ross and Mark A. Lamport

Published by Baker Academic
a division of Baker Publishing Group
PO Box 6287, Grand Rapids, MI 49516-6287
www.bakeracademic.com

Printed in the United States of America

Library of Congress Cataloging-in-Publication Data
Names: Ross, Melanie C., editor. | Lamport, Mark A., editor.
Title: Historical foundations of worship : Catholic, Orthodox, and Protestant perspectives / edited by Melanie C. Ross and Mark A. Lamport; introductions by Nicholas Wolterstorff and John Witvliet.
Description: Grand Rapids, Michigan : Baker Academic, a division of Baker Publishing Group, [2022] | Series: Worship foundations | Includes bibliographical references and index.
Identifiers: LCCN 2021043091 | ISBN 9781540962522 (paperback) | ISBN 9781540965349 (casebound) | ISBN 9781493434985 (ebook) | ISBN 9781493434992 (pdf)
Subjects: LCSH: Liturgics.
Classification: LCC BV176.3 .H57 2022 | DDC 264—dc23
LC record available at https://lccn.loc.gov/2021043091

22  23  24  25  26  27  28      7  6  5  4  3  2  1

*From Melanie:*
For my students, from whom I learn so much


*From Mark:*
To my son and sons-in-law: Daniel,
Aaron, Christopher, and Zachary

# Contents

## Part 5. Protestant Worship

# Preface

## Melanie C. Ross and Mark A. Lamport

The Worship Foundations textbook series is designed as a set of accessible yet focused studies on theological and historical liturgical themes. *Historical Foundations of Worship*, the second book in the series, is divided into five parts. Early chapters address liturgical developments all Christians held in common: the source of the stream before the traditions split into separate tributaries. The remaining sections survey Eastern Orthodoxy, Roman Catholicism, and Protestant developments that include Reformation traditions, evangelicalism, and Pentecostalism.

Although each chapter is written by a different author, this volume is united by a cluster of shared themes concerning the historical study of liturgy. The first is a word of caution against a call for repristination: the return to some perceived earlier historical ideal. Liturgical rites and practices of earlier centuries may provide "sources for inspiration, but there is no golden age that can be revived for the present," notes Bryan Spinks. And L. Edward Phillips concurs: while it may be appropriate to look to the early church for inspiration, we must "avoid assigning too much authority to an ancient practice simply because it is ancient." The reason for this, he explains, is that the truth is always messy and diverse. "Even though we claim to be the early Christians' spiritual descendants," we are separated from the early Christians by time and culture, "trying to make sense of the reports of witnesses that we only partly understand."

At the same time, a second recurring theme is the importance of learning from those who have gone before. Joanne Pierce suggests that the Middle Ages offer a balance in liturgy and worship to modern Christians who "get lost in a sea of words and a clamor of noise. There is a need to rediscover the value of silence and the experience of transcendence/mystery." Reflecting on John Calvin's legacy, Martin Tel observes, "In a culture fixated on #TheNextIdol, a religious iconoclast is an unlikely go-to conversation partner. But, with a little imagination, it is possible to recognize meaningful similarities between the landscape of worship arts today and that of Calvin's sixteenth century." The reader is especially encouraged to study the "Practical Implications for Worship" section at the end of each chapter for more of these kinds of connective threads.

A third recurring theme is that the study of liturgical history must encompass more than an analysis of worship texts. As Valerie Rempel reminds us, not all Christian traditions center their worship on recurring texts: "There is no common liturgy that unites Anabaptist and Mennonite communities of faith." J. Kwabena Asamoah-Gyadu guides us to the reflection that Pentecostal praise is "direct, spontaneous and simple," free from "dependence on such liturgical resources as prayer-books and hymn-books." John Baldovin points out that even for those communities that do share common liturgy, the experience of Christian worship "is intimately related to the social and cultural spirit of any given age. . . . We neglect the critical history of worship at our peril." In a similar vein, Joris Geldhof stresses the importance of making bridges "between the multiple shapes and forms and customs of the church's liturgy, on the one hand, and the sociocultural environments where these celebrations happen, on the other." Worship is not a disembodied activity but rather one that, in Craig Satterlee's words, always "takes place in particular assemblies within particular contexts."

Finally, the study of the past may yield surprises and insights that challenge today's status quo. "It is not enough to assume that 'this is the way we've always done it,'" writes Jennifer Davidson. "What a deceptively authoritative phrase that can be, especially when it comes to worship." Indeed, as Nina Glibetić observes in her survey of Eastern Orthodoxy, "reverence toward liturgical tradition sometimes obstructs a popular appreciation for just how much historical development has occurred."

May the chapters that follow serve as both windows (examinations of the unfamiliar) and mirrors (reflections of your own practices and experiences). Echoing Andrew McGowan, we hope that the insights and ecumenical ethos of each author helps "place the historic Christian community itself firmly before us, not merely as an interesting source but as a living reality, whose abiding relevance counters glib comparisons between past tradition and modern sensibility."

# Series Introduction

## *Nicholas Wolterstorff*

### The Structure of Christian Worship

When we participate in Christian communal worship, we engage in a distinct form of activity that I shall call *scripted*. The diverse historical streams of worship, which the writers in this volume identify and analyze, are the result of different communities of Christians following different liturgical scripts—and of following their particular scripts in different ways.

Let me introduce what I mean by *scripts* and *scripted activity* with an example from music. Suppose that you and three of your friends decide to play one of Beethoven's string quartets—Quartet no. 12, opus 127, let us say. To make that decision is to decide that you will together follow a certain set of prescriptions for a correct performance of that work. If you faithfully follow those prescriptions, you have played the work correctly; if not, you have played it incorrectly—or, if you diverge too widely from the prescriptions, you have not played it at all. Of course, a performance can be correct without being a good performance, and some good performances are incorrect at certain points.

Though Beethoven's score for his opus 127 specifies prescriptions for correct performances of the work, it does not specify all of them. It could not possibly specify all of them—matters of legato, for example, of bowing, of tremolo. The additional prescriptions are implicit in the modern Western traditions of string-instrument playing. It's the *total* set of prescriptions for a correct performance that I call the *script*—those notated in the score plus those implicit in the relevant performance practice.

Let me highlight the ontological distinctions that I have employed in these remarks. There is the *work*, Beethoven's Quartet no. 12. Since it can be multiply performed, it's a universal. There is the *performance* of the work by you and your friends at a given time and place. There is the *score* for the work, which contains a good many of the prescriptions for a correct performance of the work. And there is what I call the *script*, which is the entire set of prescriptions for a correct performance: those specified in the score plus those implicit in the performance tradition. Lots of room for mistakes!

When participating together in the worship of God, we willingly surrender a portion of our autonomy for the duration. When we assemble to worship God, we do not each do our own thing but together submit to a script, the decisive clue to the fact that we are submitting to a script being that what we do can be judged in terms of correct and incorrect, not just in terms of better and worse. I may think that a different hymn would have been better for opening the service on this particular Sunday morning, but I limit my autonomy for the time being and join everybody else in singing the prescribed hymn. Of course, not everything that we do, or how we do it, is prescribed. How loudly we sing the hymns is usually a matter of personal choice.

How do the people know what is prescribed? In some worship traditions—Orthodox, Catholic, and Episcopal, for example—a great deal of what is prescribed is specified in texts and hymnals that the worshipers follow. In other worship traditions—Pentecostal, for example—a great deal of what is prescribed is announced by the worship leader. But in every case, it will be a combination of these two. And in no case do the prescriptions specified by the texts, plus those specified by the worship leader, constitute the totality of the prescriptions; many are implicit in the worship tradition of that particular congregation.

The ontological distinctions that I employed when discussing my musical example obviously have close parallels in Christian communal worship. For every worship service, there is a *script* specifying things to be done—words to be uttered, songs to be sung, movements to be made, and so on. By reference to the script, worshipers act correctly or incorrectly.

The counterpart to the musical *score* is the liturgical text, if there is one, and the hymnal. The counterpart to the musical *work* is the sequence of actions performed when the worshipers faithfully follow the script. This is a universal; it can, in principle, be performed many times. The counterpart to the musical *performance* is, of course, what the worshipers actually do on a particular occasion.

This is a good point to introduce the discussion concerning what it is that the term "liturgy" refers to that I promised in my introduction to the first book in this series. When writers speak of *liturgy*, or of *liturgies* (plural) and *a liturgy* (singular), what are they referring to? Among the ontologically distinct types of things that I identified in the discussion above, which do they have in mind? The answer is that different writers have different things in mind, and the same writer may have different things in mind in different passages.

As I noted in my introduction to the preceding volume, participants in the Liturgical Movement of the early twentieth century used the term to refer to what the people do under the direction of their leaders—that is, to liturgical enactments. Liturgy, so understood, is the counterpart, in worship, to a musical performance.

By contract, when writers use the term "Catholic liturgy," what they usually have in mind is the prescriptions for worship specified in the Catholic missal, and when they use the term "Episcopal liturgy," what they usually have in mind is the prescriptions for worship specified in the *Book of Common Prayer*. Liturgy, so understood, is like the score for a musical work—except that, since these texts don't specify the hymns for the day, they are considerably more incomplete than most musical scores. It's because Pentecostals don't have anything like such books that they often declare themselves to be nonliturgical.

In my own writing on these matters, I have quite often spoken of *enacting* the liturgy.[1] Liturgy, so understood, is the counterpart of the musical *work*. We enact the liturgical *work* by following the liturgical *script*, thereby producing a liturgical *enactment*.

The moral is that when a writer uses the term "liturgy," one has to judge from the context which sort of entity he or she is referring to. Usually it will be rather easy to tell, and sometimes it won't make any difference.

For the assembled people to enact the liturgy for the day, different members have to fill different roles. There's the role of the people, the role of presiding minister or priest, the role of Scripture reader, the role of preacher, the role of leader of the prayers, the role of musical instrumentalist(s), and so on. Often the same person fills several of these roles.

It is this phenomenon of different roles being filled by different members of the assembly that has led a good many writers on these matters to compare enacting a liturgy to performing a drama. The similarity is indeed striking. But there is also a decisive difference. In the performance of a drama, the members of the cast play the roles of *fictional characters*. When they speak,

1. I have refrained from speaking of *performing* the liturgy because of the misleading connotations of the term.

they do not speak in their own voice but in the voice of the character they are playing. By contrast, when we together enact the liturgy for the day, we do not play the roles of fictional characters but speak in our own voice. In the Confession, *I* confess *my* sins; I do not play the role of a *fictional character* who confesses *his* sins. A liturgical enactment, when well done, will have a strong dramatic quality. But it is not the performance of a drama.

It is by all together submitting ourselves to following the liturgical script that we *together* enact the liturgy; if there were not a script that we all submitted to following, we could not enact the liturgy *together*. Let me briefly point to another way in which we limit our autonomy in order to enact the liturgy *together*.

Not only do we submit to the script in our speaking, our singing, our bodily motions. We also adjust our speaking, our singing, our bodily motions to those of our fellow worshipers. I might prefer that the hymn be sung more slowly. No matter. I adjust my pace to that of the instrumentalists and my fellow congregants. This phenomenon of adjusting what one is doing to what those around one are doing is especially familiar to those who have sung in a choir or played an instrument in an ensemble.

A point that I have several times alluded to but not highlighted is the following. All Christian liturgies originate in the worship practices of the early church, of which we get some indications in the letters of the New Testament. But over time different liturgical scripts emerged within different sections of the church, along with different ways of communicating the script for a given Sunday—by texts, by announcements, on a screen—so that now we can identify distinct liturgical traditions and practices: Coptic, Eastern Orthodox, Presbyterian, Pentecostal, and so on. This present volume is devoted to analyzing some of these script-shaped liturgical traditions and practices.

In concluding this section, let me note that when Christians assemble to enact their liturgy, almost always the actions they perform include actions that are not, strictly speaking, actions of worship. Confessing to God that we have wronged God is not adoration of God, nor is petitioning God. The justification for nonetheless speaking of the enactment of a liturgy as a *worship* service is that worship is the all-embracing context. To call the entirety of the liturgical enactment a "worship service" is to use the term "worship" as a synecdoche: a part is used to stand for the whole.

## Christian Liturgy and Christian Scripture

In this introduction I have devoted my discussion thus far to identifying a fundamental structural feature of Christian communal worship—namely, when Christians assemble to worship God, they surrender part of their autonomy for the time being so as together to engage in the scripted activity of worshiping God. Let me close our discussion by pointing to a fundamental and pervasive feature of the *content* of Christian worship. Christian liturgy is suffused with Christian Scripture.

This suffusion takes a number of distinct forms. The most obvious form is that in most Christian liturgical enactments, one or more passages from Scripture are read and a sermon or homily is delivered based on those passages. If one or more of the passages read is a narrative, as it often is, the reading amounts to a retelling of that part of the biblical story. The retelling of some part of the biblical story is not confined to the reading of Scripture, however. It also occurs when the minister retells some part of the story in their own words, or in words prescribed by the script. The most obvious example of this last is the retelling of a part of the biblical story in the eucharistic prayer.

Not only are Christian liturgical enactments replete with retellings of parts of the biblical story, they are also replete with repetitions of episodes that the biblical stories narrate. The people praise God, just as people in the biblical narratives praised God; they intercede with God, just as people in the biblical narratives interceded with God. Sometimes, in their praise or intercession, the people repeat the very words used by persons in the biblical narrative. This is most obvious when the people pray the Lord's Prayer.

A central component in traditional Christian liturgical enactments is the celebration of the Lord's Supper, the Eucharist. Jesus himself, in his institution of the Supper, employed the fundamental category for understanding what is taking place when we celebrate the Supper: we imitate what Jesus and his disciples did in that last supper of our Lord as a *memorial* or *remembrance* of him.

The idea of doing something *as a memorial* or *as a remembrance* of some person or event in the biblical narrative has application beyond our celebration of the Lord's Supper. It is, for example, the basic category for understanding the church's celebration of the various seasons of the church year. Our celebration of Christmas is a memorial or remembrance of Christ's birth; our celebration of Good Friday is a memorial or remembrance of Christ's crucifixion; our celebration of Easter is a memorial or remembrance of Christ's resurrection. And so forth.

We could identify yet other ways in which Christian Scripture is suffused in Christian liturgical enactments. For example, the washing of feet on Maundy Thursday is a *reenactment* of Christ's washing of the feet of his disciples. But enough has been said to make my point.

Many have tried to capture, with a single concept, the many and diverse ways in which Christian Scripture suffuses Christian liturgies. The concepts most commonly used for this purpose are *enactment* and *reenactment*. It is often said that by participating in the liturgy we *enact*, or *reenact*, "the story of salvation," or "the biblical narrative," or "the redemptive work of Christ." No doubt something like this fits some of the ways in which Scripture suffuses Christian liturgies, but not all. It doesn't fit, for example, praying the Psalms. Content with not having a concept that fits all the cases, we should note and celebrate the diverse ways in which Christian Scripture suffuses Christian liturgies.

# Introduction

## *John Witvliet*

As we engage with the subject matter of this volume, we are invited into a pilgrimage through the history of Christian worship. Whether we are paging through a book of family photos or absorbed in a historical documentary, museum exhibit, or a book like this, we have a choice to make about whether we will take in the information being offered as tourists or as pilgrims. Are we primarily interested in a mere diversion? Or are we seeking something deeper, open to learning that is transformative, soul-engaging, and, thanks to the work of the Holy Spirit, profoundly sanctifying?

The way of the pilgrim begins in love—as we turn from self-absorption toward deep attentiveness toward neighbors near and far. In nearly every village, neighborhood, and social media network, each of us encounters Christians who worship quite differently than we do, singing different songs with different instruments or no instruments at all, presenting public Bible readings according to starkly different reading plans, preaching and praying with quite different sensibilities about how lengthy and formal these practices should be, practicing baptism and the Lord's Supper with quite different gestures, postures, and explanatory frameworks. As a Protestant Christian, I love my Catholic and Orthodox neighbors when I learn about the feast days and baptismal celebrations that are so central to their sense of identity in Christ. I love my Pentecostal neighbors when I learn the story behind a heartsong that they carry with them into moments of challenge and stress. One powerful motivation for studying the history of worship is to better know and understand people whom God has placed in our lives from traditions quite different from our own.

When we begin to search for the stories behind the cherished practices of our neighbors, we are quickly confronted by the stunning pluriformity of liturgical practices that have developed in multitudes of denominations across thousands of distinct subcultures across hundreds of years. The mathematics are staggering: imagine what would be required for us to deeply learn the inner dynamics of twenty or thirty Christian practices across even the two hundred more populated denominations that have emerged across eighty generations in what today are two hundred or so countries. As if this isn't wondrous enough, we then discover that throughout these eighty generations, so many influential figures were themselves amateur (or professional) historians, inviting us to pay attention to how they studied history and employed historical reasoning in their discernment. This can become challenging to manage as we become aware, for example, of how nineteenth- and twentieth-century liturgical reforms were based on a certain understanding of how the sixteenth-century reformers drew on fourth-century liturgical sources and their roots in ancient biblical metaphors and narratives! All of it invites us to see ourselves in relation to a long procession of historical inquirers—going way back to the remarkable acts of historical meaning-making we see on display in so many Old Testament historical books and in the four Gospels and the Acts of the Apostles.

What begins in an act of love toward a neighbor ends in wonder and astonishment and the breadth and diversity of Christ's body, the pluriformity of Christian worship practices. The fact that we can even contemplate this pluriformity is a gift. What remarkable access we have today to artifacts, archaeological sites, and other historical documents from across the range of Christian traditions. In each of the last eight generations, serious students of worship have been graced to live through periods of groundbreaking paradigm shifts in the study of liturgical history, thanks to archaeological discoveries, improved scholarly editions of key primary sources, and insightful analytic studies of any number of sources and time periods. In nearly every topic area covered in doctoral research seminars a generation ago, there are now new shelves full of books and rich online repositories of sources that offer new insights. As we learn to see each individual source, topic, and time period in light of all of this work, we also find that our view of the entire landscape of liturgical history changes. Given the rapid expansion of all this knowledge, it seems likely that we have only begun to clarify what this means for our vision of Christianity as a whole and our place in it. A book like this is a significant resource to assist with this undertaking, offering us at once a view of the whole and deep insight into particular practices and traditions from scholars who are sympathetic to their subject, with expertise in some of the many specialties related to the study of the complexities of Christian liturgical practices. As you read this book, give thanks to God for the historians, archaeologists, editors, librarians, copyists, historical preservationists, collectors and curators, risk-taking interpreters, and pastoral pedagogues whose labors are bearing fruit as we learn together.

Not infrequently, our forays into all these sources will not only inspire us but also unsettle us as we discover communities, traditions, and time periods filled with conflict, mixed motives, disruption, and variance in practice that call into question so many of our most cherished assumptions. Deep, pilgrimlike engagement with this material challenges us to set aside sentimental history that idealizes heroes, avoiding inconvenient facts about their vices, as well as punitive history that refuses to appreciate redemptive, life-giving episodes in even crassly fallen people. Deep, pilgrimlike engagement with this material invites us to be alert to historical interpretations that are wielded as instruments of coercion—excusing sin and twisting truth. We also become alert to the gift of prophetic interpretations that challenge these destructive ones, telling more of the truth, and forming us to be at once more humble and more courageous as we interpret the histories that shape us. To choose only one of thousands of potential examples, if slaveholders of European descent tried to evangelize chattel slaves but then withheld baptism from them, naming that hypocrisy creates a context in which justice and reconciliation can be pursued.

All of that leads us back into disciplines of ecclesial love, as we seek to honor the deepest desire expressed in Jesus's high priestly prayer that his followers would be one unified body (John 17; Eph. 4). It takes practice to learn to see believers in a vastly different cultural and historical context from our own not just as objects of study but rather as siblings in Jesus—kin in Christ. The journey is humbling and ennobling, unsettling and yet deeply grounding. Almost always, we are led toward greater caution as we consider the supposed strengths of our own traditions, greater charity as we listen in on the foibles and glories of our siblings, and greater courage for facing our own inadequacies. Our capacity to do this well depends in large measure on our awareness of how complex the interactions among Christian traditions can be. At times, the distinct Christian traditions described in this volume interact in mutually enriching ways, sharing insights, approaches, and artworks of many kinds. At other times, Christian traditions set themselves up over against others, reacting against, challenging, and even decrying developments in other parts of the body of Christ. Whereas some differences across Christian traditions are a matter of difference in patterns of emphases, others offer a stubbornly profound contrast in the most basic forms of worship.

None of us approach all this complexity from a neutral or perfectly objective point of view. And yet we can, I'm convinced, make progress in our capacity not only to acknowledge more historical data but also to see deeply into both the virtues and the vices of a given approach or time period, including our own. As a teacher of liturgical history, I have observed two things that deeply enhance this pilgrimlike learning. First, I have increasingly noticed how beautifully students respond to an invitation to study the history of worship in search of "charisms"—learning to look for Holy Spirit–given gifts that edify, encourage, and chasten the body of Christ. When we engage history in search of "successes," we set our sights too low. When we seek to identify charisms, we find ourselves looking deeper, noticing under-the-surface dynamics, celebrating fruits of the Spirit of a given historical figure that may not be apparent during their lifetime.

Second, I have learned how essential it is to study this material, whenever possible, in a collaborative context with people who have different temperaments, cultural backgrounds, and denominational histories. For many years I have taught some students from traditions with quite fixed and stable liturgical practices and many others from traditions with a high degree of flexibility, variability, and even risk-taking in their liturgical practices. Each of these broad groups has within them students motivated by different concerns. Many of my students from more fixed and stable traditions study history to discover ways that even seemingly unbending, inflexible practices have adapted and changed subtly over time. Others study history in order to explain, defend, and protect these practices. Many of my students from traditions with more variability study history in order to seek inspiration for next week's innovation or—conversely—to discover something more stable and enduring than they have known. These complex crosscurrents of motivation can make a class on the history of worship dynamic and challenging, creating conditions for mutual accountability as we discern together what is good, true, and beautiful in this unfolding story. So much of the richest learning happens when we notice how other people react to the same material. Any given student may initially be disengaged as they encounter an ancient Christian mosaic, a medieval monastic prayer book, a Reformation baptism and eucharistic liturgy, or an influential modern projection or sound technology—until they see how that same artifact excites or troubles a friend. Pilgrimage is so often enhanced in good company.

Ultimately, some of us who study this material will do so in order to discern what is best in our congregations and ministries, and for our own personal churchgoing decisions. We will act on the insights we gain here. In this regard, I have discovered two key insights from my students. When thinking about our own communities in light of our historical study, seek both to diagnose and to enrich. Our pilgrimages in the history of Christian worship will help us diagnose gaps. Studying an ancient lectionary may help some of us see how anemic some patterns of Bible reading are today or to discover strengths in how our traditions may have rebalanced our scriptural diets over time. Our pilgrimages also enrich our imagination for what is possible. A contemporary songwriter who prayerfully reviews a nineteenth-century hymnal will discover a treasure trove of metaphors and images. Whether we gain insight or inspiration, each encounter challenges us to grow in our capacity to think analogously—to discern the points of both continuity and discontinuity between a given cultural context and time period and our own. We gain insight for shaping worship services for the people we serve, as well as for nurturing the people we serve for the services we shape.

In and through all of this, our engagement with liturgical history truly comes into its own when it trains us to behold the goodness and glory of the triune God. One of the most ancient and enduring liturgical impulses across Christian traditions is to learn to engage in liturgical practices as occasions to "lift up our hearts," to "set our minds on things above" (see Col. 3:2), to behold the goodness and glory of God. The term "worship" is so frequently used as a synecdoche to title particular liturgies in some traditions and the field of liturgical studies in others precisely because doxology is a foundational spiritual practice. While there is great wisdom in being measured and cautious when speaking of the Holy One, it would be tragic if our engagement with liturgical history left us with little room for doxology. At its best, studying liturgical history forms us for beholding the goodness of the Lord. If I encounter a long historical psalm or eucharistic prayer and am turned off by its length, I will miss its beauty. But if I study its history and discover the profound ways that each unfolds the grand metanarrative of God's saving acts in history, then I am better able to participate in that unfolding text with attention on God and not the prayer's length. At its best, liturgical history invites us to listen in on testimonies of God's saints across the centuries who worshiped in ancient temples, obscure homes and villas, grand cathedrals, makeshift chapels, and on terrifying battlefields, saying,

> I have looked upon you in the sanctuary,
>     beholding your power and glory.
> Because your steadfast love is better than life,
>     my lips will praise you.

> So I will bless you as long as I live;
>     I will lift up my hands and call on your name. (Ps. 63:2–4)

Whereas a tourist seeks diversion, a pilgrim longs to gain new capacity to perceive truth, to express love, to be grasped by wonder, and to return all praise and thanks to God. May God's Spirit grace each reader of this book with this holy longing.

# PART 1

# Common Roots of Worship

# — 1 —

# Baptism

## *Bryan D. Spinks*

What we call the beginning is often the end
And to make an end is to make a beginning.
The end is where we start from.

—T. S. Eliot, *Little Gidding,*
*The Four Quartets*

Like much poetic language, the words of T. S. Eliot tease and are capable of many meanings. We may understand a beginning as a journey toward a goal, and the suggestion that the goal also makes a beginning is apropos of Christian baptism. Phillip Tovey, noting that there is an integral relationship between making disciples and baptism, has expressed it thus: "The fruit of discipleship-making is baptisms, and baptisms are a call to further disciple-making."[1] The beginning is an end, and the end is a beginning.

## Baptism and the New Testament

In Galatians, Paul writes, "For in Christ Jesus you are all children of God through faith. As many of you as were baptized into Christ have clothed

1. Phillip Tovey, *Of Water and the Spirit: Mission and the Baptismal Liturgy* (Norwich, UK: Canterbury, 2015), 3.

3

yourselves with Christ" (Gal. 3:26–27), and in his Letter to the Romans he asks, "Do you not know that all of us who have been baptized into Christ Jesus were baptized into his death?" (Rom. 6:3). In these verses Paul assumes a ritual called baptism, and he assumes his readers will be familiar with the ritual. However, neither in these verses nor elsewhere in his letters does he describe the details of this ritual. Nicholas Taylor has succinctly put it this way:

> Paul says little about the practice of Baptism. The only reference in the Pauline letters to specific occasions on which Baptism was administered is in 1 Corinthians 1.14, 16, which simply lists the people whom Paul had baptized in Corinth, with no further details. There is no indication as to how the rite related to the conversion of the individuals mentioned and their households; nor is there any mention of catechumenal instruction before and after Baptism. There is no liturgy described, no venue specified. These details form a part of the common knowledge shared by Paul and those to whom he wrote, and in many respects by other of the first generation of Christians also. Paul does not suggest that the occasions on which he administered Baptism were the exception rather than his usual practice, so we should not extrapolate too many generalizations from this brief reference.[2]

What Taylor says of Paul is true of the whole of the New Testament. To look for or to reconstruct a ritual for baptism from the New Testament writings is as misplaced as would be an attempt to construct a modern scientific manual from the creation stories of Genesis. It was simply not the purpose of the writers. Nevertheless, the New Testament is the place to begin to understand the foundational narratives of Christian baptism.

The Synoptic Gospels all attest that Jesus was baptized by John the Baptist in the river Jordan. John's baptism was for repentance, and he proclaims that one coming after him will baptize with the Holy Spirit. Although they have differences, the Synoptic Gospels describe Jesus being baptized by John, a voice announcing him as the beloved Son, and the Holy Spirit descending in the form of a dove. The Fourth Gospel does not attest that John baptized Jesus but does have the Baptist affirm that Jesus is the Lamb of God who takes away the sins of the world and who will baptize with the Holy Spirit. It is possible to see here a ritual—baptism in water, a formula, a belief that the Holy Spirit descends—and those elements are present in subsequent Christian baptismal rituals.

The formula at the baptism of Jesus stresses his unique status as the Son of God, but although Christians were and are regarded as children of God

---

2. Nicholas Taylor, *Paul on Baptism: Theology, Mission and Ministry in Context* (London: SCM, 2016), 102–3.

and fellow heirs with Christ, there is no evidence that the words concerning Jesus were used of Christians. In the New Testament we find two formulae, one of which later certainly became a baptismal formula. In Matthew 28:19 the disciples are to baptize in the name of the Father, and of the Son, and of the Holy Spirit. Some scholars have stated that this is a later addition, though their claim has no manuscript support. This may well be what the Matthean community did, on the basis of the "trinitarian" dimensions of Jesus's baptism—the Son is baptized, the Father speaks, and the Holy Spirit descends (echoing the creation narrative). Mention is made in Acts of baptizing in the name of Jesus. What is important here is that, regardless of the formula, it is a baptizing "into" (*eis* or *epi*) the name. Given the importance of the name in the Hebrew Scriptures, at the very least baptism here is understood as being poured into the person and identity of Jesus and all that he is and represents. This is probably why Paul speaks of putting on the Lord Jesus Christ (Gal. 3:27), being baptized into one body (1 Cor. 12:13), or being baptized into Jesus's death and being united with him (Rom. 6).

One important distinction of Christian baptism from that of John is its pneumatological dimension, and the baptism into the name of Jesus gives a christological dimension. The New Testament writings also give other theological dimensions and themes to baptism. There is a soteriological aspect—baptism washes away sin and saves. It has an ecclesiological dimension in that it incorporates a person into the body of Christ, the church. It is a covenant and is also concerned with the coming kingdom, and so is eschatological. Other images are death and resurrection, being born again, illumination, and stripping off and putting on. Some of these were subsequently articulated in liturgical prayers and formulae in the liturgies that developed, but no liturgy contains them all, and it is probably an overload to attempt to incorporate them all into one service.

The place of faith, and what constitutes faith, is another question that the New Testament does not give an unambiguous answer to. With John's baptism it seems that the ritual was a response to his preaching, and that also seems to be the case in Acts 2:41—an immediate response. Prior to the baptism of the Ethiopian eunuch, the eunuch gets instruction on a passage of Isaiah and then is baptized in the next body of water that he and Phillip spot. In Acts 16 the jailer hears the word, resulting in he and his family being baptized. This seems to have been a cultural norm. Most people belonged to a "household" and followed the lead of the head of the household.[3] Some households would have contained infants, and so it should be assumed that

3. See the excellent discussion in Taylor, *Paul on Baptism*, 118–23.

they too were baptized along with other members who followed the choice of the head of the household.

The Acts of the Apostles has accounts of baptism that present different sequences or patterns of the ritual. In some there is baptism followed by the laying on of hands, which is associated with the gift of the Spirit. Some followers of the Baptist who had received only the baptism of repentance have hands laid on them to complete or transform it into Christian baptism. But with Cornelius the Spirit descends first, and baptism follows. Some scholars have attempted to see some evolutionary ritual pattern in these variations, but often they read their own presuppositions back into the texts. It is better to see these as reflecting different ritual patterns that coexisted, rather than to rearrange them into a developmental pattern.

## Pre-Nicene Witnesses

Variety and different patterns and emphases are what we find in the pre-Nicene evidence. The *Didache*, a church order itself compiled from several sources, is dated by most scholars circa 80 CE, from the region of Antioch.[4] It has close affinities with the Gospel of Matthew and seems to have originated in communities that were predominantly Jewish-Christian. Baptism is in the name of the Father, the Son, and the Holy Spirit (cf. Matthew), but it also mentions baptism in the name of the Lord. There is a period of fasting by the candidates prior to baptism. What is significant is the permissive method of baptism—in living water (i.e., river, lake, baths, or cistern), warm or cold, or triple pouring. It is significant that in the house church at Dura-Europos (ca. 280) the place for baptism is too small for anything other than standing in shallow water and pouring. It suggests that water, not the amount and method, was the important factor. In the community known to Justin Martyr in Rome, as outlined in Justin's *First Apology* (ca. 165), the baptism of new members was done in private, away from the actual congregation—presumably for reasons of modesty. After the act of baptism, the newly baptized arrived at the assembly to join in worship with them. Justin's community gathered over public baths, and it may be that the baths were the place used for their baptisms.

Other important witnesses are the apocryphal works. There are two versions of the *Acts of Thomas*, Greek and Syriac.[5] Although the Syriac may be the original language, the present Syriac text seems to postdate the Greek, and

4. For a recent commentary, see Shawn J. Whilhite, *The Didache: A Commentary* (Eugene, OR: Cascade Books, 2019).

5. Relevant excerpts are in E. C. Whitaker and Maxwell Johnson, *Documents of the Baptismal Liturgy* (London: SPCK, 2003).

there are some differences between them. What emerges is different patterns of initiation. In the Greek text, some are by anointing with oil only. Others are by anointing with oil and baptism in water. Some accounts have an invocation of the Holy Spirit over the oil, and baptism is with the trinitarian formula. A lighted lamp after the baptism is also mentioned—possibly a symbol of illumination. The *Gospel of Philip* mentions a stripping off and putting on of garments, and it also discusses the importance of oil.[6] Tertullian, representing North African practice circa 200, witnesses to instruction and fasting as preparation, renouncing of the devil and his pomp, possibly a blessing of the water, baptism, anointing of the head, and the laying on of hands.[7] The cumulative evidence and witnesses illustrate differing ritual patterns across geographical areas and different Christian communities. Anointing with olive oil, either before or after the baptism, became a common element. This was part of bathing etiquette in the classical world and was regarded as having health benefits and protective qualities. Sometimes the anointing was before bathing, sometimes after, and for the wealthy it was both before and after using perfumed oil.[8] For a faith that preached the Anointed One, on whom the Spirit alighted after his baptism—who was himself prophet, priest, and king—olive oil and perfumed oil were quickly ritualized as a sign of the Spirit and of the newly baptized being anointed heirs with Christ. It was now a spiritual protection and marked the baptized as members of the royal priesthood.

## Fourth- and Fifth-Century Homilies and Liturgical Material

In the fourth century we have more information about the rites of baptism and how at least some authors understood them. We have three sets of sermons by John Chrysostom, from when he was a presbyter at Antioch; the catechetical lectures of Cyril of Jerusalem and the mystagogical lectures attributed to him (Jerusalem); the catechetical homilies of Theodore of Mopsuestia (Antioch or Mopsuestia); and homilies of Zeno of Verona and *De mysteriis* and *De sacramentis* of Ambrose of Milan, both representing Italy. In addition, we have liturgical material from the *Apostolic Constitutions*, a church order (possibly by a Eunomian who did not accept that Christ was equal in divinity to the Father) circa 360, from the region of Antioch; from the so-called *Apostolic*

6. Thomas M. Finn, *Early Christian Baptism and the Catechumenate*, vol. 1, *East and West Syria* (Collegeville, MN: Liturgical Press, 1992).

7. For some of the relevant texts, see Whitaker and Johnson, *Documents of the Baptismal Liturgy*.

8. Fikret Yegül, *Baths and Bathing in Classical Antiquity* (Cambridge, MA: MIT Press, 1992).

*Tradition* once associated with a Hippolytus; and prayers from a collection by Bishop Serapion of Thmuis and the *Canons of Hippolytus*, both reflecting Egyptian practices.

The picture that develops is of regional variations within an emerging common liturgical framework. In Jerusalem, candidates had to "sign up" before Lent, and they were given instruction during Lent leading up to baptism at Easter, which was becoming the preferred time for baptism. Toward the end of the instruction period, the Creed was "given" to the candidates. They also received exorcisms, since this instruction time may have been regarded as a time when the devil and demons would assault the candidates. On Easter Eve the candidates experienced a ritual in which they renounced the devil, his works, and powers of this world; stripped; were anointed and baptized; and, after the postbaptismal anointing, put on a white garment. Cyril gives the prebaptismal anointing a christological significance, and the postbaptismal anointing he associates with the Holy Spirit. Here we see that the two anointings, which have a parallel in secular bathing, are given theological meanings. In some later rites oil is also poured into the baptismal water, which again has a parallel in secular bathing custom.

The *Apostolic Constitutions* witnesses to a particular community, and its prayers cannot be regarded as applicable to all Christian communities of Antioch and its environs. In book 7, chapters 39–45, there is instruction, ritualized by prayer and the laying on of hands. A full description of the renunciation of Satan is given, and that is followed by the recitation of the Creed. There is a prebaptismal anointing, and then the water is blessed, and the prayer contains the following words: "Look down from heaven, and sanctify the water, [and] give it grace and power, so that he who is to be baptized, according to the commandments of your Christ, may be crucified with him, and be buried with him, and may rise with him, to be adopted in him, that he may die to sin and live to righteousness."[9] After the baptism with the triune formula, the candidates were anointed with myron (perfumed oil), followed by the laying on of hands and the recitation of the Lord's Prayer.

John Chrysostom's three sets of homilies, given at differing periods in Lent, witness to the exorcisms of candidates, the need for sponsors, the renunciation of Satan, a prebaptismal anointing of the whole body, and a triple immersion for baptism. No mention is made of a postbaptismal anointing, which has led some scholars to suggest that the rite known to him did not contain one.[10] The homilies of Theodore may have been given when he was

9. Whitaker and Johnson, *Documents of the Baptismal Liturgy*, 39.
10. Hugh Riley, *Christian Initiation* (Washington, DC: Catholic University of America Press, 1974).

a presbyter with Chrysostom in Antioch, or when he was later bishop of Mopsuestia. In his description of the renunciation of Satan, he likens it to a trial in a law court. He mentions the stripping of clothes for the baptism, the anointing, the baptism, the putting on of a white garment, and a post-baptismal anointing.

The homilies of Zeno of Verona, bishop circa 362–370, have been studied by Gordon Jeanes, who thinks it possible to reconstruct from them the service presupposed by Zeno. Jeanes posits a sequence of anointing, renunciation, entry to the baptistery, stripping, immersion, anointing with sealing, clothing with a white garment, and the paschal Eucharist. He suggests that *Homily* 1.37 might allude to renunciations.[11] Much more information can be gleaned on the practice in Milan when Ambrose was bishop. Ambrose claimed that the rite of Milan was very much like that of Rome, save for one or two differences. Candidates gathered on Saturday night at Paschal Tide, and the bishop touched their ears and nostrils, ritualizing the miracle in the Gospels when Jesus touched the ears and eyes of the deaf and dumb man. In the baptistery the candidates were anointed as athletes about to wrestle. They renounced the devil and all his works and were baptized, the water having been exorcised and blessed. There was a threefold immersion, which is described in Pauline terms of death, and so is tomblike, and this was followed by chrismation. There was also a footwashing, which differentiated the use of Milan from that of Rome. Ambrose also mentions a sealing, and it is unclear whether this was accompanied by a hand-laying and a further anointing. That is the pattern found in the *Apostolic Tradition*. In the mid-twentieth century, scholars believed this was by Hippolytus, bishop of Rome (ca. 215). More recent scholarship sees it as a composite document dating from the late third or early fourth century and reflecting several traditions. However, its description of the pattern of initiation is one that became peculiar to Rome. After baptism the candidates were anointed by a presbyter and then were taken to the bishop, where they received an episcopal hand-laying and further chrismation. This peculiar Roman episcopal ritual would eventually spin off as a separate service called confirmation.

From Egypt there are prayers for baptism in the *Euchology of Serapion*, who was bishop of Thmuis (339–360). There are no directions for how the service

---

11. Gordon P. Jeanes, *The Day Has Come: Easter and Baptism in Zeno of Verona* (Collegeville, MN: Liturgical Press, 1995). The terms "seal" and "sealing" reflect the Greek word *sphragis*, which has a range of meanings but typically indicates ownership—such as the seal on a document. "Sealing" might mean the sign of the cross made by the celebrant's thumb or finger with the oil, or the laying of the hand on the head.

was ordered, but there are prayers for catechumens, for baptism, and for oil.[12] Another document is the *Canons of Hippolytus*, a version of the *Apostolic Tradition*. The canons stress that candidates must be rigorously examined, and people with certain professions are excluded. There was a threefold immersion with creedal interrogatories, a postbaptismal anointing, a hand-laying, and a further anointing by the bishop. These two collections suggest that there was more than one use in Egypt.

The cumulative evidence from this period suggests that an interval of instruction preceded baptism and was associated with Lent, though the length differed from place to place. Candidates were separated out as catechumens, and at Easter (as the preferred time) they were baptized and incorporated as members of the church. This basic pattern falls into the "Rites of Passage" categories, made famous by Arnold van Gennep, of Separation (made catechumens), Liminality (as catechumens, no longer non-Christian, but not yet full members), and Integration (baptism). Another development, at least in the West, stemmed from the teaching of St. Augustine of Hippo, who, on the basis of the Latin mistranslation of the Greek in Romans, formulated a doctrine of original sin. This led to the belief that the unbaptized were damned, and it would lead in the medieval West to the requirement for babies to be baptized within a few days, lest they die without the saving effects of baptism.

Another question pertains to the level of undress during baptism. In the Greco-Roman world the custom at public baths differed from place to place, and in some places men and women bathed together naked. In Christian baptism the rite was not public, suggesting that candidates were naked, though in some places there is evidence that a covering was used for modesty. It appears that one of the duties of deaconesses was to anoint women candidates by rubbing oil all over their bodies. Following Greco-Roman local bathing customs, it seems that in some places the candidates were naked at baptism, and at others they were scantily dressed.[13]

## Classical Baptismal Rites of East and West

These fourth- and early-fifth-century commentaries give the main ingredients, East and West, of the liturgies that were evolving. The Eastern churches

---

12. For how the prayers might have been used, see Maxwell Johnson, *The Prayers of Serapion of Thmuis: A Literary, Liturgical and Theological Analysis*, Orientalia Christiania Analecta 249 (Rome: Pontifical Oriental Institute, 1995).

13. Bryan D. Spinks, "Much Ado about Nothing (On): Nudity and Baptism in Ravenna Revisited," *Anaphora* 8 (2014): 13–22.

were divided over the christological disputes of the fifth and sixth centuries, and so the evolving rites also took on a denominational identity. The East Syrian Baptismal Ordo is reputed to have been revised by Catholicos Iso'yabh III (ca. 649–659) and is a rite that assumes that candidates are infants. Although some of the later East Syrian commentators refer to the older "staged rites" performed over a period of time, this ordo assumes initiation in a single ritual. There is a consecration of oil and of water, and these prayers have been conformed to a pattern found in eucharistic prayers, with the inclusion of the sanctus. In this tradition oil from the *qarna* is added to the new oil—the tradition being that the *qarna* derives from a mixture of water from Christ's baptism and which flowed from his pierced side, mixed with oil by the disciples at Pentecost. It is an interesting material link with Christ's baptism.

The image of baptism as womb is quite strong in this tradition. This is even more so in the Maronite Rite, named after Jacob of Serug, which has links both with the older Syriac tradition and with the Syrian Orthodox tradition. The Maronite Rite emphasizes the image of the candidate being marked as a sheep and reborn from the womb of the font. The Syrian Orthodox tradition knew two rites, one named after a Timothy, which is no longer used, and one named after Severus of Antioch, which is the one now in use. This latter rite has two sections, which is a telescoping of the once staged rites. Tomb and resurrection are the dominant theme. The Byzantine (Eastern Orthodox) Rite has a prayer over the water that seems to have undergone only minimal development compared to other Eastern traditions. The oldest text is found in the *Barberini 336 Euchologion*, and this includes some prayers for catechumens that indicate a rite phased over time. The developed rite has a prebaptismal anointing and then, after baptism, the candidate is anointed on the forehead, eyes, nostrils, mouth, and ears with the words "the seal of the gift of the Spirit." The Armenian Rite has its own identity but has been influenced by both the Byzantine and the Latin rites. The Coptic Rite has close affinities with the earlier Egyptian *Canons of Hippolytus*, and the Ethiopic Rite follows the Coptic, with one or two variations.[14]

In the West, we have already noted that the rite of Milan was not identical to that of Rome—there were geographical differences. In addition to the use of Rome, there was a Gallican Rite, used in the Frankish lands, and also a Spanish or Visigothic Rite. One of the main differences between these and the use in Rome was that, in the former, initiation was completed by the

---

14. For the texts of these, see Whitaker and Johnson, *Documents of the Baptismal Liturgy*, esp. chaps. 3–8.

presbyter, whereas in Rome the presbyter's anointing was supplemented by an episcopal hand-laying and anointing. Over time, it was the Roman use that came to be adopted throughout the West, though it was never a "pure" Roman use, since it absorbed some things from the other Western rites. Our earliest full liturgy for this hybrid Roman Rite is found in Codex Vaticanus Reginensis Latinus 316, dating from around 750 from a nunnery in Chelles, near Paris, but seems to reflect an earlier time, circa 628–715. Although the structure of the rite assumes a series of stages throughout Lent culminating in Easter baptism, and so is for adults, the focus of the rite is on *infantes*— young children and infants.

Like the Eastern rites, this witnesses to the fact that in "Christendom" the only nonbaptized were newborn children from Christian families. In later Western baptismal rites, although there were certainly diocesan and local variations, a standard set of prayers and rituals was used, and telescoped into a single service and used for infants. The child and parents met at the church door for the first part of the service—the old catechumenate. There was an exorcism, marking the candidate with the sign of the cross, and inquiry of the name of the candidate. There were further prayers of exorcism with anointings, a reading of the gospel, the laying on of hands, and "delivery" of (now just the priest reciting) the Lord's Prayer and the Creed. On entry into the church the Litany of the Saints was recited, and the blessing of the font took place. This blessing has been formed by amalgamation of elements from Gallican and Roman usages. The Creed was recited by the candidate, followed by a threefold immersion/pouring with the Matthean formula. There was anointing and the putting on of a white cap as well as the christening garment, the chrisom. A lighted candle was also sometimes given. Ideally the episcopal rite followed. This became separated by days, then weeks, then months and years, and developed as a separate rite called confirmation and was regarded as a separate sacrament. This would cause the Reformation to reimage confirmation (as a rite of maturity after catechesis), and it has caused considerable discussion and argument in twentieth-century liturgical reforms.

## The Reforms of the Magisterial Reformers

The Eastern rites as they had developed mainly stayed intact with little textual change. The West, however, faced divisions and splits at the Reformation. Although all the reformers regarded the inherited Roman Rite as superstitious and in need of reform, they disagreed among themselves over the theology of baptism and of how to reform the liturgical rite. Martin Luther taught that the central themes of baptism were death/resurrection and justification by faith through grace. He defended infant baptism on the grounds of *fides aliena*, the faith of others. He also believed that baptism removes original sin, and exorcisms witness to the reality of Satan.

Luther authored two baptismal liturgies. The first, in 1523, removed some of the elements that he believed obscured a clearer meaning in the old rite. He removed the exorcism of salt, though still used salt, and removed the blessing of the water. In his own prayer associated with the water (known as his "flood prayer"), he articulated the belief that by his baptism in the Jordan, Christ had sanctified all water. Luther retained exorcisms, the anointings, and the giving of the white robe and the lighted candle. In the second liturgy in his 1526 rite, most of the exorcisms, the anointings, and the lighted candle were abolished. Lutheran cities followed either one or the other of these rites, though with freedom to retain or add other things, and so there is considerable variation among the Lutheran baptismal rites, and this is particularly apparent in the forms used in the Church of Sweden.[15] Luther worked with an understanding of *adiaphora*—if something wasn't specifically prohibited in Scripture, it was optional and permissible.

Huldrych Zwingli, the reformer of Zurich, worked with a different hermeneutic. Unless Scripture mandated something, it should not be used. The first rite in Zurich was that of Leo Jud, which was based on Luther's 1526 rite. Zwingli believed that sacraments were badges of Christian profession—our testimony to belief—and not something in which God gives grace. At one point he seems to have sided with the growing Anabaptist movement, which held that only believers' baptism was valid, and repudiated infant baptism. Zwingli then changed his mind and defended infant baptism, using the concept of covenant, on analogy with male circumcision in the Old Testament. Infants are baptized into the covenant because of the faith and commitment of their parents. His baptismal rite of 1525, following Jud's earlier order, was brief. The minister asked the godparents if they wished for the child to be baptized. There followed a version of Luther's prayer for the water, a reading from Mark, and baptism into the triune name. The practice of dressing the initiate in a white garment was retained. The rite ended with a dismissal in peace.

The other famous member of the Reformation trilogy was John Calvin. He drew up a rite in 1540 when minister to the French congregation in Strasbourg.

---

15. Kent Burrison, "The Saving Flood: The Medieval Origins, Historical Development, and Theological Import of the Sixteenth Century Lutheran Baptismal Rites" (PhD diss., University of Notre Dame, 2002).

Whereas for his Communion service he used Martin Bucer's Strasbourg Rite as his own basis, for his baptism rite he used a previous liturgy of William Farel for Neuchâtel of 1533. Calvin altered some of Farel's explications. There was a request for the child's name, explication, a prayer and the Lord's Prayer, a second request for baptism, an admonition (which included a paraphrase of the Creed, the Ten Commandments, and a call to live a gospel life), a reading from Matthew 19, and baptism with the Matthean formula. Then came the dismissal.

Calvin made some slight changes in his 1542 rite for Geneva. Important for Calvin was the concept of covenant, and here he followed Zwingli. However, Calvin was also influenced by Luther and regarded sacraments as rites where God's grace may be given. Of the Reformation rites, one of the most conservative was that for the Church of England, made by Archbishop Thomas Cranmer. He shared Luther's idea of original sin, and he defended infant baptism—not on the grounds of covenant but on the basis of Jesus's receiving the little children. In the *Book of Common Prayer* of 1549, he retained many things from the medieval rite, and the first part of the rite was at the church door. He seemed in fact to give ritual expression to Mark 10 and the receiving of the children. He used Luther's flood prayer. The second part of the rite was conducted at the font. He retained the giving of the white robe and anointings. A major theme was incorporation into the ark of the church. A separate blessing of water was also provided.

A more Protestant book appeared in 1552, and here the rite of 1549 is simplified. It all takes place at the font; anointings were removed, as was the white robe. The blessing of the font was modified and incorporated into the service, but the priest no longer blessed the water. A petition to bless water had to wait until the prayer book was revised in 1662. Thomas Cranmer retained a service of confirmation, reserved for the bishop and necessary for admission to Communion. He used much of the medieval rite, though without the anointing and without explicit conferral of the Holy Spirit. Other Reformation churches modified confirmation to make it a rite of maturity in the faith, after a period of instruction. This was regarded as a "topping up" or supplying the explicit faith of the candidate missing in infant baptism. That was one answer to the problem of explicit profession of faith.

The other was that developed by the Anabaptists, and then later by the English Baptists, which regarded infant baptism as no baptism and insisted on believer's baptism—at a time of maturity with a personal confession of faith. In sixteenth-century Anabaptism and seventeenth-century English Baptist churches, the mode of baptism had varied, but as the English Baptist tradition developed, the mode of baptism became submersion, or "total immersion."

The Roman Rite was standardized at the Council of Trent, and Reformation rites underwent little change, though in the eighteenth-century "age of reason" some were modified to express the rationalism of the age, particularly by downplaying sin and the power of evil.

## Some Trends in the Modern and Postmodern Era

In the modern period many Western churches, including the Roman Catholic Church, have revised their liturgies in the wake of the liturgical and ecumenical movements, and there are far too many to discuss in detail. These liturgical revisions often draw on studies of the ancient classical texts while adapting the liturgy to current pastoral and missional needs. The Roman Catholic Church produced a rite for infants and a staged series of rites for adults—*Rites of Christian Initiation of Adults* (RCIA). Confirmation can be delegated to the priest. *RCIA* took seriously the need for instruction over a period of time, and other churches have made attempts to provide similar new liturgies. In Anglicanism there was a concern to rejoin confirmation to baptism, but this remains problematic when confirmation is still reserved as an episcopal rite. There has been a new emphasis on public baptism in the presence of a congregation; this was urged by all Protestant reformers, but since the Reformation many churches resorted to private family baptisms. Some churches use seasonal material, acknowledging that not everything can be said about baptism in a liturgy, and at different liturgical seasons certain themes can be more prominent, such as new birth at Epiphany and death/resurrection at Easter.

The World Council of Churches' report *Baptism, Eucharist and Ministry* (1982) outlined commonly accepted theological themes of baptism. It urged pedobaptist churches to think carefully about how they nurtured infants after baptism, and it urged those who practice only believers' baptism to reflect on the place of infants in the church communities. It also urged churches to consider using generous amounts of water in the ritual rather than a token sprinkling; and so that all churches could accept the validity of one another's baptisms, it recommended the use of the threefold Matthean formula. This was because some smaller groups insisted on baptism into the name of Jesus only, and others, because of the concern for inclusive language, were altering the Matthean formula to Creator, Redeemer, and Sustainer.[16] Some more

---

16. This formula in English avoids masculine language, but at the expense of an orthodox trinitarian doctrine—all three persons of the Trinity are involved in creation, redemption, and sustaining the church and world.

recent studies have urged the need to engage with parents seeking baptism for their infants, using it as a mission opportunity, and also to push back against the idea that the rites should minimize or omit references to evil and the devil.[17]

## Practical Implications for Worship

What are some lessons for the postmodern, missional church? The New Testament is the source for doctrine, not liturgy. Baptismal rites of the past provide sources for inspiration, but there is no golden age that can be revived for the present. Churches need to consider what is helpful for reuse and reimaging for today's challenges. Sweet-smelling oil, a lighted candle, a white garment, and a generous use of water can all be useful symbols.[18] Baptisteries need to visually proclaim the meaning of baptism; "bird baths" and plain, small swimming pools convey nothing much; new birth in church should have the same welcoming as a new member of a family usually has. Not everything about baptism and the Christian life can be crammed into a single liturgy; careful teaching after baptism is as important as prebaptismal preparation.

## For Further Reading

Bradshaw, Paul F. "Christian Initiation." In *The Oxford Handbook of Early Christian Ritual*, edited by Risto Uro, Juliette J. Day, Richard E. DeMaris, and Rikard Roitto, 523–37. Oxford: Oxford University Press, 2019.

Ferguson, Everett. *Baptism in the Early Church: History, Theology, and Liturgy in the First Five Centuries*. Grand Rapids: Eerdmans, 2013.

Jensen, Robin. *Baptismal Imagery in Early Christianity: Ritual, Visual, and Theological*. Grand Rapids: Baker Academic, 2012.

Johnson, Maxwell E. *The Rites of Christian Initiation: Their Evolution and Interpretation*. Rev. ed. Collegeville, MN: Pueblo, 2007.

17. Sandra Millar, *Life Events: Mission and Ministry at Baptisms, Weddings and Funerals* (London: Church House, 2018); Sarah Lawrence, *A Rite on the Edge: The Language of Baptism and Christening in the Church of England* (London: SCM, 2019); Tom Clammer, *Fight Valiantly: Evil and the Devil in Liturgy* (London: SCM, 2019).

18. New symbols should be used with caution. One church I served gave a "baptismal teddy bear," which was placed in the font, and the baptism itself was administered from a bowl. The bear was a nice gesture (for infants!) but had replaced serious use of water. What did it in fact symbolize?

Rempel, John D. "Baptism: The Art of Rising from the Dead." Chapter 5 in *Recapturing an Enchanted World: Ritual and Sacrament in the Free Church Tradition*. Downers Grove, IL: InterVarsity, 2020.

Spinks, Bryan D. *Early and Medieval Rituals and Theologies of Baptism: From the New Testament to the Council of Trent*. Aldershot, UK: Ashgate, 2006.

———. *Reformation and Modern Rituals and Theologies of Baptism: From Luther to Contemporary Practices*. Aldershot, UK: Ashgate, 2006.

# — 2 —

# Eucharist

## *Andrew McGowan*

W hen Christians first gathered to celebrate and affirm their faith, the question that shaped their meetings was not "How shall we worship?" but rather "How shall we eat?" Worship of course they did, but "worship" in the ancient world was not communal ritual alone.[1] Comprising any and all aspects of devotion to the gods or God, worship could mean performing everyday civic and familial duty, as well as undertaking specific ritual acts such as sacrifices and offerings. Followers of Jesus knew that he was son and image of the God of Israel, who dwelt in Jerusalem and who was worshiped there with sacrifices and prayers, as Jesus himself had once done. Yet they also spoke of Jesus as a definitive sacrifice, and of their daily lives, too, as forms of offering. To worship him was in at least certain respects a new thing, yet their initial response was not to build temples but to meet for meals.

### From Last Supper to Eucharist

Somewhat like family gatherings and somewhat like study groups, the meetings of Christ-followers were probably most like those of *collegia*, clubs or associations with various professional, social, and religious interests. *Collegia*

1. Andrew B. McGowan, *Ancient Christian Worship: Early Church Practices in Social, Historical, and Theological Perspective* (Grand Rapids: Baker Academic, 2014), 1–17.

18

were common in the Mediterranean world in antiquity and had a communal life centered on meals.[2] Like the famous banquets of Greek philosophers, these meals included not just food and drink but what we would term religious rituals such as prayer, as well as conversation, singing, and perhaps communal reading. Christian gatherings were to retain these elements, arrayed around the meal celebrated in memory of Jesus.

While these meals began alongside sacrifices rather than in place of them, Greco-Roman meals typically included prayer as well as offering practices, such as libations. At the Christian banquets, acts of blessing or giving thanks over the bread and cup, which were their signs of community in Jesus, were quickly understood as forms of thank offering. The meal thus came to be called "thanksgiving," *eucharistia*. This name and the practice to which it pointed reflected the centrality of thanksgiving over bread and cup in stories about Jesus, not only at the Last Supper but also during the miraculous feeding stories and resurrection meals. The focus on ritualizing the meal elements themselves, which were simple yet desirable in an environment where food insecurity was typical, was the original sense in which the Eucharist was thought of as "sacrificial." Since some traditional animal sacrifices of the temple had also been known as "thanksgivings" (Lev. 7), this offering of thanks had older biblical roots too.

In the first few centuries the supper, both sacred and substantial, had different names even while a common theme of thanksgiving with and for Jesus over bread and wine—and sometimes less, or more, than these—was characteristic.[3] Sometimes it was called an *agapē*, which later came to refer to substantial meals separate from the Eucharist. In Luke and Acts, "breaking of the bread" (Luke 24:35; Acts 2:42) evokes these gatherings. Paul's famous aside (1 Cor. 11:20) about the failed Corinthian "Lord's supper" (or, better perhaps, "banquet") did not become a common name for the meal but reflected an ideal based on recognizing the real host and inspirer of this banquet, who was a model for its conduct. Women as well as men participated, and they likely led at least some of these events. Around 200 CE the apologist Tertullian depicted the Christian sacramental gathering as a dinner party with mixed company but impeccable restraint:

> Our banquet shows its purpose by its name. The Greeks call it "Love." . . .
> Before reclining, we taste first of prayer to God. As much is eaten as satisfies

2. John S. Kloppenborg, *Christ's Associations: Connecting and Belonging in the Ancient City* (New Haven: Yale University Press, 2019).

3. See further Andrew B. McGowan, *Ascetic Eucharists: Food and Drink in Early Christian Ritual Meals* (Oxford: Clarendon, 1999).

hunger; as much is drunk as suits the modest. As much is eaten as is consistent with being those who remember that even during the night they have to worship God; as much spoken, as those who know that the Lord is listening. After hand-washing and lights, each is prompted to sing, as able, a hymn to God, from the holy Scriptures or composed, so the measure of our drinking is demonstrated. The dinner-party closes with prayer, as it began.[4]


## From Banquet to Liturgy

The shift from a communal supper to a morning ritual with only token foods had both theological and logistical causes. If the idea of Jesus's presence at the meal was a persistent symbolic center, understandings of just what happened to the meal elements themselves took time to emerge. Paul had observed that some of the Corinthians had sickened or died because they partook in an unworthy manner, without specifying how or why (1 Cor. 11:27–30). The authors of the *Didache* (ca. 100) excluded the unbaptized from their "holy" food. More positively, the second-century bishop Ignatius called the eucharistic foods a "medicine of immortality."[5] A little later (ca. 160), expatriate Syrian teacher Justin Martyr wrote about the gathering in Rome, which now included readings from Scripture and an extended prayer over bread and cup, now imbued with profound significance: "For we do not take these as common bread and common drink, but just as Jesus Christ our Savior had both flesh and blood for our salvation, so have we been taught that the food which is given thanks over by the prayer of his word, and from which our blood and flesh by transformation are nourished, is the flesh and blood of the same Jesus who was made flesh."[6]

While Justin's community still seems to have eaten a substantial meal, sending food parcels to those unable to be present, soon after this the Eucharist—perhaps initially as leftovers—was being eaten in the morning, both by individuals who wanted to break their fast with Jesus and by groups who gathered to receive the sacrament in small quantities.[7] The implications of larger numbers of people played a part in the shift; around 250 the African bishop Cyprian acknowledged the impossibility of the whole community gathering for a supper

---

4. Tertullian, *Apology* 39.16–18. Translations are the author's unless otherwise indicated.

5. Ignatius, *To the Ephesians* 20.

6. Justin, *First Apology* 66.

7. See Andrew B. McGowan, "Rethinking Agape and Eucharist in Early North African Christianity," *Studia Liturgica* 34 (2004): 165–76; and Clemens Leonhard, "Morning *salutationes* and the Decline of Sympotic Eucharists in the Third Century," *Zeitschrift für antikes Christentum / Journal of Ancient Christianity* 18, no. 3 (2015): 420–42.

according to Jesus's example, noting that a now-familiar morning celebration allowed all to be present.[8] Cyprian also developed more fulsomely a view of the Eucharist as a sacrifice parallel to those of the Roman authorities, its sacred food a holy alternative menu relative to the demonic "leftovers of idols."[9]

When the emperor Constantine became Christian and built grand civic halls dedicated to the apostles, these "basilicas" became the expected venue for eucharistic celebrations that were increasingly characterized by more fixed and elaborated rituals and prayers, and with accoutrements befitting a "liturgy," originally a sort of public ceremony. Gender roles became clearer in familiar ways, and concerns about impurity, including menstruation, sometimes led to separation of sexes.

The Roman and other Western rites related to it, the liturgies of James (especially in Syria and in India), those of Basil and of John Chrysostom (typical in the Greek-speaking Mediterranean), and Armenian, Egyptian, and Ethiopian liturgies all included fundamentally similar elements: scriptural readings, prayers, and the eucharistic prayer and Communion, along with hymns from various sources. The eucharistic prayers of these rites also shared a basic structure, including an opening dialogue, a preface, and, unlike the earlier prayers, the narrative of Jesus's Last Supper, which was one way they invoked Jesus's sacrificial death more clearly as a symbolic center. Most of these liturgies now also included specific prayers for the transformation of the gifts of bread and wine by the Holy Spirit, although the Roman liturgy tended increasingly to see the recitation of the "words of institution" ("this is my body," etc.) as a moment of consecration.

## East and West

Eastern eucharistic liturgies mostly developed into still-familiar forms during the first millennium. In Byzantine liturgy a sense was developed of the celebration not only as a commemoration of the Last Supper or of Jesus's death but as participation in an angelic and cosmic liturgy of which the mystery of Jesus's death and resurrection was the center. Commentaries such as that of Maximus the Confessor (seventh century) thus interpreted the details of the service allegorically, so that apparently prosaic features such as the movement of ministers in the sanctuary were related to a much larger and more profound reality: "The descent of the bishop from the throne and the dismissal of the catechumens signifies in general the second coming from heaven of our great

8. Cyprian, *Epistle* 63.
9. Cyprian, *The Lapsed* 2.

God and savior Jesus Christ and the separation of sinners from the saints and
the just retribution rendered to each. . . . The closing of the doors and the
entrance into the holy mysteries and the divine kiss and the recitation of the
symbol of faith [Creed] mean in general the passing away of sensible things
and the appearance of spiritual realities."[10]

The preparation of the eucharistic offerings was now overlain more thickly
with the imagery of animal sacrifice, a portion of the eucharistic bread (itself
called a *prosphora*, offering) being cut and then named the *amnos*, lamb.
Such elaborations of act and meaning accompanied a decline, however, in
actual reception of the Eucharist by those attending. As Communion itself
sometimes was reduced to an annual obligation, other sensory experiences
allowed for different forms of participation.[11] From the ninth century or so, the
consecrated bread was mixed with the chalice for those who did receive and
then distributed to communicants with a spoon, a custom that has influenced
other Eastern traditions; in the Egyptian Coptic Church, Communion in one
kind (bread) was sometimes practiced, but spoons have tended to prevail.[12]

Church historians can seem embarrassed that an immediate cause of the
lasting rift between Eastern and Western Christendom was a dispute over the
exact form of eucharistic bread.[13] More recent experiences with objects such
as statues and flags should tell us that there is nothing trivial about revered
symbols. Despite the obvious connection of unleavened bread with Passover
and the biblical narrative of eucharistic origins, the oldest Christian texts
about the Eucharist—including the Gospel narratives of the Last Supper—
use the generic word for bread, *artos*. This would originally have included
both leavened and unleavened bread, the latter of which was not merely a
peculiarity related to Passover but often eaten in subsistence-level economies
and communities in antiquity, because of the short time involved between
obtaining flour and eating. The evidence for an unwavering focus on unleavened bread as a faithful imitation of Jesus's example appears clearly in the
West only late in the first millennium, although Armenian Christians were
using unleavened bread in the sixth century and probably before, and they
were in dispute (and schism) with the Byzantines over this too, long before it
became an issue with the West.

10. Maximus, *Mystagogia* 24, in *Maximus Confessor: Selected Writings*, trans. George C.
Berthold, Classics of Western Spirituality (New York: Paulist Press, 1985), 209.

11. Hugh Wybrew, *The Orthodox Liturgy: The Development of the Eucharistic Liturgy in
the Byzantine Rite* (Crestwood, NY: St. Vladimir's Seminary Press, 1990), 59–60.

12. See the description in John Patrick Crichton-Stuart Bute, *The Coptic Morning Service
for the Lord's Day* (London: Cope and Fenwick, 1908), 129.

13. Brett Whalen, "Rethinking the Schism of 1054: Authority, Heresy, and the Latin Rite,"
*Traditio* 62 (2007): 1–24.

Leavened bread, however, came to be seen as the appropriate eucharistic offering in the Byzantine East and in Syrian and Egyptian traditions, not least because it was aesthetically and economically more suited as a gift.[14] The Roman Church saw the Eastern practices as "deviation" and as an affront not only to the sacrament itself but to the apostolic authority of Rome, whose connection to Peter surely guaranteed authentic maintenance of tradition. Each side then elaborated the theological possibilities of their preferred breads; while the West accused the "Prozymites" (*zymos* is "leaven" in Greek) of dismissing the example of Jesus at the Last Supper as well as apostolic authority, the Byzantine leaders viewed the "dead" unleavened bread of the Western "Azymites" as akin to liturgical roadkill, a defiled or unworthy sacrifice. These two views, bound up in the political claims of rival bishops, fueled distinctive elements of the two strands of liturgical theology. The Western Mass thus increasingly commemorated Jesus's death single-mindedly, while the Eastern liturgy emphasized the whole paschal mystery and the renewed reality it instituted.

## The Eucharist in the West

In the medieval West the Mass (as it became known) was the center of public worship as well as private devotion. From the ninth century or so, clergy (who increased considerably in number) celebrated private Masses as part of a grand sacrificial economy in which the fate of souls was at issue. A sacrificial understanding of eucharistic celebration was not new, but its application to the deficits of personal sin, during and after earthly life, now took on a new centrality. Understandings of atonement based on satisfaction added to commodification of eucharistic celebration; more was now clearly better. More Masses would re-present the sacrifice of Jesus more often and thus please the divine, and hence benefit the souls seeking final purification in purgatory.

Penitential concerns and prayer for the many departed drove much of the change visible in medieval Western ritual as well. Priests often said multiple Masses in a day, mostly privately, and other vestiges of communal celebration such as the roles of deacons and others were lessened. Concern for the seriousness of sin and the risks of unworthy reception meant that the objective fact of the Mass being said was usually more important, and safer, than participating via Communion. Yet if eucharistic celebration was often separated from a liturgical assembly, the consecrated elements themselves (or at least the host)

14. Mahlon H. Smith, *And Taking Bread: Cerularius and the Azyme Controversy of 1054* (Paris: Beauchesne, 1978).

increasingly became the object of popular devotion outside the Mass itself.[15] Theological speculation such as that of Paschasius Radbertus (ninth century), who wrote around the same time that evidence for private Masses emerges clearly, articulated systemically the meaning of the consecrated elements as truly the body and blood of Jesus, even in isolation from the celebration itself. Whether pious practice or focused theology drove these developments is hard to say, but they accompanied each other.

The enduring high point of medieval Western eucharistic and sacramental theology was the work of Thomas Aquinas, who refined the eucharistic theory known as transubstantiation, wherein the real essences or substances of bread and wine were changed into those of Christ's body and blood, even as the outward appearance or "accidents" remained: "The body of Christ can only come to be in the sacrament by means of the conversion of the substance of bread into his body; and that which is converted into anything does not remain after the conversion."[16]

## Reformation

The reforms of Western Christianity in the sixteenth century and after included radical criticism of the purposes and theories of Western eucharistic celebration, and by extension of their forms as well. Paid private requiems, closely related to indulgences, may have been the most obvious target for Martin Luther and those who followed him. Luther and other reformers held up biblical (and to some extent patristic) models of celebration and piety that emphasized participation and simplicity, not just over against the whole political economy of Masses but also in contrast to the specific ritual and the theology attached thereto.[17] In his treatise *On the Babylonian Captivity of the Church* Luther inveighed, for instance, against restricting Communion to one kind (which had become common in the few centuries preceding, as a practical measure), against transubstantiation, and against the sacrificial economy of the Mass.[18] Yet while he rejected the specifically Thomist and Aristotelian metaphysical framework of accidents and essences, Luther was not against the idea of Christ's real presence: "The bread and wine are really

15. Nathan Mitchell, *Cult and Controversy: The Worship of the Eucharist Outside Mass* (Collegeville, MN: Liturgical Press, 1982), 66–198.

16. Henry Bettenson and Chris Maunder, *Documents of the Christian Church* (Oxford: Oxford University Press, 2011), 154.

17. Esther Chung-Kim, *Inventing Authority: The Use of the Church Fathers in Reformation Debates over the Eucharist* (Waco: Baylor University Press, 2011).

18. Bettenson and Maunder, *Documents of the Christian Church*, 210–11.

bread and wine and the true flesh and blood of Christ is in them in the same fashion and the same degree as they hold them to be beneath their accidents. . . . Fire and iron are two substances; yet they are so mingled in red-hot iron that any part is at once iron and fire. What prevents the glorious body of Christ from being in every part of the substance of bread?"[19]

Others, however, such as John Calvin and especially Huldrych Zwingli, thought more radically about the question of eucharistic presence. Calvin did affirm the reception of Jesus's body and blood in the Lord's Supper (a term that appears only around this time as a name for the Christian meal, as does "Holy Communion"), but as a spiritual reality, of which the physical bread and wine were signs:

> That sacred communication of his own flesh and blood by which Christ pours his life into us, just as if he were to penetrate into the marrow of our bones, he witnesses and attests in the Supper. And that he does not by putting before us a vain or empty sign, but offering there the efficacy of his Spirit, by which he fulfils his promise. . . . If it is true that the visible sign is offered to us to attest the granting of the invisible reality, then, on receiving the symbol of the body, we may be confident that the body itself is no less given to us.[20]

Zwingli argued more radically that the eucharistic elements were signs, not so much of an objective spiritual act of communion, but of the communion always existing in the church as Jesus's body. While least fully articulated of the key reformers' views, this last position anticipated modern ideas of signification and subjectivity, and a shift away from metaphysical understandings of the Eucharist altogether.

While the reformers theoretically sought a recovery of the patterns they discerned in the New Testament and the early church, their diverse theologies and varied forms of authority meant that what came was the shattering of the Western medieval synthesis, not its renewal. Protestant eucharistic celebration was united primarily in its use of the vernacular and in its relative austerity; the old ritual trappings of attendant bodies and objects—genuflection, vestments, and accoutrements like incense—seemed to signal theologies that were being rejected, and hence were limited or abandoned. While some Lutherans maintained use of vestments for a time (and more enduringly in Scandinavia), Calvinists and others were uncompromising. Vessels and furnishings were now chosen to emphasize the meal to which Jesus invited his guests, so that simplicity with reverence was generally the order of the day. Bread and wine

19. Bettenson and Maunder, *Documents of the Christian Church*, 210.
20. Bettenson and Maunder, *Documents of the Christian Church*, 228.

themselves were more likely to be those used every day; while the symbolism of leavening did not feature in this controversy, many reformers were skeptical of traditional unleavened wafers as hinting at a sacral quality in the physical signs themselves.

Most Protestant traditions also maintained the traditional emphasis on personal sanctity as necessary for reception, even if the eucharistic elements themselves were no longer seen as requiring reverence, and though personal confession was no longer a prerequisite. While reformers not only insisted that the Eucharist be a communal event but also urged more regular participation, these hopes were not fulfilled, joined as they were to continued dire warnings about sin, repentance, and unworthy reception. Protestantism thus enshrined the medieval wariness of eating and drinking the eucharistic elements, rather than overcoming it. Since attendance at church continued to be much more normative than actual Communion, other forms of liturgical gathering, based on occasional preaching services or the monastic daily offices of prayer, took on a new and abiding, if originally unintended, prominence. The "worship service," if not by that name, begins here.

## Catholic Reformation

Roman Catholic theology and practice did not stand still either. The shock of what seemed heresy and schism drove its leaders to a process of reflection and refinement, a Catholic Reformation whose most famous and most systematic expression was the Council of Trent (1545–1563). The Council decreed both on eucharistic theology and on the liturgy itself, establishing norms of ritual that would remain until the twentieth century. Dogmatically, the Tridentine fathers resolutely supported the doctrines of transubstantiation and of eucharistic sacrifice, and defended Communion in bread alone as well as the veneration of the sacramental elements and their use outside the context of the Mass—thus reflecting in their conciliar mirror the various claims of the reformers to the contrary.

There were common threads in both reformations nevertheless. Simplification was one; the Council sought to refine the liturgy and to clarify the essential elements of the rite, since a variety of accretions and local variations had led to confusion about essentials. Council fathers and reformers alike knew that ragged practice was not conducive to the expression of their eucharistic faith, but they differed as to what true core would or should be revealed when the dross was scraped away. A second thread was that both reforms involved a quest for greater uniformity. While the actual diversity of Protestant practice rarely achieved this, reforming controversialists and liturgists often lacked the means to impose uniformity beyond local settings. In England, concern for uniformity had preceded the promulgation of reformed liturgies, when Henry VIII sought to impose the popular Sarum Rite (largely the Roman, with some local ritual adaptations) over local variations. The idea of a *Book of Common Prayer*, introduced under Henry's son Edward VI as a restrained Protestant model, was as much driven by the quest for a "common" form of worship as by the search of a more truely reformed one.

## The Eucharist and the Modern World

Between the Reformation and the twentieth century, various Western and Eastern traditions elaborated their theologies, developed their rituals, and conducted their controversies, but deep shifts in fundamental beliefs or practices were rare. Where change did occur, it was often in the course of rediscovering older views. Theologians of the eighteenth century in England (such as the "non-jurors," freed from allegiance to the prayer book by schism) rediscovered aspects of ancient liturgy, such as in the fourth-century *Apostolic Constitutions*, and influenced many others. Some Anglicans—including John and Charles Wesley—came more actively to reconsider the idea of eucharistic sacrifice, without the medieval emphasis on purgatory or the commodifying implications, and yearned for more regular Communion. John Wesley's zeal for participation was warmer than that of most contemporary Anglicans: "Let every one, therefore, who has either any desire to please God, or any love of his own soul, obey God, and consult the good of his own soul, by communicating every time he can; like the first Christians, with whom the Christian sacrifice was a constant part of the Lord's day service."[21]

Charles Wesley's eucharistic hymns also reflect an unmistakably "high" theology. At least one of the factors that led to John's appointment of elders for Methodism, in a lasting break from Anglican polity, was a desire to ensure the availability of the sacraments on the American frontiers served by itinerants. The same reality of sparsely populated regions, however, meant American Methodism never really fulfilled John's picture of regular Communion and instead resembled other Protestant groups in the prevalence of word-centered liturgy.[22]

21. "The Duty of Constant Communion," in *The Works of the Rev. John Wesley* (New York: J. & J. Harper, 1826), 7:171.
22. Lester Ruth, "A Reconsideration of the Frequency of the Eucharist in Early American Methodism," *Methodist History* 34, no. 1 (1995): 47–58.

The Methodist movement was also among traditions that revived forms of the *agapē* feast, claiming the more festive and participatory aspect of ancient meal celebrations, but taking these to have been a separate set of practices from the Eucharist itself.[23] Some Brethren, Moravians and other Pietists, and Seventh-day Adventists have held these as simple suppers, sometimes with the "Lord's Supper" included and often incorporating another attempt at ritual retrieval, that of footwashing. While more a reflection of late antique developments than primitive ones—there were also forms of vestigial *agapē* in Eastern Orthodoxy, more akin to potluck suppers or coffee hours—these love feasts became periodic additions to the worship of these movements. In the nineteenth century, some of these same groups and others also raised the possibility (or for them necessity) of avoiding all alcohol, including at Communion, on what were primarily moral grounds, although typically some efforts were made to suggest that references to "wine" in ancient practice could be read differently.

Images of the early church also influenced the renewal of more Catholic theology in Anglican circles, at first in the theoretical forms taught by an "Oxford Movement" led by John Keble, E. B. Pusey, and J. H. Newman in the 1830s. In the following generation, forms of ceremony and ornaments reflecting Western medieval custom found new favor in Anglican as well as some English Roman Catholic circles, where the baroque had long seemed to be the aesthetic of the Council of Trent. This "Anglo-Catholicism" had at least some influence throughout Anglicanism, since while even use of a colored stole and altar candles had been unthinkable in the mid-nineteenth century, by the mid-twentieth they were ubiquitous, yet had also lost their specific significance as markers of sacrificial ritual.

## The Liturgical Movement

Through the twentieth century a remarkable period of renewal and convergence took place, again with the ancient church as an intellectual source of inspiration, but now with an eye to the demands of modernity and with an ecumenical dimension hard to imagine not long before. Shortly before the Great War, Roman Catholic monastic leaders Lambert Beauduin and Ildefons Herwegen had called for a return to more active participation in the liturgy in their tradition.[24] They began to seek models for a simplified and more com-

23. Lester Ruth, *A Little Heaven Below: Worship at Early Methodist Quarterly Meetings* (Nashville: Kingswood, 2000).

24. John Fenwick and Bryan Spinks, *Worship in Transition: The Twentieth Century Liturgical Movement* (London: T&T Clark, 1995), 23–28.

munally focused approach in ancient writings—such as the fourth-century *Catecheses* of Cyril of Jerusalem and a document enthusiastically identified as the *Apostolic Tradition* attributed to Hippolytus of Rome, a figure of the early third century. While this latter treatise is now regarded somewhat differently, it presented a model of eucharistic celebration that would underlie the most radical revision of the Roman Catholic liturgy ever undertaken.[25]

In the following generation, Catholic scholars like Josef Jungmann were joined by others such as the Anglican Gregory Dix in recovering a simpler, more participatory, and (as they saw it) more authentic eucharistic celebration via historical investigation of these and similar sources.[26] The liturgical ethos thus identified was less penitential than medieval or reformed liturgies, and implicitly lowered some of the inherited barriers to fuller participation and more regular Communion. Lay participation in responses, readings, and distribution of Communion was recovered. The shape of the rite, emphasized in Dix's work particularly, became a new focus for liturgical scholars. This included discerning a basic twofold structure wherein word and sacrament were seen as complementary within the Eucharist. Dix's claimed "fourfold shape" (taking, blessing, breaking, distributing) provided a model that put new emphasis on the first (offertory) and third (fraction) of these elements, as well as on Communion itself, in liturgical revision.

The arrival during the same period of the ecumenical movement embodied in the creation of the World Council of Churches (founded in 1948) enhanced new conversation across denominational boundaries for this Liturgical Movement. The reconstructed ancient Eucharist provided elements that were to become characteristic of many modern rites, as mainline denominations joined in the process of looking for a model older than either the disputes of the Reformation or the abuses that had driven them. A union of Anglican, Presbyterian, and Methodist churches in southern India provided opportunity for one of the first fully revised liturgies that reflected these principles and also included some elements from local orthodox practice.

For Protestants, these developments seemed somewhat catholicizing in their emphasis on the sacrament as central to worship. For Roman Catholics, however, and for the Anglicans already participating in their own Catholic renewal, the model echoed reformed understandings both in the centrality of Scripture and in the emphasis on community and meal. Nevertheless, for

25. Paul F. Bradshaw, Maxwell E. Johnson, and L. Edward Phillips, *The Apostolic Tradition: A Commentary*, Hermeneia (Minneapolis: Fortress, 2002).

26. Josef A. Jungmann, *The Mass of the Roman Rite, Its Origins and Development (Missarum Sollemnia)* (New York: Benziger Bros, 1959); Gregory Dix, *The Shape of the Liturgy*, new ed. (New York: Continuum, 2005).

some decades these models carried a great deal of weight across a remarkable variety of traditions as many denominational groups revised their liturgies to make them both more ancient and more modern. The two high points of the Liturgical Movement were arguably the reforms carried by the Second Vatican Council in its Constitution on the Sacred Liturgy (*Sancrosanctum Concilium*) in 1963, introducing use of the vernacular and many of the other features already mentioned, and the "Lima Liturgy" promulgated in the World Council of Churches in 1983, which could claim some form of support across a spectrum that included Orthodox and even some Pentecostal churches.[27] Today the worship of the Roman Catholic and Western mainline churches are indelibly marked by these revised forms. Orthodox liturgy gave only limited attention to the same developments, however, seeing their own maintenance of ancient liturgical texts as a model to which the West was now leaning. Yet just as ecumenism itself lost momentum at the end of the twentieth century, so too the Liturgical Movement was revealed to have gone only so far, as the vigor of many mainline churches seemed to stutter and the relative strength of fundamentalist and Pentecostal groups untouched by these developments became more evident. In many such communities that had remained outside the twentieth-century ecumenical conversation, the Eucharist thus remains a periodic observance at best, reflecting older evangelical patterns in most details, although the lessening of barriers based on unworthy reception may be true across the board.

If one limit of the ecumenical conversation and consensus about the Eucharist was revealed in the changing political and theological shape of contemporary Christianity, another has been shifting assumptions about eucharistic food and drink. The evolved postmedieval wafer and the teetotal cup of pietism or evangelicalism appear as modern "snack" foods in the West, more "crackers and juice" than bread and wine, and so various further changes start from this point rather than from bread and wine. More robust forms of enculturation have been proposed elsewhere or adopted out of local need. Sudanese Protestant Christians, influenced by evangelicalism and living in close proximity with Islam, have sometimes used red hibiscus tea (*karkade*) as a simulacrum of red wine, which is both rare and often considered undesirable. Elsewhere the questions have been more whimsical, if less widely adopted. East Asian Protestants have asked whether forms of solid and liquid food based on rice were not possible, Pacific Islanders have wondered about coconut products, and other Africans have suggested yams and palm wine,

---

27. Max Thurian, *Ecumenical Perspectives on Baptism, Eucharist and Ministry*, Faith and Order Papers 116 (Geneva: World Council of Churches, 1983).

all responding in part to the colonial connotations of wheat bread and grape wine. Yet these traditional elements would not have been the indigenous foods of western Europeans either, prior to the expansion of both the Roman Empire and the Roman church bearing the ambiguous gifts of ancient eastern Mediterranean cuisine.

## Practical Implications for Worship

For most Christians and for most of history, the Eucharist has been not merely an important practice but the center of worship, both because it has been understood as a command of Jesus and because of the belief, however articulated, in his presence in the celebration. The most obvious lesson of eucharistic history, then, is to celebrate it. The onus lies on any community for which Eucharist is not regular or central to "worship" to consider why, and to ponder how alternative patterns may be the results of an early modern theological accident—the failure of the Protestant reformers to bring their adherents to more regular Communion—which has been hallowed by custom. Whether "high" or "low" in theology or ritual, eucharistic celebration suggests that its own meaning and power rests not on the predetermined needs or wants of participants but on what is faithful to Christ, as an encounter with him, and hence not merely appropriate but potentially transformative.

The most interesting and fruitful moments of renewal in eucharistic practice have often been inspired by past engagement with the example and command of Jesus. These experiences place the historic Christian community itself firmly before us, not merely as an interesting source but as a living reality, whose abiding relevance counters glib comparisons between past tradition and modern sensibility. The theological reason that these historic examples have power—most fully acknowledged in Orthodox theology of the liturgy perhaps—is the possibility that when even a few gather to celebrate this meal in memory of Jesus, they join a much larger fellowship of saints and angels, who celebrate across all times and through the cosmos "by him, with him, and in him."

## For Further Reading

Berger, Teresa. *Gender Differences and the Making of Liturgical History: Lifting a Veil on Liturgy's Past.* Farnham, UK: Ashgate, 2011.

Bradshaw, Paul F., and Maxwell E. Johnson. *The Eucharistic Liturgies: Their Evolution and Interpretation.* Collegeville, MN: Liturgical Press, 2012.

Fenwick, John, and Bryan Spinks. *Worship in Transition: The Twentieth Century Liturgical Movement*. London: T&T Clark, 1995.

McGowan, Andrew B. *Ancient Christian Worship: Early Church Practices in Social, Historical, and Theological Perspective*. Grand Rapids: Baker Academic, 2014.

Wybrew, Hugh. *The Orthodox Liturgy: The Development of the Eucharistic Liturgy in the Byzantine Rite*. Crestwood, NY: St. Vladimir's Seminary Press, 1990.

## — 3 —

# Liturgical Time

## *Paul F. Bradshaw*

Ancient civilizations ordered their lives according to the natural cycles around them, the alternation of day and night, the regular phases of the moon, and the apparent annual path of the sun from the winter solstice through the vernal equinox and onward to its highest point in the sky at the summer solstice before returning via the autumnal equinox to the lowest point again at the winter solstice. And because they had no detailed knowledge of the astronomical forces that drove these movements, they invested them with religious significance. As religions developed in the course of history, they tended to retain some or all of these phenomena as the basis for marking liturgical time, continuing to recognize their symbolic value even after scientific explanations for them had replaced attributions to divine intervention. Quite often the traditional practice was retained but then endowed with a quite new meaning more closely related to the central beliefs of the particular religious tradition.

The concept of liturgical time is understood by some simply as a signpost or reminder—for example, a reminder to pray at a particular hour or a marker of an important event that took place on a particular date in the past. But for others it is something much more profound than that. Through a symbolic or sacramental experience, it is an entering into a spiritual reality, often either recalled from the past or anticipated from the future. So, for example, the Jewish Passover meal includes these words:

> In every generation a person is obligated to regard himself as if he had come out of Egypt, as it is said: "You shall tell your child on that day, it is because of this

that the Lord did for me when I left Egypt" [Exod. 13:8]. The Holy One, blessed be He, redeemed not only our ancestors from Egypt, but He redeemed also us with him, as it is said: "It was us that He brought out from there, so that He might bring us in to give us the land that He swore to our ancestors" [Deut. 6:23].[1]

The liturgy of time is often also a liturgy of place, involving a procession or pilgrimage to a particular holy site associated with the spiritual reality that is being celebrated, or at least some movement to a symbolic representation of that holy place. The ritual performed may be quite simple or it may include elaborate ceremonies. Some years ago the liturgical scholar Kenneth Stevenson proposed a useful distinction between what he termed "unitive" celebrations, in which a rich complex of saving acts are compressed into a single liturgy, and "representational" celebrations, where each individual element in the sacred story receives its own visual or symbolic expression. Between these extremes, he situated what he called "rememorative" celebrations, where some symbolic artifacts or ritual actions might be used to enhance the liturgy but no attempt is made to reproduce dramatically every detail of the story, as would be in a passion or nativity play. Popular piety always tends to eschew the stark unitive in favor of the more vivid representational (which explains why many pastors introduce live donkeys to a Palm Sunday procession), whereas effective liturgy aims at the rememorative, which provides stimulus for the senses without descending into play-acting, as though we did not know the end of the story.

In his Letter to the Galatians, Paul criticized his readers for observing "days, and months, and seasons, and years" (4:10 RSV). While biblical scholars dispute whether he was referring to their persisting in their former pagan practices or being persuaded by other Christians to adopt Jewish practices that he regarded as an unnecessary burden on them, some Reformation churches have traditionally interpreted the passage as forbidding the observance of any Christian festivals and holy days, for which in any case they could find no warrant in the New Testament, and so eliminated from their practice everything except the weekly Lord's Day.

## Day and Night

Peoples in primeval times very commonly marked the beginning and end of each day with prayer, and especially the evening, as the intense darkness of the

---

1. This translation of the Passover Haggadah can be found in Joseph B. Soloveitchik, *The Seder Night: An Exalted Evening—The Passover Haggadah*, ed. Menachem Genak (New York: Orthodox Union Press, 2009), 101.

night held many terrors for them. So, for example, we find religious ceremonies surrounding the ancient domestic lamp-lighting each evening throughout the eastern Mediterranean area, with a similar practice also being maintained in early Christian homes, where thanksgiving was made for the gift of light. Among Jews, the recitation of the Shema (the words of Deut. 6:4–9; 11:13–21; Num. 15:37–41) became standard practice twice a day in accordance with its injunction to do so "when you lie down and when you rise" (Deut. 6:7; 11:19). Alongside that, and distinct from it, there was also the custom of prayer three times a day practiced by some (e.g., Dan. 6:10). Probably originally intended to mark the sun's rising, zenith, and setting, it later became associated with the cult in the Jerusalem temple and was said to mark the times of the morning and afternoon (evening) sacrifices and the closing of the temple gates at night.

### Early Christianity

Early Christians were directed to "pray without ceasing" (1 Thess. 5:17), which was generally understood by them to mean turning their whole life into an act of prayer, an offering of themselves to God (see Rom. 12:1) but punctuated by regular and specific moments of conscious prayer. In this way they were to be ready for the return of their Lord, whenever that might be. The most common practice, doubtless derived from Judaism, seems to have been to pray not less than three times a day. In rural areas these times would almost certainly have been morning, noon, and evening, but it appears that in urban settings they were instead the hours of the day that were publicly announced in cities—the third, sixth, and ninth hours of the Roman day (approximately 9:00 a.m., noon, and 3:00 p.m.). As eschatological expectations gradually subsided, various biblical precedents instead became associated with these hours, prominent among them remembrance of the hours of the crucifixion (Mark 15:25, 33–34). We also hear of prayer in the middle of the night, apparently linked to New Testament references to the return of Jesus "like a thief in the night" (Matt. 24:43; 1 Thess. 5:2, 4; 2 Pet. 3:10; Rev. 16:15). This latter practice was not particularly arduous in a premodern society, where not much could be done during the hours of darkness and people anyway commonly broke their sleep into two parts.

By the third century Christians were being encouraged by some leaders to increase the number of times they prayed, combining the two patterns of threefold prayer to produce five hours of daily prayer—morning, third, sixth, and ninth hours, and evening—together with prayer during the night. It is of course impossible to know how many followed this counsel. In the fourth century, when the persecutions of Christians had ceased, prayer services began to be held publicly in church buildings, usually just twice a day, morning and evening. This limitation seems to have been partially for practical reasons (most people were not free to attend during the other hours of the day and it was unsafe to be outdoors at night) and partially for symbolic reasons (these two hours were understood as the spiritual fulfillment of the morning and evening sacrifices of the Old Testament). Thus, only the especially devout and those living together in nascent religious communities tended to observe the other hours of prayer. The eventual addition of prayer at bedtime enabled these communities to claim to fulfill Psalm 119:164, "seven times a day I praise you."

On the other hand, some others rejected particular times of prayer altogether and in a life of desert solitude devoted themselves to almost continuous prayer, with minimal interruptions for sleep and eating, aiming to fulfill more literally St. Paul's injunction to "pray without ceasing." However, in the course of time many of these ascetics gathered together in monastic communities, where some specific hours of prayer were observed communally, even though the members were expected to continue in prayer on their own for the rest of the time. When these communities rose for prayer during the night, they tended to forgo further sleep and extend the prayer into a vigil lasting until morning, a practice that was imitated by urban monastic communities too.

### Later Developments

Later religious orders in the West tended to adopt the spirituality of the desert ascetics but the prayer practices of the urban monastic communities, generally adding the first hour (Prime) to the other offices celebrated each day, to produce seven times of prayer during the daytime, together with a vigil office for part of each night. Each of these became longer in form as the years went by, leaving less time for other activities during the day, and, what is more, came to be imposed on all members of the clergy as well, reducing their opportunities for pastoral and other work. A minor revision and abbreviation was made after the Council of Trent in the sixteenth century.

Although all the churches of the Reformation encouraged their members to engage in some form of prayer each day, the Church of England was alone in continuing to require its clergy to celebrate a fixed pattern of daily morning and evening prayer in their churches, which it was hoped that some laypeople would attend. Drawing on some elements from the medieval services, the forms centered on the regular reading of Scripture and the recitation of all 150 psalms in order. In the twentieth century the Roman Catholic Church revised its daily offices—renamed the Liturgy of the Hours—translating them into the vernacular and reducing the number required each day.

## The Week

Different divisions of the year were used among ancient peoples, but the concept of a month loosely related to the lunar cycle was most common. It appears that the Babylonians were responsible for the further division of the lunar month into quarters consisting of seven days. This method of reckoning the passage of time was adopted in Israelite religion, observing the seventh day of each week as a rest from labor (the Sabbath) and treating the whole seven days as a memorial of creation (Gen. 1).

### Early Christianity

Although the New Testament contains some references to the first day of the week that seem to some scholars to indicate a special emphasis on that day in the earliest Christian communities (especially Acts 20:7–12; 1 Cor. 16:2), it is not until toward the end of the first century that the term "the Lord's Day" emerges to denote Sunday (Rev. 1:10; *Didache* 14.1), together with the first firm evidence that it had begun to constitute the regular weekly occasion for the celebration of the Eucharist, and that consequently any observance of the Sabbath by Christians was opposed, in order to differentiate them from nascent Judaism. Sunday was not at first viewed as replacing the Sabbath for Christians—the true Sabbath rest was to be a feature of the Age to Come—nor solely as a commemoration of the resurrection, but as a day of rejoicing in anticipation of that Age to Come. Later, explicit prohibitions of fasting or kneeling for prayer (i.e., expressing penitence) were issued with respect to that day.

Just as pious Jews had fasted twice each week, on Mondays and Thursdays, so too did Christians, but on Wednesdays and Fridays instead, so as to differentiate their practice. These days were known as "stations," a military term indicating that Christians were "on watch," especially alert for the Lord's return. Not surprisingly, Friday eventually became the more prominent of the two, because of its association with the day of the crucifixion. Especially among Christians in the eastern Mediterranean area, Saturday came to occupy something of an intermediate position, not a day when any voluntary fasting should take place but not equal in status to Sunday.

### Later Developments

The emperor Constantine in 321 made Sunday a day of rest from work for everyone except farmers. Among Christians, however, the emphasis continued to fall on its being a day for participation in eucharistic worship rather than on its being primarily a day of rest, and it was not until the Middle Ages that Sunday came to be viewed as "the Christian Sabbath," and the Old Testament commandments about the Sabbath understood to apply to Sunday. This view has continued among many Christians down to the present day, although modern biblical and historical scholarship has influenced some churches to return to an earlier understanding of the day.

## The Year

The seasons of the year held great importance in primitive societies, which were dependent on the right weather conditions for the successful growing of crops or raising of sheep and cattle. It is thought, for example, that the Jewish Passover has its ultimate roots in a spring sacrifice performed by semi-nomadic herders to ward off evil at the lambing season before they set out for summer pasture, later merged with the celebration by settled farmers of the first cereal crop of the year (the Feast of Unleavened Bread). The Feast of Tabernacles (Sukkot) also began as an autumnal harvest festival. In time all these feasts came to be reinterpreted as a memorial of the nation's deliverance from slavery in Egypt and subsequent journey through the wilderness: the Passover sacrifice of a lamb recalling the protection given to the people of Israel when God spared them from destruction in Egypt, the unleavened bread the need to escape before it had time to rise (Exod. 12), and Sukkot the time when they lived in tents on their journey (Lev. 23).

### Easter

Only one annual festival seems to have been observed by the first Jewish Christians, a transformation of the Jewish Passover, recognizing Christ as the true paschal lamb, whose sacrificial death brought them salvation (see the apparently metaphorical use of that expression in 1 Cor. 5:7, and the references to Christ as the lamb of God in John 1:29, 36, and in Revelation). Kept on the same day as the Jewish Passover, and known by the same name in Greek, *Pascha*, it too was preceded by a day of fasting, but eventually began to distinguish itself by extending the fast into the late evening, during which a vigil was kept while the Jews feasted, and the Christian eucharistic feasting only began after that.

Sometime during the second century, other Christians, too, apparently adopted the festival but did not observe it on the same day as its Jewish predecessor (the evening of the fourteenth/fifteenth of the month Nisan). Instead they located the vigil and feast on the Saturday evening following the Jewish date, after a day of fasting (no doubt counting it as their Sunday Eucharist). Toward the end of that century a dispute arose as to which form of celebration was the right one. Both sides claimed tradition in support of their practice, but those keeping Saturday/Sunday were eventually in the majority and dismissed their opponents as "Quartodecimans" (Latin for "Fourteeners") who were wrongly imitating Judaism.

Very probably because of its connection to Sunday, in the third century the meaning of the celebration shifted, from passion to passage, from a primary emphasis on the sacrificial death of Christ to his passing over from death to life in the resurrection. It may have been because of that shift in theology that at Rome and in North Africa the Easter liturgy became the preferred occasion for the baptism of new converts (see Rom. 6:3–11). The late-night hour for the Eucharist was understood as related to the time Jesus was thought to have risen from the dead, with some keeping it at midnight, others later or earlier. Because the paschal fast on Saturday followed the regular weekly day of fasting on Friday, the whole period began to be seen in the West as a *triduum*, a three-day unit of liturgical time, two days of preparatory fasting followed by a day of rejoicing, while in the East some extended the preparatory fasting to the whole week.

During the Middle Ages, however, because of the development of Holy Week liturgies and of a piety focused on the passion and death of Christ, the centrality of the Easter vigil diminished until for convenience it began to be customary to celebrate it during the day on Saturday, robbing it of the dramatic effect of darkness, and commonly including only a blessing of the water in the font and no actual baptisms then. This remained the case until, as a first step in liturgical renewal, the Roman Catholic Holy Week rites were revised in the 1950s. This included the restoration of the vigil to its former centrality in the week, with its celebration in darkness and the inclusion of baptisms where possible, and in any case the introduction of a renewal of a baptismal affirmation of faith made by the whole congregation. These changes in time brought about a similar alteration of practice in other churches and the introduction of a vigil in many cases where it had previously been unknown.

### Pentecost

There is an apparent link between the name Pentecost and the Jewish Feast of Pentecost or Feast of Weeks, occurring on the fiftieth day (Greek *pentekostē*) after Passover and celebrating both the wheat harvest (Exod. 34:22; Deut. 16:9–12) and the traditional anniversary of the giving of the law on Mount Sinai. However, there is no firm evidence for the continuation of this feast among the earliest Christians: it is suddenly attested in various sources around the end of the second century, and it always refers to a prolongation of Easter rejoicing for fifty days, not a festival on the fiftieth day, in spite of its name. Every day of the season was treated like a Sunday, with no kneeling or fasting. It was only toward the end of the fourth century that the fiftieth day began to be given special prominence, as a commemoration of the gift of the Spirit (Acts 2:1–41), and in some places of the ascension of Jesus too (Luke 24:51; Acts 1:1–12), although by the fifth century the latter had everywhere come to be sited more naturally on the fortieth day after Easter. This led in turn to the eventual breakup of the fifty-day period into a series of separate festivals, each with an octave attached. It was only in the liturgical revisions of the twentieth century that attempts were made to restore the unity of the fifty days once more.

### Holy Week

The roots of what became known in the West as Holy Week and in the East as Great Week lie in fourth-century Jerusalem, where the presence of growing numbers of pilgrims seems to have encouraged the church there to create commemorations of the events of the last days of Jesus in the places where they were thought to have happened. Thus, a procession into Jerusalem with palms was added to the celebration of Sunday at the beginning of the week (Matt. 21:1–9; Mark 11:1–10; Luke 19:29–38), with a commemoration of the raising of Lazarus (John 11) on the preceding Saturday, which subsequently altered its focus to the visit by Jesus to Bethany "six days before the Passover" (John 12:1). This latter observance was later maintained only in Eastern churches and not in the West.

Other days of the week were marked by further commemorations: on Tuesday evening a visit to the Mount of Olives, where there was a cave in which Jesus was believed to have taught his disciples and where the bishop now read Matthew 24:1–26:2; on Wednesday evening the reading by a presbyter of the continuation of Matthew (26:3–16), the account of Judas agreeing to betray Jesus. Thursday featured two celebrations of the Eucharist in the late afternoon, the first probably marking the end of the season of Lent, and the second commemorating the Last Supper. In the evening, a vigil was kept on the Mount of Olives until about 11:00 p.m., when Jesus's discourse (John 13:16–18:1), believed to have been given in that very place, was read. From midnight until dawn the people slowly processed back to the city, stopping twice on the way, once to commemorate Jesus praying and then his arrest, before ending at a representation of the cross on Golgotha.

On Friday the morning was given over to an exhibition of what was claimed to be wood from the original cross, with individuals passing by in turn to venerate it. From noon onward for three hours there was a service of readings from the Old and New Testaments related to the death of Christ, together with psalms and prayers. There followed the usual service held at this hour each day of the week, ending with a visit to the tomb of Jesus, where the account of Joseph of Arimathea asking Pilate for Jesus's body and placing it in the tomb (Matt. 27:57–61) was read. Some worshipers then kept a vigil throughout the night.

In the centuries that followed, some of these observances were gradually imitated in other churches throughout the ancient world, no doubt as a result of pilgrims to Jerusalem returning home with stories of the powerful nature of the liturgies. Other Christians might not have been able to go to Jerusalem themselves, but they could now experience what went on at the holy places symbolically in their own places of worship, and so enter into the drama of the passion. At Rome it was many centuries before a palm procession was added to the liturgy of the Sunday service, and so the Eucharist itself continued to focus on commemorating the passion, with a dramatized reading of the passion narrative from Matthew in the place of the usual Gospel reading. Similarly, many places that did not possess a relic of the cross were slow to supplement their Good Friday liturgy of the word and prayers with the entry of a large symbolic cross that people might venerate. But the introduction of the celebration of the Eucharist on Thursday evening in commemoration of the Last Supper seems to have caught on rather more quickly. This led in time to the *triduum* being thought of as extending from Thursday to Saturday rather than Friday to Sunday.

Other ceremonial acts, not derived from Jerusalem practice, also began to make an appearance in Holy Week in a number of places, with many of them eventually being imitated more widely. The aim was obviously to make the liturgical experience more vivid and "real." Thus, for example, in some places a wooden representation of a donkey was used in the palm procession; chiefly in monastic communities and royal households a solemn footwashing in commemoration of Jesus's action in John 13 was introduced on the Thursday; and in some places a piece of bread consecrated at the Thursday Eucharist was symbolically "buried," to be "resurrected" on Easter Day (a remnant of which can still be seen in the creation of an Easter Garden in many churches within the Church of England).

The most striking change to Holy Week practices in the West, however, occurred in the Good Friday liturgy. Apparently a desire grew among people to receive Communion on that most important day, but tradition held that there was to be no celebration of the Eucharist on the Friday and Saturday: the Eucharist after the Easter vigil was the Eucharist of the whole *triduum*. Borrowing a practice commonly used in Eastern churches on days when a Eucharist was not permitted, the Liturgy of the Presanctified, a compromise, was adopted, in which some consecrated bread from the Thursday Eucharist was kept until Friday and then given in Communion.

Modern liturgical revision, while maintaining most of the traditional pattern, has brought about the abolition of some lesser practices so that the essentials can stand out more clearly and has made the footwashing a central feature of the Thursday liturgy.

### Lent

The origin of this season appears to lie in an early Egyptian Christian tradition of observing a forty-day season of fasting, associated with Jesus's fasting in the wilderness (Matt. 4:1–11; Mark 1:13; Luke 4:1–13). When it was adopted more generally in the early fourth century, it was located immediately prior to the period of pre-Easter fasting and combined with the period of final preparation of candidates for baptism at Easter. Because there were not forty days of actual fasting during the season (Sunday was never a fast day, and in the East nor was Saturday), the duration was later extended to bring this about, and in the West it was later prefaced on the first day by a ceremonial imposition of ashes on each worshiper, a standard expression of mourning and repentance in the Old Testament (see Isa. 58:5; Jer. 6:26).

### Christmas and Epiphany

The reasons for the choice of December 25 and January 6 for these two festivals have been the subject of debate among scholars. Some thought that it had something to do with pagan winter solstice celebrations on those dates in the various calendars in use in the ancient world, but that theory has been weakened by the absence of any firm corroborative testimony related to January 6, and by the recent discovery that the evidence for a pagan festival of Sol Invictus (the Invincible Sun) on December 25 at Rome is very tenuous. The chief alternative hypothesis, that the dates were arrived at as a result of early Christians trying to calculate the date of the death of Jesus and deducing the date of his conception and birth from that, is also not without some weaknesses.

What can be said is that as early as the beginning of the third century attempts were being made to calculate the dates of Jesus's death and birth, with varied results, and that the Christian sect of the Basilidians in Egypt was observing January 6 as a commemoration of the baptism of Jesus. That seems to have spread to other Christians throughout the eastern Mediterranean area, who by the fourth century were celebrating the birth as well as the baptism of Jesus on that date under the name of Epiphany (in Greek, "manifestation") or Theophany ("appearance of God"). Only Rome and North Africa apparently had no such festival, but they then began to keep December 25 as the celebration of Christ's incarnation. If this was not as a counterattraction to pagan festivities previously thought to have been taking place on that date, then it is most likely to have been the result of calculating the date of the death of Jesus to have been March 25 and of believing that his conception must have occurred on the same day of the year, and hence his birth exactly nine months later.

When the Roman Christmas festival was eventually taken up in most of the Eastern churches, it celebrated Christ's birth, and January 6 his baptism. When the equivalent adoption was made of January 6 in Rome, and from there throughout the Western church, its primary focus was instead on the visit of the Magi (Matt. 2:1–12).

### Saints' Days

At first churches celebrated only the anniversary of the death of their own local martyrs, usually at the place of burial, but later the list of those commemorated annually expanded, aided by the practice of allowing relics of martyrs to be transferred to other churches, around which a cult could develop. From the fourth century onward those other than martyrs also began to be venerated, chiefly ascetic and monastic figures and former bishops, until by the late Middle Ages the majority of days in the year had the commemoration of a saint attached to them. Because the veneration included prayer to these saints for divine assistance, the whole cult of saints was subsequently rejected by most Reformation churches, who regarded Christ as the sole mediator.

## Practical Implications for Worship

The psychological impact that the various rhythms of time have on human beings and their lives ought not to be underestimated or ignored in the formulation of patterns of Christian worship. This does not mean that every such practice inherited from the past must always be retained in the present or introduced uncritically into new settings. They require careful evaluation. The aim is not to reproduce historical events to add what W. S. Gilbert called "merely corroborative detail intended to give artistic verisimilitude."[2] Nor is simply watching a drama performed to be equated with active liturgical participation (however valuable religious dramas might be in their own right). The past is recalled only in order that it may be experienced as a present spiritual reality.

The primary must also be distinguished from the secondary. However worthy are the causes for which themed Sundays are often promoted, such as "Creation Sunday" or "Mission Sunday," both they and the overabundant observance of individual saint's days should not proliferate to an extent where they obscure the fundamental character of the liturgical year as what in modern Roman Catholic thinking is described as the celebration of the paschal mystery—of the saving death, resurrection, and glorification of Christ toward which his conception and incarnation point.

## For Further Reading

Bradshaw, Paul F. *Daily Prayer in the Early Church: A Study in the Origin and Early Development of the Church Office.* Eugene, OR: Wipf & Stock, 2008.

———. *Reconstructing Early Christian Worship.* Collegeville, MN: Liturgical Press, 2010. Especially chapters 7–9.

Bradshaw, Paul F., and Maxwell E. Johnson. *The Origins of Feasts, Fasts and Seasons in Early Christianity.* Alcuin Club Collections 86. Collegeville, MN: Liturgical Press, 2011.

Brown, Peter. *The Cult of the Saints: Its Rise and Function in Latin Christianity.* Chicago: University of Chicago Press, 1981.

Chupungco, Anscar. *Shaping the Easter Feast.* Washington, DC: Pastoral Press, 1998.

Stevenson, Kenneth W. *Jerusalem Revisited: The Liturgical Meaning of Holy Week.* Washington, DC: Pastoral Press, 1988.

2. W. S. Gilbert, *The Mikado, or the Town of Titipu* (New York: A.W. Tams Musical Library, 1885), act 2.

# PART 2

# Early Christian Worship

# — 4 —

# Worship in the Early Church

## *L. Edward Phillips*

Around the year 112 CE, Pliny the Younger, Roman governor of Bithynia-Pontus on the Black Sea, wrote to the emperor Trajan for advice on how to deal with the growing number of Christians in the province. While Christians were not actively persecuted during the reign of Trajan, Christianity was still officially illegal, and when persons charged with being Christian were brought before the governor, he had to try them and mete out an appropriate punishment. His procedure for the trial was to require those accused to deny that they were Christians and to prove this by offering worship to the Romans gods and to a statue of the emperor. Those who offered to the gods were exonerated; those who did not were executed. Some of the accused who made the offering confessed that they had previously been Christians but no longer followed Christ. Pliny, consequently, wondered whether the crime was the mere fact of being a Christian in name, or whether it had to do with criminal deeds committed by Christians. To find out what sorts of criminal deeds may be involved, he interrogated those who had once professed Christianity and reported to Trajan what he discovered:

> They maintained, however, that all that their guilt or error involved was that they were accustomed to assemble at dawn on a fixed day, to sing a hymn antiphonally to Christ as God, and to bind themselves by an oath, not for the commission of some crime, but to avoid acts of theft, brigandage, and adultery,

not to break their word, and not to withhold money deposited with them when asked for it. When these rites were completed, it was their custom to depart, and then to assemble again to take food, which was however common and harmless.[1]

How should we read such evidence? The Christians gathered on a "fixed day." One may assume that this was Sunday, the Lord's Day. In Revelation 1:10, John the Elder says that he received his vision on "the Lord's day." If the Christians in Bithynia-Pontus met on the Lord's Day, this implies they adhered to the Jewish practice of organizing days into a seven-day week. Romans, however, did not widely recognize a seven-day week until after the conversion of Constantine in the fourth century, which may be why Pliny uses the vague term "fixed day."

Pliny further reports that the Christians gathered twice on their fixed day: once at dawn to sing to Christ and "bind themselves by an oath," and a second time to share "common and harmless" food. If the Christians kept the Jewish week, then they likely also kept the Jewish tradition of counting days from sundown to sundown. If the morning gathering was on the morning of the Lord's Day (Sunday), and the second gathering of the Christians was after sundown when people had finished their workday, then, according to the Jewish practice, the evening meal took place at the beginning of the following day. Is it possible that the dawn gathering Pliny reports actually took place on Saturday morning, while the evening meal took place that evening to begin the first day of the week, the Lord's Day?

I begin with this rather detailed example to show that what may seem like relatively simple evidence is actually rather complicated. Not all examples from the ancient world are quite so ambiguous, but even so, the evidence for the first two centuries is rather sparse and spread out over several geographic regions and ethnic groups. Paul Bradshaw compares the evidence for the worship practices of the early church to a children's connect-the-dot puzzle.[2] Unfortunately, we do not have all of the dots, and they are not numbered.

## Historical Reconstruction of Early Christian Worship

At the beginning of the twentieth century historians believed they could connect the various pieces of evidence from the early church to show a fairly

1. Pliny the Younger, *Letter 96*, in *Complete Letters*, trans. P. G. Walsh (Oxford: Oxford University Press, 2006), 278–79.
2. Paul F. Bradshaw, *The Search for the Origins of Christian Worship*, 2nd ed. (Oxford: Oxford University Press, 2002), 20.

coherent picture of how the early church developed practices of worship, sacrament, and daily prayer. In part, this historical work was motivated by the discovery in 1873 of a copy of the *Didache* (meaning "teaching") in a monastery in Constantinople.[3] Soon after the publication of this ancient text, most historians identified it with the *Teaching of the Apostles*, mentioned by the fourth-century historian Eusebius in his list of noncanonical texts that were "known to most ecclesiastical writers."[4] While the precise date of the *Didache* has been difficult to determine, with proposed dates ranging from the middle of the first century to the early second century, almost all agree that it is quite early, with ancient Syria or even Palestine being the most likely place of origin.[5]

The contents and arrangement of the *Didache* suggest it was written as a manual for the organization of a congregation, with special attention to the education of new members, and it describes a number of community rituals, including baptism, the Lord's Prayer, and a meal ritual it calls the Eucharist. The New Testament touched on all of these topics, but the *Didache* provided more detailed content of the ritual practices of a congregation. Historians now had new information that helped them understand even some worship practices found in the canonical Scriptures.[6]

Another major development in the history of scholarship was the identification of a text previously known as the *Egyptian Church Order* with the third-century bishop and heresiologist Hippolytus of Rome, with the title *Apostolic Tradition*. Even though a copy of the original Greek text has never been found, early twentieth-century scholars pieced together a reasonably coherent text drawing on ancient Latin, Coptic, Arabic, and Ethiopic translations. While a few important scholars had doubts about this project, at least in some of its details, most were convinced that the *Apostolic Tradition* provided a comprehensive picture of the liturgical life of the church in Rome in the early third century.[7]

3. Kurt Niederwimmer, *The Didache*, trans. Linda M. Maloney (Minneapolis: Fortress, 1998), 19.

4. *Ecclesiastical History* 3.25.6, in *The Nicene and Post-Nicene Fathers*, ed. Philip Schaff, series 2, vol. 1, available in the Christian Classics Ethereal Library, https://ccel.org/ccel/schaff /npnf201/npnf201.iii.viii.xxv.html. For other early references to the *Didache*, see Niederwimmer, *Didache*, 4–6.

5. Niederwimmer, *Didache*, 52–54.

6. See Pheme Perkins, "New Testament and Worship," in *Theological Foundations of Worship: Biblical, Systematic, and Practical Perspectives*, ed. Khalia J. Williams and Mark A. Lamport (Grand Rapids: Baker Academic, 2021), 27–28.

7. For the history of scholarship, see Paul F. Bradshaw, Maxwell E. Johnson, and L. Edward Phillips, *The Apostolic Tradition: A Commentary*, Hermeneia (Minneapolis: Fortress, 2002), 1–6.

The discovery (or, better said, recovery) of the *Didache* and the *Apostolic Tradition* contributed to an explosion of scholarly interest in early Christian liturgy in the first decades of the twentieth century. Moreover, this scholarly interest was more than mere antiquarian fascination with the past, for the twentieth century was a time of major liturgical revision among Catholics and Protestants. The work of historians supported the liturgical reformers as they sought to ground their revision of present liturgy on the foundation of the primitive church. Indeed, it is impossible to understand many of the liturgical reforms of the Second Vatican Council of the Catholic Church, the 1976 *Book of Common Prayer* of the Episcopal Church, or the worship books of the mainline Protestant churches in the United States without some understanding of twentieth-century scholarship on early Christian worship. However, it is not quite right to say these reforms were based on actual worship practices of the primitive church, which we have already noted are difficult to determine. Rather, they were based on historical reconstructions of early Christian worship that presumed a more or less coherent development from the first through the fourth centuries.

## Historical Reconstruction of Early Christian Eucharist

In 1945 the liturgical historian and Anglican monk Dom Gregory Dix put forward a compelling method for connecting the dots of liturgical development in his groundbreaking book on the history of the Eucharist, *The Shape of the Liturgy*.[8] Dix argued that in order to find the primitive core of the eucharistic rite, one had to look for the original ritual patterns rather than the text of original prayers. He proposed that the eucharistic liturgy was constructed of two parts with distinct origins.[9] The first part was a word service of lessons, psalms, preaching, and prayers drawn from what Dix accepted was the liturgy of the Jewish synagogue, though he acknowledges that rabbinic scholars do not agree on the form and content of the synagogue liturgy in the first century.

The second part was the "Eucharist proper," a table service that had its origin in Jewish meal rituals for blessing and sharing of bread and a cup, witnessed by Jesus's words and actions at the Last Supper in Matthew, Mark, and 1 Corinthians 10. These New Testament accounts indicate seven actions at the supper: "Our Lord (1) took bread; (2) 'gave thanks' over it; (3) broke it; (4) distributed it, saying certain words. Later He (5) took a cup; (6) 'gave

8. Dom Gregory Dix, *The Shape of the Liturgy* (1945; repr., London: Continuum, 2005).
9. Dix, *Shape of the Liturgy*, 36–37.

thanks' over that; (7) handed it to His disciples, saying certain words."[10] However, the early church did not long keep this sevenfold pattern, nor did it long continue to conduct the Eucharist during a complete meal. Rather, these seven actions were condensed into four: (1) Jesus took bread and a cup, (2) he gave thanks for both (the eucharistic prayer), (3) he broke the bread to begin the meal, and (4) he shared the bread and cup with them. This "four-action shape," Dix claimed, "constituted the absolutely invariable nucleus of every eucharistic rite known to us throughout antiquity from the Euphrates to Gaul."[11] By his account, no later than the early second century, the Eucharist was combined with the synagogue services to form a united service of word and table. All subsequent developments in form and content were expansions of the two-part pattern.

Dix located the earliest record of the word and table order in the *First Apology* of Justin Martyr in a brief description of worship in Rome around the year 155 CE:

> And on the day called Sunday, all who live in cities or in the country gather together to one place, and the memoirs of the apostles or the writings of the prophets are read, as long as time permits; then, when the reader has ceased, the president verbally instructs, and exhorts to the imitation of these good things. Then we all rise together and pray, and, as we before said, when our prayer is ended, bread and wine and water are brought, and the president in like manner offers prayers and thanksgivings, according to his ability, and the people assent, saying Amen; and there is a distribution to each, and a participation of that over which thanks have been given, and to those who are absent a portion is sent by the deacons. And they who are well to do, and willing, give what each thinks fit; and what is collected is deposited with the president, who helps the orphans and widows and those who, through sickness or any other cause, are in want, and those who are in bonds and the strangers sojourning among us, and in a word takes care of all who are in need.[12]

Written before the development of standard Christian terminology, parts of Justin's description sound strange to modern Christian ears. For example, "memoirs of the apostles" means the Gospels.[13] Similarly, Justin refers to the Old Testament as the "writings of the prophets." The "president" or "presider"

---

10. Dix, *Shape of the Liturgy*, 48.
11. Dix, *Shape of the Liturgy*, 48.
12. Justin, *First Apology* 67, in *Ante-Nicene Fathers* (hereafter cited as *ANF*), vol. 1, ed. Alexander Roberts and James Donaldson, https://www.ccel.org/ccel/schaff/anf01.viii.ii.lxvii.html.
13. Which Justin explains in *First Apology* 66.

was the leader of the congregation, who preached the sermon and who offered the thanksgiving for the ritual meal.

After the sermon, the congregation stood together to pray. Two chapters earlier (*First Apology* 65) Justin had described the first Eucharist of the newly baptized, and he states that following the communal prayer, the congregation shared a kiss of peace. It is likely this was a regular part of the Sunday service as well, even though he does not list the kiss of peace in chapter 67.

Regarding the prayer over the bread, wine, and water, we notice that the presider offered the prayer "according to his ability." Yet this does not mean that the presider invented the prayer on the spot. In another of his writings, *Dialogue with Trypho, a Jew*, Justin argues that Jesus instituted the Eucharist "in remembrance of the suffering which He endured on behalf of those who are purified in soul from all iniquity, in order that we may at the same time thank God for having created the world, with all things therein, for the sake of man, and for delivering us from the evil in which we were, and for utterly overthrowing principalities and powers by Him who suffered according to His will."[14] Thus while the presider did not read a prayer out of a book, the eucharistic prayer likely had an established content. Moreover, Justin makes a point of saying that the congregation responded with "Amen," which means "so be it." In other words, the congregation was expected to agree with what the leader prayed on their behalf, which implies they were expected to pay attention.

According to Justin, the basic outline of a service of Christian worship in Rome in the mid-second century was as follows:

Gathering on Sunday

Scripture readings (Old and New Testament)

Preaching by presider

Congregational prayers

Kiss of peace

Offering of bread and wine (and water) for the Eucharist

Eucharistic prayer led by presider

The people give their "amen"

Distribution of meal to the church (including those absent)

Following Dix's analysis, it is reasonable to see in Justin's account a united service of "Word" (gathering for readings and preaching) and "Table" with

---

14. Justin, *Dialogue with Trypho* 41, ANF 1:215, https://www.ccel.org/ccel/schaff/anf01 .viii.iv.xli.html.

the prayers of the congregation and the kiss of peace forming a central link between the two halves. Dix did notice one glaring omission in this description: Justin fails to mention the "fraction"—that is, the breaking of the bread that formed action three in Dix's four-action shape of the eucharistic liturgy.[15] Despite such problems, the worship order that Justin provides looks very much like the structure of more detailed liturgies centuries later, particularly in the Eastern churches, and liturgists of the twentieth century found Dix's argument compelling. Most of them accepted that Word and Table and the four-action shape of the Eucharist had been the normative order for the Sunday eucharistic liturgy in the patristic church, and they used this pattern as a template for reforming the order for the Eucharist in their official liturgical books.[16]

Scholars, moreover, could use Dix's schema to determine what might count as an early eucharistic prayer. The *Didache*, for example, refers to a meal in chapters 9 and 10 as "eucharist." *Didache* 9–10, however, does not look at all like Dix's four-action sequence. Indeed, this meal ritual begins in chapter 9 with a prayer over a cup, followed by a prayer over bread. Chapter 10 concludes the rite, "after being filled," which strongly suggests that a full meal has preceded the thanksgiving.[17] Dix argued that *Didache* 9–10 was not the Eucharist but an *agapē* meal, and this despite the structural similarity to the Last Supper account in Luke 22:14–20, which has the same pattern: cup, bread, meal, cup after the meal. Some might say this is a textbook case of making the evidence fit the theory.

If the *Didache* does not prove to be an acceptable candidate for the earliest eucharistic prayer, the *Apostolic Tradition* has a prayer that fits the criteria beautifully. As part of the rite for the ordination of a bishop, *Apostolic*

15. He filled in this gap by pointing to an example from the postbaptismal Eucharist in *Apostolic Tradition* 21.31, even though the *Apostolic Tradition* is decades later than Justin and the specific example he cites does not refer to a Word service at all. See Dix, *Shape of the Liturgy*, 131.

16. For example, the eucharistic liturgies in the *United Methodist Hymnal* (1989) have the title "A Service of Word and Table." In the previous *Methodist Hymnal* (1964), the title was "The Order for the Administration of the Sacrament of the Lord's Supper or Holy Communion."

17. Since Louis Finkelstein's work on this prayer in the early twentieth century, many scholars have considered the table prayers in the *Didache* to be Christianized versions of the Jewish table blessing. See Finkelstein, "The Birkat Ha-Mazon," *Jewish Quarterly Review*, n.s. 19 (1928/1929): 211–62. The connection has recently been challenged by Paul Bradshaw, *Eucharistic Origins* (New York: Oxford University Press, 2004), 32–35. Among the problems is that no early Jewish text of the *Birkat ha-mazon* exists, and Finkelstein has to read back from much later texts (well after the fourth century) to reconstruct a first-century *Birkat ha-mazon* by extracting the Christian material.

*Tradition* 4 describes the bishop's first Eucharist with his congregation, including, remarkably, a long prayer of thanksgiving for the eucharistic meal:

> And when he is made bishop, let everyone give the kiss of peace, greeting him. And let the deacons bring the offering to him. And when he lays his hand on the offering with the presbyters, let him say, giving thanks:
>
>> The Lord [be] with all of you.
>> And let all the people say:
>> With your spirit.
>> And he says:
>> Up, [with your] heart.
>> And the people say:
>> We have [them] to the Lord.
>> And he says, again:
>> Let us give thanks to the Lord.
>> And the people say:
>> It is worthy and right.[18]

The order thus far in the outline of this liturgy is:

Kiss of peace

Offering of the bread and wine for the Eucharist

A three-part call and response between the newly ordained bishop and the congregation in which the bishop asks permission to offer the thanksgiving

*Apostolic Tradition* 4 continues with the text of the thanksgiving prayer:

> We render thanks to you, God, through your beloved Child[19] Jesus Christ, whom in the last times you sent to us as savior and redeemer and angel of your will, who is your inseparable word, through whom you made all things and it was well-pleasing to you; you sent from heaven into the virgin's womb, and who conceived in the womb was incarnate and manifested as your Son, born of the holy spirit and the virgin; who fulfilling your will and gaining

---

18. Translation from Bradshaw, Johnson, and Phillips, *Apostolic Tradition*, 38, 40. Text amended for illustration purposes.

19. The use of the word "child" (the Latin word may also be translated "servant") rather than "son" to refer to Jesus Christ is an indication of the antiquity of this prayer. Other examples from the second century use "child" as a modifier for Jesus, but not after the third century.

for you a holy people stretched out [his] hands when he was suffering, that he might release from suffering those who believed in you; who when he was being handed over to voluntary suffering, that he might destroy death and break the bonds of the devil, and tread down hell and illuminate the righteous, and fix a limit and manifest the resurrection, taking bread [and] giving thanks to you, he said: "Take, eat, this is my body which will be broken for you." Likewise also the cup, saying: "This is my blood which is shed for you. When you do this, you make my remembrance." Remembering therefore his death and resurrection, we offer to you the bread and cup, giving thanks to you because you have held us worthy to stand before you and minister to you. And we ask that you would send your holy spirit in the offering of [your] holy church, [that] gathering [them] into one you will give to all who partake of the holy things [to partake] in the fullness of the holy spirit, for the strengthening of faith in truth, that we may praise and glorify you through your Child Jesus Christ, through whom [be] glory and honor to you, Father and Son with the holy spirit, in your holy church, both now and to the ages of ages. Amen.[20]

The *Apostolic Tradition* probably did not intend for the bishop to use these precise words. A later passage (*Apostolic Tradition* 9) says thanksgivings may be improvised so long as they are "orthodox." Extemporizing of the prayer "according to his ability," as we saw in Justin's account, was still allowed. Almost all the ancient eucharistic prayers from the fourth century onward had these elements in the same order.[21]

| Order | Technical Terms for Reference |
|---|---|
| Opening call and response | Opening dialogue |
| Thanksgiving prayer | Thanksgiving |
| Account of the Last Supper | Institution narrative |
| Remembrance of the saving work of Jesus | Anamnesis |
| Statement of offering | Oblation |
| Prayer for the descent of the Spirit | Doxology |
| Trinitarian doxology | Epiclesis |
| Amen (by the congregation) | Amen |

20. Translation from Bradshaw, Johnson, and Phillips, *Apostolic Tradition*, 38, 40. Text amended for illustrative purposes.

21. W. J. Grisbrooke, "Anaphora," in *A New Dictionary of Liturgy and Worship*, ed. J. Gordon Davies (London: SCM, 1986), 10–17.

If this prayer looks familiar, it may be because it was adapted as Eucharistic Prayer II in the Roman Missal of 1970 and in Eucharistic Prayer B, Rite II, of the 1979 *Book of Common Prayer*, to give two of many examples.

Beginning in the fourth century, eucharistic prayers further expanded to include the biblical acclamation "Holy, holy, holy" (*Sanctus*) and prayers of intercession for the world. A little later still, Western rites added the Lord's Prayer after the eucharistic prayer itself, and so on. The structure of the service of Word and Table was gradually evolving, and there were regional and even local differences. Nevertheless, liturgical historians were discovering an increasingly clear picture of the liturgical life of the early church. They found an amazing degree of coherence, so long as one did not focus too much on evidence that did not fit into this coherent picture.

## Historical Reconstruction of Early Christian Baptism

Like the way Dix and his followers found a foundational, primitive shape to the Sunday Eucharist, liturgical scholars identified a primitive pattern in the initiation rites. As with revision of the Eucharist, the historical recovery of ancient baptismal texts prompted contemporary revisions, most notably in the Catholic Church's Rite for the Christian Initiation of Adults, published in English translation in 1974.[22]

As this translation was being released, Catholic liturgical scholar Aidan Kavanagh published a book titled *The Shape of Baptism: The Rite of Christian Initiation*, echoing the title of Dix's *Shape of the Liturgy*, in which he surveys a great deal of historical work that led to the development of the new rite. He summarizes the earliest structure of baptism: "Preceded by authentic proclamation of the risen and exalted *Christos-Messiah* and by conversion, Spirit baptism by water at apostolic hand initiated one into the full life of the community in which the gospel has begun to become praxis. Here is the common ground that serves as articulation point for all the multivalent practices that enter the initiatory continuum."[23] In outline, this primitive shape is as follows:

Proclamation of the gospel

Conversion

Baptism by water and Holy Spirit

Incorporation into the church (cf. Acts 2:42)

22. Published by the International Commission on English in the Liturgy.
23. Aidan Kavanagh, *The Shape of Baptism: The Rite of Christian Initiation* (New York: Pueblo, 1978), 23.

In subsequent centuries, items in this outline would expand, but the shape would perdure. Yet, as we saw with Dix's shape, not all of the patristic examples fall neatly into this schema.

Again, the *Didache* proved to be an outlier, though not quite as much of an outlier as it had been for Dix's typology. The *Didache* begins with six chapters of moral instruction, the "Two Ways." While these six chapters contain numerous teachings that echo or even seem to quote the preaching of Jesus (especially as found in the Gospel of Matthew), they do not contain any obvious Christology, nor do they attribute the teachings to Jesus. They could easily be the teaching of a Jewish community.[24] The chapter on baptism, however, does have explicit Christian features:

> And concerning baptism, baptize in this way: Having first said all these things, baptize into the name of the Father, and of the Son, and of the Holy Spirit, in living water. But if you do not have living [i.e., flowing] water, baptize in other water; and if not in cold, then in warm. But if you do not have either, pour out water three times upon the head in the name of Father and Son and Holy Spirit. But before the baptism let the one who baptizes fast, and the baptized, and whatever others can; but you shall order the baptized to fast one or two days before.[25]

Whereas the baptisms in Acts are performed in the name of Jesus Christ, the *Didache* uses the trinitarian baptismal formula as commanded by the risen Christ in Matthew 28:19. A range of options are provided concerning the water, given local conditions, including a triple pouring over the head in the name of the persons of the Trinity. There is not, however, explicit mention of the gift of the Holy Spirit, which is another deviation from Kavanagh's primitive shape. We also see an expansion of prebaptismal preparation: fasting by the candidate, and by the one who administers the baptism, along with others in the community, as an apparent act of solidarity.

Chapter 8 provides details of community life, specifically the regular days of fasting along with the praying of the Lord's Prayer three times daily. Then follow, as has already been discussed, the prayers of the community meal. Chapter 9 explicitly links the meal with baptism: "But let no one eat or drink of your Eucharist, but they who have been baptized into the name of the Lord; for concerning this also the Lord has said, Give not that which is holy to the dogs."[26] In short, we find that the *Didache* roughly parallels and expands on

---

24. Kavanagh, *Shape of Baptism*, 39.
25. Aaron Milavec, *The Didache: Text, Translation, Analysis, and Commentary* (Collegeville, MN: Liturgical Press, 2003), 67.
26. Milavec, *Didache*, 75.

Kavanagh's primitive shape, but with moral teaching in place of the proclamation of the risen Christ, and with no explicit mention of the Holy Spirit
(other than the trinitarian name).

The *Apostolic Tradition*, which Kavanagh, following Dix, dates to the early
third century, shows a tremendous amount of expansion in the process of Christian initiation. The first stage of initiation grew into a lengthy process beginning
with the newcomers being questioned about their social status and occupations
to make sure they were able to take up the requirements of Christian discipleship. Occupations such as idol-making or acting in the theater were prohibited
and had to be abandoned. After this, the newcomers became catechumens, or
"hearers," for a period of time (possibly as long as three years), during which
they attended lectures on the Christian life and learned such practices as caring
for widows and orphans. Once catechumens proved they were keeping these
practices, they entered into a final intense period before baptism, during which
the bishop (or perhaps another minister) laid on hands and exorcised them daily.

Baptism took place at cockcrow on a Sunday morning, possibly on Easter.
The rite began with a prayer over the water as it was drawn into a pool, and
the candidates stripped off all clothing and jewelry in order to enter the water
completely naked. Then followed an elaborate ritual that entailed another
exorcism, during which the candidates renounced Satan and his works. The
baptism proper entailed a triple immersion during which candidates recited the
three articles of a form of the Apostles' Creed. There followed a postbaptismal
anointing, after which the newly baptized dressed and were led to where the
rest of the congregation had been meeting. The bishop laid hands on the candidates and offered a prayer with explicit mention of the Holy Spirit and the
reception of grace, followed by a second postbaptismal anointing, the signing
of the forehead, and a kiss. The baptized then were allowed to pray together
with the faithful for the first time, and also to join them for the Eucharist.

The rest of the *Apostolic Tradition* addresses a wide variety of topics
pertaining to church life: other fellowship meals, meals for widows, how to
care for eucharistic ministry to the sick, care for cemeteries, and a lengthy
chapter on times (and content) of daily prayer. None of these later chapters,
however, have proven as important as the process of initiation for the reform
of rites of baptism in the twentieth century.

## Historical Reconstruction of Early Christian Daily Prayer

The twentieth century also saw scholarly interest in finding an original pattern for Christian daily prayer. Clifford Dugmore proposed that the earliest

Christian pattern combined the morning and evening prayer rituals of the synagogue with a Christian pattern of the third, sixth, and ninth hours (9:00 a.m., noon, and 3:00 p.m.) for which various patristic writers offered biblical precedents, such as the time of prayer mentioned in Acts (on Pentecost the church was praying at the third hour, Peter received his rooftop vision at noon, and Peter and John went to the temple for prayer at the ninth hour).[27] Joan Walker offered a counter theory that prayer at the third, sixth, and ninth hours was the original and distinctly Christian pattern, and that it was based on the Markan chronology of the crucifixion. She cited the instruction of *Didache* 8.3 to pray the Lord's Prayer three times a day to support her theory.[28] Paul Bradshaw gave a third reading of the early testimony, drawing on the evidence from Alexandria, to suggest that the earliest daily prayer custom was a fourfold pattern of morning, noon, evening, and during the night.[29] These three assessments show that while the evidence for daily prayer in the pre-Constantinian church is well established, it is open to various interpretations. Most scholars assume that Christians, at least in part, must have drawn on Jewish precedents. However, the actual evidence for Jewish practice in the first century is even more complicated because of the diversity of Jewish groups—Pharisees and Sadducees, as well at the Therapeutae of Egypt and the Essenes of Qumran and elsewhere, *and* Galilean Jews about whom we have little evidence beyond the New Testament. Some Jews associated daily prayer with the daily temple sacrifices, and there is evidence some Christians did so as well. Some Jews justified practices by reference to Scripture, finding warrants for their practices by reference to Deuteronomy 6:4–7 or the story of the exodus. Christians similarly found prooftexts to explain their practices in Jewish Scriptures, and by the early third century with reference to Christian Scripture. The Qumran community connected daily prayer to the angelic hosts, and some Christian descriptions of daily prayer saw a connection to the cosmic, heavenly liturgy.[30]

Clearly, therefore, in the formative early centuries there was not one simple model for the origins of practices even if we consider only the Jewish sources. Yet even the human experience of basic natural phenomena, such as the rising and setting of the sun, can provoke a natural desire for morning and evening

27. C. W. Dugmore, *The Influence of the Synagogue upon the Divine Office* (Westminster, PA: Faith, 1964), 10, 47, 70, 112.

28. J. H. Walker, "Terce, Sext, and None, and Apostolic Custom?," *Studia Patristica* 5 (1962): 206–12.

29. Paul F. Bradshaw, *Daily Prayer in the Early Church* (New York: Oxford University Press, 1982), 47–49, 61–63.

30. L. Edward Phillips, "Early Christian Prayer," in *The Oxford Handbook of Early Christian Ritual*, ed. Risto Uro et al. (Oxford: Oxford University Press, 2019), 572–76.

prayer directed to the creator of the sun, the moon, and the stars. Around the year 200 CE Clement of Alexandria wrote, "Some assign definite hours for prayer—as, for example, the third, and sixth, and ninth—yet the Gnostic prays through his whole life, endeavoring by prayer to have fellowship with God."[31] The discrete times for prayer may have been arbitrary, but the goal of prayer was not.

## Practical Implications for Worship

Historians in the twentieth century tried to form a reasonably coherent picture of the early church at worship. To a large degree, that picture has had a tremendous impact on the liturgy of Christian churches today. Not only did this picture influence the revisions of mainline church worship books, it also has influenced the actual practice of congregations. In the early twentieth century, very few Protestant congregations, apart from denominations that grew out of the Restorationist Movement of the nineteenth century (the Church of Christ and Disciples of Christ), had a weekly celebration of the Lord's Supper. And while the Catholic Church always celebrated Sunday Mass, not many lay Catholics took weekly Communion until the mid-twentieth century. The recovery of regular weekly Eucharist is a major contemporary trend, and this trend developed in large measure out of the influence of twentieth-century scholarship. Justin Martyr has become a twenty-first-century worship influencer! With reforms of baptism rites in the Catholic Church, the *Apostolic Tradition of Hippolytus* has arguably been much more successful in shaping Christian worship today than it was in fourth-century Rome. The irony is that much recent scholarship no longer assumes that the *Apostolic Tradition* was composed by Hippolytus of Rome, or that it has any connection to the city, or that it all dates from the early third century.

This does not mean that we should avoid looking to the early church for inspiration. But we should avoid assigning too much authority to an ancient practice simply because it is ancient. Weekly Communion, perhaps. Adult baptism in the nude, probably not.

Finally, while a coherent historical account may be compelling, the truth is always messier and more diverse. For even though we claim to be the early Christians' spiritual descendants, separated from them by time and culture, in many ways we are like Pliny the Younger, trying to make sense of the reports of witnesses that we only partly understand.

31. Clement of Alexandria, *Miscellanies* 7.7.40.3, ANF 2:534, https://www.ccel.org/ccel/schaff/anf02.vi.iv.vii.vii.html.

## For Further Reading

Bradshaw, Paul F. *Eucharistic Origins*. New York: Oxford University Press, 2004.

Bradshaw, Paul F., and Maxwell E. Johnson. *The Origins of Feasts, Fasts and Seasons in Early Christianity*. Collegeville, MN: Liturgical Press, 2011.

Ferguson, Everett. *Baptism in the Early Church: History, Theology, and Liturgy in the First Five Centuries*. Grand Rapids: Eerdmans, 2008.

Hammerling, Roy. *The Lord's Prayer in the Early Church: The Pearl of Great Price*. New York: Palgrave Macmillan, 2010.

Jensen, Robin M. *Living Water: Images, Symbols, and Settings of Early Christian Baptism*. Boston: Brill, 2011.

McGowan, Andrew B. *Ancient Christian Worship: Early Church Practices in Social, Historical, and Theological Perspective*. Grand Rapids: Baker Academic, 2014.

Uro, Risto, Juliette J. Day, Richard E. DeMaris, and Rikard Roitto, eds. *The Oxford Handbook of Early Christian Ritual*. Oxford: Oxford University Press, 2019.

# ← 5 →

# Worship in Late Antiquity

## *Maxwell E. Johnson*

L ate antiquity, usually defined as lasting from Constantine's Edict of
Toleration (ca. 312 CE) to the fall of the Roman Empire (ca. 476),
though sometimes extended to include the reign of Pope Gregory the Great
(590–604), was a period of profound change and development for Christian
worship. The various cultural and social shifts in the Constantinian era
and beyond brought with them the need for churches to respond to those
changing circumstances. One of those responses was the first of several great
periods of what might be called liturgical reform and renewal in the history
of the church. And our contemporary knowledge of the various patterns of
worship is due, in large part, to the documentary evidence that exists from
this period. As recent liturgical scholarship has demonstrated, what we see
in this first reform or renewal is the development of what Paul Bradshaw has
called "liturgical homogeneity," wherein through a process of assimilation to
the practices of the great patriarchal and pilgrimage churches of the world—
that is, Rome, Jerusalem, Alexandria, Antioch, and Constantinople—and
through the cross-fertilization of borrowing and exchange, distinctive local
practices and theologies disappear in favor of others, becoming copied,
adapted, and synthesized.[1] Such, of course, is constitutive in the develop-

---

1. Paul Bradshaw, "The Homogenization of Christian Liturgy—Ancient and Modern: Presi-
dential Address," *Studia Liturgica* 26 (1996): 1–15.

ment of what we still call the diverse rites of Christianity, those distinct "whole styles of Christian living,"[2] to use Aidan Kavanagh's phrase—that is, numerous distinct rites existing in both East and West.

### Branches of the Church

| Rites of the Eastern Churches* | Rites of the Western Churches[†] |
| --- | --- |
| Armenian | Roman |
| Byzantine | North African |
| Coptic | Ambrosian |
| Ethiopic | Gallican (includes Celtic) |
| East Syrian | Mozarabic (includes Visigothic) |
| West Syrian | |
| Maronite | |

* All seven Eastern rites remain living liturgical traditions today among Eastern Orthodox and Eastern Catholic churches.
[†] Along with the Roman Rite, the Ambrosian (Archdiocese of Milan, Italy) and Mozarabic (Toledo, Spain) remain living liturgical traditions today.

Consequently, what is often appealed to as *the* early church's worship is but the end result of a process of assimilation, adaptation, and change in the late fourth and early fifth centuries, wherein some of the distinctive and rich theologies and patterns of an earlier period either disappear or are subordinated to others.

This fourth- and fifth-century "homogenization" in liturgical practice is easily demonstrated in the shift from a private to a public expression of Christian faith (i.e., Christianity becoming a *cultus publicus*) in the wake of Constantine's "conversion," the subsequent legalization and eventual adoption of Christianity as the official religion of the Roman Empire, the building of shrines and basilicas in the holy places of Jerusalem associated with Christ's passion, the trinitarian and christological decisions of the first ecumenical councils, and the end of the age of the martyrs. Especially is this the case with regard to the rites of Christian initiation, the eucharistic liturgy and its Great Prayer (the "Anaphora" or "prayer of offering"), the Liturgy of the Hours or daily prayer, and, not least, the feasts and seasons of what will come to be called later in history "the liturgical year." It is with these liturgical practices, especially Christian initiation and Eucharist, in this late antique context that this chapter is concerned.[3]

2. Aidan Kavanagh, *On Liturgical Theology* (Collegeville, MN: Liturgical Press, 1984), 100.

3. I have written on this topic previously and point readers, especially as it pertains to this chapter, to the second part of my essay "Worship, Practice, and Belief," in *The Early Christian World*, ed. Philip Esler (London: Routledge, 2017), 406–26.

## The Rites of Christian Initiation

Thanks to the extant prebaptismal catechetical and postbaptismal mystagogical homilies of the great "mystagogues" (i.e., Cyril [or John] of Jerusalem, John Chrysostom, and Theodore of Mopsuestia for the East, and Ambrose of Milan for the West), along with other documentary evidence such as letters, conciliar decrees, and treatises, the practices of Christian initiation in this period are easily reconstructed.[4] While some local diversity from an earlier period continued to exist, by the end of the fourth century the following came to characterize the overall pattern of the rites in the Christian East:

- The adoption of paschal baptism and the now forty-day season of Lent as the time of prebaptismal (daily) catechesis on Scripture, Christian life, and the Creed for the photizomenoi (those to be "enlightened")
- The use of scrutinies (examinations) and daily exorcisms throughout the period of final baptismal preparation
- The development of specific rites called *apotaxis* (renunciation) and *syntaxis* (adherence) as demonstrating a "change of ownership" for the candidates
- The development of ceremonies like the solemn *traditio* and *redditio symboli* (the presentation and "giving back" of the Nicene Creed)
- The increasing interpretation of the prebaptismal anointing as a rite of exorcism, purification, and/or preparation for combat against Satan
- The rediscovery and use of Romans 6 as the dominant paradigm for interpreting the baptismal immersion as entrance into the "tomb" with Christ
- The introduction of a postbaptismal anointing associated with the gift and "seal" of the Holy Spirit
- The use of Easter week as a time for "mystagogical catechesis" (an explanation of the sacramental "mysteries" the newly initiated had experienced)

Although not all of the Eastern sources in this period will associate the gift or "seal" of the Holy Spirit with a postbaptismal anointing (John Chrysostom,

4. The idea for this section is an adaptation based on themes in Maxwell E. Johnson, *The Rites of Christian Initiation: Their Evolution and Interpretation* (Collegeville, MN: Liturgical Press, 2007), 115–218. For texts of the relevant sections of the mystagogues and other documents listed above, see E. C. Whitaker and Maxwell E. Johnson, *Documents of the Baptismal Liturgy* (Collegeville, MN: Liturgical Press, 2003).

e.g., views the Spirit-gift in conjunction with the baptismal immersions themselves),[5] this will gradually become the norm and remain so throughout the various rites of the Christian East until the present day.

A similar overall ritual pattern also existed in the West, but Western sources display some significant differences. In his *De sacramentis* and *De mysteriis*, Ambrose of Milan (339–397), who baptized Augustine of Hippo at the Easter Vigil in 387, witnesses to a Milanese postbaptismal rite of footwashing (*pedilavium*) as an integral component of the rite known to him, with parallels to other Western and Eastern (East Syrian) rites but not, by his own admission, to Rome.[6] Ambrose also refers to something he calls the *spiritale signaculum* ("spiritual seal") following the postbaptismal *pedilavium*: "There follows the spiritual seal of which you heard in the lesson today. After the font there remains the 'perfecting,' when the Holy Spirit is poured down at the bishop's invocation, 'the Spirit of wisdom and understanding, the Spirit of counsel and strength, the Spirit of knowledge and godliness, the Spirit of holy fear.'"[7] Although we do not know "what ritual action—*if any*—accompanied the bishop's prayer,"[8] it is quite probable that this "spiritual seal" was but a hand-laying prayer at the conclusion of the rite, such as was known to be the case also in North Africa and Spain in this time period.[9] There exists, however, nothing equivalent to this in the later Ambrosian or Milanese liturgical traditions.

Other Western sources from Rome (e.g., the *Letter of John the Deacon to Senarius*)[10] and North Africa (Augustine)[11] indicate the presence of three public scrutinies (including even possible physical examinations) held on the third, fourth, and fifth Sundays of Lent. And, thanks to an important fifth-century letter from Pope Innocent I to Decentius of Gubbio, it is clear that at Rome itself the pattern of episcopal hand-laying with prayer followed by a postbaptismal anointing was in the fifth century being understood as an essential aspect, now associated explicitly with the bishop's prerogative in "giving" the Holy Spirit.

---

5. Whitaker and Johnson, *Documents of the Baptismal Liturgy*, 46.

6. Whitaker and Johnson, *Documents of the Baptismal Liturgy*, 180.

7. Ambrose, *De sacramentis* 3.8, ed. and trans. Gordon P. Jeanes, *Origins of the Roman Rite*, Alcuin/GROW Litergical Study 20 (Nottingham, UK: Grove Books, 1991), 8–9; Whitaker and Johnson, *Documents of the Baptismal Liturgy*, 181–83.

8. Pamela Jackson, "The Meaning of 'Spiritale Signaculum' in the Mystagogy of Ambrose of Milan," *Ecclesia Orans* 7 (1990): 94.

9. See Whitaker and Johnson, *Documents of the Baptismal Liturgy*, 140–52 (North Africa) and 153–75 (Spain).

10. Whitaker and Johnson, *Documents of the Baptismal Liturgy*, 208–11.

11. Whitaker and Johnson, *Documents of the Baptismal Liturgy*, 103.

Regarding the signing of infants, this clearly cannot be done validly by anyone other than the Bishop. For even though presbyters are priests, none of them holds the office of pontiff. For not only is it ecclesiastical custom that shows this should be done only by pontiffs—in other words, that they alone would sign or give the comforting Spirit—but there is also that reading in the Acts of the Apostles that describes Peter and John being ordered to give the Holy Spirit to those who had already been baptized. For whether the Bishop is present or not, presbyters are allowed to anoint the baptized with chrism. But they are not allowed to sign the forehead with the same oil consecrated by the Bishop, for that is used by the bishops only when they give the Spirit, the Paraclete. I cannot reveal the words themselves, lest I seem to betray more than is needed to respond to your inquiry.[12]

Just how necessary this uniquely Roman postbaptismal episcopal rite was thought to be by others, however, is debatable. While popes following Innocent tended to repeat his admonition, and so forbade presbyters from performing this rite, Pope Gregory I at the end of the sixth century can say that "if any are troubled at all by this, we concede that where bishops are absent, *even presbyters ought to anoint the baptized with chrism on their foreheads.*"[13] Therefore, in spite of Innocent's firm insistence on the physical presence of the bishop for the celebration of these rites, outside the city of Rome, where bishops were not in similar abundance, there remained long-lasting confusion about the actual need for the presence of bishops for these rites and, hence, the practice of presbyters themselves presiding at the whole rite. In fact, other Western rites—for example, North African, Gallican, Mozarabic—have nothing equivalent to this rite containing what later in history will come to be called "confirmation," when the Roman Rite itself becomes normative for western Europe, although some of these rites will include a hand-laying for the gift of the Holy Spirit (by a *presbyter*, however) and begin to refer to rites of episcopal oversight, especially in emergency situations, as "perfection" or "confirmation."[14]

The adoption of several of these ceremonies for the preparation and initiation of candidates in both East and West was undoubtedly the result of

12. Whitaker and Johnson, *Documents of the Baptismal Liturgy*, 206. See Martin F. Connell, *Church and Worship in Fifth-Century Rome: The Letter of Innocent I to Decentius of Gubbio* (Cambridge: Grove, 2002), 28–33.

13. Whitaker and Johnson, *Documents of the Baptismal Liturgy*, 206 (emphasis added).

14. See Gabriele Winkler, "Confirmation or Chrismation? A Study in Comparative Liturgy," in *Living Water, Sealing Spirit: Readings on Christian Initiation*, ed. Maxwell E. Johnson (Collegeville, MN: Liturgical Press, 1995), 202–18; Gerard Austin, *Anointing with the Spirit* (New York: Pueblo, 1985), 14–20.

the church seeking to ensure that its sacramental life would continue to have some kind of integrity when, in a changed social and cultural context where Christianity was now favored by the emperor, authentic conversion and properly motivated desire to enter the Christian community could no longer be assumed. Indeed, as the experience of Augustine himself demonstrates (*Confessions* 1.11), it became common in some places to enroll infants in the catechumenate and then postpone their baptism until much later in life, if ever. Similarly, as the rites themselves took on numerous elements that heightened dramatically the experience of those being initiated, the overall intent was surely to impress on them the seriousness of the step they were taking.[15]

It is not, however, only the baptismal candidates who regularly experienced this process. Egeria, the late-fourth century Spanish pilgrim to Jerusalem, records in her travel diary that, along with the candidates and their sponsors, members of the faithful also filled the Church of the Holy Sepulchre in Jerusalem for the daily catechetical lectures of the bishop. "God knows, lady sisters," she writes, "that the voices of the faithful who come in to listen to the catechesis are louder at those things that are said or explained by the bishop than at those things that are explained in this way when he sits and preaches in church." Further, during the week of mystagogy she notes that "the voices of those praising are such that their voices are heard outside the church." Because of this, she concludes, "In these places all the faithful follow the Scriptures when they are read in church."[16]

Designed for adult converts, the ritual process of Christian initiation in these several sources was to be short-lived, owing in part to its success in "converting" the masses. The North African controversy between "Pelagianism" and Augustine over the long-standing practice of infant initiation, and Augustine's theological rationale for infant initiation (including the reception of Communion) based on a theology of "original sin," would lead to the catechumenate's further decline, though we should not assume that infant initiation became the norm in the West until much later. At the same time, Augustine's lengthy battle with "Donatism," in the aftermath of the Diocletian Persecution (303–311 CE) over the Donatists' practice of rebaptizing Catholics and their insistence on the moral character of the baptizer in assuring the valid administration of baptism, would lead to an "orthodox" sacramental theology based on the use of proper elements and words as constituting a "valid" sacrament

15. Edward Yarnold, *The Awe-Inspiring Rites of Initiation: The Origins of the R.C.I.A.* (Collegeville, MN: Liturgical Press, 1994), 59–66.

16. Anne McGowan and Paul F. Bradshaw, *The Pilgrimage of Egeria: A New Translation of the* Itinerarium Egeriae *with Introduction and Commentary* (Collegeville, MN: Liturgical Press Academic, 2018), 190–92.

with Christ himself underscored as the true sacramental minister. If Augustine himself knew an initiation rite similar to those summarized above,[17] his own theological emphases, born in the heat of controversy, would set the agenda for a later Western medieval sacramental theology focused on "matter" and "form," the *quamprimum* ("as soon as possible") baptism of infants, and an objective sacramental validity ensured by what Western Scholastic theology would refer to as an *ex opere operato* understanding, based on the performance of the "work" itself with Christ as the guarantor of its validity.

## The Eucharistic Liturgy and Its Great Prayer (the Anaphora)

Christianity as a *cultus publicus*, increasingly favored by the state, began taking on the appearance of other contemporary religions—temples, altars, a visible priesthood, and so on—and its worship therefore took on more of the features of the worship of other religions.[18] Its number of adherents grew, and so it occupied larger and grander buildings than before (i.e., basilicas). As John Baldovin has noted, the use of basilicas was particularly important, for their adaptation and use "signified the move of Christian worship into public space. The basic basilican form was that of a public meeting place—as imperial court, court of justice, or assembly hall, etc. It was transformed on a longitudinal axis to meet the requirements of Christian processions, many of which began in outdoor spaces."[19] James White adds that, with the termination of the basilica in its semicircular apse, "the bishop simply took the place of the judge on the throne in the apse, flanked by presbyters. In front of him stood the altar table, first wood, later stone. Eventually low screens railed in a space in front of it for the singers, and an ambo (pulpit) accommodated readings; the rest was open congregational space where the people stood, usually divided by sexes. For well over a thousand years the posture of worship was standing."[20] With regard to this, preaching was done from the chair until the locus shifted to the ambo, a shift credited to John Chrysostom as being the first to preach from the ambo rather than the chair.[21]

17. William Harmless, *Augustine and the Catechumenate*, rev. ed. (Collegeville, MN: Liturgical Press, 2014), 79–87.
18. Some ideas in this section are adapted from themes in Paul F. Bradshaw and Maxwell E. Johnson, *The Eucharistic Liturgies: Their Evolution and Interpretation* (Collegeville, MN: Liturgical Press, 2012), 61–136.
19. John Baldovin, "Christian Worship to the Eve of the Reformation," in *The Making of Jewish and Christian Worship*, ed. Paul F. Bradshaw and Lawrence A. Hoffman (Notre Dame, IN: University of Notre Dame Press, 1991), 165.
20. James White, *A Brief History of Christian Worship* (Nashville: Abingdon, 1993), 72.
21. See White, *Brief History*, 69.

Closely related to these architectural shifts, worship became more formal in style and incorporated ritual and symbols from the civic world around to suit this new setting. Hence, there was a rapid growth in ceremony in this period; many aspects of the imperial court were adopted, with incense, processional lights, and ornamental fans becoming common. The result of all this, at least in the major cities, says Baldovin, "was what Aidan Kavanagh has called 'liturgy on the town,' the use of public streets and places as well as shrines and basilicas for an open manifestation of Christianity as now the dominant religious force in the society. Similarly, different churches and shrines were increasingly employed for liturgy on different feast days and fast days creating systems that have been called 'stational liturgy.'"[22]

Consequently, the possibility now of large crowds within Christian liturgical assemblies led to the rites themselves being expanded precisely at those points where greater order in the assembly was needed (i.e., at the entrance of clergy and community, at the presentation or transfer of the eucharistic gifts to the altar, and at the distribution of Communion), with the result that diaconal directions (e.g., "let us stand," "let us kneel"), litanies, psalmody, chants, and prayers became regular elements. Robert Taft has referred to these various places of processional movement in the eucharistic liturgy as "soft spots," which tend to attract various elements to those locations in the rite over time.[23] That is, what liturgical scholars refer to as a "liturgical unit"— consisting of a procession covered by a chant and concluded by a collect, and closely associated with the entrance of clergy and community at the beginning of the liturgy, at the presentation or transfer of the eucharistic gifts to the altar, and at the distribution of Communion—would now become a regular component of the eucharistic liturgy. This would give rise to various *Introits* or "Entrance Hymns," opening collects (prayers), "Offertory" or "Great Entrance" chants and "prayers over the gifts" at the preparation or transfer of the eucharistic offerings, and various chants and prayers related to before, during, and after the reception of Communion. In time and in both East and West, these "soft spots" would attract even more elements, often making the earlier "liturgical units" themselves difficult to uncover or discern. It is, of course, here at these "soft spots" where somewhat later elements such as the *Kyrie Eleison* and *Gloria in Excelsis* in the West or various antiphons in the East such as *Ho Monogenes* ("Only Begotten One") or the *Trisagion* ("Holy God, Mighty God, Immortal One, have mercy upon us") will be attached

22. Baldovin, "Christian Worship," 165.

23. Robert Taft, "The Structural Analysis of Liturgical Units: An Essay in Methodology," in *Beyond East and West: Problems in Liturgical Understanding* (Rome: Pontifical Oriental Institute, 1997), 187–202.

to the "entrance" or opening rites and elements such as the Our Father, the *Agnus Dei,* and the invitation ("Holy things for the holy") to the reception of Communion. At the end of this period, with the additions known to have been added by Pope Gregory the Great (e.g., the *Kyrie Eleison* at the beginning), the overall structure of the Roman Rite and, at least, the Byzantine Rite (which, with considerable expansion, will become the dominant eucharistic rite in the Christian East in following centuries) may be outlined as follows:

| Byzantine Rite | Roman Rite |
| --- | --- |
| Prothesis (preparation of the bread and wine) | |
| Entrance with *Trisagion* | Introit psalm |
| | Greeting |
| | *Kyries* |
| | *Gloria in Excelsis* |
| | Collect (opening prayer) |
| Epistle reading | Epistle reading |
| | Alleluia (gradual) |
| Gospel reading | Gospel reading |
| | Dismissal of catechumens |
| Homily | Homily |
| Litany | Intercessions (disappearing) |
| Dismissal of catechumens | |
| Prayer of the faithful | |
| | Kiss of peace (eventually moved) |
| Great entrance (of bread and wine) | Offertory psalm (bread and wine presented) |
| | Prayer over the gifts |
| Kiss of peace | |
| Anaphora ("St. Basil" or "St. John Chrysostom") | Eucharistic prayer ("Roman Canon") |
| Lord's Prayer | Lord's Prayer |
| Elevation | |
| Fraction rite | Fraction rite |
| | *Agnus Dei* (added in seventh century) |
| Invitation to Communion ("Holy things for the holy") | |
| Communion | Communion with psalm |
| Litany and thanksgiving prayer | Post-Communion prayer |
| Dismissal | Dismissal |

Documents (e.g., *Apostolic Constitutions* 8 and *Egeria*) also show that various categories of noncommuning people—for example, catechumens, *photizomenoi* (those elected to baptism), and penitents preparing for reconciliation—were regularly dismissed from the assembly with rites that included hand-laying and prayer before the Eucharist proper began. In one of his homilies John Chrysostom laments not only that the liturgical assemblies are now filled with gossipers, revelers, and pickpockets but that even several of the faithful are leaving before the Eucharist, and, as a result, various dismissal rites for them are added.[24] In the West such *missa* or dismissal rites, especially the dismissal of catechumens, would eventually suggest the term *missa* or "mass" for the Eucharist itself.

If eucharistic liturgies expanded at these points, however, they tended to contract at others. In the liturgy of the Word, for example, the number of biblical readings would gradually be limited to two in most traditions, and, generally, both would be from the New Testament. Nevertheless, preaching itself was anything but neglected. Eastern sources from this period indicate that *several* homilies would regularly be given at the Sunday Eucharist, with any presbyters present preaching first and the bishop last.[25]

By far, one of the most significant developments in this period was the standardization of written texts of the eucharistic prayer, the Anaphora, a process related, at least in part, to the need for liturgical texts to express orthodox teaching against trinitarian and christological heresy and, undoubtedly, to the increasing lack of proficient and prayerful extemporizers.[26] Along with this, although the precise origins of their anaphoral use remains debated, the *sanctus* hymn of Isaiah 6,[27] the institution narrative and its accompanying anamnetic offering language, even "consecratory" epicleses of the Holy Spirit, and numerous intercessions now became fixed structural components of these anaphoral prayers resulting from a process of cross-fertilization (i.e., the borrowing of elements across ecclesial boundaries).[28] The integration of these elements into specific anaphoras resulted in the classic anaphoral

24. Robert Taft, "The Inclination Prayer before Communion in the Byzantine Liturgy of St. John Chrysostom: A Study in Comparative Liturgy," *Ecclesia Orans* 3 (1986): 29–60.

25. See Paul F. Bradshaw, *Liturgical Presidency in the Early Church* (Nottingham, UK: Grove, 1983), 17.

26. Allan Bouley, *From Freedom to Formula: The Evolution of the Eucharistic Prayer from Oral Improvisation to Written Texts* (Washington, DC: Catholic University of America, 1981).

27. In addition to Bradshaw and Johnson, *Eucharistic Liturgies*, 111–23, see Bryan Spinks, *The Sanctus in the Eucharistic Prayer* (Cambridge: Cambridge University Press, 1991); and Robert Taft's two-part article, "The Interpolation of the Sanctus into the Anaphora: When and Where? A Review of the Dossier," *Orientalia Christiana Periodica* 57 (1991): 281–308; 58 (1992): 531–52.

28. John R. K. Fenwick, *Fourth Century Anaphoral Construction Techniques*, Grove Liturgical Study 45 (Nottingham, UK: Grove, 1986); and Fenwick, *The Anaphoras of St. Basil and*

patterns of different traditions called, for example, Antiochene, West Syrian, or Syro-Byzantine (e.g., the anaphoras known as "St. Basil" and "St. John Chrysostom"), Alexandrian ("St. Mark"), and Roman and Ambrosian (the "Roman Canon"), with Ambrose of Milan being the first witness to this eucharistic prayer.

### Anaphoral Structures in East and West

| Antiochene/West Syrian/Syro-Byzantine | Alexandrian | Roman |
|---|---|---|
| ("St. Basil/St. John Chrysostom") | ("St. Mark") | ("Roman Canon") |
| Dialogue | Dialogue | Dialogue |
| Preface (invariable) | Preface (invariable) | Preface (variable by feast and/or season) |
|  | Intercessions |  |
| Sanctus/Benedictus | Sanctus | Sanctus/Benedictus |
| Post-Sanctus |  | Post-Sanctus (*Te igitur, Memento Domine, Communicantes, Hanc Igitur*) |
|  | Epiclesis I | *Quam oblationem* |
| Institution narrative | Institution narrative | *Qui pridie* (institution narrative) |
| Anamnesis (Memorial) | Anamnesis (Memorial) | Anamnesis (*Unde et memores, Supra quae*) |
| Epiclesis | Epiclesis II | *Supplices te* |
| Intercessions |  | Intercessions (*Memento etiam, Nobis quoque, Per quem*) |
| Final doxology | Final doxology | Final doxology |

Together with this anaphoral development, a theological concern for "consecration" of the bread and wine into the *typos, antitypos, figura,* or *homoioma* of the body and blood of Christ develops further with requests that the bread and wine might be revealed as or changed to become Christ's body and blood. Cyril (John) of Jerusalem attributes this to the activity of the Holy Spirit in the epiclesis,[29] and Ambrose of Milan to the recitation of the words

---

*St. James: An Investigation into Their Common Origin*, Orientalia Christiana Analecta 240 (Rome: Pontifical Oriental Institute, 1992).

29. Cyril of Jerusalem, *Lectures on the Christian Sacraments: The Procatechesis and the Five Mystagogical Catecheses ascribed to St. Cyril of Jerusalem*, trans. Maxwell E. Johnson (Yonkers, NY: St. Vladimir's Seminary Press, 2017), 125.

of Christ (the institution narrative) by the priest.[30] From this point on, East and West will tend to approach the question of eucharistic "consecration" from these differing points of view, although one should not assume that these are hardened theological positions in this time period, nor will consecration by the epiclesis of the Holy Spirit ever become the only approach of the Christian East.[31] Further, what must not be neglected in all of this is that the whole ecclesiological connection to eucharistic presence that we see in the West, especially in Augustine, in the context of the Donatist controversy, is concerned with what Communion ultimately signifies. That is, the sharing of Communion signifies the ultimate union between Christ and the church and, hence, the unity of the whole Christ (the *totus Christus*), Head and members, what later Scholastic theology would refer to as the *res tantum*.[32]

Mystogogical teaching on the "awesome" and "fearful" nature of eucharistic participation, as well as noncommuning attendance on the part of a now largely "nominal" Christian assembly, will lead to, and be fostered by, allegorical interpretation of the liturgy itself as a kind of dramatic reenactment of the life of Christ. Here various liturgical elements (e.g., the transfer of the gifts to the altar and the anaphoral epiclesis) become interpreted in relation to moments in Christ's passion and resurrection.[33] Along with an increased theological emphasis on the sacrificial nature of the Eucharist, a split develops between the liturgy and Communion reception to such an extent that the Eucharist becomes almost exclusively a clerical affair and eucharistic participation becomes focused on individual contemplation of the "meaning" of the ceremonies and symbols of the rite itself. Aided by the increase of anaphoral intercessions for a variety of categories of people (living and dead) and other needs, the Eucharist was thus seen increasingly as being "offered" for those "needs," even in the words of Cyril (John) of Jerusalem as a "propitiatory sacrifice."[34] But, to be fair, theology stressed the "commemorative" or "memorial of Christ" aspect of this eucharistic "sacrifice," and for that matter, in spite of the preponderance of offering language in the Roman

30. R. C. D. Jasper and G. J. Cuming, *Prayers of the Eucharist: Early and Reformed*, ed. Paul F. Bradshaw and Maxwell E. Johnson, 4th ed. (Collegeville, MN: Liturgical Press Academic, 2019), 196 (hereafter cited as *PEER4*).

31. On this see Michael Zheltov, "The Moment of Eucharistic Consecration in Byzantine Thought," in *Issues in Eucharistic Praying in East and West*, ed. Maxwell E. Johnson (Collegeville, MN: Liturgical Press, 2010), 263–306.

32. Joseph Wawrykow, "The Heritage of the Late Empire: Influential Theology," in *A Companion to the Eucharist in the Middle Ages*, ed. Ian Levy, Gary Macy, and Kristen Van Ausdall (Leiden: Brill, 2012), 74–75.

33. See Yarnold, *Awe-Inspiring Rites*, 216.

34. Cyril of Jerusalem, *Lectures on the Christian Sacraments*, 125–27.

Canon, the principal understanding even there is that of the Eucharist as the church's great *sacrificium laudis* (sacrifice of *praise*).[35] Robert Taft summarizes the early Christian and Eastern approach to this issue:

> There is one single offering of the Church within which several things happen. These things are expressed in various ways and moments according to the several pre-reformation traditions of East and West, all of which agree on the basic ritual elements of their traditions. These classical anaphoras express that the Eucharist is a sacrifice, the sacramental memorial of Christ's own sacrifice on the cross, in which the Church, repeating what Jesus did at the Last Supper, invokes God's blessing on bread and wine so that it might become Jesus' body and blood, our spiritual food and drink. . . . All attempts to squeeze more out of the words of the prayer . . . are inferences that can only be made by imposing on the text the results of later theological reflection and/or polemics.[36]

## Daily Prayer (the Liturgy of the Hours)

During this period, patterns for daily prayer from within the first three centuries evolved into different types of daily, public, communal prayer, especially at morning and evening. Thanks to the seminal work of Anton Baumstark, two types stand out with great clarity: the *cathedral* (or *parochial*) and the *monastic*.[37] While some scholars have challenged this designation, the terms remain helpful descriptions of what some have called "two ways of praying" in this late antique period.[38] That is, "cathedral prayer" is so named because of the variety of ministries employed in its performance and on account of its interpretation as the priestly prayer of the whole church in praise and intercession, and because it made use of a number of "select" elements (e.g., psalmody) and "popular" ceremonies (e.g., candle lighting and incense). The core of morning prayer was the daily use of Psalms 148–50 and either Psalm 63 or 51, and evening prayer regularly used the hymn *Phōs Hilaron* ("O Gladsome Light") to accompany an evening ritual of lamp lighting (*lucernarium*)—the ultimate origins also of the candle lighting and *Exsultet* of the Easter Vigil liturgy—as well as Psalm 141 (East) and Psalm 105 (West). Various litanies and lengthy prayers of intercession were regular components of both morning

---

35. *PEER4*, 2007. See also Maxwell E. Johnson, "Recent Thoughts on the Roman Anaphora: Sacrifice in the *Canon Missae*," *Ecclesia Orans* 35 (2018): 217–51.

36. Robert Taft, "Understanding the Byzantine Anaphoral Oblation," in *Rule of Prayer, Rule of Faith: Essays in Honor of Aidan Kavanagh, O.S.B.*, ed. Nathan Mitchell and John F. Baldovin (Collegeville, MN: Liturgical Press, 1996), 53–54.

37. Anton Baumstark, *Comparative Liturgy* (London: SPCK, 1958).

38. Paul Bradshaw, *Two Ways of Praying* (Nashville: Abingdon, 1995).

and evening prayer, with the response of *Kyrie Eleison* sung after each petition, and neither homilies nor the reading of Scripture was generally included. By the end of the fifth century, even daily offerings of incense also became characteristic.[39]

Together with *Apostolic Constitutions* 8, our best witness to the "cathedral office" is the pilgrim Egeria. Along with describing a rather full *cursus horarum* for the day, including not only morning and evening prayer but also an early morning (monastic) vigil and prayer at the third (*terce*), sixth (*sext*), and ninth (*none*) hours in the Holy City, Egeria is an invaluable witness to an early Sunday morning Resurrection Vigil, which will come to be a characteristic "cathedral" or "parochial" service leaving its traces throughout the Christian East:

> As soon as the first cock has crowed, the bishop immediately comes down and goes into the cave at the Anastasis. All the doors are opened and the whole crowd goes into the Anastasis, where very many lights are already lit, and when the people have entered, one of the presbyters recites a psalm and all respond; after this a prayer is made. Then one of the deacons recites a psalm, similarly a prayer is made; a third psalm is also recited by one of the clergy, a third prayer is also made and the commemoration of all. . . . Behold, censers are brought into the cave of the Anastasis so that the whole Anastasis basilica is filled with the smell. And then where the bishop stands inside the enclosure, he takes the gospel and comes to the door, and the bishop himself reads [the account of] the Lord's resurrection. When he has begun to read it, there is such a groaning and moaning from everyone and such tears that the hardest person could be moved to tears that the Lord had undergone such things for us. So, when the gospel has been read, the bishop comes out and is led with hymns to the Cross and all the people with him. Then one psalm is recited and a prayer is made. Then he blesses the faithful and the dismissal is done. And as the bishop comes out, all come to his hand.[40]

The "monastic" type of daily prayer had its origins among the growing ascetical communities in the deserts of Egypt and Syria. If praise and intercession characterized the cathedral office, the emphasis in the monastic office was on meditation and contemplation geared toward spiritual perfection in the monastic life. Whether prayed alone in cells or in community, the content of the monastic office was the psalms, recited (or sung by a soloist with some communal response) in their biblical order, alternating with periods of silence,

39. Robert Taft, *The Liturgy of the Hours in East and West: The Origins of the Divine Office and Its Meaning for Today* (Collegeville, MN: Liturgical Press, 1986), 31–56.
40. McGowan and Bradshaw, *Pilgrimage of Egeria*, 153–54.

prostrations, and concluding prayers. Lengthy Scripture readings tended to be included as well, and the offices themselves were oriented toward the goal of "ceaseless" contemplative prayer.[41] Our best source for the monastic office, at least for its Egyptian version, is John Cassian, a Western monk who went to Egypt in his younger days and now sought to reform monasticism in Gaul according to an Egyptian model, based, at least in part, on what Taft calls "a somewhat idealized Egyptian office," which Cassian presents as a reliable witness to the entire country.[42] Nevertheless, if his witness has to be received with some caution, in his *Institutes* 2 and 3 Cassian does provide helpful information to us. We learn from him, for example, that the Egyptian monastic office was only twice daily, morning and evening, that it consisted of twelve psalms in each office (with the twelfth psalm having an "alleluia" refrain or response), that the *Gloria Patri* doxology ("Glory to the Father and to the Son and to the Holy Spirit") concluded the psalmody as a whole, and that Scripture reading from both Testaments occurred on weekdays but only from the New Testament on Saturdays and Sundays.[43]

The influence of monasticism on ecclesial life in general during this period had profound consequences for the cathedral office. Not only were many of the leading bishops of this period monks themselves, but the development of "urban" monasteries closely connected with local churches would lead to a hybrid or mixed office that combined both cathedral and monastic elements as well as the retention of the early pattern of prayer at the third, sixth, and ninth hours and at various intervals during the night.[44] One of the best examples of this mixed office in the West is the influential *Rule of St. Benedict*, where morning prayer (*lauds*) is essentially a "cathedral office," with the same psalmody, including Psalms 67, 51, and 148–50, assigned to every morning, and evening prayer (*vespers*) a "monastic office," with Psalms 110–47 constituting a recurring weekly *cursus* recited in order, with four of these psalms assigned to each evening.[45] In the Western Middle Ages, beginning with the emperor Charlemagne's assistant Benedict of Aniane, the use of *The Rule of St. Benedict* will shape monasticism as predominantly "Benedictine."

In addition, while some nonbiblical hymns make their appearance in the eucharistic liturgy during these centuries in the East, the majority of early

---

41. Taft, *Liturgy of the Hours*, 57–73.

42. Taft, *Liturgy of the Hours*, 58.

43. Taft, *Liturgy of the Hours*, 58–60. For an English translation of Cassian's *Institutes*, see E. C. S. Gibson, trans., *The Works of John Cassian*, in *Nicene and Post-Nicene Fathers*, series 2, vol. 11 (Grand Rapids: Eerdmans, 1964).

44. Taft, *Liturgy of the Hours*, 75–140.

45. See Timothy Fry, *The Rule of St. Benedict in English* (Collegeville, MN: Liturgical Press, 1982), 42–46.

Christian hymns, including even the *Gloria in Excelsis* (*Apostolic Constitutions* 7), have their origins in this context of daily prayer. When, for example, Augustine describes the corporate singing at Ambrose's cathedral in Milan (*Confessions* 10), which he notes was instrumental in his conversion, it is quite likely that what he refers to is some form of "Ambrosian" office hymns.[46]

## The Liturgical Year

If Christian initiation, Eucharist, and the Liturgy of the Hours achieve their "classic" forms in the late antique period, so too do the various feasts and seasons of the liturgical year become organized into traditional fixed patterns.[47] Together with the Nicene decision on the date for *Pascha* or Easter (i.e., the first Sunday after the first full moon after the vernal equinox) and the widespread adoption of paschal baptism,[48] so a forty-day "Lent"—probably as a synthesis of an Alexandrian post-Epiphany, forty-day period of baptismal preparation and fast with other prepaschal and/or prebaptismal preparation periods elsewhere[49]—makes its universal appearance as a time for the final preparation of baptismal candidates and penitents, and ascetical preparation for the faithful. Here as well, a fully developed Holy Week and "Paschal Triduum" (i.e., the three days measured from Thursday evening to Easter Sunday evening) are to be noted, with Egeria witnessing to a "Palm Sunday" procession of palms and a Good Friday rite that included both the reading of the Johannine Passion (John 18–19) and the veneration (kissing) of a relic of the cross, a relic closely guarded by deacons to ensure that none of the "faithful" would bite off a portion and steal it.[50] All of these celebrations would move from Jerusalem to the West, although at Rome "Palm Sunday" would remain the day for the reading of the Matthean Passion (Matt. 26–27) and only in the Middle Ages would it acquire the palms procession from elsewhere in the West (Gaul). In none of the earliest traditions did Holy (Maundy) Thursday evening or Good Friday include a celebration of the eucharistic liturgy. Rather, the paschal fast itself (distinct from the Lenten

---

46. On early Christian liturgical music, see Johannes Quasten, *Music and Worship in Pagan and Christian Antiquity* (Washington, DC: National Association of Pastoral Musicians, 1983).

47. On the liturgical year for this period, see Paul F. Bradshaw and Maxwell E. Johnson, *The Origins of Feasts, Fasts and Seasons in Early Christianity* (Collegeville, MN: Liturgical Press, 2011).

48. See Paul Bradshaw, "'*Diem baptismo sollemniorem*': Initiation and Easter in Christian Antiquity," in Johnson, *Living Water, Sealing Spirit*, 137–47.

49. See Nicholas Russo, "The Origins of Lent" (PhD diss., University of Notre Dame, 2009).

50. McGowan and Bradshaw, *Pilgrimage of Egeria*, 176.

forty-day fast) began on Thursday evening, and since the celebration of the Eucharist was seen as incompatible with fasting, it was not celebrated until the Paschal Vigil.

The "fifty days" of the Easter celebration also become fully liturgicized during the centuries corresponding to the chronology of Luke-Acts. Although Pentecost Sunday was originally a unitive celebration of Jesus's ascension and the gift of the Holy Spirit, by the beginning of the fifth century the fortieth day of Easter had become a separate *feast* of the ascension and Pentecost the *feast* of the Holy Spirit, now separated by nine days of preparation. In spite of an earlier tradition that forbade fasting and kneeling during the "fifty days," some Western churches resumed both practices in the time between ascension and Pentecost, thus effectively changing the Easter season from fifty days to forty.

The Western celebration of Christmas on December 25 and the Eastern celebration of Epiphany on January 6 were adopted universally during these centuries. Traditional scholarship has tended toward what is called the "history of religions hypothesis," that December 25 and January 6 were chosen to counteract already-existing pagan solar cults. More recent scholarship has been sympathetic to what is termed the "calculation hypothesis," that dates for Christmas and Epiphany were based on what was believed to be the date of Jesus's crucifixion and conception (either March 25 or April 6), leading to birth feasts a perfect nine months later, either on December 25 or on January 6.[51] Whatever the ultimate origin of the dates for these feasts, influenced, undoubtedly, by the continuing popularity of the pagan solar cults (at least in the West) and a concern for christological orthodoxy, Christmas and Epiphany (Theophany) became the feasts of the incarnation par excellence and, at least in the East, Epiphany would become focused exclusively on Jesus's baptism as the revelation of his identity and divine Sonship. Although Jesus's baptism forms the content of Epiphany in some Western traditions as well (e.g., northern Italy), at Rome Epiphany focused on the visit of the Magi (Matt. 2:1–12) as the manifestation of salvation to the Gentiles. A season of preparation for these feasts also begins to make its appearance in some sources, but the full development of "Advent" itself, whether as "Marian" (East) or "eschatological" (West), is a later phenomenon.

The filling out and universalizing of the "sanctoral" cycle is also a characteristic of this period as relics of the martyrs and their cult were increasingly "transferred" to other churches. Together with martyr feasts, this period also

---

51. In addition to Bradshaw and Johnson, *Origins of Feasts*, 123–70, see Thomas J. Talley, *The Origins of the Liturgical Year* (Collegeville, MN: Liturgical Press, 1986), 91–162.

witnessed to the inclusion on local liturgical calendars of influential bishops and ascetics as exemplary models of faith. Biblical saints, especially the Virgin Mary after the proclamation of the *Theotokos* doctrine at the Council of Ephesus (431), make their appearance as well. Often connected to the building and dedication of churches in her honor, the feasts of "Mary Theotokos," later her "Dormition" or "Falling Asleep" (August 15), her "Nativity" (September 8), the "Annunciation" (March 25), and the "Presentation" of Christ to Simeon and Anna (February 2) are well in place by the fifth century in the East. All four would be adopted subsequently by Rome and, with the addition of a *Roman* feast on January 1 commemorating the *Theotokos* decree of Ephesus, would remain the only "Marian" feasts on the general Roman calendar until the fourteenth century.[52]

Traditional scholarship has argued that the concern for dates, the multiplication of feasts, and the development of Holy Week in this period, where numerous moments of the passion of Christ are now ritualized, is the result of a new "historicizing" mentality that replaced an earlier eschatological orientation.[53] But, in underscoring a concern for dates even in the pre-Nicene period (e.g., the "Quartodeciman" *Pascha* on 14 Nisan of the Jewish calendar, which equals March 25 and April 6 on the Julian calendar), recent scholarship has suggested that there is no necessary contradiction between "history" and "eschatology" and, thus, no reason to posit a new mentality to account for these developments.[54] Rather, in places like Jerusalem it would be only natural to expect that Christians would want to visit the holy places and to celebrate there the events associated in Scripture with Christ's life. Especially with the imperial funding and building of basilicas at those places, such development was inevitable.

## Practical Implications for Worship

As we have seen, Christian worship in the late antique period is the story of development, change, accommodation, and adaptation. The diverse churches of East and West emerge at the end of this period with a rather homogeneous liturgical structure, style, and theological interpretation. If some important and distinctive elements remain within the various liturgical traditions, the

52. See Bradshaw and Johnson, *Origins of Feasts*, 171–214.
53. Gregory Dix, *The Shape of the Liturgy* (London: Dacre, 1945), 303–96.
54. See Talley, *Origins of the Liturgical Year*, 1–32; John Baldovin, *The Urban Character of Christian Worship: The Origins, Development, and Meaning of Stational Liturgy* (Rome: Pontifical Oriental Institute, 1987), 102–4; and Robert Taft, "Historicism Revisited," in *Beyond East and West*, 31–49.

challenges of doctrinal heresy and the changed sociopolitical climate of late antiquity result, nevertheless, in relatively similar rites for initiation, Eucharist, daily prayer, and the liturgical year, as well as common perceptions about the meaning of those rites: baptism as participation in Christ's death and resurrection; the Eucharist as the celebration and reception of Christ's body and blood, the bread and wine being changed by either the Holy Spirit or the words of Christ from the Last Supper; daily prayer, the Liturgy of the Hours, or the Divine Office as the common prayer for the whole church (laity, clergy, and monks alike); and the feasts and seasons of the liturgical year providing the calendrical framework for the life of the church in the world.

At the same time, it should be noted, especially with regard to the challenges of doctrinal heresy, that worship not only was formed by but also helped in forming orthodox Christian teaching.[55] Orthodox trinitarian and christological doctrine developed, in part at least, from the church at prayer, as the baptismal-creedal profession of faith gave rise to the "official" creeds themselves, as prayer *to* Christ contributed to an understanding of him as *homoousios* with the Father, as the Holy Spirit's "divine" role in baptism shaped the theology of the Spirit's divinity, and as early devotion to Mary as *Theotokos* gave rise to the decree of Ephesus. While "orthodoxy" means "right thinking," not giving "right glory" to God, such right thinking often developed from the doxology of the church, where several of these doctrines were prayed liturgically long before they were formalized dogmatically. So it has been ever since. The practice of Christian worship forms the belief of the church (*ut legem credendi statuat lex supplicandi*, "that the law of supplication might establish the law of believing"). In turn, worship itself is formed further by that belief and, further still, continues to form people into believers and disciples of the crucified and risen Lord.

## For Further Reading

Alexopoulos, Stefanos, and Maxwell E. Johnson. *Introduction to Eastern Christian Liturgies*. Collegeville, MN: Liturgical Academic, 2021.

Bradshaw, Paul F. *The Search for the Origins of Christian Worship*. London: SPCK, 2002.

Bradshaw, Paul F., and Maxwell E. Johnson. *The Origins of Feasts, Fasts and Seasons in Early Christianity*. Collegeville, MN: Liturgical Press, 2011.

---

55. See Maxwell E. Johnson, *Praying and Believing in Early Christianity: The Interplay between Christian Worship and Doctrine* (Collegeville, MN: Liturgical Press, 2013).

Johnson, Maxwell E. *Praying and Believing in Early Christianity: The Interplay between Christian Worship and Doctrine.* Collegeville, MN: Liturgical Press, 2013.

———. *The Rites of Christian Initiation: Their Evolution and Interpretation.* Collegeville, MN: Liturgical Press, 2007.

McGowan, Andrew B. *Ancient Christian Worship: Early Church Practices in Social, Historical, and Theological Perspective.* Grand Rapid: Baker Academic, 2014.

# PART 3

# Eastern Orthodox Worship

# — 6 —

# History of Orthodox Worship

## *Nina Glibetić*

Orthodox Christianity is widely acknowledged as placing a preeminent emphasis on the liturgy in the life and mission of the church. Many Western pilgrims to the Holy Land or elsewhere have been struck by the complex rites fostered by the ancient communities in Christianity's homeland of the Near East.[1] Similarly, official ecumenical declarations between Western and Eastern Christians often highlight the importance of liturgy to Orthodox Christians.[2] This centrality of worship is likewise seen through common interpretations of the word "orthodox" itself. While etymologically stemming from the Greek expression "correct belief" (from *orthos*, "correct," and *doxa*, "belief"), the double meaning of the word *doxa* as also representing "glory" or "praise" has led many to define orthodoxy as "correct worship."[3] For all the importance of liturgy within the Orthodox Christian tradition, a scholar tasked with writing a general summary on the historical themes of Orthodox

---

1. For an example, see the observations made throughout William Dalrymple, *From the Holy Mountain* (London: HarperCollins, 1997).
2. As Vatican II's ecumenical decree *Unitatis redintegratio* puts it, "Everyone knows with what love the Eastern Christians celebrate the sacred liturgy, especially the eucharistic celebration, source of the Church's life and pledge of future glory." See *Unitatis redintegratio*, chapter 15, accessible in English at https://www.vatican.va/archive/hist_councils/ii_vatican_council/documents/vat-ii_decree_19641121_unitatis-redintegratio_en.html.
3. See the definition in A. Edward Siecienski, *Orthodox Christianity: A Very Short Introduction* (New York: Oxford University Press, 2019), 2, 110.

worship is immediately faced with a challenge. The designation "Orthodox" can be used for a variety of ecclesiastical traditions, some of which have not been in communion with one another for sixteen centuries. Thus, before setting about any description of Orthodox Christian ritual and its history, one must first define what one intends to refer to by the expression "Orthodox" worship.

## Nomenclature

The name "Orthodox Christianity" can designate several churches. With the exception of the Roman Catholic Church and those Christian traditions stemming directly or indirectly from late medieval Catholicism (the Anglican Communion, Evangelical Lutheranism, Anabaptist traditions, etc.), a vast number of historic Christian churches have tended to refer to themselves as "Orthodox." For example, we find "Orthodox" within the titles of the Russian Orthodox Church and the Coptic Orthodox Church, although these two ecclesiastical bodies are entirely distinct. Western literature often problematically groups all non-Western Christians into a single "Orthodox" category.[4] The communities they intend can be subdivided into three categories.

The first comprises what some call "Eastern Orthodox" churches (e.g., Greek Orthodox, Russian Orthodox, Georgian Orthodox, Serbian Orthodox). These jurisdictionally independent churches are in communion with one another and celebrate according to one liturgical tradition known as the Byzantine Rite, owing to its historical associations with the Eastern Roman—that is, Byzantine—Empire. The geographic label of "Eastern" here is nothing more than a western European indication that these churches were historically found to their east, predominantly in the eastern Mediterranean, the Caucasus, and Eastern Europe.

The second group of Orthodox churches usually designates those communities variously known as Oriental Orthodox, non-Chalcedonian Orthodox, or Miaphysite Orthodox Christians. These traditions subscribe to Miaphysite Christology and have historically rejected the Council of Chalcedon (451 CE), even if recent ecumenical dialogue has resulted in mutual acknowledgment of significant christological agreement between Chalcedonian and non-Chalcedonian Christians.[5] Oriental Orthodox likewise stem from ancient

4. See, e.g., the denominational categorizations of the influential World Christian Database: Todd M. Johnson and Gina A. Zurlo, eds., *World Christian Database* (Boston: Brill), https://worldchristiandatabase.org/.

5. See especially the two historical statements of agreement made by the Joint Commission of the Theological Dialogue between the Orthodox Church and the Oriental Orthodox Churches in 1989 (Anba Bishoy Monastery, Egypt) and 1990 (Chambésy), published in *The*

Christian churches and include the following communities: the Coptic Orthodox Church of Alexandria, Syriac Orthodox Church of Antioch, Armenian Apostolic Church, Malankara Orthodox Syrian Church (Indian Orthodox Church), Ethiopian Orthodox Tewahedo Church, and Eritrean Orthodox Tewahedo Church. These six churches are all in communion. Yet in contrast to the "Eastern Orthodox" who celebrate a common liturgical heritage, the "Oriental Orthodox" subscribe to four distinct liturgical rites—namely, the Coptic, the Armenian, the Ethiopic (followed also in Eritrea), and the West Syriac Rite (followed also by the Malankara Church).

To these two categories of Orthodox Christians we can add a third—namely, the Assyrian Church of the East. This relatively small church today stems from an ancient community that was historically located outside the borders of the late antique Roman Empire. At its height, it stretched from Mesopotamia to China and thus represented the geographically largest church of the Middle Ages. The Assyrian Church of the East historically rejected the third ecumenical council of Ephesus (431 CE), and within outdated scholarship it is sometimes referred to as the Nestorian church. While it does not use the term "Orthodox" in its formal title, it does employ the term "Catholic" in its long title, a practice found among some other Orthodox churches as well.[6] The Assyrian Church of the East has its own liturgical tradition known as the East Syriac Rite.

Taken together, these three groups of Orthodox Christians include over 285 million people around the globe.[7] Though principally residing in central, southeastern, and eastern Europe, North and East Africa, the Middle East, and India, Orthodox Christians span all continents, with sizable communities today also in western Europe, Australia, and North and South America. If the term "Orthodox" is used in this broadest sense to encompass the various historic Christian traditions that developed outside the Western framework, then the label applies to at least twenty-three distinct groups (or more, depending on how one counts them) who practice one of six liturgical rites of the Christian East. Furthermore, within a single liturgical tradition, such as the Armenian or Coptic Rite, there is a range of identities and liturgical practices in each church's homeland and their various diaspora communities across the globe. It is also important to note that nearly all Eastern Christian branches

---

*Dialogue between the Eastern Orthodox and the Oriental Orthodox Churches*, ed. Christine Chaillot (Volos, Greece: Volos Academy, 2016).

6. The Holy Apostolic Catholic Assyrian Church of the East, as self-described on the official website: https://www.assyrianchurch.org/home/.

7. Johnson and Zurlo, *World Christian Database*, https://worldchristiandatabase-org.proxy .library.nd.edu/wcd/#/homepage/main-page.

have a Catholic counterpart—that is, an ecclesiastical community composed of former members of one of these churches who have entered into communion with the pope usually after a period of contact with Catholic missionaries and/or during a period of Catholic political governance. These Eastern Catholic churches are in communion with the Roman Catholic Church but worship according to their own historical liturgical tradition, with varying degrees of Latinization.

Despite the great variety among various Orthodox communities, the grouping together of Christians as diverse as Russian Orthodox and Eritrean Orthodox is not entirely without reason since some common features emerge, especially in comparison to the post-medieval West. As the patristic scholar Andrew Louth asserts, "In many ways, Eastern Orthodox and Oriental Orthodox feel much closer to each other than either do to the West."[8] At the same time, providing a history of worship across these diverse traditions and rites is simply not possible within the span of a single chapter. For the purposes here, I will provide an overview of the historical stages and themes of the most widely practiced and studied of these worship traditions—namely, that of the Eastern Orthodox Church, whose liturgical heritage is known to scholarship today as the Byzantine Rite. From here forward, I will be using the terms "Orthodox" and "Eastern Orthodox" interchangeably, and exclusively in reference to the Eastern Orthodox Church as defined above.

## Place of Liturgy in Eastern Orthodox Life

To demonstrate the position of liturgy within the Eastern Orthodox tradition, scholars have often called on the colorful narrative on the conversion of the Kievan Rus'. This legendary account is preserved in the *Russian Primary Chronicle*, the oldest historical narrative of the East Slavs. Attributed to Saint Nestor, a monk from the Kievan Monastery of the Caves who lived from the mid-eleventh to the beginning of the twelfth century, the chronicle recounts that in the year 987 the ruler of the Kievan Rus', Grand Prince Vladimir (r. 980–1015), sent envoys out to inquire about the religions of neighboring nations in order to ascertain which one to adopt for his nation. Among the places they visited was Constantinople, capital of the Byzantine Empire, where the envoys visited the famous cathedral church of Hagia Sophia to witness the liturgy. Upon their return to Vladimir, they reported the following:

8. Andrew Louth, *Introducing Eastern Orthodox Theology* (Downers Grove, IL: InterVarsity, 2013), xv.

When we journeyed among the Bulgars (Muslims), we beheld how they worship in their temple, called a mosque. . . . There is no happiness among them. . . . Their religion is not good. Then we went among the Germans (Latin Christians), and saw them performing many ceremonies in their temples; but we beheld no glory there. Then we went to Greece, and the Greeks led us to the edifices where they worship their God, and we knew not whether we were in heaven or on earth. For on earth there is no such splendor or such beauty, and we are at a loss how to describe it. We only know that God dwells there among men, and their service is fairer than the ceremonies of other nations. For we cannot forget that beauty. Every man, after tasting something sweet, is afterward unwilling to accept that which is bitter, and therefore we cannot dwell longer here.[9]

Persuaded by their report, Vladimir adopted Christianity and married the Byzantine princess Anna. His people, too, accepted the new faith and received baptism in the Dnieper River, thereby inaugurating what would eventually emerge as the largest Orthodox denomination, the Russian Orthodox Church. The question of the degree of legendary elaboration within the *Primary Chronicle* is of secondary importance for our purposes here. What is striking is that the oldest extant Slavic memory of conversion to Christianity records *worship* as the motivating factor. According to this legend, Vladimir is not ultimately persuaded by theological or political argument. Rather, it is the liturgical celebration in its full glory at Hagia Sophia that ultimately draws the Rus' prince into the Orthodox Christian fold.

Such an emphasis on the liturgy within Eastern Christian ecclesial identity is not isolated to medieval accounts. It is also highlighted by contemporary theologians.[10] The twentieth-century Orthodox theologian Georges Florovsky writes, "Christianity is a liturgical religion. The Church is first of all a worshipping community. Worship comes first, doctrine and discipline second."[11] Likewise, Alexander Schmemann anchors his theological anthropology on the claim that humans are ultimately characterized as worshiping beings, or *Homo adorans*:

In the Bible to bless God is not a "religious" or "cultic" act, but the very way of life. . . . All rational, spiritual and other qualities of man, distinguishing him

9. *The Russian Primary Chronicle: Laurentian Text*, trans. and ed. Samuel H. Cross and Olgerd P. Sherbowitz-Wetzor (Cambridge, MA: Medieval Academy of America, 1953), 111.

10. As evident in the thought of Nicholas Afanasiev, Alexander Schmemann, and John Zizioulas. See Alexander Schmemann, *For the Life of the World: Sacraments and Orthodoxy* (Crestwood, NY: St. Vladimir's Seminary Press, 2002); and Schmemann, *The Eucharist: Sacrament of the Kingdom*, trans. Paul Kachur (Crestwood, NY: St. Vladimir's Seminary Press, 1987).

11. Georges Florovsky, "The Elements of Liturgy in the Orthodox Catholic Church," *One Church* 13, nos. 1–2 (1959): 24.

from other creatures, have their focus and ultimate fulfillment in this capacity to bless God, to know, so to speak, the meaning of the thirst and hunger that constitutes his life. "Homo sapiens," "homo faber" . . . yes, but first of all, "homo adorans." The first and basic definition of man is that he is the priest. He stands at the center of the world and unifies it in his act of blessing God, of both receiving the world from God and offering it to God.[12]

In other words, one finds within Orthodox Christianity an affirmation that worship and praise of God is the intended telos of all human activity, and not just of cultic or ritual-liturgical acts.

Yet while there is no doubt about the centrality of the liturgy in the Eastern Orthodox (and other Orthodox) churches, this should not be thought of as a uniquely "Orthodox" or an especially "Eastern" characteristic. Rather, in this respect the Eastern Orthodox Church reflects a shared, ritually centered identity common to both East and West for much of premodern history. Indeed, Eastern Orthodox Christians are only "especially liturgical" insofar as they have maintained an emphasis on liturgy that characterized many ancient and medieval societies at large.[13] Furthermore, one must not interpret this emphasis on liturgy as diminishing the importance of other activities, such as theological reflection (including academic theology) or charitable and missionary engagement, which are often viewed as extending out of and representative of the church's praise of God—that is, liturgy.

## Key Features of the Eastern Orthodox Liturgy in Historical Context

Outside observers often note that Eastern Orthodox liturgy (and Oriental Orthodox liturgy) involves a complexity of gestures, movements, texts, images, and hymns. The multisensory stimulation, including sight (icons, vestments, etc.), sound (chant, prayers, responses, etc.), and smell (incense), is viewed by Orthodox theologians not only as aiding a didactic purpose but as directing the entire human person toward union with God. The Orthodox tradition does not know of an equivalent to the Western medieval "low Mass"—that is, the celebration of the Eucharist through spoken words only, without the solemnization of chant nor the use of incense. Instead, the multisensory dimensions of worship have historically been fostered across diverse Orthodox communities irrespective of congregation size or liturgical occasion, while

---

12. Schmemann, *For the Life of the World*, 14–15.

13. The reasons for the diminishing of ritual centrality in the European West and the colonized "new" world are connected to several influential historical movements. See Edward Muir, *Ritual in Early Modern Europe* (Cambridge: Cambridge University Press, 2005).

the musical and artistic components of liturgy have long interacted with, and been influenced by, local culture and artistic expression.

## Prayer Posture

What the Eastern Orthodox tradition regards as an essential relationship between the human body and humanity's worship of God is manifest in a variety of ways, including in the liturgical posture of worshipers. Pews found in many contemporary Orthodox churches in North America and elsewhere are of recent introduction, adopted under the influence of Western worship traditions. Recent years have seen attempts to halt their introduction or to remove them where previously adopted.[14] Orthodox churches do tradition- ally have places for people to sit and rest during services, but these have historically been benches or seat stalls (*stasidia*) placed to the sides of the nave. The unencumbered, open nave, which is the norm to this day for many Orthodox across the globe, enables a good deal of movement both in the form of liturgical processions and by individuals attending worship.[15] Rarely are Orthodox worshipers fixed to one spot throughout an entire liturgical service.

One of the significant ways in which an open floor plan has affected worship is evident in the gesture of full prostrations—that is, the act of kneeling down and touching one's head to the floor typically in conjunction with making the sign of the cross. Full prostrations are testified across medieval sources as a regular component of both corporate worship and private prayer. This full-body gesture is not indiscriminate to the day of the week or liturgical season. Viewed as an act of humility, deference, and penance, the Council of Nicaea in 325 deemed kneeling inappropriate for the festive commemora- tion of Christ's resurrection and forbade it on Sundays and throughout the fifty days from Easter Sunday until Pentecost Sunday, a liturgical principle largely maintained in contemporary Orthodox churches.[16] The oldest extant Byzantine liturgical manuscripts already testify to a specific prayer service for

14. Such views can be found in popular literature, including parish websites: "A Call for the Removal of Pews in Orthodox Churches," St. George Serbian Orthodox Church, https://www .stgeorgehermitage.org/removethepews. Cf. Andriy Chirovsky, "Anathema 'Sit': Some Reflec- tions on Pews in Eastern Christian Churches and Their Effects on Worshippers," *Diakonia* 15 (1980): 167–73.

15. Depending on cultural context, some Orthodox churches maintain gender separation, with men and women standing on opposite sides of the nave.

16. On this liturgical canon, previously also maintained in the West, see the two-part article by Gabriel Radle, "Embodied Eschatology: The Council of Nicaea's Regulation of Kneeling and Its Reception across Liturgical Traditions," *Worship* 90 (2016): 345–71, 433–61.

reintroducing kneeling at the close of the Pentecost season.[17] Such a service continued to be used throughout the centuries and is maintained to this day. The altering postures of the human body within Orthodox worship mark the liturgical seasons and reveal the church's liturgy as both a venue for working out one's salvation through penance and also a space and time in which Christians experience a foretaste of eschatological fullness and joy.

### Sights

One of the defining sensory characteristics of Eastern Orthodox churches today is the arrangement and decoration of worship spaces, with church walls and ceilings often filled with frescoes depicting biblical scenes, saints, and events in the life of the church. Icons of Christ and the saints are usually available for veneration, while a prominent location in the church is reserved for an alternating icon depicting the particular feast or saint being commemorated on any given day. Such extensive use of visual imagery in Byzantine worship is part of a long tradition. It is attested in many extant late antique and medieval Byzantine churches, from the mosaic decoration of Constantinople's cathedral church of Hagia Sophia, to the frescoes of late medieval village churches in Greece. Though only a small number of pre-Constantinian worship spaces have survived, those extant to this day, such as the third-century church of Dura-Europos or the Christian burial sites of the Roman catacombs, reveal that images donned prayer spaces from the first centuries of Christianity. At the same time, Byzantine liturgical iconography particularly flowered after the defeat of iconoclasm in the ninth century.[18]

Particularly relevant for Byzantine worship is the emergence of the iconostasis. Located between the nave and the sanctuary, the iconostasis takes its origin from the marble structure of small columns and architrave known as the templon and common to many late antique Christian basilicas. In the Middle Ages, spaces between the templon columns come to be filled with icons, with prominent places given to Christ and the Theotokos (literally "God bearer," the common Orthodox title for the Virgin Mary).[19] The ico-

17. Stefano Parenti and Elena Velkovska, *L'eucologio Barberini gr. 336. Seconda edizione riveduta* (Rome: CLV-Edizioni Liturgiche, 2000), 226–28.

18. Obtaining its name from the Greek words for "icon" and "to break," the iconoclasm controversy refers to tensions over the use of icons that shook the Byzantine world in the eighth and ninth centuries. See Leslie Brubaker and John Haldon, *Byzantium in the Iconoclast Era, c. 680–850: A History* (Cambridge: Cambridge University Press, 2011).

19. On the historical development of the iconostasis, see the collection of articles in Sharon Gerstel, ed., *Thresholds of the Sacred: Architectural, Art Historical, Liturgical, and Theological Perspectives on Religious Screens, East and West* (Washington, DC: Dumbarton Oaks, 2007).

nostasis continued to develop over time, and in the postmedieval period many regions adopted wooden-carved icon screens with multiple registers depicting apostles, prophets, and scenes from the life of Christ.

Orthodox theologians stress that the iconostasis ought not to be viewed as a wall or a barrier intended to block access to the sanctuary and the altar therein.[20] To the contrary, it brings attention to the removal of the separation between heaven and earth achieved by Christ. This is evident in the ways that the iconostasis is repeatedly penetrated, including the gestures of clergy entering and exiting the sanctuary, and especially through the bringing out of the consecrated eucharistic gifts for the communion of the laity.[21]

While iconography and the arrangement of worship space have important aesthetic roles, Byzantine liturgical commentators do not regard these features as mere decoration, nor simple mimetic devices. Rather, icons are conceived of as "windows" into heavenly realities intended to bring the viewer into the mystery of the incarnate Logos and his church.[22] Conceived in this way, the iconostasis serves as a window into the mystery of the Eucharist achieved on the altar behind it. This is especially evident in the iconography on its central doors, which typically consists of the annunciation. Just as Mary's *fiat* helped bring about the physical incarnation of Christ, the iconostasis proclaims that the Eucharist is an extension of Christ's incarnation.

### Sounds

The Orthodox tradition has various musical systems for the singing of psalms, biblical odes, and hymns. Orthodox chant is traditionally performed according to the ancient system in which hymnography is assigned to eight musical modes. This system first emerged within the early liturgical tradition of Jerusalem and subsequently spread to other liturgical rites.[23] Since the local rite of Jerusalem represents one of the primary constituent elements of the synthesized Byzantine Rite, it would become a mainstay of the Byzantine

20. This is a common motif in Orthodox theological reflection on iconography. See Pavel Florensky, *Iconostasis*, trans. Donald Sheehan and Olga Andrejev (Crestwood, NY: St. Vladimir's Seminary Press, 1996), 62.

21. For comparison with Gothic screens in the medieval West, see Jacqueline Jung, *The Gothic Screen: Space, Sculpture, and Community in the Cathedrals of France and Germany, ca. 1200–1400* (New York: Cambridge University Press, 2013).

22. See Elizabeth Zelensky and Lela Gilbert, *Windows to Heaven: Introducing Icons to Protestants and Catholics* (Grand Rapids: Brazos, 2005).

23. Peter Jeffery, "The Earliest Christian Chant Repertory Recovered: The Georgian Witnesses to Jerusalem Chant," *Journal of the American Musicological Society* 47, no. 1 (1994): 1–38; Stig Frøyshov, "The Early Development of the Liturgical Eight-Mode System in Jerusalem," *St. Vladimir's Theological Quarterly* 51, nos. 2–3 (2007): 139–78.

tradition that all hymnography is assigned to one of the eight modes, a liturgical practice that continues to this day.

Even if early Byzantine liturgical manuscripts assign hymns to specific modes, scholars are unable to ascertain the precise melodies and stylization used within the earliest phases of Byzantine liturgical history. Much of early Christian music was transmitted orally. The first known form of Byzantine notation, known as "paleo-Byzantine notation," appears to have been intended for aiding a cantor with the details of musical performance practice for a specific hymn, but it does not provide complete melodies. Only with the emergence of "Middle Byzantine notation" starting around the twelfth century are the main features of Byzantine liturgical chant fully discernible. Byzantine chant tradition is monophonic (i.e., in unison), although the use of a drone or holding note known as an "ison" goes back centuries.

Alongside the main line of Byzantine chant development, a myriad of local variations in chant likely existed across the medieval Orthodox Christian world. Notable examples include the Znamenny chant of the Russian Orthodox tradition and the unique polyphonic tradition of Georgia,[24] as well as many variations and developments of Byzantine chant attested across the diverse Orthodox churches of the Balkans.[25] The use of Western-style choral music came into Orthodox liturgical practice originally via the Russian court in the seventeenth century. Gradually, Western choral forms came to be adapted to local melodies, producing a rich genre of Orthodox polyphonic choral music in use across multiple Orthodox traditions today.

### Engagement with the Bible

Sacred Scriptures are embedded in Byzantine worship in a host of ways. On the most basic level, biblical readings from the New Testament feature as part of the eucharistic liturgy. The backbone of the Liturgy of the Hours consists in the distribution of the Psalter across the week, with other texts from the Old Testament read at various points throughout the liturgical year. Historically, biblical texts were principally transmitted through liturgical books, many of which continue to be used today. Acts and Epistles are preserved in the Apostolarion, and many Old Testament readings in the Prophetologion. Other biblical readings are found in liturgical books containing propers (specific texts and hymns for a given day), such as the Triodion and Pentecostarion

24. The online website Georgian Chant provides extensive academic bibliography as well as musical samples: http://www.georgianchant.org/.

25. These are discussed in Elena Toncheva, "The Idea of Polyphony" (in Bulgarian), *Bulgarian Musicology* 3 (2001): 3–13.

used for the cycle of movable feasts connected to Easter, and the volumes of the Menaion used for the fixed-date feasts of the liturgical year. Given their use across the daily services of the Liturgy of the Hours, the psalms have their own book—namely, the Psalter. The Gospels are found in an Evangelion. This liturgically privileged book is not only used for proclaiming the appointed Gospel reading of a given day, it is also a revered liturgical object viewed as an icon of Christ, the Word made flesh. Gospel books are elaborately decorated, carried in liturgical processions, venerated by clergy and laity, and used by clergy for the blessing of the worshiping community. This last practice was recently adopted by the Roman Catholic tradition from Eastern Orthodoxy.[26]

It would be amiss to consider the Bible as operating within Orthodox worship only through direct biblical readings. Rather, the Bible permeates Eastern Orthodox worship through feasts commemorating biblical events, homilies based on biblical readings, iconographic depictions of biblical stories, and liturgical hymnography. The rich medieval hymnographic tradition resulted in a large body of liturgical poetry sung at every service of each day. As Derek Krueger and others have discussed, these hymns do not just commemorate biblical feasts; they also invite liturgical participants to interpret their own lives through biblical themes.[27] The hymnographical tradition encourages the Eastern Orthodox worshiper to view the Bible not as a past recounting of salvation history but as a vehicle for reading oneself into that history in the present day.

### Liturgical Calendar

The Eastern Orthodox Church follows the so-called Julian calendar, established under Julius Caesar and used by most Christians into the sixteenth century. Basing himself on Jesuit Roman astronomers and mathematicians, Pope Gregory XIII slightly reduced the Julian calendar in order to bring it into more precise conformity with the solar year. His modification resulted in the "Gregorian calendar" that was gradually adopted by all Western Christians. For the celebration of Pascha (Easter) and all dates related to the moveable cycle of feasts, all Orthodox churches except for the Finnish Orthodox Church continue to follow the computus according to the ancient Julian calendar. Thus, Eastern Orthodox usually do not celebrate Easter on the same day as Western Christians, although the two calendar systems do occasionally align.

26. See Marco Benini, "The Blessing with the Book of the Gospels: A Recent Adoption from the Byzantine to the Roman Rite," *Antiphon* 24, no. 1 (2020): 50–66.

27. Derek Krueger, *Liturgical Subjects: Christian Ritual, Biblical Narrative, and the Formation of the Self in Byzantium* (Philadelphia: University of Pennsylvania Press, 2014).

In 1923 several Orthodox churches (i.e., Constantinople, Albania, Bulgaria, Greece, Romania) adopted revisions to the Julian calendar to likewise bring it into better conformity with the solar year. Owing to advancements since the Gregorian reform, this revised Julian calendar is currently the most in line with the earth's solar year. It presently aligns with the Gregorian calendar for the next several centuries. However, these adaptations are applied only to the fixed cycle of feasts (Nativity, Annunciation, Transfiguration, etc.) and not to the moveable cycle.

## Practical Implications for Worship

The Eastern Orthodox churches have preserved and built up a rich liturgical tradition over the centuries. Given the Orthodox emphasis on continuity in worship practices, those guiding worship services do not have the same function as worship planners in many Western denominations, since the texts and hymns for all the days are already stipulated by the tradition itself. Thus, clergy and choir directors or cantors concentrate their energies primarily on properly executing the received tradition in an edifying manner according to the cultural and musical norms of their local Orthodox community. Whereas conformity of prayer and hymnographic texts across the Orthodox churches might strike some as static, Orthodox faithful tend to see their tradition as dynamic. This is because it represents a joining of one's voice in the present age to the history of God's saving economy by praying along with the saints, who too prayed these very services in generations past, in the timeless liturgy of the church before the ageless God.

At the same time, the Orthodox liturgical tradition has undergone significant development through the centuries. Reverence toward liturgical tradition sometimes obstructs a popular appreciation for just how much historical development has occurred in the Orthodox churches. Conserving prayers and practices from the early centuries of Christianity, the Byzantine Rite also incorporates developments from subsequent centuries, such as the flowering of hymnography or the use of the opaque iconostasis. There are many other examples as well. The gradual dissolution of the female diaconate in the Middle Ages is one feature that has generated recent discussion in some contemporary Orthodox circles.[28] Another topic of critical evaluation has been how the late medieval standardization of monastic rules has impacted

---

28. Petros Vassiliadis, Niki Papageorgiou, and Eleni Kasselouri-Hatzivassiliadi, eds., *Deaconesses, the Ordination of Women and Orthodox Theology* (Newcastle upon Tyne, UK: Cambridge Scholars, 2017).

the fasting practices expected of laity.[29] These and other conversations are indicative of contemporary attempts to balance faithfulness to the received tradition with mindfulness of the church's historical diversity and attentiveness to perceived needs in the present day.

## For Further Reading

Galadza, Daniel. *Liturgy and Byzantinization in Jerusalem*. Oxford: Oxford University Press, 2018.

Krueger, Derek. *Liturgical Subjects: Christian Ritual, Biblical Narrative, and the Formation of the Self in Byzantium*. Philadelphia: University of Pennsylvania Press, 2014.

Marinis, Vasileios. *Architecture and Ritual in the Churches of Constantinople: Ninth to Fifteenth Centuries*. Cambridge: Cambridge University Press, 2014.

Meyendorff, Paul. *Russia, Ritual, and Reform: The Liturgical Reforms of Nikon in the 17th Century*. Crestwood, NY: St. Vladimir's Seminary Press, 1991.

Roberson, Ronald G. *The Eastern Christian Churches: A Brief Survey*. Rome: Pontifical Oriental Institute, 2005.

Taft, Robert F. *The Byzantine Rite: A Short History, American Essays in Liturgy*. Collegeville, MN: Liturgical Press, 1992.

29. Nina Glibetić, "Reflections on the Crete Document Regarding Orthodox Fasting Practices," in *Voices of Orthodox Women on the Holy and Great Council*, ed. Carrie Frost and Nathan Symeonides (New York: Greek Orthodox Archdiocese of America, 2018), 16–22.

## — 7 —

# Icons and Eucharistic Theology

### *Nicholas Denysenko*

The Eastern Orthodox Church has produced a rich heritage of eucharistic theology and iconography. The sources for eucharistic theology are diverse, including late antique and medieval liturgical commentaries, modern theologians, and the liturgical texts and contexts. These sources represent diverse regional liturgical traditions such as Antioch, Palestine, Constantinople, Mount Athos, and Thessalonika, among others. Theological literature defending and explaining the veneration of icons dates from the eighth century, and the icons themselves are primary sources of theology.

This chapter presents a survey of the primary features of Orthodox eucharistic theology and iconography. The presentation acknowledges the breadth of figures who contributed to these two theological traditions but limits the feature to a selection of sources. The treatment of eucharistic theology analyzes three distinct traditions: Byzantine liturgical commentaries, the texts and ritual context of the Divine Liturgy, and modern Orthodox theologians. This portion of the chapter introduces the theology of Germanus of Constantinople, Nicholas Cabasilas, Nicholas Afanasiev, Alexander Schmemann, and a selection of liturgical texts. The presentation on the theology of icons begins with a review of the iconoclastic controversy, analyzes the significance of the new interior decoration of the Middle Byzantine church, and explains the meaning of icons by engaging thinkers such as John of Damascus and Leonid Ouspensky. Readers will discover that these two dimensions of Orthodox theology share a crucial intersection: participating in the Divine Liturgy and venerating icons create an encounter with the living God that brings God's reign into the present and has the capacity to transform the faithful into God's witnesses.

## Byzantine Liturgical Mystagogy

A handful of authoritative commentaries on the Divine Liturgy represent the Orthodox tradition of eucharistic theology. The classical Byzantine liturgical mystagogies are attributed to Maximus Confessor (seventh century), Patriarch Germanus of Constantinople (eighth century), Nicholas and Theodore of Andida (eleventh century), Nicholas Cabasilas (fourteenth century), and Symeon of Thessalonika (fifteenth century). This section presents an analysis of the eucharistic theology of Germanus of Constantinople and Nicholas Cabasilas.

### Germanus of Constantinople (ca. 632–ca. 740)

Germanus wrote his liturgical mystagogy between 715 and 730 CE. The mystagogy was influential, as it was printed in Greek and some of the first Slavonic editions of the Divine Liturgy, lending it quasi-official status as an explanation of the Divine Liturgy. Germanus adopts a more traditional approach to mystagogy by relating the components of the Divine Liturgy to historical events in the life of Christ. His description of the liturgy explains each component as communicating the passion, death, and resurrection of Christ. Germanus illustrates this point directly, as the priests' movement in "unbelted phelonia" points to Christ's going to the "crucifixion carrying His cross."[1]

Germanus interprets the Great Entrance as a cosmic gathering of "seraphim, saints, and righteous" who lead Christ the King on a procession to the mystical sacrifice. The Great Entrance is an elaborate rite, a procession with the ministers carrying the gifts of bread and wine to the holy table for the offering. Germanus sees the paschal mystery in this ritual act and interprets it as a representation of Christ's crucifixion on the cross and burial in the tomb.[2] Germanus's presentation of the Divine Liturgy in these sections is thoroughly christological, encompassing the economy of salvation from incarnation to burial, the liturgy being an act performed by one united church of earth and heaven. In summary, Germanus presents the liturgy itself as an icon that expresses the church's christological profession while uniting the church with angelic worship of God in heaven through the Holy Spirit.

---

1. St. Germanus of Constantinople, *On the Divine Liturgy*, trans. Paul Meyendorff (Crestwood, NY: St. Vladimir's Seminary Press, 1984), 67.
2. Germanus, *On the Divine Liturgy*, 89.

### Nicholas Cabasilas (ca. 1322–ca. 1392)

Cabasilas expounded his eucharistic theology in the fourteenth century, late in the Byzantine period. He presents his eucharistic theology in two collections of writings. The commentary on the Divine Liturgy is a classical mystagogy devoted to the Eucharist. *The Life in Christ* is a treatise on the rites of initiation, an explanation of these liturgies as participation in the divine life of God.

Cabasilas's explanation of the meaning of the Eucharist in *The Life in Christ* is also significant because of the powerful themes of sacramental theosis. Cabasilas had already presented baptism and the anointing with chrism as mysteries that bring the participant into an intimate union with Christ. For example, he describes the rite of anointing with chrism as "imparting the energies of the Holy Spirit" and the chrism itself as bringing in "the Lord Jesus himself," through whom the participant has access to the Father.[3]

Cabasilas's exposition of the transformation that occurs through Holy Communion is also an instance of sacramental theosis, a strong statement on how participation in the liturgy contributes to the process of becoming like God. Cabasilas asserts that Christ leads participants to the holy table and that they are "transformed into his own state" through Communion. He uses evocatory language of intimate union to describe this transformation, marveling at the commingling of our minds, wills, bodies, and blood with Christ's.

In summary, the mystagogues define the liturgy as a commemoration of Christ's paschal mystery. The approach employed by Germanus is not merely a reference to a past event, as he invites the participant to partake of the paschal mystery by depicting the liturgical rituals as symbols of Christ's passion. Germanus's emphasis on the paschal mystery illustrates the prominent Christology of Orthodox eucharistic theology. Cabasilas describes liturgical participation as leading to an intimate union with Christ, a type of sacramental theosis. What is consistently present is a teaching that one encounters the living God through participating in the Eucharist.

## Christology and Pneumatology in the Liturgical Texts and Rituals

The Orthodox texts and rituals express traditional Chalcedonian Christology and pneumatology. These features stand out in fixed components: the Monogenes hymn, the Trisagion hymn, the Anaphora, and the rites of preparing the bread and the cup for Holy Communion.

3. Nicholas Cabasilas, *The Life in Christ*, trans. Carmino J. deCatanzaro (Crestwood, NY: St. Vladimir's Seminary Press, 1974), 106–7.

### The Monogenes Hymn

The emperor Justinian added the Monogenes hymn to the liturgy in the sixth century in response to the controversies surrounding the human and divine wills of Christ.[4] The text of the Monogenes hymn is a fixture in the current Orthodox liturgy—it is sung at every Divine Liturgy as the Troparion on the second antiphon.

> Only-begotten Son and Logos of God, being immortal, You condescended for our salvation to take flesh from the holy Theotokos and ever-virgin Mary and, without change, became man. Christ, our God, You were crucified and conquered death by death. Being one with the Holy Trinity, glorified with the Father and the Holy Spirit: Save us.[5]

The Monogenes hymn functions as a mini-creed, sung toward the beginning of the Divine Liturgy to proclaim and preserve the Chalcedonian teaching that Jesus Christ is perfect God, evident in Christ's identity as the immortal Word of God from the Gospel of John. The hymn proclaims Christ as perfectly human, taking flesh from a virgin (the ever-virginity of Mary is necessary to claim that Christ's nature did not change). The hymn also professes Christ as united with the Holy Trinity. The author of the Monogenes drew from the Nicene-Constantinopolitan Creed to compose this short hymn. Singing the Monogenes at every Divine Liturgy enhances the Chalcedonian christological feature of Orthodox liturgy. Participants essentially sing the Creed twice—first in abbreviated form with the Monogenes, and then later in its full form.

### The Trisagion Hymn

The Trisagion hymn is another fixture of the Orthodox liturgy, occurring immediately prior to the responsorial psalmody, readings, and homily. The text of the hymn follows, with variants in brackets:

> Holy God, Holy Mighty, Holy Immortal, have mercy on us. (three times)
> Glory to the Father and to the Son and to the holy Spirit, now and ever and unto ages of ages. Amen.

4. Juan Mateos, *La Célébration de la parole dans la liturgie byzantine: Étude historique*, Orientalia Christiana Periodica 181 (Rome: Pontifical Oriental Institute, 1971), 49–53.

5. "The Divine Liturgy of St. John Chrysostom," Greek Orthodox Archdiocese of America, https://www.goarch.org/-/the-divine-liturgy-of-saint-john-chrysostom.

Holy immortal, have mercy on us.

[Dynamis!]

Holy God, Holy Mighty, Holy Immortal, have mercy on us.

Some of the non-Chalcedonian churches of the East, like the Coptic Church, have additional phrases attached to each "holy." These include "born from the virgin," "crucified for us," and "rose from the dead." These variants, which originated in fifth-century Antioch, enhance the christological dimension of the Trisagion.[6] The Byzantine church excluded such variants and emphasized the trinitarian meaning of the Trisagion hymn.

The Trisagion hymn inaugurates the proclamation of the word of God during the Orthodox liturgy. Historically, the Trisagion hymn expresses both Christology and trinitarian theology. The non-Chalcedonian variant identifies Christ as the addressee of the Trisagion, and the alternatives are explicitly paschal. The first part of the Divine Liturgy, with the Monogenes and Trisa-gion hymns, is saturated with explicit and implicit expressions of Orthodox Christology.

## Eucharistic Theology of the Anaphoras of John Chrysostom and Basil of Caesarea

The Orthodox Church celebrates four liturgies, of John Chrysostom (CHR), Basil the Great (BAS), the Presanctified Gifts (PRES), and James of Jerusalem (JAS). The church uses CHR for most of the liturgical year. BAS is appointed to the Sundays of Lent and a number of solemn feast days. The church prays PRES on appointed weekdays of Lent and Holy Week—it is essentially Vespers with a rite of Holy Communion. JAS is rarely used in practice.

These liturgies are attributed to their respective authors for numerous reasons. John Chrysostom himself introduced the liturgy with which he was familiar in Antioch to Constantinople, which was likely the anaphora of the twelve apostles.[7] The entire liturgy came to carry Chrysostom's name.

Robert Taft has argued persuasively that John Chrysostom edited the anaphora of the twelve apostles used in Antioch.[8] The anaphora of CHR is a precious source of Christology.[9] CHR is quite brief, referring to God's love

---

6. Mateos, *La Célébration*, 101–2.

7. For an English translation of this text, see R. C. D. Jasper and G. J. Cuming, eds., *Prayers of the Eucharist: Early and Reformed* (Collegeville, MN: Liturgical Press, 1990), 124–28.

8. Robert Taft, "The Authenticity of the Chrysostom Anaphora Revisited: Determining the Authorship of Liturgical Texts by Computer," *Orientalia Christiana Periodica* 56, no. 1 (1990): 5–51.

9. English translation in Jasper and Cuming, *Prayers of the Eucharist*, 129–34.

for the world and sending of the Son to grant it life. CHR bears the personal touch of John Chrysostom in the use of apophatic language to describe God in the preface (ineffable, invisible) and in multiple references to the Trinity. The anamnesis thanks God for Christ's life-giving death and resurrection, making specific mention of the cross, tomb, resurrection on the third day, ascension into heaven, and second coming. Despite CHR's brevity, it expresses a poignant Christology and trinitarian theology.

The Byzantine version of BAS is considerably longer than CHR and expresses an elaborate Christology.[10] In the post-Sanctus, BAS summarizes the fall of humanity in the Old Testament and turns to a classical soteriological scheme with the transitory phrase "but when the fullness of time had come." This section expresses Chalcedonian Christology, emphasizing Christ's divinity as the creator of the universe who knew no beginning and yet condescended to save humankind. BAS uses Pauline phrases to accentuate Christ's condescension, stating that Christ did not regard it as "robbery" to be equal to the Father but nevertheless "emptied himself" to take on the body of humanity's "lowliness." BAS states that Christ obtained the Christian community as a chosen people, royal priesthood, and holy nation through baptism and anointing with chrism, and then turns to Christ's voluntary passion and death on the cross—offered as a ransom that liberated humankind from captivity to sin.

The post-Sanctus of BAS is unusually long, most likely the work of multiple editors. This section of the Anaphora is essentially a synthesis of patristic soteriology of late antiquity. The references to Christ's activity in liberating the liturgical community from sin through baptism and anointing is particularly noteworthy—it is a brilliant literary device that enfolds the community hearing the prayer into the larger narrative of divine activity on behalf of humankind.

The liturgies also express the pneumatology of the Orthodox Church in the epicletic fruits of Communion, when the church prays that all who partake of the bread and cup would be united into the fellowship of the Holy Spirit. Furthermore, the epiclesis occurring at this point in the liturgy is not the only petition for the descent of the Holy Spirit. Holy Communion begins with the ritual acts of fraction and commixture and with the addition of hot water to the cup. During the commixture, the presider places the Lamb (consecrated bread) into the cup and says, "The fullness of the Holy Spirit."[11] The deacon pours the blessed hot water into the cup, saying, "The fervor of the Holy Spirit."

10. See Jasper and Cuming, *Prayers of the Eucharist*, 114–23.
11. See "Divine Liturgy of St. John Chrysostom," https://www.goarch.org/-/the-divine -liturgy-of-saint-john-chrysostom.

Taft observes that the pouring of hot water into a cup of wine already mixed with water had domestic origins.[12] Adding hot water to wine was a common practice in ancient dining culture, and it was natural to add hot water to the common Communion cup used for liturgical practice. Taft suggests that the practical purpose of cutting wine with water might have been theologized, since communicants do not partake of a dead cadaver but of the living Christ, who is manifest in the warm and sanctified contents of the cup.[13] Boris Bobrinskoy asserts that the Holy Spirit is constantly at work in all the liturgical rituals, including the Eucharist, by conforming participants to Christ.[14] The Spirit is active and present at multiple times of the liturgy, and the addition of the warm water to the cup is simply another instance of epiclesis.

The Orthodox liturgy, then, invites liturgical participants to receive the salvation offered by Christ to humankind in the Anaphora. The Anaphora functions like a liturgical creed by synthesizing Chalcedonian Christology and trinitarian theology and invoking the descent of the Holy Spirit on the assembly for its sanctification on multiple occasions.

## Modern Orthodox Theologians: Afanasiev and Schmemann

In the twentieth century, the Orthodox Church joined many other Christian churches in experiencing a eucharistic revival. An examination of historical sources contributed to a renewal of traditions that had fallen into disuse. Modern Orthodox theologians such as Nicholas Afanasiev and Alexander Schmemann followed the principle of renewing tradition to update the church.

### Nicholas Afanasiev (1893–1966)

Afanasiev was a member of the large and diverse cohort of Russian intellectuals who escaped the Soviet regime and took refuge in the West.[15] He wrote prolifically and embraced the ecumenical ideal of returning to one church, an *una sancta*. His best-known work is a magisterial study of Christian ecclesiology, and he also wrote a shorter but equally significant work on the Eucharist.[16]

12. Robert F. Taft, *The Precommunion Rites*, vol. 5 of *A History of the Liturgy of St. John Chrysostom*, Orientalia Christiana Analecta 261 (Rome: Pontifical Oriental Institute, 2000), 442–44, 467.

13. Taft, *Precommunion Rites*, 468–69.

14. Boris Bobrinskoy, *Communion du Sainte-Esprit* (Bégrolles-en-Mauges, France: Abbaye de Bellefontaine, 1992), 161–92.

15. Michael Plekon, *Living Icons: Persons of Faith in the Eastern Church* (Notre Dame, IN: University of Notre Dame Press, 2002), 152–56.

16. Nicholas Afanasiev, *Trapeza Gospodnia* [The Lord's Supper], Lex Orandi (Kiev, Ukraine: Khram Agapita Pecherskogo, 2003), 11–14. See also Plekon, *Living Icons*, 163–67.

Three of Afanasiev's contributions are particularly noteworthy for Orthodox eucharistic theology. The first is his identification of the church as a gathering in one place, with the assembly of the apostles in Acts 2 functioning as the antecedent for each contemporary eucharistic assembly.[17] The Holy Spirit descends on each local assembly in the present just as the Spirit descended on the apostles in the past. The church is manifest, or visible, when it gathers for the Eucharist. The second contribution concerns the restoration of the orders of the church. Afanasiev transforms the meaning of concelebration from a number of clergy standing around the same table to the church itself gathered together. He identifies the bishop and the laity as the concelebrants of the liturgy. This teaching changes the relationship between the clergy and the laity and restores the meaning of the Eucharist as a dialogue and gift exchange between the whole church—the laity together with the clergy, with the bishop presiding—and God. Afanasiev's thesis on the concelebration of the laity is connected to his study of the church and identification of the laity as an order of the church. Afanasiev interprets the liturgical evidence of baptism and anointing with chrism in late antiquity as a rite ordaining people to the order of the laity.[18] This holy order is not inferior or subservient to the orders of the clergy, and it calls for apostolic witness and service in both the church and the world together with the clergy. The resumption of frequent Holy Communion to continually nourish the laity for this crucial ministry was a practical outcome of Afanasiev's macro-level ecclesiology.

### Alexander Schmemann (1921-1982)

Schmemann is the most renowned of the contemporary Orthodox theologians. His eucharistic theology is scattered throughout his publications—one cannot locate a convenient synthesis of the whole in one essay, chapter, or passage. Schmemann embraced Afanasiev's ecclesiology and provided the final major push for the implementation of the initiative of a eucharistic revival.[19] For Schmemann, this revival amounted to the return to the experience of the fathers, whose participation in the liturgy shaped their theology.[20] In practical terms, Schmemann implemented what his predecessors had outlined—the

17. Afanasiev, *Trapeza Gospodnia*, 79–83.

18. Nicholas Afanasiev, *The Church of the Holy Spirit*, trans. Vitaly Permiakov, ed. Michael Plekon (Notre Dame, IN: University of Notre Dame Press, 2007), 23–31.

19. Alexander Schmemann, *The Eucharist: Sacrament of the Kingdom*, trans. Paul Kachur (Crestwood, NY: St. Vladimir's Seminary Press, 1987), 16–19.

20. Alexander Schmemann, "Liturgical Theology, Theology of Liturgy, and Liturgical Reform: A Debate," in *Liturgy and Tradition: Theological Reflections of Alexander Schmemann*, ed. Thomas Fisch (Crestwood, NY: St. Vladimir's Seminary Press, 1990), 42–43.

resumption of frequent Communion, so that each Divine Liturgy would include Communion as its fulfillment.

Schmemann's primary objective was theological. The point of the liturgy is the assembly's ascent to heaven to partake of the life of God.[21] Having partaken of God, the assembly returns to the world to witness to this experience of joy, to be citizens of God's reign in the world, and to make the eschatological future manifest in the present.[22]

Schmemann emphasized a second aspect of the eucharistic revival that remains a work-in-progress for the Orthodox churches. Schmemann was often harshly critical of the Western scholastic medieval system, which he claimed limited liturgy to a mere subfield in the larger universe of dogmatic theology.[23] He abhorred the notion of a transactional sacrament, where an appointed minister performs a holy task that produces grace for a recipient. Renewing the practice of frequent Communion would be the most practical and theologically significant way of correcting the liturgical deficiency of interpreting sacraments as acts that grant individuals access to divine grace. Transforming the participating community into a living cloud of witnesses capable of pursuing God's mission in the world is the point of the Eucharist.

Schmemann's efforts produced numerous notable outcomes. His emphasis on the communal nature of the Eucharist and the manifestation of God's reign in the world through Communion took an important first step when church leaders responded positively to the call to restore frequent Communion. The contemporary Orthodox enterprise of eucharistic theology remains incomplete for numerous reasons, however. The primary task for the current generation of theologians is to clean the church of the culture of sacrament as transaction, and to develop new threads of eucharistic theology that envision a tangible transformation of the cosmos through the church, including the healing of broken social orders.

## The Theology of Icons

The icon is a two-dimensional image depicting Jesus Christ, Mary, a saint, or a holy event. Icons adorn personal, private, communal, and public spaces. Icons appear in all sizes—they are painted on wood and canvas, printed on enamel, and reproduced in small cards that are easily distributed to masses of people.

21. Schmemann, "Liturgical Theology," 143.
22. Alexander Schmemann, *Church, World, Mission: Reflections on Orthodoxy in the West* (Crestwood, NY: St. Vladimir's Seminary Press, 1979), 31.
23. For example, see Alexander Schmemann, *Of Water and the Spirit: A Study of Baptism* (Crestwood, NY: St. Vladimir's Seminary Press, 1974), 54–55.

Traditionally, Eastern Christian churches adorn the interior spaces of their temples with icons. The iconostasis is the most recognizable feature of Orthodox interior configuration and decoration. Even a humble church with limited financial means has some variant of a wall of icons one encounters upon entry, with the holy table and sanctuary through the doors in the middle of the wall.

There is no universal order for interior decoration, but there are patterns that apply to most church buildings.[24] The interior dome or ceiling occupies the most prominent place, oriented spatially to invite the assembly to look up to heaven with God looking down. An image of Jesus Christ is usually placed in the dome. The apse in the sanctuary is the second primary position, often occupied by Mary Theotokos, Jesus's mother, sometimes alone with arms uplifted in the orans (praying) gesture, and sometimes holding Christ. In some edifices, the apse depicts the mystical supper, the twelve disciples receiving Communion in the form of bread and cup from Christ, six disciples on each side of Christ, who stands at the center. The icons on the iconostasis have two fixtures—Mary Theotokos to the left of the door and Christ to the right. The patron saint of a church also typically appears on the wall, accompanied by archangels or other saintly figures. The pattern of positioning icons of Mary (left) and Jesus (right) accompanied by other beloved saints also applies to personal space.

### The Iconoclastic Controversy

Orthodox tradition claims that the evangelist Luke painted the first icon, of Mary Theotokos. Icons appeared as early as the second century. The debate on the legitimacy of venerating icons began to rage toward the end of the seventh century and was not resolved until the mid-ninth century, in 843. History implicates iconoclast emperors such as Leo III and Constantine V as notorious opponents of icon veneration who implemented policies that removed icons from public spaces and churches.[25] Supporters of icon veneration (iconodules) responded to episodes of imperial iconoclasm by convoking councils, including the gathering in Nicaea in 787, the seventh ecumenical council.

Leslie Brubaker suggests that the origins of the iconoclastic controversy were complex and therefore irreducible to a debate on violating God's commandment.[26] Brubaker analyzes the emergence of iconoclasm within the larger

24. Hans-Joachim Schulz, *The Byzantine Liturgy: Symbolic Structure and Faith Expression*, trans. Matthew O'Connell (New York: Pueblo, 1986), 50–59.

25. Leslie Brubaker, *Inventing Byzantine Iconoclasm* (London: Bristol Classical, 2012), 24–29.

26. Brubaker, *Inventing Byzantine Iconoclasm*, 5–7.

political context of the Eastern Roman Empire of the late seventh and eighth centuries. The shrinkage of the imperial realm and the realization that the rising Islamic power was going to remain in place for the foreseeable future contributed to a period of reflective questioning.[27] The Quinisext Council (Trullo) of 691–692 declared increasing control over religious practices, including the proper form for depicting Christ and distinctions between good and bad icons.[28] Brubaker suggests that students need to examine the context of the battle over icons carefully, since some of the church historians accusing Leo III for iconoclastic acts were writing as long as eighty years after the episode, or represent the attempt of high-ranking church officials to maintain control over pious practices influencing the church from the bottom up.[29] In this case, theological priority was again at stake, with church officials arguing that honoring the Trinity was more important than venerating relics and icons with piety.

The debates on icons and the ultimate victory of the iconodules resulted in a theology of the icon as incarnation and a radical change in art and architecture. Hans-Joachim Schulz describes the transformation of the interior of the church in the Middle Byzantine era, beginning in the ninth century following the triumph of the icon in 843.[30] Schulz details the adornment of the interior with icons of Christ, Mary, the saints, and the theophanies recorded by Christian history. Liturgical ritual, song, movement, and image combined to place the participants in the midst of the announcement of salvation, presented in detail in word, sound, and image. The interior iconography of the Middle Byzantine church enhanced the experience of salvation through an intense engagement of all the senses, especially the eyes.

### Theological Treatises on the Icon

The debate on icons engendered an explosion of iconography and a number of treatises explaining the legitimacy of venerating icons. John of Damascus, Theodore the Studite, and Germanus are three of the many theologians defending the veneration of icons. John of Damascus distinguished between worship and veneration, asserting that worship is offered to Christ, who is truly God, whereas participants venerate Mary and the saints on icons.[31] These

27. Brubaker, *Inventing Byzantine Iconoclasm*, 16–19.
28. Brubaker, *Inventing Byzantine Iconoclasm*, 17.
29. Brubaker, *Inventing Byzantine Iconoclasm*, 27–29.
30. Schulz, *Byzantine Liturgy*, 50–59.
31. John of Damascus, *On the Divine Images: Three Apologies Against Those Who Attack the Divine Images*, trans. David Anderson (Crestwood, NY: St. Vladimir's Seminary Press, 1997), 21–22.

figures can be depicted on icons because they appeared in the flesh and were seen by human eyes. He adds that no one worships the matter of paint and wood, but instead offers worship to the "Creator of matter," noting that the matter has been glorified.[32]

John of Damascus's teaching that icon veneration involves gestures and petitions of worship to a living person yields a significant feature of the meaning of icons. Icon veneration is both personal and dialogical, an act of real communication between the participant and the holy figure. The notion of the icon as a symbol of personal communication contributed to the popular description of icons as "windows into heaven," with the holy figure hearing the petition of the participant. During the dialogue of icon veneration, the holy figure is present in person but not in nature.

### Wonder-working Icons as Holy Relics

Icon veneration communicates the notion of the real presence of saints in the present. The presence of the holy ones is occasionally reported in extraordinary theophanic appearances. Orthodox history includes multiple instances of wonder-working icons, with miracles performed by the holy figure. Mary Theotokos defending a city from attack and reports of healings of diseases are common examples of such theophanies.[33] Frequently, a tangible sign accompanies the wonder-working icon, especially when fragrant myrrh streams from icons. Wonder-working icons produced episodes of profound local piety and veneration, with the icon carried in procession, and the anniversary of the manifestation of the saint recorded on the local calendar and commemorated by the eucharistic liturgy. In this sense, the calendrical commemoration of a wonder-working icon follows the late antique pattern of the progress of the cult of the saints.[34]

Local festal commemorations gradually become universal when the icon travels to another location for a visitation, often attracting large crowds of the faithful petitioning the saint for deliverance from afflictions and woes. These festivals tend to cluster around the cult of Mary Theotokos, whose appearances are associated with the Nikopoia and Hodegetria icons of the Byzantine period,

32. John of Damascus, *On the Divine Images*, 61–62.
33. For background reading on wonder-working icons, see Bissera Pentcheva, *Icons and Power: The Mother of God in Byzantium* (University Park: Pennsylvania State University Press, 2006); Vera Shevzov, "Icons, Miracles, and the Ecclesial Identity of Laity in Late Imperial Russian Orthodoxy," *Church History* 69, no. 3 (2000): 610–31; Jim Forest, "Icons and Miracles: An Intensity of Faith," *Christianity and Crisis* 45, no. 9 (1985): 201–5.
34. Peter Brown, *The Cult of the Saints: Its Rise and Function in Latin Christianity* (Chicago: University of Chicago Press, 1981), 9–12.

along with the Vladimir, Pochaiv, and Iveron icons. These feasts elevate the significance of the icon so that its story becomes a narrative ritualized within the Eucharist, an instance of divine favor compatible with salvation history. Scholars such as Bissera Pentcheva also note that wonder-working icons of Mary projected an image of maternal power in the Byzantine imperial context.

The personal and private veneration of icons accompanies their role in the church's public liturgy. While the windows-into-heaven motif continues to dominate the popular interpretation of icons, the icon also functions as a mirror, showing humanity what it is to become by receiving Christ's invitation to come and follow him.[35] Leonid Ouspensky states that the icon reveals the glorified and recreated human nature one can attain through the Christian life.[36] For example, the participants see the face of Christ in the icon—this means that they are seeing Christ in themselves, the recreated divine image given to humankind through Christ's incarnation. In practical terms, the icon as a mirror is an exhortation to faithful participants to receive the grace of Christ and become like him.

The veneration of icons became popular in the Eastern Christian world following a fierce struggle for control over the details of communal and personal ritual practice. The bottom-up piety of icon veneration won the day and resulted in the redecoration of Byzantine church interiors and the hegemony of incarnational theology through symbolic mediation. Icons feature the presence of the saints, and they are therefore siblings of the late antique cult of holy relics. Byzantine icon veneration stresses the petitions of the faithful and the positive response of the holy figure, sometimes in extraordinary theophanies and miracles. God's invitation for the transformation of the faithful to become like Christ by beholding him in the icon as a mirror remains an essential feature of this phenomenon.

## Participation in the Life of God

This presentation of Orthodox eucharistic theology and icon veneration appears to present two mutually exclusive ritual practices. Icon veneration certainly influenced worship, and it is compatible with the assurance of real presence in the consecrated bread and cup. It is also a visual depiction of the proclamation of salvation history announced from the Scriptures and hymnography of Orthodox liturgical tradition.

35. Leonid Ouspensky, *Theology of the Icon*, trans. Anthony Gythiel (Crestwood, NY: St. Vladimir's Seminary Press, 1992), 1:156–60.
36. Ouspensky, *Theology of the Icon*, 1:164–65.

I conclude with one thread that connects this presentation of eucharistic theology and icon veneration in the Orthodox Church. The section on eucharistic theology mentions Cabasilas's interpretation of the liturgy as an experience of intimate union with God. Schmemann uses the language of ascent to interpret the liturgy as a veritable experience of communion with God followed by return to the world for mission. Icons are likewise similar—a real dialogical and personal union between faithful and holy one takes place, with the absence of bodily nature.

These three examples illuminate a bridging of the gap between earth and heaven, present and future. Participating in the Eucharist and venerating icons bring the community of faithful into the future outside the laws of time to receive divine grace. For the Orthodox Church, then, the Eucharist itself is a living icon of the promised life to come, the participation of a living community of the present with the communion of saints outside time in the life of God.

## Practical Implications for Worship

The theology of the icon and Eucharist described in this chapter draws from classical treatises, influential theologians, and the liturgical texts. It might be more accurate to depict these theological explanations as the "official" theology of the church, especially given the long life and broad influence of the thinkers in question. One should embrace these theologies with the understanding that the people who participate in liturgy do not have the luxury or convenience of settling down with liturgical texts to consider their application for everyday life. The texts, icons, and ritual gestures embrace all participants in the narrative of Christ's salvation of humankind and invite them to partake of the life of God. It is likely, however, that there is a gap between the participant's experience of liturgy and its official explication. Most participants never hear the actual text of the Anaphora and do not have access to fundamental instruction on what Orthodox liturgy is and does.

Many realities contribute to this gap between official liturgical theology and the people's experience, including impoverished liturgical celebration and the people's inability to become fluent in the language and grammar of liturgy. In general, the people get snapshots of the good news the liturgy proclaims and invites the participant to receive. If the Anaphora is said silently, they join the singing of the Trisagion. If the cantor hurries through the Creed, they may have sung the Monogenes hymn. The popular piety accompanying the veneration of icons contributed to filling this gap. For everything the people may have misunderstood or were simply never able to access in the liturgy, their veneration of icons proclaimed the fundamental story of Christ's salvation and invited them to enter into a dialogue with God and the communion of saints. The people's pious devotional practices have always compensated for distant liturgical offices that spoke primarily to the elite, and they will continue to do so. The continued existence of a gap between the people's experience of liturgy and the fullness of the good news it communicates beckons theologians and pastors to commit to bridging that gap, an enterprise that will require them to commence a dialogue with the people themselves.

## For Further Reading

Calivas, Alkiviadis. *The Liturgy in Dialogue: Exploring and Renewing the Tradition.* Essays in Theology and Liturgy 5. Brookline, MA: Holy Cross Orthodox Press, 2018.

Denysenko, Nicholas. *Theology and Form: Contemporary Orthodox Architecture in America.* Notre Dame, IN: University of Notre Dame Press, 2017.

Ouspensky, Leonid. *Theology of the Icon.* 2 vols. Translated by Anthony Gythiel. Crestwood, NY: St. Vladimir's Seminary Press, 1992.

Rentel, Alexander. "Byzantine and Slavic Orthodoxy." In *Oxford History of Christian Worship*, edited by Geoffrey Wainwright and Karen Westerfield Tucker, 254–306. Oxford: Oxford University Press, 2006.

Schmemann, Alexander. *Liturgy and Tradition: Theological Reflections of Alexander Schmemann.* Edited by Thomas Fisch. Crestwood, NY: St. Vladimir's Seminary Press, 1990.

Taft, Robert F. *The Byzantine Rite: A Short History.* American Essays in Liturgy. Collegeville, MN: Liturgical Press, 1992.

# PART 4

# Roman Catholic Worship

## — 8 —

# Medieval Catholic Worship

## *Joanne M. Pierce*

To understand the importance of Western medieval worship, one must grasp the complexity of the medieval period itself; it was not a monolithic block of unvarying customs and social structure. There were ongoing changes and geographical variations in culture, language, politics, economics, art, theology, and spirituality. It lasted over a thousand years and involved European countries stretching from Greenland to the medieval Kingdom of Hungary, and from Norway to northern Africa and the Middle East. In this chapter,[1] the medieval period is divided into three parts: early Middle Ages (eighth to tenth century), high Middle Ages (eleventh to thirteenth century), and late Middle Ages (fourteenth to early sixteenth century). However, these boundaries are not clear-cut; rather, they are fuzzy edges, each blending into the next.

### Early Middle Ages (Eighth to Tenth Century)

By the beginning of the eighth century, the shape of Christianity in western Europe had changed dramatically from its earlier contours. Earlier Christian

---

1. Many historians would mark the beginning of the Middle Ages with the fall of the last Roman emperor in the West (476), while others might begin as early as the legalization of Christianity (313) or as late as the pontificate of Gregory the Great (d. 604).

churches in England and Ireland had adopted Roman liturgical practice. Missionaries were sent from these islands back into continental Europe, working to convert others of the Germanic tribes who had remained beyond the orbit of imperial Rome. To the north and east, for example, the Low Countries, Scandinavia, and parts of eastern Germany and Poland, tribes kept to their old gods. The Franks, largely Catholic[2] Christians since the conversion of their king, Clovis (between 496 and 508), had become united as a single kingdom under his Merovingian dynasty.

To the south, Muslim armies from Arabia had conquered Christian North Africa in the seventh century. The same would happen in Europe when, in 711, Muslim armies crossed the Straits of Gibraltar, establishing an Islamic caliphate on the Iberian Peninsula. They continued to advance north of the Pyrenees, stopped only by the Franks under Charles Martel ("the Hammer"), chief general and palace officer of the Merovingian kings, at the Battle of Tours (732).

Charles Martel's son, Pepin (Pippin) the Short, eventually succeeded him and, with the approval of Pope Zachary, deposed the last Merovingian king (Childeric III) and assumed the title King of the Franks. This Carolingian dynasty would remain in power until the end of the tenth century. Pepin's son Charlemagne (Charles "the Great") continued to strengthen ties with the popes in Rome; both pledged to assist the popes in their struggle against domination by the Lombard rulers in the north and south of Italy. The outcome of this alliance was not just Charlemagne's inheriting the title King of the Franks from his father but also his later coronation (800) by Pope Leo III as Holy Roman emperor (*Imperator Romanorum*). This would change the balance of power between the West and the East (controlled by emperors in Constantinople, where the Roman Empire had never fallen) and influence the history and culture of western Europe for centuries to come.[3]

Most of Europe at this time was still largely rural. There were a few larger town-cities, with their own small cathedrals and bishops in residence. There may have been smaller "parish" churches on the outskirts of towns or in villages, but in rural areas peasants and serfs worshiped in "proprietary" churches, belonging to the local lord and staffed with a priest hired by him. Monasteries, located in distant or rural areas, were important centers for local liturgical ministry, and the hours of the Divine Office were celebrated

2. Here "Catholic" is in the sense of Nicene Roman Christianity. Arian Christianity had also been adopted by some Germanic tribes in late antiquity.

3. However, the century after Charlemagne's death (814), western Europe became increasingly divided into smaller kingdoms, and the office of Holy Roman emperor would become elective rather than purely hereditary.

daily, usually for any to attend. Charlemagne supported Benedictine monasticism above other types as one way to provide liturgical and spiritual unity within his realm. Many Benedictine monasteries trained certain monks to be scribes, working daily in the monastery's "writing room" (*scriptorium*), producing copies of manuscripts ordered by bishops, courtiers, or other nobles for liturgical, spiritual, or educational use. Manuscript production expanded under the reign of Charlemagne, who ordered each bishop in his territory to maintain a "cathedral school" in his diocese.

### Theological Issues in the Liturgy

During this early medieval period, a few important theological issues shaped liturgical spirituality and devotional practices. The first is the theological understanding of what it means to state that during the celebration of the Eucharist, the bread and wine really become the body and blood of Christ. Earlier Christians had various ways of referring to the ultimate mystery of the Eucharist, but in the early medieval West, attention was beginning to focus on how to explain this mystery more clearly. An important discussion of the question took place in the mid-ninth century between two Benedictine monks living in the same monastery.[4] No official decision was made at this point, but the "physicalist" interpretation became increasingly dominant: that the real presence of Christ in the Eucharist was identical with the "historical" body and blood of Christ.[5]

The second theological issue that becomes pronounced during this period is an elaboration of the teaching about the afterlife. First, the doctrine of purgatory, a place of purification for the souls of the faithful who died with lesser sins left unabsolved, spread more widely. Mentioned by St. Augustine (d. 430) and developed more fully by Pope Gregory the Great (d. 604), Catholics believed that prayer on behalf of the deceased could help reduce their "time" spent in purgatory. This spurred an increase in the practice of priests celebrating private Masses for deceased individuals at the request of their friends and relatives. Such requests were accompanied by an offering, later a monetary stipend, to the priest.

Related is the development of belief in limbo, a state of the afterlife in which the deceased is not subject to the eternal punishment of hell but cannot

4. Paschasius Radbertus and Ratramnus, of the Abbey of Corbie, north of Paris.

5. As opposed to a spiritual reality present in the consecrated physical elements, a spiritual reality that is more truly real than any material reality, following Plato. See Nathan Mitchell, *Cult and Controversy: The Worship of the Eucharist Outside Mass* (Collegeville, MN: Liturgical Press, 1990), 73–86. Already miracle stories about the consecrated bread and wine were spreading in monastic circles (see below).

be admitted to the bliss of heaven and the presence of God. Since baptism was considered mandatory for salvation,[6] those who died without baptism were understood to spend eternity in a state of "natural happiness," but still deprived of the presence of God. Liturgically, concern focused on unbaptized infants. The result was the expectation that an infant born to Catholic parents should be baptized soon after birth.[7]

The third theological focus involved a jurisdictional shift involving the veneration of saints. As in antiquity, men and women of exceptional holiness came to be venerated after their deaths by local and regional Catholic communities. Pilgrimages might be made to their graves, or their bodies moved to chapels or churches that would be treated as shrines to those saints. Increasingly, parts of a saint's remains might be sent to different churches or monasteries, with the goal of promoting and expanding their *cultus* (accepted liturgical veneration). At the end of the tenth century, however, the approval of saints was taken out of the hands of the local bishop and transferred to the more centralized authority of the popes.[8] Eventually, this became a formalized procedure supervised by officials in the Curia.[9] The increasing number of saints were now proclaimed formally by Rome, and although the feast days of some were still celebrated only locally or regionally, others were given a more prominent place in the liturgical calendar and were celebrated more universally in western Europe.

### Liturgy: The Mass

The early medieval period was a crucial period for the development of liturgical books, including those containing the various prayers, readings, music, and rubrics required for the celebration of the Eucharist or, as it came to be called in the Latin West, the Mass.[10]

The Roman Mass usually included two readings, the second of which was always taken from one of the Gospels. However, the selected readings

6. With some exceptions—e.g., catechumens preparing for baptism but who died or were killed before receiving it were understood to have been saved by "baptism of desire."

7. Following the teaching of earlier theologians (Tertullian, *On Baptism* 17, and Pope Leo the Great, *Letter* 16, 6), if an infant was sickly or struggling after birth, anyone could administer a simple "emergency" baptism with water and the trinitarian formula ("I baptize you in the name of the Father and of the Son and of the Holy Spirit. Amen.").

8. The first saint to be officially canonized by a pope was St. Ulrich of Augsburg in 993.

9. The Curia was the bureaucratic structure of offices making up the administrative structure of the Roman Catholic Church, headed by the pope. It was the job of these officials to evaluate the worthiness of the candidate for sainthood as well as the claims of miracles taking place as a result of individuals praying to the candidate to intercede on their behalf.

10. Derived from the dismissal formula: *Ite, missa est.*

appointed for the Mass, arranged according to the liturgical calendar, came to be collected in books of their own called lectionaries. One book, the epistle lectionary or epistolary, held the "epistle" readings—that is, readings taken from books other than the four Gospels. The other contained the readings from the Gospels assigned for the Mass—the gospel lectionary or evangeliary.

A similar process took place with the various prayer texts that made up the liturgical celebration. The central prayer of the Mass was the single eucharistic prayer,[11] called the Roman Canon,[12] with three variable prayers at other points in the rite, known as collects or orations (*orationes*).[13] Each day had its own set of collects, called a Mass formulary. The formularies for individual Masses on Sundays and weekdays were written down in small booklets at first, called *libelli* (little books). These booklets were collected locally and bound together in single volumes for private use[14] or for the use of a particular church. These collections became the basis for the development of the sacramentary, the book of prayers used by the priest or bishop for the celebration of Mass.

The "stage directions" for each celebration were also originally written down in *libelli*. The structure and gestures of the Mass, or *ordo missae*,[15] would not change much for a Mass on a weekday or on an ordinary Sunday, but for different seasons (e.g., Lent), holy days, or feast days (e.g., Holy Week and Easter), the ceremonies would be more complex, involving other ritual elements not used at other times of the year. Some of the earliest are the Roman orders (*ordines Romani*)[16] for several liturgical services.[17]

A sacramentary is formed when these Mass formularies and *ordines* are edited together in a single volume. The eighth and ninth centuries were critical in the evolution of the sacramentary, for reasons that involved both theology and politics. Under the Frankish kings, sacramentary material from Rome became interpolated with regional sacramentary content, resulting in two

11. From the Greek, meaning "to give thanks."

12. The word "canon" comes from Greek and means "measure," "rule," or "list." From the ninth century on, it became the practice for the priest to recite the canon in a low voice or whisper ("silent" canon).

13. These were an opening prayer (the collect or *collectio*), an offertory prayer (the secret or *secreta*), and the prayer after Communion (*post communio*).

14. The earliest collection we have is the Verona Sacramentary (Verona, Codex Veronensis LXXXV), a seventh-century copy of formularies dating back at least a hundred years or more.

15. The same word used in English as "order" of service; the plural is *ordines*.

16. These can be found in *Les ordines Romani du haut Moyen-Âge*, ed. Michel Andrieu, 5 vols. (Leuven: Spicilegium Sacrum Louvaniense, 1930–1961). Some of these *ordines* were mixed with Gallican elements.

17. Later, these directions were referred to as *rubrics* (from *ruber/rubeus*, "red"), because scribes would write them in red ink, to distinguish them from prayer texts and other recited texts, written with black ink.

distinct sacramentary traditions. Earlier Gallican[18] texts were used for political reasons to supplement the Roman structures and strengthen the political and cultural effort to unify the kingdom. The earlier is known as the "Gelasian"[19] group, and the later, compiled under Charlemagne, is called the "Gregorian"[20] sacramentary tradition.[21]

### Liturgy: Confirmation

There were several official, public rituals practiced in Western Catholic liturgy during these centuries. Certain of these were more fundamental in the lives of all Catholics, while others were more limited in frequency and participation.[22] Perhaps the most important development at this time involved the ancient liturgy of Christian initiation.

As mentioned above, the medieval practice of baptism was affected by the developments in Christian cosmology. Initial conversions of tribal groups often involved both the chief and all other members of the group, adults and children alike; more complete catechetical instruction was reserved for later, effectively rendering the earlier formal catechumenate obsolete. Because of the high infant mortality rate, newborns were usually baptized within a few days of birth. On the other hand, the final anointing/chrismation of the process of Christian initiation (which came to be referred to as "confirmation") re- mained reserved to the bishop in the wider Roman Rite. In these early medieval centuries, this meant that while the children of nobles, usually baptized by a bishop, would be baptized and confirmed at the same time, many ordinary Catholics were only confirmed when (and if) the local bishop visited a town or village. Gradually, the meaning of this final anointing focused on the idea of "strengthening by the gift of the Holy Spirit" for older children and young adults who had already been baptized and were now facing the challenges of adult life.

18. "Gallican" refers here to earlier Mass texts in use in the area the Romans knew as Gaul—that is, parts of modern France and western Germany. Parts of Gaul had been Catholic Christian (as opposed to the Arian Christianity that some Germanic tribes had accepted) for more than two centuries.

19. So named because the text was originally attributed to Pope Gelasius.

20. So named because the Roman material was originally attributed to Pope Gregory the Great.

21. Charlemagne also adapted the style of liturgical chant then in use at Rome to further strengthen liturgical unity. With possible influences from earlier Gallican chant, this monophonic style became known as Gregorian chant (attributed to Pope Gregory the Great).

22. However, it is important to note that an authoritative list of the seven fundamental "sacraments" had not yet been made. Only in the late twelfth century would theologians define certain rites as official primary ritual acts of the church.

## High Middle Ages (Eleventh to Thirteenth Century)

The next three centuries were a period of critical change for medieval Christianity and its liturgy. Western Europe was developing from an agricultural to an urban civilization. In addition, except for a few areas such as the Baltic countries, much of Europe had adopted Roman Christianity by the end of the eleventh century. The office of Holy Roman emperor continued, but the empire itself covered a smaller section of central Europe. Catholic kingdoms had been reestablished in northern Spain, and larger, more centralized monarchies were developing in other areas, such as Scandinavia, France, and England.

Church and state remained intertwined, in increasing tension since the weak papacy of the tenth century had become revitalized and strengthened under the leadership of clerics influenced by reforms that had taken place in Benedictine communities in the tenth and eleventh centuries. Many important bishops continued to govern territories including or beyond their dioceses as "prince-bishops," leading to a clash between the reforming Pope Gregory VII (d. 1085) and Emperor Henry IV (d. 1106) on the selection and liturgical installation of abbots and bishops, known as the Investiture Controversy. The issue was settled by the Concordat of Worms (1122), leading to a partial disentanglement of church and states in these matters. The spiritual and political power of the popes continued to increase into the thirteenth century, and it was during this century that the popes more consistently referred to themselves as "Vicar of Christ" rather than "Vicar of Peter."

The end of the eleventh century also saw the beginning of another religious/political/military movement: the Crusades. The major Crusades lasted through the end of the thirteenth century, all directed at gaining, and then regaining, control of the Holy Land and nearby territories. For approximately one hundred years, the Middle East was divided into Crusader states, and after the reconquest of Jerusalem by Saladin (1187), unsuccessful attempts were made to regain it. Initially, the Crusades were seen theologically as penitential pilgrimages to the lands where Jesus Christ had lived and preached—not just to visit the shrines located there but to liberate them from the hands of Muslim "infidels."[23]

Another lasting effect of the Crusades on Catholic Christianity was the increasing devotional interest in the historical life of Jesus and other biblical figures, especially those depicted in the Gospels. This new spiritual movement had several effects. First, a lively interest in new "relics" pertaining to Christ,

---

23. Other waves of the crusading movement were directed against other groups of "infidels" within Europe, including violent attacks on local Jewish communities and more organized warfare against heretical groups like the Albigensians in France and the Hussites in Bohemia.

Mary, and others from the Holy Land, brought back by returning Crusaders, sparked a vigorous "trade" in these venerated objects. Second, a more flexible form of religious life developed, marked by apostolic poverty and ministerial mobility, and especially suited to the growing urban nature of medieval society. There were the mendicant ("begging"[24]) religious orders; the most notable groups were the Dominicans (the Order of Preachers), founded by the Spanish Dominic de Guzmán (d. 1221), and the Franciscans (the Order of Friars Minor, or "Little Brothers"), founded by the Italian Francis of Assisi (d. 1226). Unlike monks, who were pledged to a settled religious life in monasteries relatively removed from society, these new groups of friars ("brothers"[25]) traveled frequently for study, preaching, and other ministerial duties.[26]

Intertwined with these other factors was the development of another key medieval institution. The cathedral and monastic schools of the early Middle Ages led to the formation of some of the great universities of Europe. Centered originally on groups of teachers, universities grew as more students gathered in these cities to study disciplines such as theology, philosophy, and law. Earlier theologians and philosophers had utilized Platonic frameworks for their teaching and writing. Medieval theologians referred to as scholastic theologians[27] stressed the idea of *fides quaerens intellectum* (faith seeking understanding),[28] emphasizing the role of reason in exploring God's revelation and the natural world. Early scholastic theologians utilized Platonic frameworks in their teaching and writing. But a revolution occurred in scholastic theology at the turn of the thirteenth century with the reintroduction of several works by another ancient philosopher, Aristotle, into western Europe. Despite errors in translation and confusion with non-Christian commentaries,[29] Aristotle's philosophical categories were embraced by many scholastic theologians.

### Liturgical Life: Eucharist and Mass

The understanding and celebration of the Mass during the high Middle Ages changed in several ways during this period. Some changes took place during the eleventh century. At the beginning of that century, continuing a trend that had begun earlier, the *ordo missae*[30] was expanded to include

24. From the Latin *mendicare*, "to beg."
25. From the Latin *frater*, "brother."
26. Women who wished to join the Franciscans or Dominicans were required to remain cloistered within their convents.
27. From the Latin *schola*, "school."
28. Inspired by Augustine, *Sermon 43*, ¶4.
29. Many of Aristotle's works had been earlier preserved and studied by Muslim scholars.
30. The invariable structure or "order of Mass."

numerous "private" prayers for the bishop or priest celebrant to recite during certain points in the Mass ritual (so-called soft spots[31]) where actions or chanting took place without assigned "official" prayers. These prayers were often penitential in nature, asking God for pardon and purification. By midcentury, the number of these prayers had increased greatly. Along with Pope Gregory VII's reforms for clerical life came a liturgical reform, in which he moved to rid the *ordo missae* of these excessive elements. Many of these private prayers were dropped, although a few were retained.

Scholastic theology also had an impact on eucharistic devotional activity. As discussed above, the prevailing "physicalist" notion of understanding the presence of the body and blood of Christ in the consecrated elements was stressed in the collections of miracle stories concerning, most frequently, the eucharistic host.[32] If the consecrated host[33] was the physical body of Christ, and Christ was really the incarnation of the Son, the Second Person of the Trinity equal to God the Father and God the Holy Spirit, then the host could be understood as a literal "piece" of God.[34]

With the introduction of Aristotelian philosophy, scholastic theologians could discuss the presence of Christ in a different way. An object is composed of a substance, its inner reality, and accidents, external physical characteristics that might distinguish one object from another but do not affect the inner *esse* ("is-ness" or being) of the object itself. So, after the words of Christ ("This is my body . . . This is my blood") were recited during Mass, the substance (the inner reality) changed from "breadness" or "wineness" to the body and blood of Christ. However, the external accidents, the "appearance" of bread and wine, remained the same. This explanation is referred to as transubstantiation; the Council of Trent (1545–1563) would later describe this doctrine as *aptissime*[35] for understanding the eucharistic mystery.

31. See Paul Bradshaw and Maxwell E. Johnson, *The Eucharistic Liturgies: Their Evolution and Interpretation* (Collegeville, MN: Liturgical Press, 2012), 71–72; and Robert F. Taft, *Beyond East and West: Problems in Liturgical Understanding* (Rome: Pontifical Oriental Institute, 1997), 187–202.

32. One common theme was the doubting monk (or other person), unconvinced of the real presence of Christ in the eucharistic bread and wine, who experiences a vision at Mass: a piece of bleeding flesh instead of the host, and a cup of actual blood instead of the consecrated wine. For more on medieval eucharistic miracles, see Miri Rubin, *Corpus Christi: The Eucharist in Late Medieval Culture* (Cambridge: Cambridge University Press, 1991), 108–29.

33. The bread used for the celebration had by this time been prepared in smaller, thinner discs referred to as hosts, from the Latin word *hostia*, "sacrificial offering/victim."

34. This literalism sometimes formed the basis of superstitious practices or tales. A traveler might be tempted to take a host and sew it into the hem of his cloak for protection, or a farmer place a host into the dirt of a newly plowed field, to improve his harvest.

35. Meaning "most apt or appropriate."

Benediction was another ritual developed to encourage adoration of Christ present in the consecrated host[36] and to offer a blessing with the host to those gathered. The host would be placed in a transparent container, which was part of an embellished stand so that it could be seen by the faithful.[37] Called a monstrance,[38] this would become an important and elaborate liturgical vessel in the late Middle Ages and the early modern era, a mark of Roman Catholic devotion that would distinguish it from Protestant belief and practice.

The sacramentary also underwent changes during this time. Influenced especially by the liturgical needs of the Franciscans,[39] the full missal became a more widely used book by priests. In a single, portable volume, the missal contained all the texts necessary for the celebration of Mass (prayers, rubrics, and readings) as well as some of the chants. A similar process took place with the texts and chants for the Divine Office, resulting in the production of the breviary, a portable collection of prayers, readings, and some chants[40] arranged in one or more volumes according to the season.

### Liturgy: Other Rites

During this period, some rituals diminished in importance,[41] while others became more widespread. Perhaps the most critical theological development in general was the acceptance by scholastic theologians of a list of the seven primary rites of the Catholic Church: baptism, confirmation, Eucharist, penance, matrimony, orders/ordination, and extreme unction ("last anointing"). These were proposed by the theologian Peter Lombard (d. 1160) in book 4 of his text *The Sentences*[42] (ca. 1150), a theological compendium that became a standard required text for theological students in the thirteenth and fourteenth centuries and, in some areas, into the sixteenth century.

36. From antiquity, some of the consecrated bread or hosts would be reserved in the church building for the sick or the dying. The Fourth Lateran Council (1215) required that these be kept locked up somewhere safe. The use of the tabernacle, an embellished locked box, became more common for this need.

37. There were other styles of monstrance designed for holding relics.

38. From the Latin *monstrare*, "to show."

39. The Franciscans based their missal on that used by the Roman Curia. For the texts of the Franciscan Missal and Breviary, see S. J. P. Van Dijk, *Sources of the Modern Roman Liturgy*, vol. 2 (Leiden: Brill, 1963).

40. More complete books of chant for Mass or Office or both, with roots in the Carolingian period, were also widely produced at the time: the antiphonary (*antiphonale*), the gradual (*graduale*), and the troper (*troparium*).

41. For example, priestly involvement with trials by ordeal, earlier conducted in connection with liturgical blessings and the celebration of Mass, was forbidden in the early thirteenth century by the Fourth Lateran Council (1215).

42. *Libri Quattuor Senteniarum* (The Four Books of Sentences).

Several of these sacraments, as well as other rites, took a more stable ritual shape during this period. Marriage, for example, was by no means an obvious candidate for the list, since it had clearly existed long before the first century CE and was originally a domestic rite arranged in stages between families. Apart from a special blessing over the bride during the celebration of Mass (the "nuptial blessing"), church rituals for the exchange of consent, vows, and rings only appear during the eleventh century and become more elaborate over the following two hundred years. Ordination liturgy expanded to include lesser church offices (minor orders) as well as the ancient bishop, priest, and deacon.[43] Penitential practice underwent an evolution from public penance performed for serious sin, to a stress on oral confession of all sins,[44] followed by an assigned penance and then a later absolution by a priest. The penance/absolution sequence was eventually flipped, with the absolution granted after the private confession under the assumption that the penance would be performed later. Extreme unction is essentially rooted in the anointing of the sick.[45] However, over time this anointing became part of the rites for the dying, reserved only for the seriously ill.[46]

Other rites of the church were still considered to be important in preparing the recipient to receive God's grace. Rituals like the profession of religious vows, the coronation of a monarch, or the blessing of an abbot/abbess were also collected in liturgical books: the Ritual (*Rituale*), which came to contain rites for either a priest or a bishop to perform (e.g., baptism or the blessing of a women after childbirth) and the Pontifical, rites reserved for a bishop alone (e.g., ordination or the dedication of a church). The Processional would contain texts to be sung for liturgical processions, which were conducted on certain feast days and other holy days. While some rubrics, prayer texts, and chants might be common to all these liturgies, it is important to remember that there was a good deal of local variation as well.

## Late Middle Ages (Fourteenth to Early Sixteenth Century)

The late medieval period was a time of both disruption and ferment for several interrelated reasons. The fourteenth century has been called "the calamitous

43. The minor orders were porter, lector, exorcist, and acolyte; subdeacons were understood to be one of the four major orders.

44. Confession was later restricted to a priest alone. The practice of auricular confession was influenced by the Benedictine monastic practice of spiritual mentoring/direction of junior monks by senior monks.

45. Based on James 5:14–15.

46. As later descriptions would note, for those "in danger of death." Confession (if the dying person was able) and the reception of Communion (*viaticum*) were also part of these "last rites."

fourteenth century"[47] for good reason. A convergence of natural and political disasters struck Europe during this period. The climate cooled, bringing about what has been called a little ice age; summer temperatures dropped, harvests failed, and millions suffered from hunger and starvation. In addition, an outbreak of bubonic plague (later referred to as the Black Death[48]), brought by merchant ships returning from the East,[49] ravaged the Continent and Great Britain midcentury (1347–1353).[50] This century also witnessed periods of intense warfare between England and France over conflicting claims to the French crown, the Hundred Years' War (1337–1453), devastating parts of modern France and Belgium.

The clergy were subject to the same stresses as the laity. Many died; others fled in search of safety, abandoning their communities. The institutional church itself was destabilized by political forces as well. Pope Boniface VIII (d. 1303) came into conflict with the powerful French king, Philip the Fair (d. 1314), when he claimed papal supremacy over both spiritual and secular leaders. The pope was quickly captured by French forces and beaten; he died soon after. In 1309 one of Boniface's successors, Clement V (d. 1314), moved the papal Curia from Rome to Avignon, a town that, at that time, was close to the French border. For most of that century, the papacy resided there under French influence: the Avignon papacy.[51] Pope Gregory XI returned the papacy permanently to Rome in early 1377 but died soon after. The validity of Roman election that followed was later disputed, and another papal election was held in Avignon, resulting in both a pope in Rome (Urban VI) and a second in Avignon (Clement VII). This split in the papacy came to be called the Western (or Papal) Schism.

This schism had a profound impact on Catholicism. Already reeling from the suffering and chaos caused by famine, plague, and war, the rulers and peoples of western Europe now found themselves divided over which pope to accept as legitimate. Specialists in canon law from some of the major universities were unable to reach consensus on the legality of these elections, and the Council of Pisa (1409) was convoked to come to a resolution. A third pope (Alexander V) was elected, but neither the Roman nor the Avignon popes conceded their positions. The schism was finally resolved when, at

47. Barbara Tuchman, *A Distant Mirror: The Calamitous 14th Century* (New York: Random House/Ballantine, 1987).

48. From the Latin *atro* (dark, black, bleak) and/or *atrox* (frightening, terrible); see Ole Benedictow, "The Black Death: The Greatest Catastrophe Ever," *History Today* 55, no. 3 (2005), https://www.historytoday.com/archive/black-death-greatest-catastrophe-ever with bibliography.

49. The area of Crimea, although the plague originated further east in Asia.

50. Estimates of the total death toll range from 30 to 60 percent of the total population.

51. This is also referred to as the Babylonian Captivity of the Church.

the prompting of Sigismund (the future Holy Roman emperor),[52] one of the papal claimants (Pope John XXIII)[53] convoked another council at Constance (1414–1418). The claimants from the Roman, Avignon, and Pisan lines either abdicated or were declared deposed,[54] and in 1417 a new pope was elected: Pope Martin V.

It was also in the fourteenth century that the early Renaissance and Reformation movements began, with transitional figures including the poets Dante (d. 1321) and Petrarch (d. 1374), the artist/architect Giotto (d. 1337), and the priest-theologians John Wycliffe (d. 1384) and Jan (John) Hus (d. 1415). In the fifteenth century, the influence of the Renaissance and its "rediscovery" of classical antiquity was more widely felt. With the fall of Constantinople to the Muslim Ottoman Turks (1453), new copies of classical and early Christian sources poured into the West along with Christian refugees. This new material boosted the fresh intellectual and artistic urge to "return to the sources" that would shape secular and religious life into the sixteenth century. This new movement, humanism,[55] swept over Europe, supported by political leaders in both southern and northern Europe.[56]

### Liturgy: The Mass

One important factor in the history of the Mass was the invention of the printing press in Europe in the mid-fifteenth century. A printed edition of the Roman Missal[57] was first published in Milan in 1474. Although other variations of this Missal were printed in other parts of Europe, this 1474 edition was essentially the one used in preparing the universal Roman Missal (1570) called for by the later Council of Trent. Until then, other regional Catholic missals continued to be printed and used in many parts of Europe.[58]

52. At the time of the council, Sigismund was king of the Romans and of Hungary.

53. John XXIII was a pope of the Pisan line and was later declared to have been an "antipope."

54. Their removal was justified using a theological teaching called "conciliarism": the view that a general (ecumenical) council of the whole church had authority over any individual member, including the pope. Conciliarism was later condemned as heretical by Pope Pius II (1460).

55. Renaissance humanism stressed the value of human action and achievement, fueled by renewed interest in the languages, arts, and literature of ancient Greece and Rome.

56. Several European princes and nobles—especially in Italy—were leaders, including some of the popes (rulers of the Papal states themselves). The university-educated members of the wealthy merchant classes throughout Europe also assumed leadership roles, especially in areas of Germany, the Low Countries, and England.

57. This was the version used by the papal Curia in Rome.

58. All of these used the Roman Canon; variations would be found in the calendars, some prayer texts and rubrics, some chants, and certain readings.

The adoration of the consecrated host became more fervently practiced in the later Middle Ages. During this period, it became common for the priest, after consecrating the host, to pause and hold it up over his head for all the congregation to see.[59] On the basis of visions experienced by the thirteenth-century mystic Julianna of Liège, the local bishop established a feast celebrating the Eucharist itself: the Feast of Corpus Christi (the Body of Christ). Although added to the universal liturgical calendar later in the thirteenth century, the feast was not widely celebrated in western Europe until the early fourteenth century. The Mass of that day was usually preceded by a public procession surrounding a priest carrying a monstrance in which a consecrated host would be displayed.[60]

Early voices for reform included English priest and academic John Wycliffe, who criticized several abuses in the church during his career.[61] One of his theological topics was the scholastic doctrine of transubstantiation. He suggested that the eucharistic species (the bread and the wine) had, in effect, two natures: a material, "earthly" nature, and a spiritual, "divine" nature. After the consecration, the bread and wine remained bread and wine in their material nature but became the body and blood of Christ in their spiritual nature.[62]

Wycliffe's ideas influenced the Bohemian (Czech) priest and theologian Jan (John) Hus. Hus also attacked several abuses in the church; one of his concerns was the withdrawal of the cup from the laity. Since the thirteenth century,[63] laypeople had been permitted only the consecrated host when receiving Communion and were not allowed to drink the consecrated wine. Hus insisted that both clergy and laity receive the bread and the wine.[64] Like Wycliffe, he also questioned the doctrine of transubstantiation, suggesting that the real presence of the body of Christ in the consecrated bread does not replace the inner reality of the bread itself, a kind of consubstantiation.[65]

59. This came to be called the elevation. By this time it was usual for the priest to recite the prayers of the Mass with his back to the people facing the apse of the church or the wall against which the altar was placed.

60. The feast was observed on the Thursday following Trinity Sunday, the first Sunday after Pentecost. Pentecost Sunday, celebrating the descent of the Holy Spirit on the apostles (Acts 2:1–13), is itself the seventh Sunday after Easter. So Corpus Christi was celebrated in the late spring or early summer.

61. Wycliffe's English followers, known as Lollards, remained active in England into the sixteenth century.

62. Alessandro Conti, "John Wycliffe," *Stanford Encyclopedia of Philosophy*, Spring 2017 edition, https://plato.stanford.edu/entries/wyclif/#4.3.

63. In many regions, this became the practice earlier.

64. This belief came to be known as *utraquism* (from Latin meaning "under both kinds").

65. Hus's teaching is known as *impanation* ("within [the] bread"); the broader idea of consubstantiation refers to the presence of both substances, body and bread, at the same time.

Hus was invited to attend the Council of Constance to defend his views but was instead put on trial and executed as a heretic (1415). Both Wycliffe and Hus have traditionally been considered forerunners of the Reformation; Hus's followers (Hussites) continued to be active in Bohemia and neighboring areas into the seventeenth century.[66]

### Other Rites

Despite the practice of auricular confession in the sacrament of penance, individuals might engage in stricter, private penitential practices. One form of this "self-mortification" was flagellation—that is, whipping oneself on the back with knotted ropes or small whips. Originally practiced by individual monks in monasteries, the practice spread more widely among individual Christians. In the fourteenth century, in response to a popular belief that God had sent the plague as a punishment for the sins of Christendom, groups of men known as flagellants would engage in a form of public penance by making a kind of pilgrimage from town to town and whipping themselves along the way. The flagellant movement—active in parts of Italy, Austria, and Germany—was eventually condemned as heretical, but groups of flagellants continued to be active sporadically throughout the later medieval period despite attempts to suppress them.

Also related to penitential practice was the system of issuing indulgences. Prayer for the dead was considered a way of applying the extraordinary "merit" of Christ and the saints to shorten their time of purgation before admission to heaven. Offering up one's own physical suffering or engaging in fasting and giving alms to the poor were also considered meritorious, as was making a pilgrimage or donating an offering of money to the church. As time went on, these "offerings" took on the character of a purchase. The practice of buying and selling indulgences was roundly criticized by many Christian humanists as an example of church corruption in direct contradiction to the example of the early Christians. Other pious acts, like going on pilgrimage, were also considered to be a distraction to the quiet, daily routine of prayer and work at home.[67]

---

66. The Hussite Wars (1419–1434) resulted in a compromise accepted by all except the most radical Hussites (the Taborites); it restored Communion with both bread and wine to the laity in Bohemia.

67. The Dutch Catholic humanist Erasmus (d. 1536) wrote a satirical dialogue/colloquy on this topic, "Pilgrimage for Religion's Sake" (1526). The superstitious approach to the veneration of the saints was one of his key points. Some of his reformer contemporaries, like Huldrych Zwingli (d. 1531), would go further, accusing people of effectively worshiping the saints, treating them like little gods/goddesses.

## Practical Implications for Worship

In North American culture, "facts" are key. Facts can be discovered by experience, research, or controlled experimentation, and are concretely verifiable. It is "truth" that seems to have become increasingly relativized, individualized, and uncertain. Therefore, in some ways, the "worlds" of medieval Christianity seem quite alien, repressively intolerant, rigorously structured, and woefully (or willfully) ignorant. To be accused of "medieval" thinking today is not a compliment.

And yet there are connections important for us today. The importance of communal liturgical participation, for example, was part of the reason that the Second Vatican Council of the Roman Catholic Church (1962–1965) was called. Its focus on "updating," especially in liturgical renewal and ecumenical dialogue, was propelled by the urgency to promote "active participation" of the laity as well as the clergy in the worship life of the Catholic Church and beyond—including other churches. The translation of the Roman Catholic liturgy into English allowed Catholics and other Christians to recognize common points of belief and practice. The recentering of the Scriptures in Catholic liturgy has also built bridges among Christians. Contemporary Christians should be more energetic in shaping the unity without uniformity evident in medieval Christianity through more opportunities for shared prayer among Christians, especially in a society that increasingly seems to find religion itself to be either irrelevant or, worse, a source of division and hostility. As was true in the Middle Ages, local prayer, local worship, local connections come first.

The Middle Ages can also offer an example of balance in liturgy and worship, despite its extremes that are all too evident. Modern Christianity can focus too narrowly on sheer communication and get lost in a sea of words and a clamor of noise. There is a need to rediscover the value of silence and the experience of transcendence/mystery as well, in ways consistent with our own traditions. Medieval worship had a place for procession, music, and festivity as well as for quiet daily prayer, silence, and examination of conscience. The use of social media that might isolate individuals can and does offer opportunities. Some religious communities offer websites that provide individuals with brief meditation aids that can be used for "centering" breaks at the computer. Short versions of the monastic hours of prayer can be (and already are) adapted and made available online.

Medieval Christianity also made a clear connection between worship and action. Attending Mass and receiving Communion, confessing sins and receiving absolution, and joining a procession in honor of a local saint were never acts that remained unconnected to the pattern and needs of daily life.

Setting aside funds for the poor, contributing to hospices for the sick, and recognizing the goodness of God's creation were all nourished by the pattern of liturgical prayer that structured each year, day in and day out. In the same way, Christian worship should reinforce responses to contemporary problems and not remain separate from them. For example, water was blessed and used for baptism and as a part of other blessing rituals. How does this experience influence our recognition of environmental problems like drought, water pollution, and global warming? When the gospel parable of the rich man and the beggar Lazarus is proclaimed on Sunday, what is our response to the homeless on Monday? Who are the saints, the "holy" men and women of today, and in what ways can we learn from their example?

Clearly, some of the insights of medieval life and liturgy can offer guidance to contemporary Christians struggling in worship to answer the question that echoes down through the centuries: What is truth?

## For Further Reading

Giottos, Helen, and Sarah Hamilton. *Understanding Medieval Liturgy: Essays in Interpretation*. New York: Routledge, 2016.

Larson-Miller, Lizette, ed. *Medieval Liturgy: A Book of Essays*. New York: Routledge, 2019.

Levy, Ian, Gary Macy, and Kristen van Ausdall, eds. *A Companion to the Eucharist in the Middle Ages*. Brill's Companions to the Christian Tradition 26. Leiden: Brill, 2011.

"Medieval Liturgy." Arc Humanities Press (CARMEN Worldwide Medieval Network). https://bibliography.arc-humanities.org/medieval-liturgy/.

Palazzo, Eric. *A History of Liturgical Books: From the Beginning to the Thirteenth Century*. Translated by Madeline Beaumont. Collegeville, MN: Liturgical Press, 1998.

Pierce, Joanne M. "Medieval Christian Liturgy." *Oxford Research Encyclopedia of Religion*, May 9, 2016. https://doi.org/10.1093/acrefore/9780199340378.013.84.

Rubin, Miri. *Corpus Christi: The Eucharist in Late Medieval Culture*. Rev. ed. Cambridge: Cambridge University Press, 2008.

Vogel, Cyrille. *Medieval Liturgy: An Introduction to the Sources*. Revised and translated by William G. Storey and Niels Krogh Rasmussen. Washington, DC: Pastoral Press, 1986.

## — 9 —

# Reformation in the Catholic Church

### *John F. Baldovin*

I t would be inaccurate to think that Catholic worship remained totally
static after the Council of Trent or that liturgical reform in the Catholic
Church began only with Vatican II—or for that matter even in the nineteenth century. Reform of the church was very much in the minds of those
gathered for the Council of Trent (1543–1563) and had been ever since the
fourteenth-century schism in the West and the reform councils of Constance
(1414–1418) and Basel-Ferrara-Florence (1431–1445). Even though Catholic
liturgy changed little in terms of content after Trent, various efforts at reform
continued all the way up until Vatican II. Moreover, since the text of the
liturgy does not constitute the entirety of Christian worship, we must take
account of the social and cultural elements that actually made the liturgy a
lived experience. So, while the various texts of the Catholic liturgy remained
the same for the most part, the actual experience and cultural environment
of the liturgy evolved significantly. The purpose of this chapter is to survey
those changes and efforts at reform. As we shall see, many of the reform
efforts between the sixteenth and twentieth centuries prefigured the reforms
of Vatican II.

## The Council of Trent and Its Aftermath

The Council of Trent was convoked in order to respond to the many challenges posed to the Roman Catholic Church by the churches of the Reformation. But, as mentioned above, Trent was also a council of the Catholic reform. For this reason, the term "Catholic Reformation" is much more useful than "Counter-Reformation." Part of the council's response was the promulgation of a number of doctrinal decrees. Given the nature and scope of the reformers' critiques, a number of these decrees dealt with sacraments and liturgy. Among these were a general decree on the sacraments (1551), a decree on baptism and confirmation (1551), a decree on the Eucharist (mainly eucharistic real presence, in 1551), a decree on Communion (denying the necessity of Communion in both kinds, in 1563), and finally a decree on the sacrifice of the Mass (1563). Each of these decrees responded to specific positions held by the reformers—for example, insistence on Communion in both kinds or on the use of the common language (vernacular) instead of Latin.[1] On the other hand, these doctrinal decrees avoided taking sides in the controversies among the various schools of Catholic theology. They only affected the actual practice of worship in matters like withholding the Communion cup from the faithful and protecting the liturgical use of Latin.

The council also issued a number of decrees specifically aimed at needed reforms, such as insisting that bishops be residents in their dioceses or the establishment of seminaries. One of the more important of these was issued toward the very end of the council, the 1562 decree "Decree on Things to Be Observed and Avoided in the Celebration of Mass."[2] Although a preparatory commission had enumerated seventy-eight abuses with regard to the liturgy of the Eucharist, the final decree was relatively brief. In general terms, it condemned the celebration of Masses for financial gain and superstitions like amassing a series of Masses to be said for the dead or relating monetary gain to the number of candles on the altar at a particular liturgy. It also decreed that the missals be stripped of Mass formulas for unworthy intentions, like success in business or hunting. The decree also ordered that the Eucharist be

1. For a good summary, see Paul Bradshaw and Maxwell Johnson, *The Eucharistic Liturgies: Their Evolution and Interpretation* (Collegeville, MN: Liturgical Press, 2012), 281–92. For the doctrinal decrees, see Heinrich Denzinger and Peter Hünermann, eds., *Enchiridion Symbolorum Definitionum et Declarationum de Rebus Fidei et Morum* (*Compendium of Creeds, Definitions and Declarations on Matters of Faith and Morals*), Latin and English, 43rd ed., (San Francisco: Ignatius, 2012), §§1600–1760 (hereafter cited as DH).

2. Council of Trent, "Decree on Things to Be Observed and Avoided in Celebrating Mass," in *Decrees of the Ecumenical Councils*, vol. 2, *Trent to Vatican II*, ed. N. Tanner et al. (Washington, DC: Georgetown University Press, 1990), 736–37.

celebrated only in churches and chapels and not in private houses. Finally, the council left the concession of Communion in both kinds (i.e., the permission for the laity to receive from the cup) to the discretion of the pope.[3]

Similarly, Trent, as it was concluding in 1563, left the actual reform of the liturgy to the pope. And so a commission was established.

Since, as became the case with Vatican II, a council itself could not do the detailed work of liturgical reform, Pope Pius IV was asked to take up the task. He, and then his successor Pope Pius V, entrusted the revision of all the liturgical books to the Roman Curia, which first produced the Roman Breviary (known better today as the Divine Office or Liturgy of the Hours) in 1568. Prior to Trent, in 1535 Pope Clement VII had commissioned the Spanish Franciscan cardinal Francisco Quiñones to produce a reformed breviary. In the humanist spirit of the times, Quiñones produced a book with private recitation that trimmed off legendary nonscriptural readings, as well as antiphons and responsories that were better suited to choral recitation. It also contained more and longer biblical passages. One can see here the similarities with morning and evening prayer in the Church of England put together by Archbishop Thomas Cranmer. Despite the enormous popularity of the *Breviary of the Holy Cross*, as it was known, the post-Tridentine commission did not accept it as a whole but basically retained the traditional breviary, now stripped of legendary material.[4]

The Roman Missal followed in 1570 and with very little revision remained the basic Catholic Mass book until Vatican II. It was not an entirely new production, of course, but was based on the medieval liturgy of Rome that was first printed in 1474, which itself reproduced the Roman Catholic Mass as it had been celebrated since the twelfth century. In addition, commentary and rubrics had been compiled by the papal master of ceremonies Johannes Burchard in 1501 and served as the basis for the introductory material to the Missal. The Missal of 1570 was mandatory for the whole Catholic Church. The only exceptions to this rule were churches (e.g., Milan or Toledo) and religious orders (e.g., the Dominicans) that had rites that were over two hundred years old.[5]

3. DH §176. See Reinhold Theisen, "The Reform of the Mass Liturgy and the Council of Trent," *Worship* 40 (1966): 565–83. Perhaps the best commentary on the material covered in this chapter and on which I will rely extensively is Enrico Cattaneo, *Il Culto Cristiano in Occidente: Note Storiche* (Rome: CLV-Edizioni Liturgiche, 1978), 360–617; here at 368–70.

4. See Robert Taft, *The Liturgy of the Hours in East and West: The Origins of the Divine Office and Its Meaning for Today* (Collegeville, MN: Liturgical Press, 1993), 310–11.

5. See Joseph Jungmann, *The Mass of the Roman Rite*, trans. Francis Brenner (Notre Dame, IN: Ave Maria, 2012), 1:138; Cattaneo, *Culto*, 371–78; Andrew Cameron-Mowat and Keith Pecklers, "History of Liturgy from Trent to Vatican II," *New Catholic Encyclopedia*, 2nd ed. (Detroit: Gale, 2003), 8:660–64.

As Pius V made clear in the promulgation of the Missal of 1570, one of the aims of the revision was to return to the pristine form it had in the age of the church fathers. A further goal was to provide uniform liturgies throughout the church. Prior to this the liturgies of the Roman Rite shared a family resemblance but were colored by places in which they originated; for example, the most popular rite in England was the Sarum (Salisbury) Use. Attempting such uniformity could not have succeeded prior to the invention of movable print in the fifteenth century. Returning to the earlier liturgies of the church, however, was easier said than done since the process was hampered by the state of historical research into the liturgy, a limitation that was greatly overcome in subsequent centuries.[6]

In 1582 Pope Gregory XIII, who also revised the Julian calendar and gave us the one presently in use, approved a new Roman calendar. Liturgical calendars have the tendency to accrue new feasts and observances like barnacles on a ship. The new calendar greatly reduced the number of feast days as well as some poetic material (Sequences) that had proliferated over time. As we shall see below, reducing feast days was also a social issue since it involved an economic concern (feast days without work) that became a consideration in the eighteenth-century Enlightenment efforts at liturgical reform.

A Vatican Congregation of Rites, which supervised the uniformity of the liturgy throughout the church, was established in 1588. The Roman Pontifical (the book containing all the ceremonies proper to bishops, such as ordinations and confirmation) was published in 1596. It was followed by the rubrical directions for bishops, the Ceremonial of Bishops, in 1600. Finally, the Roman Ritual containing rites used by priests (baptism, penance, marriage, and anointing of the sick) appeared in 1614. Except for the ritual to which some local practices could be attached, these books had to be used by all the churches of the Roman Rite.

Real participation in the liturgy—that is, in the liturgy itself rather than devotional practices like the rosary—was not a concern of the post-Tridentine Catholic reform. Theologians like Robert Bellarmine in the late sixteenth century (and many after him) vigorously opposed the translation of the liturgy into the language of the people, even for devotional purposes. This may seem appalling, but we should be careful about imposing our modern standards of participation on this period. As Josef Jungmann wrote with regard to the Missal of 1570, "To have gone farther and deeper say, in the direction of a stronger communion between priest and people, would have

6. See Jungmann, *Mass*, 1:133–41.

demanded different spiritual conditions among the faithful."[7] Resistance to translating the liturgy lasted a long time. In 1661 French translation of the missal had been condemned by Pope Alexander VII, who also forbade any further translations.[8]

## The Arts in Catholic Worship—Post-Tridentine Developments

As mentioned above, the church's worship does not consist in texts alone. And so, even though the texts of the Roman liturgy were (rigidly) standardized in the wake of the Council of Trent, the actual experience of worship was influenced by societal, cultural, and artistic developments.

Ever since the early Middle Ages, liturgical music had been the province of monks and choirs. Elaborate polyphonic music had been developed beyond plainchant during the late medieval period. Despite myths to the contrary, the Council of Trent never considered banning polyphonic music, and the work of sixteenth-century composers like Giovanni da Palestrina, Tomás Luis de Victoria, and Orlando di Lasso among others was extremely popular and remained so throughout the sixteenth and early seventeenth centuries. This unaccompanied vocal music was gradually replaced by more florid compositions with instrumental accompaniment by musicians like Claudio Monteverdi and Marc-Antoine Charpentier in the seventeenth century. Instrumentally accompanied choirs were characteristic of the cultural period known as the baroque. Some of the musical Mass settings by later composers like Franz Joseph Haydn, Wolfgang Amadeus Mozart, and Johann Sebastian Bach overshadowed the celebration of the Eucharist itself. The music of nineteenth-century composers like Ludwig van Beethoven, Hector Berlioz, and Franz Schubert were more like concert pieces that could easily be divorced from the liturgy.

At the same time, in Germany, hymns that had been popular outside the liturgy were introduced into the Mass to counteract the Protestants. This practice became a primary way for the people to participate in a liturgy that otherwise was the sole preserve of the clergy.[9] Thus there was a tension between popular participation represented by vernacular hymns and retaining

7. Jungmann, *Mass*, 1:138.

8. Jungmann, *Mass*, 1:143. On the history of the vernacular, see Keith Pecklers and Gilbert Ostdiek, "The History of Vernaculars and Role of Translation," in *A Commentary on the Order of Mass of the Roman Missal*, ed. Edward Foley et al. (Collegeville, MN: Liturgical Press, 2011), 35–72; and Keith Pecklers, *Dynamic Equivalence: The Living Language of Christian Worship* (Collegeville, MN: Liturgical Press), 2003.

9. Jungmann, *Mass*, 1:146, 154–57.

the tradition of choral music represented by chant, polyphony, and later classical compositions accompanied by instruments. To some extent that tension still exists.

In the nineteenth century the use of Gregorian chant became a symbol of the Catholic Restoration after the Enlightenment and the French Revolution. The center of the Gregorian revival was the Abbey of Solesmes, refounded in 1833 by the Benedictine Prosper Gueranger. At the beginning of the twentieth century, Pope Pius X, in some ways considered the initiator of the modern Liturgical Movement, strongly encouraged the restoration and use of Gregorian chant shortly after he was elected pope.

Architectural style also differentiated Catholic worship sharply from that of Protestants and Anglicans. Given the evangelical heritage of the Reformation, many Protestant churches tended to become open auditory spaces (with seating) that favored preaching as a main feature of worship. On the other hand, Catholic church building started to move away from the compartmentalized spaces of medieval Gothic cathedrals with their choirs separated from the nave, the area for the laypeople, by barriers such as rood screens. Catholic church architecture that took its inspiration from the Catholic Reformation's emphasis on eucharistic presence and the Mass as a representation of the sacrifice of Calvary tended now to focus primarily on the main altar with a monumental retable or reredos and a tabernacle that contained the reserved eucharistic bread. Thus, the churches of the Renaissance and baroque styles became elaborate throne rooms for the Blessed Sacrament. At the same time this focus was surrounded by elaborate and glorious church decoration, especially in the ceiling vaults of churches like the Gesù and the Sant'Ignazio in Rome.[10] As Jungmann put it, "The interior of the church has become a great hall filled with sensuous life."[11]

All in all, the baroque period used lavish ostentation to counteract the somewhat rationalist aspects of the Protestant Reformation. Besides music and art such ostentation was evident in devotional practices, foremost among them the Corpus Christi processions with the consecrated sacrament through the streets.[12]

The Catholic Enlightenment of the eighteenth century favored a return to a classical style of church architecture with its clean lines. This was especially true in the United States, where a classical revival helped Catholics blend

10. For example, see David Stancliffe, *The Lion Companion to Church Architecture* (Oxford: Lion Hudson, 2008), 167–91.

11. Jungmann, *Mass*, 1:150.

12. Joseph Jungmann, "Liturgical Life in the Baroque Period," in *Pastoral Liturgy* (Notre Dame, IN: Ave Maria, 2014), 80–101.

in with their fellow citizens. But just as with music, Romanticism and the Catholic Restoration of the nineteenth century saw the rebirth of Gothic architecture (or the neo-Gothic) as the ideal form of church building. The popularity of the neo-Gothic style went far beyond Catholics, but its first ardent promoter was the English Roman Catholic Augustus N. W. Pugin.[13] In the twentieth century, even before Vatican II, Catholics began to experiment with modernist architecture in church buildings. Some typical examples are the Church of Notre Dame du Haut at Ronchamp (France) by Le Corbusier, Corpus Christi in Aachen (Germany) by Rudolf Schwartz, and the Abbey Church of St. John's (Collegeville, Minnesota) by Marcel Breuer. And, just as has been the case with music, the tension between a more participative rational style and a more elaborate and traditional style of church architecture has persisted up to the present.

## Liturgical Scholarship

As was noted above, one aim in the production of the Roman Missal of 1570 was to remove accretions to the Mass over time by going back to the age of the fathers of the church. But the state of historical research in the sixteenth century made that kind of research unfeasible. The seventeenth and eighteenth centuries, however, saw a virtual explosion of historical scholarship with the editions of early liturgies in both East and West. Research into early Christian sources was characteristic of both Anglican and Catholic scholars. Some of the outstanding Catholic scholars were Giuseppe Tomasi, Pierre LeBrun, Edmund Martène, Ludovico Muratori, Jean Mabillon, and Eusebius Renaudot. They edited the early texts of the Latin and Eastern liturgies. Possessing reliable ancient texts like the fourth-century *Apostolic Constitutions* made it possible to begin thinking that the liturgy was not completely fixed.

But the slow and laborious historical-critical work of editing early sources had to wait to bear practical fruit until the twentieth century with influential Catholic scholars like Anton Baumstark, Edmund Bishop, Bernard Botte, and Josef Jungmann.

## Jansenism, Gallicanism, and the Enlightenment

Even though the texts of the liturgy did not change in the centuries following Trent, as we have already seen, social, intellectual, and cultural elements

13. Stancliffe, *Church Architecture*, 219–37; for contemporary reactions, see 245–69.

influenced the lived experience of the liturgy. One of these issues, emblematic of the Enlightenment reaction of the seventeenth and eighteenth centuries, was participation in the Eucharist especially vis-à-vis the vernacular and the frequency of receiving Holy Communion. As to the frequency of Communion, at the Fourth Lateran Council (1215) the church legislated the reception of penance and Communion at least once a year. From time to time reformers like Ignatius of Loyola, the founder of the Jesuits, recommended more frequent Communion. The French Jansenists of the seventeenth and eighteenth centuries were vigorous opponents of what they considered the laxism of the Jesuits and put strict requirements on the reception of Communion.[14] Jansenism was, however, a complex movement. Given their revival of the theology of St. Augustine, the Jansenists turned to the patristic period for inspiration. There they found liturgies that bespoke the participation of the laity. This led them to arguing for translating the liturgy as well as the Bible into the vernacular.[15] As we saw above, the translation inspired by them was condemned by Pope Alexander VII. Despite such condemnations, church figures continued to argue for a vernacular liturgy, among them in 1787 John Carroll, an American priest who later became the first bishop of Baltimore.

Another French movement, which was in some ways heir to the Jansenists and featured in post-Tridentine Catholic liturgical life, was neo-Gallicanism. The Roman Rite, strictly speaking, was not the only form of late antique and early medieval liturgy in the West. Other rites included the Ambrosian (Milan), Mozarabic or Visigothic (Spain), and Gallican (mainly France and Germany). As we have seen, the Tridentine reform mandated a uniform liturgy for all rites more recent than two hundred years old, and so the Mozarabic Rite was retained in Toledo, the Ambrosian Rite in Milan, and the Dominican Rite for the Order of Preachers. The Gallican rites, however, had long since disappeared. Yet the notion of independent Gallican rites persisted and was applied to the local liturgies of the French churches, hence neo-Gallican. And so the neo-Gallican liturgies became symbolic of a certain independence from Roman centralization.

Eighteenth-century Enlightenment Catholicism represented a strong reaction to baroque Catholicism and was particularly strong in areas under the control of the Holy Roman Empire. Many of its proposed reforms were decreed by a regional council held in Tuscany (part of the empire), the Synod of Pistoia in 1786 during the reign of Emperor Joseph II. The contents of its

14. F. Ellen Weaver, "The Neo-Gallican Liturgies Revisited," *Studia Liturgica* 16 (1986): 57.
15. See F. Ellen Weaver, "Scripture and Liturgy for the Laity: The Jansenist Case for Translation," *Worship* 59 (1985): 510–21.

decrees can only be summarized here. In general, the reforms proposed aimed at a simplification of the liturgy, greater lay participation, and an elimination of superstitious practices. The Mass was to be viewed as a corporate activity in which the people participate with the priest and therefore the vernacular should be introduced. The people should receive Communion during the Mass at the same time as the priest. (Normally Communion was distributed either before or after the celebration.) There should be only one altar in each church, and it should be unencumbered by decoration or relics; that is, it should look more like a table. The breviary was to be shortened, legendary elements eliminated, and more Scripture inserted.[16] Feasts that took up many days in the year should be less frequent.[17] The synod was strongly and swiftly condemned by Pope Pius VI in 1794 in a constitution titled *Auctorem Fidei*.[18] Ironically, in a significant swing of the pendulum, all these ideas of Pistoia were later adopted by Vatican II.

Before turning to the nineteenth century we should not neglect to note two examples of what we would call today liturgical inculturation. In the seventeenth century the Jesuit missionaries in China attempted to adapt the Christian method and devotional practices to the mentality of the people, especially with regard to how they honored their ancestors. Their effort resulted in what was called the Chinese Rites controversy. After strong opposition from the Franciscans and Dominicans, Pope Clement XI condemned the Jesuit effort.[19] Finally we should mention the Jesuit missions among the indigenous peoples of Paraguay (and today's Brazil and Argentina) in the seventeenth and eighteenth centuries.

## Restoration Catholicism in the Nineteenth Century

One may argue the Enlightenment came to a crashing halt with the reaction to the French Revolution of the late eighteenth century. What ensued was a turn to Romanticism. For our purposes it could be called the Catholic Restoration. Architecturally, as we have seen, it was characterized by a certain

16. See Albert Gerhards, "Die Synode von Pistoia 1786 und ihre Reform des Gottesdienstes," in *Liturgiereformen I*, Liturgiewissentschaflichte Queelen und Forschungen 88, ed. Martin Klöckener and Benedikt Kranemann (Munster: Aschendorff, 2002), 496–510; Jungmann, *Mass*, 1:153–56.

17. People were not allowed to do manual labor on feast days, and therefore there was a social and economic factor involved in eliminating many of them. See Cattaneo, *Culto*, 430, 448–54.

18. Pius VI, *Constitution Auctorem Fidei*, 1794, in DH §§2630–74.

19. David Mungello, ed., *The Chinese Rites Controversy: Its History and Meaning* (Nettetal, Germany: Steyler, 1994).

nostalgia for the Middle Ages and neo-Gothic architecture. Musically it was characterized by a revival of Gregorian chant, especially at Solesmes, and the Caecilian movement in Germany.[20] Guéranger, who refounded the Benedictine Abbey of Solesmes in 1833, was an adamant proponent of Roman centralization and thus an opponent of neo-Gallicanism. Solesmes became the inspiration for a liturgical movement that spread to the abbeys of Beuron in Germany (1863) and Maredsous in Belgium (1899). The latter became the motherhouse of two abbeys that were extremely influential in the twentieth-century Liturgical Movement: Mont César (Kaisersberg) in Leuven, Belgium (1899), and Glenstal in Ireland (1927).

Hand in hand with the monastic revival went the development of a Catholic theology that rejected the Scholastic method that had been dominant since the twelfth century. This development was associated with the so-called Tübingen school and Johann Adam Möhler. This theological movement began to develop a new ecclesiology that had its roots in the early church and the idea of the people of God. It was Möhler's student Franz Anton Staudenmaier who first introduced liturgy as a subject within theology as opposed to canon law and rubrics.[21]

## The Twentieth Century

The beginnings of the modern Liturgical Movement can be traced to several sources. The first was the appeal for a revival of Gregorian chant by the newly elected Pope Pius X in 1903. In promoting this liturgical reform Pius was reacting to the sorry state that church music had fallen into. For much of the eighteenth and nineteenth centuries, as we have noted above, liturgical music had become lavish and operatic. This was even true of chant itself.[22] Pius's affirmation of active participation in the liturgy as the true and indispensable source of the Christian spirit was later adopted as a major principle by Vatican II's liturgy constitution: "Filled as We are with a most ardent desire to see the true Christian spirit flourish in every respect and be preserved by all the faithful, We deem it necessary to provide before anything else for the sanctity and dignity of the temple, in which the faithful assemble for *no other object than that of acquiring this spirit from its foremost and indispensable*

---

20. On the nineteenth-century Romanticism and the Caecilian movement, see Anthony Ruff, *Sacred Music and Liturgical Reform: Treasures and Transformations* (Chicago: Liturgy Training, 2007), 75–129, 272–91.

21. See John Baldwin, "The Development of the Liturgy: Theological and Historical Roots of *Sacrosanctum Concilium*," *Worship* 87 (2013): 517–32.

22. See Ruff, *Sacred Music*, 209–42.

*font, which is the active participation in the most holy mysteries and in the public and solemn prayer of the Church.*"[23]

Two years after this Pius made an official call for more frequent Communion, a move that Jungmann called "a milestone of liturgical history."[24] This led eventually to ending the practice of distributing Communion before or after the Mass, although even up until Vatican II the distribution of Communion coincided with the eucharistic prayer. That is, another priest appeared from the sacristy to distribute Communion while the celebrant was continuing the eucharistic prayer.

A second starting point of the modern Liturgical Movement came with a Belgian former diocesan priest, Lambert Beauduin, who entered the monastery of Mont César in 1906. In 1909 he participated in the Belgian Congress of National Works. His address there, which stressed a more widespread pastoral understanding of the liturgy, is regarded by many as *the* beginning of the twentieth-century Liturgical Movement.[25]

The pastoral turn of the Liturgical Movement led to a number of important developments that paved the way for the liturgical reform of Vatican II: bilingual hand Missals, communal singing of the stable or "ordinary" parts of the Mass like the "Holy, holy, holy" in Latin, and the "dialogue Mass" in which the people responded to the priest in Latin.[26]

At the same time liturgical scholarship proceeded apace, especially in monasteries like the German Abbey of Maria Laach, founded in 1903 from Beuron. Two of its outstanding monks, Kunibert Mohlberg and Odo Casel, were responsible for major advances in liturgical renewal. Mohlberg edited the old Latin Mass books. His editions served as important sources for those preparing the Vatican II reform. Casel, whose theology of the Christ cult-mystery was an attempt to replace the current Scholastic theology of the sacraments, was a major influence on many theologians who incorporated his basic insights in the theology that informed the Vatican II liturgy constitution. Another major German liturgical figure was the theologian Romano Guardini, who introduced eucharistic celebrations facing the people to university students in the 1930s.

The Liturgical Movement spread to many European countries—in particular to Austria with the Augustianian Pius Parsch, who wrote a multivolume

23. Pope Pius X, *Tra le sollecitudini*, November 22, 1903, https://adoremus.org/1903/11/22/tra-le-sollecitudini/ (emphasis added).

24. Jungmann, *Mass*, 1:160.

25. See Keith Pecklers, *The Unread Vision: The Liturgical Movement in the United States of America 1926–1955* (Collegeville, MN: Liturgical Press, 1998), 12.

26. Jungmann, *Mass*, 1:162–63.

guide to the feasts and observances of the liturgical year, and to France, where a national pastoral center for liturgy (Centre Nationale de Pastorale Liturgique) was founded in Paris in 1947 followed by a major center for study, the Institut Supérieur de Liturgie in 1956. The movement was brought to the United States in the 1930s by a monk of St. John's Abbey in Collegeville, Minnesota, Virgil Michel. Father Michel founded the major American liturgical journal *Orate Fratres* (later *Worship*) in 1926.[27] He soon found collaborators in a number of American Catholic clergy, among them H. A. Reinhold, Reynold Hillenbrand, Martin Hellriegel, Gerald Ellard, Frederick McManus, and Michel's own successor as editor of *Orate Fratres*, Godfrey Diekmann, OSB.[28]

We should add here that the Liturgical Movement in the United States, and indeed on the European continent and Great Britain as well, was heavily intertwined with a social vision and concern that we would call social justice today. Whether seeking to restore the riches of medieval worship in the face of the bleakness of the Industrial Revolution or understanding how a truly pastoral liturgy could confront the needs of contemporary society, the pioneers of liturgical reform knew that liturgy was a religious form that could be isolated from the rest of life. In addition to concern for social justice, the Liturgical Movement lent itself to the promotion of ecumenism. Beauduin himself founded a bi-ritual monastery devoted to ecumenism especially with the Orthodox at Amay-sur-Meuse in Belgium. The monastery later moved to Chevetogne. He was also involved in the Malines Conversations, ecumenical talks between Catholics and Anglicans in the 1920s. Investigation of early sources inspired a kind of natural affinity among Protestant, Catholic, Anglican, and Orthodox liturgical scholars, who continue that cooperative enterprise to this day.

The final chapter in this history of Roman Catholic worship from Trent until the eve of Vatican II begins after World War II with Pope Pius XII in his 1947 encyclical letter, *Mediator Dei*.[29] Despite some misgivings, this letter constituted a major papal endorsement of the main lines of the twentieth-century Liturgical Movement. As a follow-up, Pius XII established a commission for the reform of the liturgy in 1948. The fruit of this commission was a number of

27. See surveys by André Haquin, "The Liturgical Movement and Catholic Liturgical Revision," in *The Oxford History of Christian Worship*, ed. Geoffrey Wainwright and Karen Westerfield Tucker (Oxford: Oxford University Press, 2005), 696–704; and Pecklers, *Unread Vision*, 1–23.

28. For brief biographies of the leaders of the nineteenth- and twentieth-century Liturgical Movement, see Robert Tuzik, ed., *Leaders of the Liturgical Movement* (Chicago: Liturgy Training, 1990).

29. Pope Pius XII, *Encyclical Letter Mediator Dei* (On the Sacred Liturgy), http://www.vatican.va/content/pius-xii/en/encyclicals/documents/hf_p-xii_enc_20111947_mediator-dei.html.

changes that inspired the more radical revisions of Vatican II: the permission for evening Mass, the shortening of the fast before Communion, a revision of the Psalter of the Divine Office, permission for the use of the vernacular in some rituals other than the Eucharist, a major revision of the Easter Vigil (1952), and finally the revision of the rest of the Holy Week liturgies (1956).

## Practical Implications for Worship

This brief survey of the history and reformation of the Catholic liturgy from Trent to the eve of Vatican II has demonstrated that although texts changed little from the period following Trent, a great deal happened with regard to the lived experience of Catholic worship. We have seen an ebb and flow of attitudes toward the liturgy from the consolidation of Catholicism after Trent to the lavish extravagance of the baroque to the reaction of Enlightenment Catholicism to the Romantic Catholic Restoration and finally to the modern Liturgical Movement, which owed a great deal to the renewed study of the Bible and the writings of the early church. Therefore, the first practical implication of these developments is to recognize that the experience of Catholic worship, like Christian worship in general, is intimately related to the social and cultural spirit of any given age. Discerning the significance of social and cultural change should show us that we neglect the critical history of worship at our peril.

A second implication has to do specifically with ongoing Catholic debates in eucharistic theology and the theology of the ordained ministry. An international liturgical congress was held at Assisi in 1956. It was an important event with speeches by the likes of Augustin Cardinal Bea, who was later to become the chief ecumenical officer of the church; Giacomo Cardinal Lercaro, who became the chair of the post–Vatican II commission on reforming the liturgy; and Josef Jungmann, the Jesuit liturgical historian whose 1949 massive history of the Mass on the Roman Rite had a profound effect on liturgical scholarship and on Vatican II itself. But the congress is perhaps best known for the allocution given at its conclusion by Pope Pius XII. In this speech the pope reiterated the support he had given to the Liturgical Movement in the encyclical *Mediator Dei* and also addressed several controversial points of Catholic doctrine—for example, priests concelebrating at the eucharistic sacrifice and the question of the nature of Christ's real presence at the Eucharist. These remain points of contention in Catholic theology to this day.

Finally, and perhaps most significantly, although modern languages had been allowed in some of the church's sacramental rites, Pope Pius XII attempted to end speculation on the use of the vernacular language in the Mass, saying, "The Church has serious reasons for retaining steadfastly in the Latin rite the unconditional obligation of the celebrating priest to use the Latin language, and, likewise, for insisting that the Gregorian chant at the holy sacrifice shall be in the language of the Church."[30] It is revealing that Pius XII was not cited even once in Vatican II's Constitution on the Sacred Liturgy. Within ten short years of his speech, the exclusive use of Latin in Catholic liturgy was to become a dead letter and a new era of Catholic worship was to begin. Sometimes conclusions that seem final turn out not to be final at all.

## For Further Reading

Botte, Bernard. *From Silence to Participation: An Insider's View of Liturgical Renewal.* Translated by John Sullivan. Washington, DC: Pastoral Press, 1988.

Bugnini, Annibale. *The Reform of the Liturgy 1948–1975.* Collegeville, MN: Liturgical Press, 1990.

Jungmann, Joseph. *The Mass of the Roman Rite.* Vol. 1. Translated by Francis Brenner. Notre Dame, IN: Ave Maria, 2012.

Pecklers, Keith. *The Unread Vision: The Liturgical Movement in the United States of America 1926–1955.* Collegeville, MN: Liturgical Press, 1998.

Tuzik, Robert, ed. *Leaders of the Liturgical Movement.* Chicago: Liturgy Training, 1990.

Wainwright, Geoffrey, and Karen Westerfield Tucker, eds. *The Oxford History of Christian Worship.* Oxford: Oxford University Press, 2005. Especially chapters 8, 9, 23, 27.

White, James. *Roman Catholic Worship: Trent to Today.* New York: Paulist Press, 1995.

30. See Pecklers, *Dynamic Equivalence*, 82.

# — 10 —

# Vatican II and the Liturgical Renewal Movement

*Joris Geldhof*

The history of Roman Catholic worship in the past century—at least the liturgy of the Roman Rite as it is celebrated in the West—is a very complex and multifaceted story. It is intrinsically linked to what many continue to call with reverence and respect the Liturgical Movement and is marked by an absolute highlight, the Second Vatican Council (1962–1965). The goal in this chapter is first to characterize in broad strokes the Liturgical Movement, with a specific emphasis on western Europe; then to focus on the enormous achievement of Vatican II and the major document on the liturgy that it promulgated, *Sacrosanctum concilium*; to continue with a discussion of the practical implementation of the encompassing liturgical reform ensuing from the council; and to finally offer some reflections about where the church stands now.

It is both interesting and appropriate to take stock, for the life of worship of millions of Catholics has gone through a period of turmoil and confusion during the past five to six decades, whereas one could meaningfully argue that

---

Much in this chapter is based on lecture notes I published in Dutch. See Joris Geldhof, *Liturgie en sacramenten: een inleiding*, 4th ed. (Leuven: Acco, 2020), esp. 154–70.

the liturgy is there, above all, to provide stability, quiet, and focus. It is fair to say—beyond a blind enthusiasm for the Second Vatican Council but even more so beyond an exaggerated attitude of repulsion and dismay—that the past hundred years of Roman Catholic liturgy have been a cocktail of failures and successes, and that the future is open, provided that one learns equally from the good things and from those that went not so well.

## The Early Liturgical Movement

Both for practice and for the study of Christian worship, the Liturgical Movement has been of enormous importance. At the same time, it is a difficult phenomenon because it was so diverse and heterogeneous. The history of the Liturgical Movement is not the story of a linear development, the unfolding of a single vision, or the execution of a plan, but a story of trial and error, of successful and failed initiatives, of a lot of trying and dragging on and a serious amount of frustrations. Above all, however, it is a story of many different people who have developed an admirable energy and worked for a vision they passionately embraced.

As a starting point of the Liturgical Movement in Catholicism, scholars usually refer to some tendencies in the nineteenth century, in which the relaunch of monastic life after the French Revolution appears to have been decisive. Thus, in 1833 Dom Prosper Guéranger (1805–1875) reestablished the famous Benedictine St. Peter's Abbey of Solesmes in western France. Guéranger stood up as a fervent advocate of the Roman liturgy, which meant, among other things, that he was a fierce opponent of the neo-Gallican liturgies that had developed in several French dioceses in the seventeenth and eighteenth centuries. He was in favor of uniformity and of Roman authority and therefore in fact a barely concealed ultramontanist. An important vehicle for the creation of liturgical uniformity was the resurgence of Gregorian chant, for which the Abbey of Solesmes became famous at the instigation of Guéranger. Gregorian chant was seen as the only authentic musical form that fits the Roman Rite.

In addition, Dom Guéranger made himself known as someone who gave the study of the liturgy a big boost. With his *Institutions liturgiques* he inspired many scholars and clerics to write all kinds of articles on liturgical themes. His famous *L'année liturgique*, which, incidentally, remained unfinished, served as a model for combining historical knowledge, theological insights, and pastoral praxis relating to the liturgical year (*historique, mystique, pratique*). Numerous other noted representatives of the Liturgical

Movement after him dealt with elaborate commentaries on the liturgical feasts and times, their origins, their development, and their significance, in order to initiate believers into the opulent riches of the various celebrations of Christ, Mary, and the saints.

In the 1860s two German brothers, Maurus and Placidus Wolter, came to Solesmes. There they found the inspiration to raise the Abbey of Beuron in Baden-Württemberg from the ashes. Beuron itself would not only play a leading role in the early Liturgical Movement—among other things because of the renowned art school and the specific style that was developed there—but would also be remarkable through two (re)foundations: Maria Laach in the Rhineland (1892) and Maredsous in Belgium (1872). From Maredsous a house of study was established in Leuven in 1888 for monks studying at the university. The community was first led by Gerard van Caloen (1853–1932), under whose initiative a first popular missal was published for the needs of those attending Mass, and later by Robert de Kerchove (1846–1942). The latter was also commissioned to see where a new abbey could be founded in Leuven. Soon after the acquisition of the first few plots on the hill of the same name, Keizersberg Abbey came into being in 1899. The first abbot was Robert de Kerchove and the first prior Dom Columba Marmion (1858–1923). Both of them cocreated the religious and intellectual atmosphere within which Lambert Beauduin could flourish and "found" the Liturgical Movement.

Octave Beauduin (1873–1960) was ordained a priest of the Diocese of Liège in 1899 and, in that capacity, active in the workers' apostolate. However, despite his sincere commitment and enthusiasm, he did not see his spiritual hunger fulfilled. That is why in 1906, at the age of thirty-three, he entered the still young Abbey of Keizersberg and adopted the monastic name Lambert. There he was particularly impressed and influenced by the spiritual conferences, approach, and personality of Marmion. This grand figure opened up to him the unfathomable richness of Scripture, the Liturgy of the Hours (the Divine Office), and the Eucharist. Through prayer and study Beauduin discovered the inestimable profundity and fertility of the idea of the mystical body of Christ. As early as 1907 Marmion entrusted a course in ecclesiology to his pupil. Slowly but surely, Beauduin's desire grew to express what he had experienced and to translate it to the whole people of the church. For, in his opinion, laity and clergy were both unjustly devoid of the spiritual depth of the liturgy.

It is a speech given by Dom Lambert Beauduin in September 1909 at a congress of the Oeuvres Catholiques in Mechelen that is considered the symbolic and actual launch of the Liturgical Movement. The title of the speech was *La vraie prière de l'église* (The true prayer of the church), with which he of course alluded to the liturgy.[1] In it, Beauduin referred to Pope Pius X's motu proprio about church music, *Tra le sollecitudini*, in which the pope advocated an *actuosa participatio* (active participation) of the faithful in the public worship life of the church. The subsequent initiatives taken by Beauduin, with which he took many in tow, were numerous and well organized, thanks to the abbey community of which he was a member.

In 1914 Beauduin published a programmatic essay in which he explained his ideas in a more systematic way. The title was *La piété liturgique*, in which the concept of *piété* does not simply mean piety, and certainly not in a purely affective-devotional sense, but should rather be translated with "spirituality," as relating to the life of faith in all its dimensions.[2] Central to the first chapter is the above-mentioned quotation from Pius X about active participation, by means of which Beauduin actually emphasized that with the Liturgical Movement he wished above all to render a service to the church, in line with his personal "discovery" of what it means to participate (actively) in the body of Christ.

*La piété liturgique* consists of two parts of approximately the same length. In the first part, Beauduin reexamines the essence of the liturgy and asks himself why it did not find its way into the lives of ordinary Christians in his time. Among these factors, individualism is particularly disastrous. Beauduin therefore understands the liturgy as essentially social, public, and collective. It is also striking that he strongly insists on the hierarchical and sacred character of the liturgy, for ulterior promoters of the Liturgical Movement may find this surprising. In the second part, Beauduin reflects on the relation of the liturgy to asceticism, prayer, preaching, and theological science, respectively. In all cases he makes a plea for an intrinsic bond, which according to him ought to be strengthened. But he does by no means compromise on the primacy of the liturgy in these relations.

Back in Germany at the outset of the twentieth century, Ildefons Herwegen (1874–1946) entered the Abbey of Maria Laach in 1895, becoming abbot in 1913 and remaining so for more than three decades until his death. In this capacity he would establish himself as one of the greatest promoters of the Liturgical Movement in Germany (and beyond). He succeeded in getting almost the whole of his abbey involved in that story, with, as was the case at

---

1. Together with commentary by André Haquin, the original text was republished in a special issue of *Questions Liturgiques* on the occasion of the hundredth anniversary of the 1909 event: Lambert Beauduin, "La vraie prière de l'Église," *Questions Liturgiques/Studies in Liturgy* 91 (2010): 37–41.

2. Lambert Beauduin, *Liturgy: The Life of the Church*, trans. Virgil Michel (Farnborough, UK: Saint Michael's Abbey, 2003).

Keizersberg, a combination of scientific work, pastoral involvement, spiritual deepening, and—not unimportantly—the use of art.

Particularly noteworthy for liturgical scholarship is the founding of the journal *Jahrbuch für Liturgiewissenschaft*, the first issue of which appeared in 1921 and which became the *Archiv für Liturgiewissenschaft* in 1950, and of the Ecclesia Orans book series. In addition, mention should be made of the scientific series Liturgiewissenschaftliche Forschungen and Liturgiewissenschaftliche Quellen, which were later brought together in one series. In the crypt of the abbey, the first so-called *Gemeinschaftsmesse* (or *missa dialogata*) was celebrated in 1918, in which the people (instead of the acolyte or deacon, as the rubrics stipulated) expressed certain acclamations and responses in their mother tongue.

Several monks entered the abbey, who would play a gigantic role in the scientific work that accompanied the Liturgical Movement. A supporter of the first hour of Herwegen, Dom Kunibert Mohlberg (1878–1963), should certainly be mentioned. He was trained in philology and history and provided a historical-critical edition of important liturgical manuscripts from antiquity. However, the best-known name in this context is that of Dom Odo Casel (1886–1948), who was in charge of the abbey's scientific journal from 1921 to 1941 and, like his fellow brother Mohlberg, wrote many historical and philological essays.

Dom Odo Casel was also at the origin of the *Mysterienlehre*, which understood the liturgy and the celebration of the sacraments primarily as mysteries, partly in line with the mystery religions of the ancient world. Casel's most important book was *Das christliche Kultmysterium* (1932), in which several studies on the concept of mystery, the liturgical year, and the Eucharist were brought together.[3] On the theological level Casel was guided by Pauline and Johannine passages, by the church fathers, by liturgical documents from the ancient world, and by a connection between God's plan of salvation, revelation, and the ensuing history of salvation. An important concept connected to Casel's theory is that of the *Mysteriengegenwart*, literally the "presence" of "mysteries," but one could comment that it is slightly tautological.

During his life as a monk, Casel had also been spiritual adviser to the female convent of Herstelle. One of the sisters there was Aemiliana Löhr (1896–1972), who is considered one of his most important students and who published an intriguing book titled *Das Herrenjahr* (lit., "the year of the Lord"), completely steeped in Caselian mystery theology.[4] Although this aspect is often overlooked

3. Odo Casel, *The Mystery of Christian Worship* (New York: Crossroad, 1999).
4. Aemiliana Löhr, *The Mass through the Year*, 2 vols. (London: Longmans, 1959).

and hardly anyone knows Löhr today, it is crucial to point out that, despite obvious clerical tendencies, the Liturgical Movement was not merely a matter of innovation among celibate men.[5] It could have hardly been as successful as it has been if this was the case; it needed a broad reception in the life of God's people.

Not a monk of the abbey, but at home at Maria Laach and also a personal friend of Herwegen and other monks, was the priest of the Diocese of Mainz Romano Guardini (1885–1968). He wrote the first book in the abbey's Ecclesia Orans series under the title *Vom Geist der Liturgie* (*The Spirit of the Liturgy*, 1918),[6] even before obtaining the degree of doctor of theology at the University of Bonn.[7] The book struck like a bomb and was a great success. Guardini dealt with, among other things, the seriousness and the playfulness of liturgy, and meticulously explained what liturgy has to do with "logos" and truth.

Furthermore, Guardini wrote in the very first issue of the *Jahrbuch für Liturgiewissenschaft* an article titled "Über die systematische Methode in der Liturgiewissenschaft" (On the systematic method in liturgical studies). In it he develops, among other things, the idea that the liturgy is "etwas Verbindliches," by which he means both that it is connecting (people, among themselves and to God; in other words, it establishes communion) and that it has something obliging, in the sense of not remaining just free or noncommittal. Another high-profile contention from that article is the parallel that Guardini sees between *Liturgiewissenschaft* (liturgical science) and *Rechtswissenschaft* (law studies).

Romano Guardini did not leave anything untouched on a pastoral level either. He was the great inspirer of the Quickborn Movement, which offered many young adults an authentic experience of the liturgy, worship, and the life of faith. The center of the movement was Burg Rothenfels, located on the banks of the river Main between Würzburg and Aschaffenburg. Guardini excelled in enthusing young people to live a life anchored in the liturgy and prayer. His inspiration marked the lives of many, who later remembered their experiences at the Burg with great pleasure. A chapel was redecorated in the castle keep. For that Guardini collaborated with the architect Rudolf Schwarz (1897–1961), who was an important advocate of the Liturgical Movement, especially after World War II, with many other innovative designs for churches.

---

5. Katherine E. Harmon, *There Were Also Many Women There: Lay Women in the Liturgical Movement in the United States 1926–59* (Collegeville, MN: Liturgical Press, 2012).

6. Romano Guardini, *The Spirit of the Liturgy*, trans. Ada Lane, Milestones in Catholic Theology (New York: Crossroad, 1998).

7. Joseph Ratzinger's 2000 essay is clearly conceived with a wink to Guardini. Joseph Ratzinger, *The Spirit of the Liturgy* (San Francisco: Ignatius, 2000). One could argue that Guardini's influence on Ratzinger can also be observed in the latter's Jesus trilogy and other works.

## The Liturgical Movement between World War II and Vatican II

Between the Second World War and the Second Vatican Council things developed swiftly, with several "successes," collaborations, and reforms. Consequently, the "dossier" of the liturgy was very well prepared on the eve of the Second Vatican Council, and the constitution on the liturgy, *Sacrosanctum concilium*, was the first document to be approved by the council fathers—something they did by an overwhelming majority. During the council everything was set in motion for the practical reform of the liturgy.[8] It helped that there were so many people from different countries who already knew each other well from before the council. In this context, four clusters of events, initiatives, and documents deserve to be highlighted.

First, we need to look at the magisterium—that is, the teaching authority of the church as embodied (in Catholicism) by the hierarchy of bishops and popes. In 1947 the encyclical *Mediator Dei* (*et hominum*) by Pope Pius XII was published. It was the very first encyclical in church history to deal explicitly and exclusively with the worship of the church. The reception of the encyclical was mainly enthusiastic among the representatives of the Liturgical Movement. The intention to really make something of it was reinforced, and the critical points made by the pope—such as the danger of "archaeologism" and possible exaggerations in liturgical theory that did not pay sufficient attention to what is uniquely Christian (e.g., certain interpretations of the *Mysterienlehre*)—could actually be endorsed. It was also noted in the reception of the encyclical that *Mediator Dei* had strong similarities in content with an earlier encyclical of Pius XII, *Mystici Corporis*, which appeared in 1943 and in which the church was referred to as the mystical body of Christ.

The second cluster is the reform of the Easter vigil and then Holy Week as a whole.[9] After the encyclical, the restoration in glory of the Easter vigil, which had become a true symbolic record for the lamentable state in which the liturgy had entered in the eyes of the Liturgical Movement, constituted another highlight.[10] In the post-Tridentine period, the Easter vigil, instead of a festive and public celebration on the eve of Easter, had deteriorated into a private prayer of the priest on the morning of Holy Saturday. It had sadly become anything but an event in which the faithful could actively participate.

---

8. Piero Marini, *A Challenging Reform: Realizing the Vision of the Liturgical Renewal 1963–1975*, ed. Mark R. Francis and Keith F. Pecklers (Collegeville, MN: Liturgical Press, 2007).

9. Patrick Prétot, "La réforme de la semaine sainte sous Pie XII (1951–1956): Enjeux d'un premier pas vers la réforme liturgique de Vatican II," *Questions Liturgiques/Studies in Liturgy* 93 (2012): 196–217.

10. Robert Amiet, *La veillée pascale dans l'Église latine*, vol. 1, *Le rite romain* (Paris: Cerf, 1999).

To this end, stimulated by many partisans of the Easter vigil and by thorough scholarship, such as *Le mystère pascal* by the French Oratorian Louis Bouyer (1913–2004),[11] the pope approved in 1951 the decrees that revalued the Easter vigil and restored it to its old form, with the blessing of fire and the rite of light, the readings from Scripture, the renewal of baptismal vows, the Eucharist, and so on. Not much later, in 1955, in the same spirit, the whole of Holy Week was reviewed and reformed. International and interdisciplinary committees were set up for these two reforms. Their secretary was none other than the Italian Lazarist Annibale Bugnini (1912–1982), who would later become one of the architects of the postconciliar reform of the liturgy.

Third, the establishment of several institutes in different countries—we will look at only France and Germany here—cannot be underestimated. They were the result of different kinds of cooperation and were differently integrated in ecclesiastical and academic centers. But what they had in common was that they promptly undertook a mountain of work and that they were led by very enthusiastic and competent figures.

In Paris, the Centre de Pastorale Liturgique (CPL) was founded as early as 1943 and was subsequently incorporated into the services of the French Bishops' Conference. The foundation was mainly the work of some forward-looking Dominicans, notably Aimon-Marie Roguet (1906–1991) and Pie Duployé (1906–1990). The periodical *La Maison-Dieu*, the first volume of which appeared in 1945, was linked from the outset to the CPL, now transformed into the SNPLS (Service national de pastorale liturgique et sacramentelle). For the very first issue of *La Maison-Dieu*, Dom Lambert Beauduin wrote a programmatic article.

The Institut Supérieur de Liturgie (ISL) was also founded in Paris in 1956 within the contours of one of the most prestigious private universities of the Catholic Church in France, the Institut Catholique de Paris. The intention was to turn it into a research and study center where specialists in the history and sources of the liturgy would be trained, who in turn could design, teach, and staff liturgy programs all over the country and beyond. The first director was the Belgian Benedictine Dom Bernard Botte (1893–1980) from Keizersberg Abbey, who was succeeded by the Dominican and medieval liturgy specialist Pierre-Marie Gy (1922–2004). Renowned professors at the ISL include Pierre Jounel, Irénée-Henri Dalmais, Jean-Yves Hameline, Paul De Clerck, Louis-Marie Chauvet, and Patrick Prétot.

11. Louis Bouyer, *Le mystère pascal: Méditation sur la liturgie des trois derniers jours de la Semaine Sainte* (Paris: Cerf, 2009). The original version appeared in 1945 in the renowned Lex Orandi series.

In 1947 the Liturgisches Institut was established in Trier; from 1989, the year of the reunification of Germany, it was officially called Deutsches Liturgisches Institut. Its first director was Johannes Wagner; he was in charge from 1950 to 1985, after which he was succeeded by Heinrich Rennings. This institute combines efforts in the field of the liturgy of the German dioceses. It acquired a strong reputation as a center of expertise and established excellent links with like-minded people in France. It still publishes the journals *Liturgisches Jahrbuch* and *Gottesdienst* and puts an impressive library at the service of anyone interested in liturgy.

Fourth, there were trend-setting international meetings associated with the Liturgical Movement, which had in the meantime acquired an explicitly international character. The pioneers in different countries knew each other, there were exchanges and collaborations, and certainly the academics were generally well acquainted with the professional literature that appeared in different languages. Of particular importance was the Liturgical Congress of Assisi in 1956.[12] It was attended by about fifteen hundred people from most European countries, but also some from other continents; however, one could not participate unless one had received an invitation. It was directed by the Congregation of Rites under the leadership of Cardinal Gaetano Cicognani. The theme was the liturgy and/as pastoral ministry, but the hot question of the celebration of the liturgy in the vernacular could not be discussed. It is no surprise that this theme, which had touched hearts so much and had become yet another symbolic dossier, was nevertheless touched on. This happened, for example, in the contribution to the congress by the Austrian Jesuit and renowned liturgical historian Josef Andreas Jungmann (1889–1975).

### Sacrosanctum Concilium

Despite some opposition from the Congregation of Rites, the Vatican dicastery who had been in control of liturgical affairs in the Roman Catholic Church since 1588 (i.e., in the immediate aftermath of the Council of Trent), there were high expectations with respect to the document on the liturgy sent to the council fathers just prior to their first gathering at the Vatican in the autumn of 1962. The work that had been done in preparation of this so-called schema was broadly appreciated by bishops as well as by theological commentators.[13]

---

12. Keith F. Pecklers, *Liturgy: The Illustrated History* (Mahwah, NJ: Paulist Press, 2012), 172–73.

13. A wealth of information about how the liturgy constitution came into being can be found in Hermann Schmidt, *La constitution de la sainte liturgie: texte, genèse, commentaire, documents* (Brussels: Lumen Vitae, 1966).

And although it was otherwise planned, the liturgy document was decided to be the first one for the council to deal with. During its first sessions the council appointed a special liturgy commission whose task it was to take care of the redaction of the text and to thereby carefully include the observations that individual council fathers had made, either through their interventions in the basilica or in written form. The members of this commission worked hard on the necessary revisions and additions between the closure of the first session and the late summer of 1963.

During the second autumn the council fathers then gathered again in St. Peter's Basilica in Rome in October and November 1963, and they discussed the final version of the text in fifteen meetings, making final suggestions for improvements and modifications. It was clear that the liturgy was dear to the heart of the council fathers. They considered it something at the very core of the life of faith, which therefore needed to be approached with utmost care. They also underscored the pastoral pertinence of the celebration of the sacraments—which partially explains why the issue of the vernacular language was among the most fiercely debated points. The final vote on the liturgy constitution, which received the name *Sacrosanctum concilium* after the first Latin words of the text, took place on December 4, 1963. An impressive majority of 2,162 council fathers approved the text, forty-six were opposed, and seven cast an invalid vote.

The document consists of 130 paragraphs spread over eight chapters. The logic behind the ordering of the material follows a classical classification, with primacy of place yielded to the Eucharist, then the other sacraments (and sacramentals), and subsequently the Liturgy of the Hours, the liturgical year, liturgical music, and the relation between liturgy and the arts. In each of these chapters, *Sacrosanctum concilium* sets out elements for a fundamental theological vision first, before it discusses matters of a more practical nature.

However, the most innovative and to some extent the most important chapter of the document is the first. It is also the most elaborate one, with forty-two paragraphs in sum—meaning that it contains one-third of the entire text. The chapter stands out in that it reflects a thorough theological vision on the foundation, the meaning, and the significance of the church's worship. It roots the liturgy in the economy and history of salvation, and thus in God's revelation to humankind (§5). It centers on the mediatory role of Christ and the multiple ways in which he is present in the liturgy and the sacraments (§7). It staunchly promotes the full, conscious, and active participation of the faithful (§14). It puts forward the idea that the celebration of the liturgy is the "source" and the "summit" of all the church's activities (§10). And it establishes a vision for an encompassing reform of the liturgy, so that the true spirit of the liturgy may permeate all the layers and the members of the church.

It is important to underline that, according to Vatican II and *Sacrosanctum concilium* in particular, liturgy is not *just* liturgy. It is not *just* an area requesting special attention or a sector of policy next to other sectors. To the contrary, the liturgy is intimately interwoven with the church as a whole; in and through it the church comes to fruition and manifests itself. Therefore, it is meaningful to acknowledge, in hindsight, that the very fact that the council fathers had started with a discussion of the liturgy, and the fact that they so enthusiastically approved the document about it, set the agenda for the council as a whole.[14] In other words, *Sacrosanctum concilium* is more than just a document about one aspect of the church's life. Its very essence is at stake.

## Implementation of the Liturgical Reforms

After the promulgation of *Sacrosanctum concilium*, the church faced the enormous challenge to execute the practical work of the liturgical reform called for by the council fathers. Not only was the scope of the task enormous but the exact direction of the march was open to interpretation, which inevitably gave rise to discussions and conflicts. In some cases fairly precise guidelines had been given, in others this was only vaguely the case, and in yet others points of reference were completely lacking. In any case, there was no straying to get out of the starting blocks. Still during the council, Pope Paul VI founded the Consilium ad exsequendam Constitutionem de sacra Liturgia, the commission for the implementation of the liturgy constitution. Cardinal Giacomo Lercaro (1891–1976) was reinstated as president of this new body, and the already mentioned Annibale Bugnini was named secretary. Thanks to Bugnini's memoirs the concrete course of the liturgical reform is relatively well documented.[15]

The main objective of the Consilium was the production of new *editiones typicae* of the liturgical books in Latin, which then had to be translated into all possible national and vernacular languages under the guidance of local bishops' conferences. Within the Consilium, a central umbrella level and a whole number of *coeti* (working groups) were established, dealing with specific aspects of the liturgical reform (e.g., the *ordinarium* of the Eucharist, the

14. Massimo Faggioli, *True Reform: Liturgy and Ecclesiology in* Sacrosanctum Concilium (Collegeville, MN: Liturgical Press, 2012).

15. Annibale Bugnini, *The Reform of the Liturgy (1948–1975)*, trans. Matthew O'Connell (Collegeville, MN: Liturgical Press, 1990).

lectionary, infant baptism, and ordinations). Each *coetus* had a responsible leader who was in contact with the central administration. There were meetings per working group and general meetings. Both specialists in liturgy and bishops were represented in the Consilium, and care was taken to reach a sufficiently large consensus in the procedures for approval. There was also—in some cases very intense—consultation with the highest level, the pope (in this case Paul VI).

In the course of the years, official documents were produced which provided both normative and practical answers to further questions raised by the liturgy reform. In the meantime, five such documents have appeared: *Inter oecumenici* (1964), *Tres abhinc annos* (1967), *Liturgicae instaurationes* (1970), *Varietates legitimae* (1994), and *Liturgiam authenticam* (2001). The first three of these documents still leaned strongly against the pressing practice of liturgical reform in full development. It was only later that *Varietates legitimae* addressed additional questions concerning the inculturation of the liturgy.

The promulgation of *Liturgiam authenticam* in 2001 was uplifting, because in the eyes of many theologians it seemed as if acquired principles for translating the liturgy according to the model of "dynamic equivalence" had suddenly become suspect, and as if because of this the document *Comme le prévoit* of 1969 had been consigned to the wastepaper basket. All in all, this is a very complicated history, in which the role of the International Commission on English in the Liturgy (ICEL) in the English-speaking world has certainly had a decisive influence on the politics of the Vatican. In any case, Pope Francis has in the meantime, through the motu proprio *Magum principium*, again placed a greater responsibility on the bishops' conferences when it comes to translating and publishing official versions of the liturgical books.[16]

## Practical Implications for Worship

What can we learn today from this intriguing history of the Liturgical Movement and its absolute culmination point, the promulgation of the Second Vatican Council's constitution on the liturgy, *Sacrosanctum concilium*? I limit myself to three thoughts.

First, it has become clear how important academic scholarship is for the church's life of worship and prayer and for the celebration of the feasts and the sacraments. Any attempt at driving a wedge between the "pastoral" or

---

16. Kevin W. Irwin, *Pope Francis and the Liturgy: The Call to Holiness and Mission* (Mahwah, NJ: Paulist Press, 2020).

"practical" side of liturgy and the serious study of it at universities or other institutions of higher learning does not do justice to the integrative view on liturgy as it was promoted by the Liturgical Movement and Vatican II. In this context, a special role may be attributed to theologies of liturgy and liturgical theologies worthy of that name—that is, theologies that attempt to build bridges between pure historical or textual research and contemporary real-life situations by consistently repeating and explaining that liturgy and sacraments are rooted in the divine-human encounter.

Second, building bridges is also necessary between the multiple shapes and forms and customs of the church's liturgy, on the one hand, and the sociocultural environments where these celebrations happen, on the other. Recently, there have been some worries about the still increasing impact of secularism on the church, not only in the West but also in other parts of the world. I think that defensive strategies are unfruitful, both those that aim at protecting the church's liturgy and therefore take an aggressive stance toward secular culture, and those that, inversely, uncritically embrace secularism and consequently despise anything that the liturgical tradition of the church stands for. As usual, wisdom here means sailing a safe middle course and doing the laborious efforts of subtle discernment.

Third, and finally, I would like to mention again the notion of the liturgical spirit, which was prominent in the emerging Liturgical Movement as well as in *Sacrosanctum concilium*. The liturgical spirit entails a fine-tuned sensitivity for what liturgy really is and does, and is meant to pervade the entire church's mentality. Individual believers, clergy, and laity—no less than its structures, institutions, documents, and discourses—should all be permeated by a truly liturgical spirit when they reach out to the poor, when they sing God's praises, when they take care of souls, when they draw inspiration from Scripture, when they express gratitude for grace and when, in so doing, they prepare the kingdom, and—maybe above anything else—when they embody Christ's call for unity.

## For Further Reading

Beauduin, Lambert. *Liturgy: The Life of the Church*. Translated by Virgil Michel. 3rd ed. Farnborough, UK: Saint Michael's Abbey, 2003.

Ferrone, Rita. *Liturgy: Sacrosanctum Concilium*. Rediscovering Vatican II. Mahwah, NJ: Paulist Press, 2007.

Geldhof, Joris. *Liturgy and Secularism: Beyond the Divide*. Collegeville, MN: Liturgical Press, 2018.

Guardini, Romano. *The Spirit of the Liturgy*. Translated by Ada Lane. New York: Crossroad, 1998.

Irwin, Kevin W. *What We Have Done and What We Have Failed to Do: Assessing the Liturgical Reforms of Vatican II*. Mahwah, NJ: Paulist Press, 2013.

Pilcher, Carmel, David Orr, and Elisabeth Harrington, eds. *Vatican Council II: Reforming Liturgy*. Adelaide, Australia: ATF Theology, 2013.

# PART 5

# Protestant Worship

# — 11 —

# Lutheran Practices of Worship

## *Craig A. Satterlee*

The Augsburg Confession (1530), the principal confession of faith of the Lutheran Church, makes clear that the Lutheran Reformation was fueled by theological conviction—"we cannot obtain forgiveness of sin or righteousness before God through our merit, work, or satisfactions, but . . . we receive forgiveness of sin and become righteous before God out of grace for Christ's sake through faith"[1]—and not worship practice. Understanding themselves as a reforming movement within the Roman Catholic Church, Lutheran reformers were generally conservative in terms of worship practices. The Augsburg Confession declares,

> The Mass is celebrated among us with greater devotion and earnestness than among our opponents. The people are instructed more regularly and with the greatest diligence concerning the holy sacrament, to what purpose it was instituted, and how it is to be used, namely, as a comfort to terrified consciences. In this way, the people are drawn to Communion and to the Mass. . . . Moreover, no noticeable changes have been made in the public celebration of the Mass, except that in certain places German hymns are sung alongside the Latin responses for

---

1. "The Augsburg Confession," article 4, in *The Book of Concord*, ed. Robert Kolb and Timothy J. Wengert (Minneapolis: Fortress, 2000), 38.

the instruction and exercise of the people. . . . Thus, the Mass remains among us in its proper use, as it was observed formerly in the church.[2]

Nevertheless, Martin Luther's (1483–1546) most significant sacramental writing, *On the Babylonian Captivity of the Church* (1520),[3] laid the foundation for worship and sacrament that all Protestant traditions build on.

## On the Babylonian Captivity of the Church

In *On the Babylonian Captivity of the Church*, Martin Luther extends to worship, sacrament, and pastoral care the Reformation's overriding concern that salvation is a free gift from God that cannot be earned by human efforts. The sacraments, then, are signs and promises of God's gift of salvation, instituted by Christ, and all humans can do is receive them in faith. For Luther, the word "promise," by which he means a scriptural promise expressed as a word of Christ and treated as an imperative to us—"Do this" and "Go therefore and . . . baptize"[4]—is the key to defining a sacrament. Applying this standard to the medieval sacramental system, Luther reduces the number of sacraments from seven to two: only baptism and the Eucharist possess "both the divinely instituted sign and the promise of forgiveness of sins"[5] and qualify as sacraments. Luther asserts that, while these two sacraments are God-given promises to the faithful, the antichrist has captured them, and current practice denies true Christians freedom in the gospel, just as Israel was captive in Babylon. Luther devotes the remainder of the treatise to expounding on the problems with the seven medieval sacraments.

Luther asserts that the Mass is bound by three captivities: withholding the cup from the laity; using the term "transubstantiation"—the conversion of the bread and wine of the Eucharist into the body and blood of Christ at consecration, with only the appearances of bread and wine still remaining—as the required formula for defining Christ's presence in the Eucharist; and making the Mass into a sacrifice, a work people offer God to obtain favor, rather than a gift from God. The only sacrifice humans can offer God are responses of faith, as we offer our prayer, praise, and service to God. Luther's critique of the Mass as sacrifice challenged not only worship but also the accepted

2. "The Augsburg Confession," article 24, in Kolb and Wengert, *Book of Concord*, 68.
3. Martin Luther, "The Babylonian Captivity of the Church, 1520," in *Luther's Works*, American Edition, ed. Jaroslav Pelikan and Helmut T. Lehmann (Philadelphia: Muehlenberg and Fortress; St. Louis: Concordia, 1955–1986), 36:11–126 (hereafter cited as *LW*).
4. Matt. 26:26–28; 28:19; Mark 14:22–24; Luke 22:19–20; 1 Cor. 11:24.
5. Martin Luther, "Large Catechism," in Kolb and Wengert, *Book of Concord*, 457.

understanding of the ordained priesthood, who offered the sacrifice, and church finances, which came from people paying for priests to offer the sacrifice on their behalf.

Luther offers little critique of baptism. Since God is the actor in sacraments, while we physically baptize, God actually baptizes.[6] Luther writes, "Baptism, then, signifies two things—death and resurrection, that is, full and complete justification."[7] The captivity of baptism is that Christians forget the genuine promise God makes to the faithful that salvation applied in baptism is a free and lifelong gift.

Luther had a very high opinion of penance. However, he reluctantly determined that, despite the command and promise in John 20:22–23, penance lacked a command of Christ and a material sign, and therefore did not qualify as a sacrament. Confirmation, ordination, marriage, and extreme unction are not sacraments because they are not based on God's instituting word. While they are not to be scorned, these rites are not guaranteed to be effectual signs of God's promise to those who receive them in faith, since they lack the essential words of Christ necessary to make them sacraments.

## Luther and Liturgical Reform

While bold in theological critique, Luther was restrained in actual worship reform. In 1523 he wrote, "The service now in common use everywhere goes back to genuine Christian beginnings."[8] Whenever possible, Luther sought to preserve what he considered to be the ancient worship forms. Moreover, he was pastorally sensitive to preserve the people's piety and not scandalize them with sweeping changes. For him, a break with the past could be justified only by the authority of the Word of God.

Luther defended practices and piety many of his impatient followers felt were more in keeping with the medieval past than the Reformation. Luther called these practices *adiaphora*—matters indifferent to effecting salvation. Unless a practice communicated something obviously false, Luther could accommodate it. So the elevation, vestments, and images tended to remain rather than be abolished. They were firmly lodged in popular piety, and Luther saw no need to trample on them. Eventually, tolerance for adiaphora became the Lutheran approach to matters that were scripturally neutral yet had great popular appeal.

6. Luther, "Babylonian Captivity of the Church, 1520," *LW* 36:62.
7. Luther, "Babylonian Captivity of the Church, 1520," *LW* 36:67.
8. Martin Luther, "Concerning the Order of Public Worship, 1523," *LW* 53:11.

## The Mass

In 1521 liturgical reform became necessary when Pope Leo X excommunicated Luther. Luther published a reformed Mass in 1523 (in Latin) and in 1526 (in German). He retained a basically traditional shape for the Mass. In keeping with his theological conviction, he removed everything that, in his view, reflected a theology that contradicted Scripture and the gospel. While Luther intended his rites for local use rather than to be normative everywhere, his popularity resulted in his work being widely imitated.

To eliminate any sense of sacrifice, Luther discarded the eucharistic prayer, except for the words of institution, which resulted in Lutherans understanding that these words alone effect the consecration of the bread and wine. Luther brought to its logical conclusion a medieval eucharistic trajectory, developed from the teachings of Ambrose of Milan (ca. 339–397), that the words of institution alone consecrate; therefore, everything else could be eliminated. Since the canon was always recited in silence during the Mass, the laity had never heard it and few were likely to notice this change. In fact, the ceremonial they could observe was virtually unchanged. Therefore, despite Luther's repudiation of the doctrine of transubstantiation, the average worshiper would find it difficult to differentiate between transubstantiation and Luther's teaching that Christ is present in, with, and under the bread and wine.

Luther believed that by virtue of baptism all Christians are called to minister to one another in whatever station they might find themselves placed. At Mass, Christians are not spectators who passively participate, but play their own priestly role through active participation. Luther therefore intended that laypeople commune frequently; regrettably, this was a radical shift as most laypeople communed only at the very greatest festivals. To receive both the bread and the cup at every celebration required laypeople to envision themselves as priests, who communed and received both elements weekly or even daily.

Luther understood that, for people to actively participate, worship must be accessible to them. The vernacular, or the language of ordinary people, allowed people to pray together so all could hear and speak as one body. Thus, Luther made increasing use of German.

Luther also employed music as a means by which all could exercise their priestly ministry. He considered music one of God's greatest gifts. He endeavored to structure the *German Mass* so major portions of it could be sung in German paraphrase. In the *German Mass*, lessons are chanted by the priest, and the congregation joins in singing standard parts such as the Creed and the German *Sanctus*—a paraphrase of Isaiah 6. By the end of 1523, while the Mass was still in Latin, Luther had begun to write vernacular hymns. By the end of the sixteenth century, a whole series of hymns of the day had been codified to accompany each Gospel reading in the Lutheran Sunday service. Exercising their priestly role, the congregation participated fully in the singing of hymns and the rest of the liturgy. As a result, Lutheran worship became intrinsically musical, and hymns were understood as a way to teach faith.

### Baptism

Among Luther's greatest contributions is a baptismal piety, a baptismal spirituality, or even a baptismal way of living.[9] His entire life was a celebration of baptism, because he found in baptism both lifelong assurance that God has forgiven our sin and daily motivation to live as those who belong to Christ. For Luther, baptism is a sign, promise, and participation in what God does for humanity in the life, death, and resurrection of Jesus Christ. He argued that God's promise in baptism "should swallow up your whole life, body and soul, and give it forth again at the last day, clad in the robe of glory and immortality."[10] He declared, "There is no greater comfort on earth than baptism." Baptism is "so great, gracious, and full of comfort, we should diligently see to it that we ceaselessly, joyfully, and from the heart thank, praise, and honor God for it."[11] Luther is said to have made the sign of the cross over himself daily while reminding himself that he was baptized. In so doing, he found the courage to face each day. He encouraged Christians to "regard baptism and put it to use in such a way that we may draw strength and comfort from it when our sins or conscience oppress us, and say: 'But I am baptized. And if I am baptized, I have the promise that I shall be saved and have eternal life, both in soul and body.'"[12] The goal of Luther's baptismal spirituality was that all Christians live each day trusting in the assurance that they are saved.

Luther published two baptismal rites. His rite of 1523 retained most of the medieval ceremony, and the only change most people would notice was the exclusive use of German. Luther added his "flood prayer" over the font, which connects each baptism to the Old Testament events of Noah's flood and the Red Sea crossing.[13] In 1526 Luther produced a revised baptismal rite with significant changes. He removed a number of secondary ceremonies, including blowing on the child, the *ephphatha* (see Mark 7:34), two anointings, and the

9. See Dennis L. Bushkofsky and Craig A. Satterlee, *The Christian Life: Baptism and Life Passages*, Using Evangelical Lutheran Worship (Minneapolis: Augsburg Fortress, 2008), 2:4–9.
10. Luther, "Babylonian Captivity of the Church, 1520," *LW* 36:69.
11. Martin Luther, "The Holy and Blessed Sacrament of Baptism, 1519," *LW* 35:34, 42.
12. Luther, "Large Catechism," in Kolb and Wengert, *Book of Concord*, 462.
13. Martin Luther, "The Order of Baptism, 1523," *LW* 53:19–40.

giving of the candle. Luther retained marking the child with the sign of the cross, the flood prayer, the use of Mark 10:13–16 ("Suffer little children"), renunciation of the devil, questions on the creed, dipping or submersion (Luther's preferred method), and giving of the white robe.[14]

Luther wanted to retain penance as an important part of people's piety. He deplored the confession of sins by numbers and type but advocated confession of all that burdened one's conscience. He provided two forms for confession to a priest (1529 and 1531), although he allowed that any Christian, by virtue of baptism, could pronounce another forgiven. The rites were simple in form so that people could confess their sins without cataloging them by type and number. Most important, satisfactions[15] or acts of penance were not to be imposed to receive God's absolution.

Luther did not consider confirmation a sacrament because it too does not have a divine promise connected to it by which it delivers salvation. For pastoral reasons, Luther was willing for the pastor to examine children and lay hands on them in confirmation. Differing conceptions among Lutherans led to confirmation becoming something of a graduation exercise, in which children publicly show their knowledge of the Christian faith.

### Preaching

One of the greatest changes Luther brought about was in the form and function of preaching as worship. Luther held preaching in such high regard that he called it the *viva vox Christi* and the *viva vox evangeli*—the living voice of Christ and the living voice of the gospel.[16] For, when the gospel is preached, the Holy Spirit produces faith in those who hear the gospel. In addition to producing faith, preaching also teaches the basics of Christianity and liberates the people from the intermediary authority of the hierarchy. Luther therefore stressed the importance of hearing the Word of God expounded "since the preaching and teaching of God's Word is the most important part of divine service."[17] In fact, Luther declared that "a Christian congregation should never gather together without the preaching of God's Word and prayer."[18] He restored biblical preaching to the Mass, included sermons in morning and evening prayer (matins and vespers), and insisted that even weddings and other public occasions include preaching.

14. Martin Luther, "The Order of Baptism Newly Revised, 1526," *LW* 53:61–90.

15. Satisfactions are actions taken to make amends for committed sins.

16. *LW* 52:206; see also *Martin Luther's Werke*, Kritische Gesamtausgabe, 73 vols. (Weimar: Herman Böhlaus Nachfolger, 1883–2009), 12:259, 8–13; 12:259; 12:275.

17. Martin Luther, "The German Mass and Order of Service, 1526," *LW* 53:68.

18. Luther, "Concerning the Order of Public Worship, 1523," *LW* 53:11.

Preaching was also strengthened by Luther's reform of the liturgical calendar. Luther endeavored to keep the major festivals with the long-established Epistle and Gospel readings. His chief reform was to observe only the Lord's days and the festivals of the Lord. He retained Circumcision, Epiphany, Purification, and Annunciation as feasts of Christ. Luther thought all the feasts of the nonbiblical saints should be abolished, or if anything in them deserves observing, it should be brought into the Sunday sermon.

Luther's reform of daily public prayer—matins and vespers—in his *German Mass* (1526) also strengthened preaching. Luther intended these services be used primarily in schools and so retained Latin as well as German for some of the psalms, canticles, and readings. Most prayers were in the vernacular in parish churches and spoken so the congregation could both hear and understand. A feature of all these services is the emphasis on the systematic reading of Scripture; Luther insisted an entire chapter be read at each service. On Sundays there was a sermon on the Epistle at matins, on the Gospel at Mass, and on the Old Testament lesson at vespers.

Yet Luther's chief contribution to improving preaching in worship was his own example.[19] Suddenly confronted with the task of teaching many former priests to preach, Luther produced a series of postils or sermon collections for them to imitate. Luther's sermons are scriptural, usually affirming a literal rather than allegorical interpretation. His approach is to deal with Scripture in a direct and earthy manner. His goal is to explain Scripture rather than moralize the congregation. Luther's sermons are not rhetorical; his style is folksy and anecdotal, aimed at helping people visualize the biblical narrative using vivid examples from everyday life.

### Ordination

Luther understood baptism as initiating Christians into the "priesthood of all believers," and inaugurating each Christian's ministry to the community and the community's ministry to that person. Through baptism, all became priests and assumed a priestly role in church and society. In keeping with this baptismal theology, Luther initially insisted that ordained ministry is purely functional, "for whoever comes out of the water of baptism can boast that he is already a consecrated priest, bishop and pope, although of course it is not seemly that just anybody should exercise such office. . . . There is no true, basic difference between laymen and priests, . . . except for the sake of office and work, but not for the sake of status."[20] Later on, Luther was more inclined

19. Fred W. Meuser, *Luther the Preacher* (Minneapolis: Augsburg Fortress, 1983).
20. Martin Luther, "To the Christian Nobility of the German Nations," *LW* 44:128–29.

to stress ordained ministry as Christ's gift and legacy to his church. Luther came to regard ordination as part of the divine order. "The public ministry of the Word," he wrote, "ought to be established by holy ordination as the highest and greatest of the functions of the church."[21] Ordination, while not essential to a Christian community, is highly desirable and in accord with God's intention for the church. Luther produced a rite for "The Ordination of Ministers of the Word" (1539), which culminated in the presbyters imposing their hands on the ordinands while the principal ordinator[22] says the Lord's Prayer.[23]

### Pastoral Rites

Luther did not consider marriage a sacrament. His marriage rite (1529)[24] is perhaps his most conventional. It follows local custom in a simple exchange of vows and rings at the church door. Luther added Matthew 19:6, "What God has joined . . . ," giving the impression that marriage is indeed a sacrament. Marriage is then pronounced, and all process into the church for Scripture readings, a sermon, and a blessing.

### Funerals

Luther eliminated vigils, Masses for the dead, processions, purgatory, and anything else done on behalf of the dead to secure their salvation, since salvation was purely by the grace of God. Instead, funerals proclaimed the resurrection with comforting hymns, and anything suggesting purgatory was avoided. Luther provided no rites for extreme unction or anointing of the sick.

---

After Luther's death in 1546, Lutheran worship developed in diverse ways in different regions. Continuing the medieval approach of a variety of similar rites for different dioceses and religious orders, Lutherans saw no need to impose uniformity through standardized rites. While Lutherans shared "justification by grace through faith" as a common liturgical criterion, various cities and principalities developed rites based on combinations of Luther's rites, the prevailing local practices, and the local reformer's own preferences. Most of the regional churches underwent similar experiences, made unique by their cultural and social differences.

21. Martin Luther, "Concerning the Ministry, 1523," *LW* 40:11.
22. The ordinator is the person who is ordaining.
23. Martin Luther, "The Ordination of Ministers of the Word, 1539," *LW* 53:110–16.
24. Martin Luther, "The Order of Marriage for Common Pastors, 1529," *LW* 53:124.

## A Brief History of Lutheran Worship

Scholars approach the history of Lutheran worship as five overlapping periods: Lutheran orthodoxy (1550–1700), Pietism (1650–1800), the Enlightenment (1700–1800), restorationism (1800–1950), and ecumenism (1950–2020). Issues from these periods continue to find expression in Lutheran worship today.

### Lutheran Orthodoxy

The period of Lutheran orthodoxy (1550–1700) represents the century following Luther's death, in which the Reformation went from a movement to an institution. As the Lutheran reformation spread, new church orders were produced to provide standards and forms for congregations to use. More importantly, a distinctively Lutheran way of being Christian developed.

Lutheran piety was shaped by many factors. Lutherans made widespread use of Luther's catechisms, which became the basis of popular belief, to teach their children through memorization. Lutheran worship reinforced catechetical instruction through preaching and the repetition of hymns. Lutheran piety included a strong commitment to the doctrine of the real presence of Christ in the Eucharist, a belief made more important by controversy with non-Lutherans.

In this period, a central schematic for a place of worship evolved. Lutherans emphasized the ability of the whole congregation to see and hear all that happened at the altar, pulpit, and font. These three loci became the central focus of buildings, often arranged so that pulpit, altar, and font were located near one another in front of the congregation. Lutherans came to appreciate a burst of natural light above the altar.

The chief liturgical controversy of this period was over what constituted adiaphora and therefore what was theologically allowed. Should all visual images, ceremonial, and practices that the reformers themselves had not explicitly condemned as endangering true doctrine be retained? Generally, traditionalism prevailed, and existing churches were not purified of images, although not many were introduced in new buildings. Much of the medieval ceremonial remained, especially those things that emphasized the real presence of Christ in the Eucharist.

Despite Luther's goal to celebrate Holy Communion more frequently, in practice it became less frequent, as it had been too radical a change from medieval practice for the laity to embrace. The first half of the service, the ante-communion, became the usual Sunday celebration.

Confession was usually linked to announcement of intention to commune. Saturday evening confessional vesper services were observed in some areas and do not seem to have been supplanted by confession to another layperson. A rite of confirmation gradually came to be common, partly because of the close connection between church and school. The result was public examination of the children before the congregation with some form of laying on of hands or blessing by the pastor.

The composition of church music for congregational use, both service music and hymn tunes, continued. Luther's colleagues and successors contributed to the writing of hymns as a way of combining teaching and worship. In this period, the tradition of Lutheran worship as heavily invested with music was reinforced and the foundation laid for further development.

### Pietism

The period of Pietism (1650–1800) reflects a time of disenchantment with conventional church life and an attempt to find a warmly personal religion. It was not a doctrinal rebellion but a desire for a stronger and more intimate sense of community within existing church structures. The focus of Pietism was the small group gathered for prayer and discipline. The small group provided new times and places for worship in addition to the parish community. Pietism became a strong force in much of Lutheranism and influenced groups including the Moravians and, through them, the Methodists.

The small groups often met twice weekly in private homes for worship, which consisted of Bible reading and prayer. This approach to worship brought an entirely different style, characterized by intimacy, to the worshiping community. Individuals shepherded one another in reflecting on and sharing their own relationship with God, and the community exercised pastoral care by stressing a disciplined life. In turn, the spiritual discipline of these small groups reinforced the worship life of the congregation.

A later form of Pietism developed in Norway under the leadership of Hans Nielsen Hauge (1771–1824) and was brought to the United States by Norwegian immigrants. Essentially a rebellion against the state church, then under Danish dominance, the Hauge movement, like earlier Pietism, placed little emphasis on set liturgical forms and the sacraments.

Some of the most long-lasting legacies of Pietism are found in hymns such as "O Sacred Head, Now Wounded" and "Soul, Adorn Yourself with Gladness." The greatest of all Lutheran musicians, Johann Sebastian Bach (1685–1750), himself deeply influenced by Pietism, expressed his faith and devotion within a traditional Lutheran piety. Bach worked within the traditional calendar and lectionary to produce several series of cantatas based on the Gospel reading for each Sunday and other feasts, which were reflective of

Lutheran Pietism. He also composed cantatas for concert occasions, including his Mass in B Minor, Christmas Oratorio, Magnificat, and St. Matthew and St. John passions.

### The Enlightenment

The period of the Enlightenment (1700–1800) brought the triumph of word over sacrament. The Enlightenment attempted to understand Christianity exclusively in rational terms. God was portrayed as contemplating the universe without interfering in its operation. Sacraments came to be discounted as God's unlikely intrusions into human life. As a result, the Enlightenment tended to suppress what sacramental piety still survived, while maintaining sacraments as biblical commands, and therefore obligatory, but celebrated infrequently.

The decline in sacramental life was accompanied by a corresponding discarding of much surviving ceremonial, although less so in Sweden, where it survived relatively intact. Architecturally, preaching churches emerged as balconies lined church walls to bring a larger number of worshipers close to the pulpit.

Morality became the characteristic sermon subject, and religion an instrument for the improvement of human society. With no expectation that God would act, all of worship became a means of teaching morality. This represented a major shift in Lutheran worship, one that has not entirely disappeared, especially in preaching.

### Restorationism

The period since 1800 has seen major efforts at restorationism. In 1817, when Frederick William III (1770–1840) attempted to combine Lutherans and Reformed in one church, many Lutherans felt pushed toward greater awareness of their own Reformation heritage. For example, Germany saw a resurgence of a Lutheran type of service, with its form derived from the medieval Mass and Luther's reforms, and a revival in sacramental life.

Lutherans in America experienced a very different reality. In 1748 Henry Melchior Muhlenberg (1711–1787), influenced by Pietism and rationalism, prepared a handwritten liturgy for Lutherans in Philadelphia. The period that followed saw a variety of liturgical books in use by various emigrant groups. Following Muhlenberg, Lutherans were attracted to the prevailing revival system in American Protestantism, with its almost complete indifference to historical patterns of worship and sacrament. American Lutheranism was faced with whether it would totally accommodate the culture or be distinctive.

Things became more complicated in the 1840s with a new influx of Germans who possessed an orthodox kind of Lutheran piety, a result of the restoration movement in Germany, while the later arrival of Scandinavians brought large numbers of Norwegian Pietists. These differences were somewhat diminished by the gradual movement from worship in European languages to English. Lutherans of all sorts increasingly used English hymnody. A series of liturgical books in English created ever-increasing collaboration among Lutheran bodies, especially centered on the recovery of an authentic Reformation pattern of worship. The Common Service (1888) and the *Common Service Book* (1917) are the highlights of this collaboration.

### Ecumenism

The period since the mid-twentieth century witnessed Lutherans moving beyond Lutheranism into a new ecumenical era. The various Christian traditions increasingly borrowed from each other and collaborated in developing new possibilities. The catalyst for this cooperation was the changes in Roman Catholic worship since Vatican II. Lutherans embraced many Catholic reforms, including the Sunday lectionary, use of a variety of eucharistic prayers, and revised pastoral rites.

In America, Lutherans are losing any distinct ethnic and cultural identities, a fact illustrated by the mergers of most of the Lutheran bodies, leaving only two major groups (and numerous small groups) by 1988—the Evangelical Lutheran Church in America and the Lutheran Church–Missouri Synod. A number of Lutheran bodies collaborated in the *Service Book and Hymnal* (1958), which broke Lutheran precedents by introducing a full eucharistic prayer despite Luther's removal of most of the canon. Lutherans returned to a much more exegetical style in preaching and a richer liturgical calendar.

In 1966 the Missouri Synod proposed the production of a common service book, something long cherished among American Lutherans. This invitation led to the establishment of the Inter-Lutheran Commission on Worship, which was active until 1978 and eventually produced the *Lutheran Book of Worship* (1978). Later, a Task Force on the Occasional Services was appointed to produce a volume of *Occasional Services* (1982), which included special occasions in the church year, weddings, funerals, and ordination. At the last moment, the Missouri Synod withdrew, producing its own book, *Lutheran Worship* (1982), setting American Lutheran church bodies on distinct paths.

Both books—*Lutheran Book of Worship* and *Lutheran Worship*—reflect sixteenth-century practice while being cognizant of early church practice and ecumenical trajectories. Weekly Eucharist is presented as normative, and provision is made to celebrate the Eucharist using only the words of institution instead of a full eucharistic prayer. Luther's baptismal piety is celebrated with an emphasis on baptism throughout all services. Importance shifted from confirmation, which was reframed as one of many occasions to remember and affirm one's baptism, to baptism itself. All services are highly musical, and a large number of Lutheran chorales are included among the hymnody. Ecumenically, Lutherans adopted the Revised Common Lectionary, an expanded calendar, and a fuller cycle of Holy Week celebrations. Freestanding altars have been moved away from the wall, and fonts given a more prominent place.

The years since the publication of *Lutheran Book of Worship* and *Lutheran Worship* have seen considerable change. Congregations increasingly use electronic resources in worship. Lutherans are aware and appreciative of the world's cultural diversity and seek to move beyond their European and Scandinavian roots, celebrating Lutheran worship in languages other than English. Changes in vernacular languages call Lutherans to discern what is appropriate language for worship, especially language used to name God. Lutherans are also discerning how to maintain their musical heritage as forms of music expand and congregations' resources for musical performance decline.

Responding to these changes, the Evangelical Lutheran Church in America and the Evangelical Lutheran Church in Canada produced *Evangelical Lutheran Worship* (2006); the Lutheran Church–Missouri Synod and the Lutheran Church–Canada produced *Lutheran Service Book* (2006). *Lutheran Service Book* enjoys status as an official worship book; *Evangelical Lutheran Worship* is commended for use. *Lutheran Service Book* strengthens Lutheran roots; *Evangelical Lutheran Worship* stretches to reach beyond them. Both include Luther's Small Catechism. *Evangelical Lutheran Worship* adds "Thanksgiving for Baptism," a gathering rite celebrating Luther's baptismal piety.

For many, *Lutheran Service Book* has become a source of unity. It is a careful blending of the best of *The Lutheran Hymnal* and *Lutheran Worship*. It offers treasured melodies and texts that have nourished God's people for generations as well as a foray into global hymnody. *Lutheran Service Book* provides five settings of the Divine Service, maintains traditional language for both humanity and God, and places great emphasis on the treasury of hymns between its covers.

*Evangelical Lutheran Worship* embraces a pattern of worship—gathering, word, table, and sending—rather than a set liturgy as uniting the church in worship. "The Holy Spirit gathers the people of God around Jesus Christ present in the word of God and the sacraments, so that the Spirit may in turn send them into the world to continue the ingathering mission of God's reign."[25] This pattern, together with words, actions, and songs handed down through the ages, expresses the Spirit's work of uniting an assembly of one time and place with the church of every time and place. Since worship takes place in particular assemblies within particular contexts, congregations embrace "freedom and flexibility" in worship by making use of ample variety in ceremony, music, and liturgical form based on this pattern. Ten musical settings of Holy Communion highlight the increased diversity of expression. In this way, the church better responds and is responsible to the cultural diversity of the world it serves. Thus, *Evangelical Lutheran Worship* is intended as a core rather than a comprehensive resource.

## Practical Implications for Worship

While justification by grace through faith remains the compass for Lutheran worship, what constitutes adiaphora is equally alive, especially as Lutherans move from an established Divine Service to a pattern and Lutheran worship books become one resource among many. Worship planners and leaders must understand the movement of the liturgy and the meaning of its parts and consider the operative theology in the choices they make.

Is worship simply a way of packaging the gospel or does liturgy shape the message of justification? Worship planners and leaders must answer this question as they weigh opportunities and limitations of worshiping. How do we balance proclaiming the gospel to the world and the preference and taste of the congregation?

The dynamics of Lutheran orthodoxy, Pietism, and the Enlightenment remain operative in Lutheran worship. They are manifested in the conflict of "traditional" (orthodoxy) and "contemporary" (Pietism) worship. Enlightenment influence can be found in the academic form and content of sermons and in the limited way in which sacraments are sometimes celebrated. The restoration question of whether American Lutherans will assimilate or remain distinctive is very real. Even as Lutherans desire to embrace diversity and grow beyond their ethnic roots, many congregations cling to "traditional" practices out of fear that, without them, they lose their reason to exist. Worship planners and leaders would benefit from understanding the breadth of the Lutheran family in their congregation.

25. "Introduction," in *Evangelical Lutheran Worship, Leaders Desk Edition* (Minneapolis: Augsburg Fortress, 2006), 6.

After working for decades to move to weekly Eucharist, Lutherans are now facing a shortage of clergy. Since many find asking congregations to celebrate Communion less frequently disingenuous, Lutherans will need to revisit their understanding of ordination and the possibility of lay presidency. In moving forward, more than theological conviction, worship practices—including the vernacular, music, and worship leadership—will define what Lutherans mean by the church as "the assembly of all believers among whom the gospel is purely preached and the holy sacraments administered according to the gospel."[26]

## For Further Reading

Luther, Martin. "The Babylonian Captivity of the Church, 1520." In *Word and Sacrament II*, edited by Abdel Ross Wentz, 11–126. Vol. 36 of *Luther's Works*, American Edition, edited by Jaroslav Pelikan and Helmut T. Lehmann. Philadelphia: Fortress, 1959.

———. *Liturgy and Hymns*, edited by Ulrich S. Leupol. Vol. 53 of *Luther's Works*, American Edition, edited by Jaroslav Pelikan and Helmut T. Lehmann. Philadelphia: Fortress, 1965.

Lutheran World Federation. *Nairobi Statement on Worship and Culture: Contemporary Challenges and Opportunities*. Geneva: Lutheran World Federation, 1996.

Senn, Frank. *Christian Liturgy: Catholic and Evangelical*. Philadelphia: Fortress, 1999.

Truscott, Jeffrey A. *The Sacraments: A Practical Guide*. Christian Heritage Rediscovered Series 22. New Delhi: Christian World Imprints, 2016.

Vajta, Vitmos. *Luther on Worship: An Interpretation*. Philadelphia: Muhlenberg, 1958.

26. See "The Augsburg Confession," article 7, in Kolb and Wengert, *Book of Concord*, 42.

# — 12 —

# Calvinist and Reformed Practices of Worship

## *Martin Tel*

O n any given Sunday morning the average worshiper would be hard-pressed to suggest any ways the reformer John Calvin might have influenced their experience in worship. This would be true even for those in churches with Calvinist roots, such as Presbyterian, Reformed, Congregationalist, and some Baptist denominations. But Calvin might fare even worse with those who have a little bit of liturgical or church history knowledge. If and when Calvin does make it into the curriculum of worship studies, most of the press is in the negative: no choirs, no instruments, no hymns, no paintings, no stained glass . . . no, no, no!

It is true that the Calvinist worship tradition did less to produce artifacts that might invite disinterested contemplation, like musical compositions that would later be performed in concert halls, or visual art that would find its way into a museum. Scholarship that assumes the superiority of "high art" inevitably puts the Calvinist tradition at a disadvantage. The Calvinist tradition's greatest contributions will be marked in the way that worship arts were redirected to support liturgical function and engage the entire assembly in its worship of God. Many of the reforms instituted by the Reformed tradition are now simply assumed, but at the time the shifts were seismic.

The twenty-first century has seen an incredible growth in programs of "worship studies." This is a healthy development in an era of global markets and seemingly limitless choices. Positively, many walls of division between Christians are being dismantled. Christian worship is being enriched by a freer and increasingly fair exchange of gifts and ideas in the worldwide church. But, given the global proclivity toward commoditization, the choices faced by worship leaders pose incredible challenges. There is a critical need for discernment. A reappraisal of Calvin's reforms instigated centuries ago might help us to navigate a way through our modern dilemma.

## Elements of Worship

### Liturgical Freedom and Order

Regarding the Reformed liturgy, it should not be too surprising that there is not a recognizable "Calvinist liturgy" today. Though Calvin is often considered the fountainhead of the Reformed Church movement, there are no denominations that bear his name. His reforms of worship were explored and formulated within a community of theologians, including Philip Melanchthon, Martin Bucer, William Farel, Theodore Beza, and John Knox. Calvin and his colleagues did not dictate a new liturgy to replace the Roman Rite. Rather, they developed principles and models that could then be received and adapted as the Reformed Church movement spread across cultures and down succeeding generations. Though there would be no prescribed liturgy, there was certainly a sense of order. Model services were published and adopted in Reformed centers within books with titles such as *La forme des prières* (Geneva), *Kirchenordnung* (Heidelberg), and *Book of Common Order* (Scotland).

### According to Scripture

The freedom engendered in the Reformed tradition operated within a scriptural framework. Though the "regulative principle" (that nothing should be allowed in worship except that which Christ through Scripture expressly commands) is often associated with Calvinism, it is a later Puritan development. What Calvin promoted was the reform of worship according to Scripture.[1] This would lead to the purging of many elements of the Roman Rite that were deemed contrary to Scripture. There was, for instance, a removal of all ceremony associated with the veneration of saints. The number

---

1. For further reading, see Hughes Oliphant Old, *Worship Reformed according to Scripture*, rev. ed. (Louisville: Westminster John Knox, 2002).

of festival services (e.g., saints' days or other liturgical "holy days") was radically reduced.

Calvin's theological exegesis of the sacraments of baptism and the Lord's Supper found expression in the liturgy. No longer would baptisms be held in private services in a corner of the church building; rather, the sacrament would be celebrated in the midst of the gathered congregation within the regular worship service. The celebration of the Lord's Supper likewise found a new expression in the worship service. The liturgy would always include an exposition of the meaning of the sacrament. Participants partook of both the bread and the wine. We do know that Calvin himself wished for a more frequent celebration of the sacrament, but the Genevan magistrates reduced this to four times per year.[2] Though Calvin did not retain the rite of confession as a sacrament, he retained public confession in the service. And, of course, preaching is a hallmark of Calvin's liturgical reform. Not only should the service be ordered according to Scripture but great care—and ample time!—must be devoted to the reading and exposition of God's Word.

### Worship Music

Calvin writes about prayer in worship, "As for the public prayers, there are two kinds: the first are made with word only, the others with song."[3] With regard to public spoken prayers, such as those modeled in *La forme de prières*, it is understood that the prayer belongs to the people, though prayed by one person.[4] However, sung prayer should be uttered by everyone. Though we now take this for granted, at the time this was revolutionary. Not only would the voices of common men be heard in the service, but women's voices would also be welcomed. This proved to be controversial. One contemporary critic of Calvin's reforms wrote, "Was the practice of the ancient and wise Christianity like the young and foolish Calvinism, which allows women to sing in church? 'Let her keep silent,' says Paul; 'let

2. Though Calvin wrote idealistically of celebrating the Lord's Supper whenever the people gathered for a full worship service (based on Acts 2:42), in practice he balanced this with his desire for people to be prepared for each celebration of the sacrament. What he ultimately argued for in Geneva was a monthly celebration, as was the practice in Strasbourg. For further reading, see Elsie McKee, *The Pastoral Ministry and Worship in Calvin's Geneva* (Geneva: Librairie Droz, 2016), 250–57.

3. Elsie McKee, ed., *John Calvin: Writings on Pastoral Piety* (New York: Paulist Press, 2001), 94.

4. For a translation of some public prayers composed by Calvin, see McKee, *John Calvin*, 210–45. The spoken prayer, though uttered by one person, is nevertheless understood as the prayer of the entire assembly, not as a collection of individuals. See Nicholas Wolterstorff, "Thinking about Church Music," in *Music in Christian Worship*, ed. Charlotte Kroeker (Collegeville, MN: Liturgical Press, 2005), 10.

her sing,' says Calvin."[5] The critiques may have been driven in part by the allure of this new way of singing, particularly for worshipers who found themselves literally surrounded by the congregational "choir." One young Roman Catholic student wrote in a letter his observations of the Protestant singing in Strasbourg in 1545: "[The psalm] is sung by everyone, men and women together. . . . I never imagined that it could be as pleasant and delightful as it is."[6]

With regard to what was sung in worship, Calvin points to the Psalms: "When we have looked thoroughly everywhere and searched high and low, we shall find no better songs nor more appropriate to the purpose than the psalms of David which the Holy Spirit made and spoke through him. And furthermore, when we sing them, we are certain that God puts the words in our mouths, as if He Himself were singing in us to exalt His glory."[7] He calls the book of Psalms "An Anatomy of all the Parts of the Soul," for, he writes, "there is not an emotion of which any one can be conscious that is not here represented as in a mirror."[8] As Jesus taught us to pray through the words of the Lord's Prayer, the book of Psalms, in an expansive way, molds the church in the life of prayer. There is no need to look elsewhere. Indeed, argues Calvin, why allow the potential for heresy by introducing songs of human composure?

One of Calvin's greatest achievements was the editorial oversight of a complete Psalter for public singing, completed in 1562. In the prefaces to the various editions of this French Psalter, Calvin offers some explicit theological and biblical framework for church music. Implicit tenets of a Reformed theology of church music can be mined from the lyrical and musical settings themselves.

With regard to the paraphrases of Hebrew poetry, it is helpful to consider Calvin's concern for translation into the vernacular. Worship in the vernacular is, after all, a hallmark of the Reformation traditions. But Calvin also casts the *poetry* of the Psalms into a vernacular form. Calvin wished for the Psalms to match Western expectations for poetry, including meter, poetic foot (or scansion), and rhyme, such as could be sung to a recurring tune. Casting the ancient text into a contextualized lyrical form would aid in the memorization of and deep connection with these prayers. Calvin would in fact require

5. For more of Florimond de Raemond's critique, translated by Elsie McKee, see her article "Context, Contours, Contents: Towards a Description of the Classical Reformed Teaching on Worship," *Princeton Seminary Bulletin* 16, no. 2 (1995): 172–201.

6. Quoted and translated by Howard G. Hageman in *Pulpit and Table: Some Chapters in the History of Worship in the Reformed Churches* (Richmond: John Knox, 1962), 27.

7. From Calvin's foreword to the 1543 French Psalter; McKee, *John Calvin*, 96.

8. From Calvin's 1557 preface to his commentary on the Psalms; McKee, *John Calvin*, 56.

two complete "vernacularizations" of the Psalms: a faithful translation for preaching and teaching, and a lyrical paraphrase to accommodate the congregation's sung prayers.

Calvin turned to two of the finest French poets of his day: Clement Marot and Theodore Beza. The full sense of each original psalm is captured in the paraphrases, while avoiding adding elements or ideas that are not present in the Hebrew. Where the reformer might see in the psalm a prophecy that was fulfilled in the new covenant, such interpretations were left to preaching and not added to the psalm.[9] The poetic elements of scansion and meter and rhyme were enjoined to interpret each psalm. For instance, a psalm of ecstatic praise might have a very punctuated meter and rhyme scheme, such as Psalm 47 with its rapid series of twelve five-syllable phrases. In contrast, a penitential psalm might have a more drawn-out meter. For instance, the phrases of Psalm 51 are ten to eleven syllables long. The rhyme of the first phrase is not answered until more than thirty syllables later. Both the long phrases and the delayed resolution of the rhyme create a sense of extension and longing. Throughout the French Psalter we find the uncovering of meaning at the microlevel of the poetry.

Turning to the melodies of the Genevan Psalter, we find even more insights into Calvin's approach to worship music. Though we do not know the sources of all the tunes, Calvin seems to rely heavily on Louis Bourgeois. A cursory survey of the tunes suggests that there were established parameters that would ensure they remained simple and accessible for a congregation of mostly untrained singers. For example, the entire Psalter is limited to only two note values. Almost without exception the settings are monosyllabic (one note per syllable). Intervals between notes favor stepwise motion.

The goal for simplicity, however, did not result in uniformity. The "long" and "short" notes are often deftly arranged so as to create a rousing syncopation. This is best illustrated in Psalm 47, where successive pairs of five-syllable lines collide, like the clapping of two five-fingered hands. Music of the period had not yet been locked into our conventional modes of major and minor. The Psalter melodies explore a broad range of scales, such as the plaintive Phrygian mode of Psalm 51. Calvin, in his preface, explains that these scales or modes can powerfully impact how the singer understands and reacts to the psalm text.[10] Melodies could also employ text painting in order to bring to the fore the overall tenor of a particular psalm.[11] Consider how the tumbling

9. This contrasts with Martin Luther's psalm paraphrases (see his *Aus tiefer Not*) and later English-language psalmody developments, most notably in the "psalm imitations" of Isaac Watts.

10. McKee, *John Calvin*, 95.

11. Text painting (or word painting) is a compositional technique in which the music mimics the literal meaning of the text.

Dorian melody of Psalm 23 flattens out, reposes, right at its center, before resuming its flow. The plummeting initial interval and slow rise at the opening of Psalm 130 is similarly evocative. In all, the French Psalter presented 110 unique meters and 125 new melodies, which, taken together, demonstrate the role that meter and music can play in uncovering the meaning of Scripture. This sophistication, all the while, was held in tension with the need for congregational accessibility. The paraphrases and the tunes were considered to be inseparable and were published as such.[12]

Having determined the repertoire for the singing congregation, Calvin ventures further in prescribing how the assembly will sing. If there is one thing that people might know about Calvin's ideas of worship music (beyond his emphasis on the Psalter), it is that he did not allow for instruments in church. As radical as this may seem to us today, it could be understood as a return to a norm of Christian worship. Many today refer to unaccompanied singing as *a cappella*, an Italian phrase that literally translates "as in the chapel." It had been assumed that the most distinctive way that Christians had worshiped in past centuries, and most notably in the early church, would have been without instruments. Calvin appeals to unaccompanied singing on theological as well as historical grounds, but his practical intentions are also clear. The introduction of instruments, or harmony, or choral singing into the liturgy may distract singers and, over time, will overwhelm the primacy of the congregation's voice. Calvin recognizes and points to the inclination of music composers and directors toward complexity of form. Without established boundaries the congregation in all likelihood would return to the passive role it played in the era leading up to the Reformation.

One might wonder how Calvin managed this new mode of congregational song. Consider the scenario: The masses had no experience singing together in the church. Even if they had familiarity with group singing outside the church, they were now confronted with more than 150 new texts[13] and 125 new melodies. His rhetoric against the singing of choirs notwithstanding, Calvin enlisted the help of school children in teaching the new psalm paraphrases to their families and to the assembled congregation.[14]

12. The persistent printing of the French Psalter with the corresponding melodies is quite different from the Psalter practices that will emerge in English-language Psalters.

13. In addition to the Psalms, the French Psalter included a metrical version of the Decalogue (the Ten Commandments) and the Nunc Dimittis (Song of Simeon).

14. Charles Garside Jr., "The Origins of Calvin's Theology of Music: 1536–1537," *Transactions of the American Philosophical Society* 69, no. 4 (1979): 10. This might suggest that Calvin was not so much opposed to choirs in church, but that he rejected the choir that sang in place of the congregation. Calvin approves of rehearsed singers who teach and lead the congregation. Nevertheless, there is evidence that outside the city of Geneva there were Reformed

Though the Psalter was produced as a songbook for communal worship, its use was not limited to the church service. In the preface, Calvin notes that the singing of psalms should cross over to all spheres of life: at home, at work, at court, at leisure. The strictures against choral singing and instruments did not carry outside the worship services. As soon as the Psalter was published, choral settings of these psalms appeared, including homophonic and polyphonic settings by Claude Goudimel and Louis Bourgeois. One would expect that these psalms, typical of secular songs of this era, would be accompanied by instruments, particularly the lute. Though in large churches the unaccompanied singing of the psalms was probably quite slow, domestic and more intimate settings would allow for more flexibility in tempos, freeing the original rhythms to shine as the composers intended.

Once the Psalter was established, adherents to the Reformed faith embraced wholeheartedly their new way of singing. So serious was their identification with these psalm texts and melodies that any attempt to meddle with them might be met with swift and decisive action. At one point Bourgeois himself spent a day in prison for making alterations to a psalm melody without authorization.[15] More poignantly, there are accounts of Reformed martyrs singing these psalms as they were burned at the stake. Indeed, the Psalter is a hallmark of the Calvinist Reformation.

## Worship Space

With respect to the worship space, Calvin and his colleagues in the Reformed movement inherited their environment from the Roman Church. Ideals they may have had about space would be constricted by stone and mortar. Where called for and possible, alterations were made. Calvin can be listed among the iconoclasts of the Reformation, though he counseled a measured approach. Over time inherited elements that the reformers considered idolatrous or simply distracting were removed from the worship space, including organs, statuary, relics, stained glass, and other artwork. Many larger cathedrals had rood screens that physically separated the clergy's celebration of the sacrament of Holy Communion (the Mass) in the choir of the church from the onlooking (or overhearing) laity in the

---

congregations in the countryside that struggled to establish congregational singing. It would appear that strong leadership and perhaps literacy were key to the success of this new ideal of congregational singing of psalms.

15. John Witvliet, "The Spirituality of the Psalter in Calvin's Geneva," in *Worship Seeking Understanding* (Grand Rapids: Baker Academic, 2003), 217n60.

nave of the church. Where possible, the reformers removed these barriers as well as the altars affixed to walls.[16] Worship spaces were retrofitted so that the preaching of the word (pulpit) and the administration of the sacraments (font and table) would take place in close proximity to the gathered congregation.[17]

The interior of the sixteenth-century Reformed worship space might be described as sober and spare. The medieval church had increasingly sought to create a sacred and heavenly environment within the walls of the church in contradistinction to the secular and profane world outside. Calvin rejects this separation. Literally and figuratively, the Reformed tradition would flood the worship space with unfiltered light. The building should not attempt to create a heaven on earth, but the hearts of the faithful will be raised to heaven when they worship in spirit and truth.

## Interpretations of the Reformed Tradition

### Development of a Reformed Architecture

The environment in which the congregation worships is formative. One may argue that "form follows function," but this does little good if the congregation inherits the form with walls and pillars that are sometimes meters thick. Such was the case for the Reformed movement. The best one could do would be to redecorate (or undecorate!) and move the furniture. This has been noted above. But when opportunities arose in Calvinist lands to begin to design and build their own churches, we can observe formal shifts meant to reflect the Reformed understanding, or function, of worship. These new Reformed worship spaces emphasized proximity of the congregation to both the Word and sacraments. The architectural choir of the old cathedral has been removed. The congregation is now the choir.

---

16. In some worship spaces where rood screens could not be removed, the cordoned-off choir (clergy space) was repurposed as a separate room for the congregation to gather for the Lord's Supper. For a pictorial and theological exposition of Reformed worship space, see Donald J. Bruggink and Carl H. Droppers, *Christ and Architecture: Building Presbyterian/Reformed Churches* (Grand Rapids: Eerdmans, 1965). With respect to the Reformed repurposing of Roman Catholic spaces, particularly the high altar and the rood screen, see pages 81–90. For a description of the rood screen's impact on worship, see Robert Kingdon, "The Genevan Revolution in Public Worship," *Princeton Seminary Bulletin* 20, no. 3 (1999): 264–80.

17. Because Calvin wished for a clean break from any lingering veneration of the font or table as holy objects, the Communion table was set up and a bowl of water was brought in only for those services in which these sacraments would be celebrated. See McKee, *Pastoral Ministry and Worship*, 55–57, 422–24.

## The Directory for Worship

The liturgies of Geneva, Heidelberg, and Edinburgh did not ossify into set liturgies. Rather, they were taken as models. In the English-speaking Calvinist lands, most notably in the Presbyterian (Church of Scotland) wing of the church, the Reformed liturgy was interpreted through the *Directory for Worship*.[18] The directory established the principle of order and freedom. Particular elements of worship are deemed essential (assembling, reading of Scripture, confession, preaching, thanksgiving, singing of psalms, sacraments). A basic sequence is outlined as well as the general layout of the prayers. But the directory stops short of creating any uniform liturgy for the churches. This principle of freedom within a common theological and confessional assent remains a hallmark of churches in the Reformed tradition.

The proverbial middle ground of the "directory" approach to worship has at times been contested. Puritans in the church, wary of any infiltration of a "prayer book," at times forbade the reading of any prayers in the worship service, a reproach of Calvin and the first generations of the Reformed tradition, including John Knox. One may presume that these Puritans' felt need to forbid the reading of prayers was a reaction to the promotion or practice of the same. Over time the desire for formative modes of worship did foment movements advocating more prescriptive liturgies.[19] While these movements would remain on the periphery of Reformed worship, they did help lead several Reformed denominations to explore and produce liturgical resources and, in some cases, comprehensive model liturgies. In 1906 the Presbyterian Church (USA) published its first *Book of Common Worship*.[20] Though the *Book of Common Worship* was never binding, the authorization for its use by the largest North American Presbyterian denomination signaled an emerging openness to prepared prayers and liturgies and, for some, a desire for a composite liturgy that could provide more uniformity and express more ecumenicity. Much of the later enthusiasm for liturgical forms was prompted

18. The first *Directory for Worship* was produced by the Westminster Assembly (1640–1649) along with the Westminster Confession of Faith and Catechisms and modeled on John Knox's *Book of Common Order*. For a concise explanation of the *Directory for Worship*, see Stanley R. Hall's article "A Directory for Worship: What It Is, What It Does," *Reformed Worship* 22 (December 1991): 42–43.

19. The nineteenth-century Mercersburg Theology movement, under the leadership of John Williamson Nevin and Philip Schaff, proved to be particularly influential for constituencies of the Reformed tradition who desired a more robust and prescriptive liturgical form.

20. Now in its sixth iteration, the *Book of Common Worship* (Louisville: Westminster John Knox, 2018) includes a brief history of the book (xxvii–xxxiv). For a thorough history, see Harold M. Daniels, *To God Alone Be Glory: The Story and Sources of the Book of Common Worship* (Louisville: Geneva, 2003).

by the Second Vatican Council and the ensuing liturgical reform movement, particularly in mainline Protestant churches.[21] But, for all the desire that these leaders may have had for a uniform Reformed liturgy, it is the directory approach that has persisted.[22]

## The Psalter and the Introduction of Hymns

As the Calvinist expression of the Reformation spread to other lands, most notably Scotland, parts of Germany, Hungary, and the Netherlands, so too did Calvin's general guidelines regarding congregational song. For the most part the lyrics were limited to the Psalms, sung in unison and without accompaniment.[23] But Calvin's care for lyrical beauty was lost in translation. The French Psalter was translated directly, and rather hastily, into Dutch and German and indirectly into Hungarian. Pieter Datheen's Dutch translation was so inflexible that it was nigh unsingable with the original rhythms of the French Psalter. This meant that psalm singing would become associated with a stringing together of long notes, known as isorhythmic singing. Though aesthetically diminished, this sort of psalm singing was heartily embraced. The fervent singing of "Genevan Psalms" became an emblem of the young Reformed faith, and in some circumstances the psalms became anthems of resistance against foreign political powers. As this sort of singing settled into the services of the churches, a new Calvinist aesthetic of psalm singing emerged, though different from what Calvin himself may have imagined.

In English-speaking lands, Calvin's vision for lyricism and melodic interpretation was further distorted. While there was some attempt to import Calvin's Psalter through an English translation, in the end it was not successful. Queen Elizabeth I, not convinced by the metrical and rhythmic variety, referred to the French psalm settings as "Genevan jigs." Prior to the Reformation the English had established a practice of translating ancient poetry,

21. For more, see chap. 10, "Vatican II and the Liturgical Renewal Movement."

22. If anything, Presbyterian denominations today have developed a new interpretation of the *Directory for Worship*, which focuses more on the freedom and less on the order.

23. The Reformed churches of the Netherlands proved to be an exception with regard to instruments. Most Dutch churches retained their pipe organs. Though the organs would not sound during the service, they might play before and after the service—ideally music based on tunes from the Psalter. But by the early seventeenth century organs began to be employed to lead the psalm singing. Because the singing congregation was so loud, a new, uniquely Protestant school of organ building developed and blossomed. The new aesthetic of the organ mirrored and matched the vocal sound produced by the congregation. These organs continued to lead robust psalm singing in the Netherlands for centuries. Many instruments survive from the earliest days of Protestant psalm singing, providing an echo of the intensity of the singing congregation.

including the biblical Psalms, into English verse. The most common meter for this practice was alternating lines of eight and six syllables, referred to as English ballad meter. Thomas Sternhold, serving in the royal court in the last years of Henry VIII and first years of Edward VI, produced thirty-seven psalm versifications by the time of his death in 1549. These were printed that same year together with seven versifications by John Hopkins. The English Protestant refugees, many of whom fled to Strasbourg and Geneva, used these psalms as the starting point for a complete Psalter. The collection, first printed in 1562, came to be referred to as the "Old Version," or the "Sternhold and Hopkins." The most enduring versification from this book is William Kethe's setting of Psalm 100: "All People That on Earth Do Dwell."[24]

Despite some fine examples of English poetry, the Old Version and successive English-language Psalters fell further and further short of John Calvin's ideals. Because psalm paraphrases came to be mostly constricted into lines of either eight or six syllables, there is no intentional correlation between meter and the sense of the psalm. Furthermore, most of these versifications were fashioned and printed without melody. Though this would enable easier access for the congregation—the entire Psalter could be sung to just a few common tunes—the lyrical interpretation modeled by Calvin through melodic mode, line, and rhythm is completely lost.

By securing the finest poets of the French language, Calvin hoped for the versifications of his Psalter to be not only exegetically sound but also winsome for succeeding generations of worshipers. A cursory survey of successive English Psalters suggests that this standard was abandoned. In fact, some Puritan strains of Calvinism reacted adversely to lyrical beauty, taking it as an indication that biblical fidelity had been compromised. This would lead to a particular Psalter aesthetic for English-language Calvinists that, regardless of any demerits, was embraced and defended. For many a Puritan, it formed the conduit for fervent and earnest engagement in the liturgy of the Lord's Day.[25]

Over time this severe aesthetic of psalm singing began to crack. By the end of the eighteenth century, Calvinists were confronted with a new type of psalmody through the "imitations"[26] of Isaac Watts, a Puritan of another stripe. An adherent of the Independent (Congregationalist) movement, he

---

24. For further reading and bibliography, see J. Michael Morgan's "English Language Metrical Psalters of the Sixteenth Century," in *Hymns and Hymnody: Historical and Theological Introductions*, ed. Mark A. Lamport, Benjamin K. Forrest, and Vernon M. Whaley (Eugene, OR: Cascade Books, 2019), 2:64–77.

25. For further reading and bibliography, see Morgan's "English Language Metrical Psalters," 2:150–63.

26. Isaac Watts, *The Psalms of David Imitated in the Language of the New Testament and Applied to the Christian State and Worship* (London: n.p., 1719).

was a gifted hymnwriter and wordsmith. Hymns, though not permitted for congregational song, were often published as devotional literature.[27] But it was Watts's psalm paraphrases that would forever alter the landscape of congregational singing in English-language Calvinist churches. In one sense, Watts harkens back to Calvin's concern for lyrical beauty. A comparison of his paraphrase of Psalm 23, "My Shepherd Will Supply My Need," to the beloved Scottish Psalter's (1650) "The Lord's My Shepherd, I'll Not Want" will bear this out. But Watts also represents a radical departure from Calvin's principle of adhering to the biblical psalm. Watts is not content to leave scriptural exegesis to the preacher. In his words, Watts insists that David be converted into a Christian. And so we receive Watts's setting of Psalm 72: "Jesus Shall Reign Where'er the Sun."

Eventually most Calvinists in North America accepted Watts and his approach to psalmody, which in essence opened the door to hymnody and led to the rather abrupt demise of psalm singing.[28] These Calvinists found themselves in a liturgical free market of ideas. Without broader cultural undergirding, the resolve to forgo hymns, musical instruments, and choirs gave way. And while the principles of order and freedom set forth in the *Directory for Worship* have endured, they no longer provide the liturgical cohesion for Reformed denominations that they once did.

## Practical Implications for Worship

If in fact worship in the Calvinist traditions has morphed into something that the reformer could not have imagined, this does not mean that Calvin's theology of worship should be disregarded. Nor should it be taken as an appeal for a Reformed repristination, a return to some earlier ideal. An overview of this "evolution"—for the Calvinist, *semper reformanda*—provides ample fodder for reflection. Calvin's own ideals evolved during his relatively short life. Had he not been exposed to the congregational singing of Strasbourg, some wonder whether he would have embraced the practice at all. Through various publications leading up to the final and complete Psalter, we observe a developing liturgical theology. Calvin could not have anticipated how his publications and teachings about worship and music would travel from a

---

27. See Christopher N. Phillips, *The Hymnal: A Reading History* (Baltimore: Johns Hopkins University Press, 2018).

28. For further reading and bibliography, see Rochelle A. Stackhouse, "Isaac Watts: Composer of Psalms and Hymns," in Lamport, Forrest, and Whaley, *Hymns and Hymnody*, 2:197–209; and Martin Tel, "North American Metrical Psalters," in Lamport, Forrest, and Whaley, *Hymns and Hymnody*, 3:190–203.

sixteenth-century Swiss city through place and time, interacting with languages and cultures and sensibilities. But this does not make Calvin irrelevant to our current situation. The emerging field of worship studies would do well to reengage Calvin as an interlocutor. Consider these areas that are ripe for Calvinist interrogation:

- *Worship space.* What is at the center in the worship space? To what must all have access? What are the idolatries (or potential idolatries) in the worship space? Of which physical objects or symbols might the people be tempted to say, "We can't worship without it"? What are the rood screens (or potential rood screens) in our worship space? Is there anything (physical, visual, aural, or symbolic) that "screens" some people out or reduces the active engagement of the "laity" (those without leadership function)? How might barriers creep in? (Clericalism is pernicious.) Does the seating arrangement and the acoustical environment of the worship space encourage the congregation to function as the primary voice for the sung elements of the service?

- *Order and freedom in worship.* Is there *order* in the service? What guides and directs this ordering? Many consider written or prepared prayers to be less spiritual. Why is this? Do you believe that the Holy Spirit works through planning? What might be the shortcomings of extemporaneous worship? Is there *freedom* in the service? Many (particularly high-liturgy converts) cling tightly to scripted or "prayer book" ordos. What are the theological pitfalls of this approach?

- *Music in worship.* What is the correlation between the musical style of a song and its function in worship? What criteria might help us determine the fittingness of musical (and other) arts in support of the liturgy?[29] How do we balance musical complexity with congregational accessibility? Should the congregation have primary voice in the sung portions of the worship service? Do they? What aspects of worship arts ministry diminish the voice of the congregation? (Think of this not in terms of what must be eliminated but rather in terms of what must be disciplined, or what warrants our care and vigilance.) Do we regularly sing songs and prayers that "God puts in our mouths" (i.e., psalms and other lyrical portions of Scripture)? What guardrails do we have in place to ensure

---

29. Nicholas Wolterstorff develops his idea of "fittingness" in his book *Art in Action: Toward a Christian Aesthetic* (Grand Rapids: Eerdmans, 1980), particularly pages 96–121, and in his chapter "Thinking about Church Music," in *Music in Christian Worship*, ed. Charlotte Kroeker (Collegeville, MN: Liturgical Press, 2005), 3–16. See also Frank Burch Brown, "Religious Music and Secular Music: A Calvinist Perspective, Re-formed," *Theology Today* 60 (2006): 11–21.

that what we sing in worship is scriptural? What "soundtrack" are we curating for the congregation? How many songs might a congregation be able to contain in its memory bank? Given that there are literally tens of thousands of songs at our disposal, how do we choose? How will we cultivate the songs that we have chosen? What roles might children and youth play in the rehearsal and teaching of the church's songs? (This should not be confused with catering to children and youth. Though there is a place for this, the Calvinist model suggests an intentional mentoring of children and youth for leadership.)

These questions only scratch the surface. Any one of them could form the basis for a worship and arts team discussion, a module in a worship arts course, or a proposal for a PhD dissertation. Or they might help a faithful church musician reorient the landscape of their ministry. Calvin's writings and influences on worship and music have been perennially neglected. In a culture fixated on #TheNextIdol, a religious iconoclast is an unlikely go-to conversation partner. But, with a little imagination, it is possible to recognize meaningful similarities between the landscape of worship arts today and that of Calvin's sixteenth century. Contrary to many people's assumption, Calvin has more to say than "no." He offers us a way forward through lessons in discernment.

## For Further Reading

Hageman, Howard G. *Pulpit and Table: Some Chapters in the History of Worship in the Reformed Churches*. Richmond: John Knox, 1962.

Maag, Karin. *Lifting Hearts to the Lord: Worship with John Calvin in Sixteenth-Century Geneva*. Grand Rapids: Eerdmans, 2016.

McKee, Elsie, ed. *John Calvin: Writings on Pastoral Piety*. New York: Paulist Press, 2001.

———. *The Pastoral Ministry and Worship in Calvin's Geneva*. Geneva: Librairie Droz, 2016.

Old, Hughes Oliphant. *Worship Reformed according to Scripture*. Rev. ed. Louisville: Westminster John Knox, 2002.

Witvliet, John D. *Worship Seeking Understanding: Windows into Christian Practice*. Grand Rapids: Baker Academic, 2003.

# — 13 —

# Anglican and Episcopal Practices of Worship

## *Euan Cameron*

To a degree unusual in the history of the churches derived from the sixteenth-century Reformation, the Anglican and Episcopal traditions receive their distinctive character through their liturgy. Worship binds these traditions together more than doctrine, or even an episcopal polity. The reformer with the greatest claim to be regarded as the founder of the tradition, the martyr-archbishop Thomas Cranmer (d. 1556), made the most impact on the Church of England by framing the worship of the church.[1] Cranmer was by no means insignificant as a theologian; but in contrast to the leaders of continental European Protestantism, his theological contributions rank behind his achievements in liturgy.[2] Over the centuries, the defining of the Anglican tradition through worship, rather than through the details of doctrine, tended to broaden the range of ways in which the tradition could be understood. The liturgy offered minimal guidance in "peripheral" matters, such as vestments or gestures in worship; so Anglican worship could, by preference, look like evangelical Protestantism or late medieval Catholicism.

---

1. See in general Diarmaid MacCulloch, *Thomas Cranmer: A Life* (New Haven: Yale University Press, 1996).

2. See *The Works of Thomas Cranmer*, ed. John Edmund Cox, vols. 15–16, Parker Society (Cambridge: Cambridge University Press, 1844–1846).

This flexibility and diversity within the tradition has only increased in the course of the last century or so; it allows some Anglicans to deny that they are Protestant and others to affirm that identity with equal conviction. The contrast with modern Lutheranism is striking.

One should stress that "Anglican," as an English rather than a Latin word, gained currency as a label fairly late in the story of the Church of England and its communion of churches. The term was used in the mid-seventeenth century by a handful of polemical writers who sought to distinguish the Church of England from the reformed Protestant churches of Europe but not much thereafter until the nineteenth century.[3] The term "Anglicanism" came into currency under the influence of John Henry Newman and the Oxford Movement, as a means to call the Protestant nature of the Church of England into question.[4] Until the emergence of the Scottish Episcopal Church, informally after the 1688 revolution and more formally after the death of Charles Edward Stuart in 1788, and the formation of the Protestant Episcopal Church in the United States of America in the 1780s, there was no family of "Anglican" churches; there was only the Church of England, defined by statute and governed by the Crown. Historians use the term "Anglican" to describe the ethos, polity, and worship of the Church of England long before 1800, but the term, as currently used, is a late coinage.

## Origins and Development of the Tradition

Churches of the continental Reformation first came into being because reformers challenged Catholic teaching and modes of worship, which they argued had departed from the gospel. Polity, and the relationship both with the Roman Catholic hierarchy and with secular authorities, lagged behind changes in doctrine and worship practices. The crisis in England played out in the reverse order to that in Germany or the Swiss Confederation—governance

3. For some early uses of the term "Anglican Church," see Peter Heylyn, *Theologia veterum, or, The summe of Christian theologie, positive, polemical, and philological, contained in the Apostles creed, or reducible to it according to the tendries of the antients both Greeks and Latines: in three books* (London: Printed by E. Cotes for Henry Seile [. . .], 1654), 5, 368; Heylyn, *Ecclesia restaurata, or, The history of the reformation of the Church of England* [. . .] (London: Printed for H. Twyford, T. Dring, J. Place, W. Palmer [. . .], 1660–1661), 91–92; Heylyn, *Cyprianus Anglicus, or, The history of the life and death of the Most Reverend and renowned prelate William, by divine providence Lord Archbishop of Canterbury* [. . .] (London: Printed for A. Seile, 1668), 41.

4. Note uses of the terms "Anglican" and "Anglicanism" in John Henry Newman (1801–1890), *Tracts for the Times, no. 90: Remarks on Certain Passages in the Thirty-nine Articles*, 2nd ed. (n.p.: n.p., 1841), 11, 77–78.

considerations came first, then worship and belief. In the early 1530s, intellectuals marshaled by Thomas Cromwell (d. 1540)—a bureaucrat-administrator who rose from the household of Thomas Wolsey (d. 1530)—persuaded King Henry VIII (r. 1509–1547) that he was morally and historically entitled to substitute his authority for that of the pope over the Church in England (known in Latin as *Anglicana Ecclesia*). The key steps were taken in the Act in Restraint of Appeals (1533), which excluded Roman jurisdiction in a narrow range of types of church lawsuits; then the Act of Supremacy (1534) "corroborated and confirmed" the (allegedly) already existing authority of the king to adjudicate all religious causes whatsoever. The king then delegated his supremacy to his chief minister, Thomas Cromwell, as "vicegerent in spirituals" to plunder the church's wealth.[5]

Henry proved to be better at defining his dislikes (the Roman papacy, but also Martin Luther) than achieving a coherent position for his church. Piecemeal doctrinal statements were issued, bewilderingly seeming to head in different directions, according to the play of factions at court and the king's own wayward sense of his own infallibility.[6] Worship remained in medieval Latin; the Act of Six Articles of 1539 prescribed the continuance of "private masses," apparently including Masses for the dead, though the wording of the act suggests that the king may have confused these with low Masses for small congregations.[7] Cautious liturgical change began in the last years of Henry's reign. The "Great Litany" in English, issued in 1544, was the first enduring element of Cranmer's liturgy to appear. It abbreviated its medieval Latin model by omitting the names of saints. The text included the inflammatory petition "From all sedycion and privey conspiracie, from the tyranny of the bisshop of Rome and all his detestable enormyties, from all false doctrine and heresye, . . . Good lorde deliver us."[8]

5. The most recent authoritative account of the story is that of Peter Marshall, *Heretics and Believers: A History of the English Reformation* (New Haven: Yale University Press, 2017), 163–266.

6. A case for the consistency of the king's religious policies, not persuasive to me, is found in G. W. Bernard, *The King's Reformation: Henry VIII and the Remaking of the English Church* (New Haven: Yale University Press, 2005).

7. See the Act of Six Articles, in G. B. Adams and H. Morse Stephens, eds., *Select Documents of English Constitutional History* (New York: Macmillan, 1918), 253–59 and esp. 255: "It is meet and necessary that private masses be continued and admitted in this the king's English Church and congregation, as whereby good Christian people, ordering themselves accordingly, do receive both godly and goodly consolations and benefits; and it is agreeable also to God's law."

8. "Exhortation and Litany (1544)," http://justus.anglican.org/resources/bcp/Litany1544/Exhortation&Litany_1544.htm. See also the discussion in Bryan D. Spinks, "Liturgy and Worship," in *The Oxford History of Anglicanism*, vol. 1, *Reformation and Identity, c.1520–1662*, ed. Anthony Milton (Oxford: Oxford University Press, 2017), 151.

The seeds of change were sown in the king's last years and months. Henry's last queen, Catherine Parr, evaded court conspiracies against her, as did Archbishop Cranmer. The tutelage of the young King Edward VI (r. 1547–1553) was entrusted to moderately reforming Renaissance scholars and their aristocratic patrons. In 1549 Thomas Cranmer largely devised, and the king's government issued, the first *Book of Common Prayer*.[9] The book was prescribed to be used throughout the kingdom and to replace all previous liturgical texts for public worship. The work condensed heavily adapted select translations from the medieval Sarum Missal (for the Eucharist), Breviary (for Morning and Evening Prayer), and Manual (for pastoral offices) into a single book entirely in English. The fourth key medieval liturgical text, the Pontifical, was supplanted by the Ordinal issued in 1550.[10] Notwithstanding the borrowings, Cranmer infused the text with his own reformed theology. The 1549 book would later enjoy some popularity with those who loved high liturgical forms. At first it pleased few people. Conservatives excoriated any worship in the vernacular; progressive reformed theologians—English and visitors from other parts of Europe—disapproved of its concessions to medieval practice. The prayer book was substantially revised into a new edition in 1552, which adopted a more unambiguously Protestant tone.[11]

The 1552 book had barely a year of use before Edward VI died in the summer of 1553 and was succeeded by his Catholic half sister Mary I (r. 1553–1558). Catholic worship was restored almost immediately. The restoration of church lands plundered by previous monarchs was abandoned, and brutal persecution was unleashed on those steadfast Protestants who could not take flight into exile or take refuge in equivocation or abjuration. With Mary's death in 1558, Elizabeth I (r. 1558–1603) reinstated, in a now polarized political atmosphere, royal supremacy over the church and the *Book of Common Prayer*. This 1559 book modified the 1552 book, omitting some of its most partisan language.[12] It defined "Anglican" worship for around a century. Yet in Elizabeth's first decades it appeared more likely that the liturgy would be

9. For the background to the first *Book of Common Prayer*, see Marshall, *Heretics and Believers*, 323–25; Spinks, "Liturgy and Worship," 148–61. For the text, see Brian Cummings, ed., *The Book of Common Prayer: The Texts of 1549, 1559, and 1662* (Oxford: Oxford University Press, 2011), and "The First Book of Common Prayer," http://justus.anglican.org/resources /bcp/1549/BCP_1549.htm.

10. For the texts of the Ordinal, see http://justus.anglican.org/resources/bcp/1549/Bishops _1549.htm, http://justus.anglican.org/resources/bcp/1549/Priests_1549.htm, and http://justus .anglican.org/resources/bcp/1549/Deacons_1549.htm.

11. The 1552 book is published as *The Book of Common Prayer: printed by Whitchurch 1552; commonly called the Second Book of Edward VI* (London: William Pickering, 1844).

12. For the text of the 1559 book, see Cummings, *Book of Common Prayer*.

a casualty of an increasingly tense political situation. From Convocation of
1563 and successive parliamentary sessions up to 1586, attempts were made
either to revise the *Book of Common Prayer* in a more distinctly reformed
direction or to replace it altogether.[13] Such demands, suppressed with bureaucratic determination by the queen's last archbishop of Canterbury, John
Whitgift (r. 1583–1604), resurfaced in the petition presented to King James I
on his accession in 1603.

The seventeenth century saw massive upheavals in the life of the Church
of England. Yet in the first two decades, regular worship was dominated by
theological preaching. Clergy as different as the reformed Richard Bernard and
the moderate poet George Herbert regarded preaching as the primary duty
of the minister.[14] Gradually, a small but influential group of ceremonialists
pushed back against this fixation with preaching, especially on the doctrine
of divine election. Richard Montagu (1577–1641) resisted the idea that the
doctrine of the Church of England was equivalent to that of the reformed
churches of Europe, to the fury of fellow clergy.[15] Clergy patronized by Bishop
Richard Neile (1562–1640) argued that prayer and sacramental worship should
take a larger place in church life, and that the sacraments should be surrounded with more ceremony, beauty, and reverence. Critically—and in the
end disastrously—this tight-knit group obtained the ear of King Charles I
(r. 1625–1649). The clique dominated not only the most important bishoprics
but, in bishops William Laud (d. 1645) and William Juxon (d. 1663), several
important offices of state as well. Suspicion of "Arminianism" (the label
imprecisely applied to the group's theological tastes) led to uproar and the
cessation of Parliament between 1629 and 1640. What made the crisis acute
was, in part, another innovation in worship. The Church of Scotland, which
had a hybrid episcopal and presbyterian polity, was in 1637 directed by its
bishops to use a version of the *Book of Common Prayer*, enriched with additional saints, in place of its Genevan-style worship.[16] The ensuing protest

13. For this period, see Marshall, *Heretics and Believers*, chaps. 15–16.
14. See Richard Bernard, *The Faithful Shepheard: or, the Shepheard's Faithfulnesse* [. . .]
(London: Hatfield and Bill, 1607); George Herbert, "The Countrey Parson preacheth constantly,
the pulpit is his joy and his throne . . ." *A Priest to the Temple: or, the Countrey Parson His
Character and Rule of Holy Life* (London: Maxey and Garthwait, 1652), chap. 7.
15. Richard Mountagu [sic], *A gagg for the new Gospell? No: a nevv gagg for an old goose*
[. . .] (London: Printed by Thomas Snodham for Matthew Lownes and William Barret, 1624).
On the larger story of this movement, see Nicholas Tyacke, *Anti-Calvinists: The Rise of English
Arminianism, c. 1590–1640* (New York: Oxford University Press, 1987).
16. *The Booke of Common Prayer, and Administration of the Sacraments: And other parts of
divine service for the use of the Church of Scotland* (Edinburgh: Robert Young, 1637). Though
at one stage known colloquially as "Laud's Liturgy," scholarly opinion now regards this book
as much more the work of the Scottish bishops than of William Laud.

and rebellion forced the king to call the English Parliament. Outrage over the religious and political policies of the monarchy produced an impasse that, by early autumn 1642, turned into civil war.

The civil wars of 1642–1648, aside from their catastrophic consequences for society in the three kingdoms, dealt a grievous blow to the Church of England. In 1645 Archbishop of Canterbury William Laud was executed for treason, and the use of the *Book of Common Prayer* was proscribed. With the episcopate disgraced, the liturgy banned, and the monarchy abolished, the Church of England entered on a fifteen-year period of partial suppression and partial clandestinity.[17] With the restoration of Charles II (r. 1660–1685), it was understood that the Church of England would be restored, though many hoped in some way to include those who had ministered in mainstream non-episcopal ministries in the Interregnum. In the end, the outcome was a stern insistence on subscription to the *Book of Common Prayer*, the Articles of Religion, and the episcopal order; the threat of expulsion hung over those who refused and was carried out in 1662. For the first time a substantial nonconforming or dissenting body of mainstream Protestants arose in England, inhibited by legal restrictions. Meanwhile the *Book of Common Prayer* was revised again, avoiding the extremes of either Protestant objectors or avant-garde ceremonialists. The 1662 *Book of Common Prayer* has, by historical accident, been the "official" liturgy of the Church of England ever since, though since the late twentieth century multiple and theoretically "alternative" liturgies have supplanted it in most parish churches. It embraced a moderate approach, rearranging elements in some services and including some nods to both ceremonial and reformed preferences.

Political events and the spectacular incompetence of Charles II's Roman Catholic brother James II (r. 1685–1688) contributed to the affirmation of the reformed identity of the church. The Stuart monarchs sought to suspend the penal laws against dissenters as a way of (coincidentally) liberating Catholics. The fear of Catholicism led to such suspicion of King James II that, when he prosecuted for sedition leading Church of England bishops who had petitioned against an edict suspending the penal laws, the mood in the country allowed William III of Orange, with his wife Mary, James II's daughter, to invade England and, over the years 1688–1691, to establish their rule in the three kingdoms. Some of the highest of High Church bishops refused to break their oaths to the old king and were replaced. After unsuccessful attempts to

17. For the mid-seventeenth century, see Spinks, "Liturgy and Worship," 161–67; Judith Maltby, *Prayer Book and People in Elizabethan and Early Stuart England* (Cambridge: Cambridge University Press, 1998).

include dissenters in the church, legal toleration (though not full civil equality) was granted to Protestants worshiping outside the Church of England.[18] Early in the eighteenth century the debates within the Church of England focused more on questions of polity than questions of liturgy; the *Book of Common Prayer* established itself as the unquestioned book of worship of the church, though the Methodist Societies would in due course modify the style of worship considerably. In the meantime the established Church of Scotland was confirmed in its presbyterian structure and reformed worship; the Church of Ireland remained the church of an elite minority.

The English colonies in North America came into being through various impulses, of which religion was by no means the least significant. The Virginia Colony—established with the founding of Jamestown in 1607—ostensibly adopted Church of England worship from the start, though the fragile and soon dispersed nature of the settlements along with the lack of funds made effective church ministries very difficult.[19] Plymouth Plantation, established ,y a Separatist sect in 1620, always included a significant proportion of nonmembers of the church in its ranks.[20] Meanwhile the Massachusetts Bay settlements were founded in the 1630s by members of the Church of England who passionately rejected both the politics and the liturgical choices of Charles I's bishops. Though not intending to be dissenters (and probably understanding themselves to be the true embodiment of what the Church of England should have been), the ministers of these colonies abandoned the *Book of Common Prayer* and formed self-supporting church structures, permanently estranged from the home country.[21]

The Church of England in the colonies, though chronically underfunded, over time developed parochial structures and institutions of education. In the colonial period, it never had its own bishops. Clergy were ordained, mostly by the bishops of London, and sent across the ocean to serve communities that most had never seen.[22] With the Revolutionary War of 1775–1783, those

18. For the liturgical history of this period, see Bryan D. Spinks, "The Book of Common Prayer, Liturgy, and Worship," in *The Oxford History of Anglicanism*, vol. 2, *Establishment and Empire, 1662–1829*, ed. Jeremy Gregory (Oxford: Oxford University Press, 2017), 253–69.

19. For the Episcopal Church in the colonial period, see Robert W. Prichard, *A History of the Episcopal Church* (Harrisburg, PA: Morehouse, 2014), chaps. 1–3.

20. On Plymouth see most recently Carla Gardina Pestana, *The World of Plymouth Plantation* (Cambridge, MA: Harvard University Press, 2020).

21. For some of the historic polity documents of the New England churches, see [General Association of Connecticut], *The Ancient Platforms of the Congregational Churches of New England; with a Digest of rules and usages in Connecticut, and an appendix, containing notices of congregational bodies in other states* (Middletown, CT: Hunt, 1843).

22. See James B. Bell, "Anglican Clergy in Colonial America Ordained by Bishops of London," *Proceedings of the American Antiquarian Society* 83, no. 1 (1973): 103–60.

loyal to Church of England worship had to reconceive church and worship, despite suspicion of being loyalists to the Crown. An influential early leader, William White of Philadelphia (1748–1836), proposed that, if need be, the episcopate should be instituted for the church without episcopal succession.[23] In the end, a different solution was found. The high clericalist Samuel Seabury (1729–1796) of Connecticut was chosen to seek consecration as a bishop in Britain. Unable to take the oath to the Crown required of English bishops (a requirement abolished shortly afterward), he sought out the Scottish Episcopalians, whose bishops declined the oath of allegiance and consecrated him in 1784. By dexterous diplomacy the democratic instincts of the Pennsylvanians and the clericalism of Seabury's Connecticut came together in the first convention of the Protestant Episcopal Church of the United States in 1785. Liturgical projects were proposed from both extremes: Enlightenment moderates proposed stripping out much of the traditional language of the prayer book, while Seabury and his allies urged a higher liturgical tone, in part because of undertakings made to the Scots bishops at his consecration. In the end, the first Episcopal *Book of Common Prayer* of 1789 amounted to a relatively modest adjustment of the 1662 book, with the state prayers altered and some detail changes.[24]

The nineteenth century brought momentous change to the ethos and culture of what became known as the "Anglican" traditions. Differences opened up, in England and the United States, between evangelicals who cherished the memory of the Protestant reformers (combined with an emphasis on personal conversion) and those who aspired to strengthen in the church a sense of its divinely authorized mission, above and beyond political contingencies. The "High and Dry" Anglicans resisted concessions made in English law to dissenters and Roman Catholics; those in the United States aspired to increase the quality, numbers, authority, and visibility of the clergy and episcopate.[25] Over the course of the 1830s and 1840s, a separate movement arose, initially known as "Tractarian" from its series of polemical pamphlets on church affairs

23. The case was made in William White, *The Case of the Episcopal Churches in the United States considered* [. . .] (Philadelphia: David C. Claypoole, 1782).

24. For the various liturgical proposals and the ultimate first *Book of Common Prayer* of the Protestant Episcopal Church, see Bishop Seabury's Communion Order at http://justus .anglican.org/resources/bcp/Seabury.htm, the proposed 1786 book at http://justus.anglican.org /resources/bcp/1786/BCP_1786.htm, and the 1789 book at http://justus.anglican.org/resources /bcp/1789/BCP_1789.htm.

25. On High Church sentiment in the nineteenth century, see Robert M. Andrews, "High Church Anglicanism in the Nineteenth Century," in *The Oxford History of Anglicanism*, vol. 3, *Partisan Anglicanism and Its Global Expansion 1829–c.1914*, ed. Rowan Strong (Oxford: Oxford University Press, 2017), 141–64.

published as *Tracts for the Times*.[26] Theoretical, learned, and academic at first, the Tractarians sought to define Anglican identity as Christianity derived from its late antique and early medieval roots, from the mission of Augustine of Canterbury and the ascetics of the age of Bede. That entailed marginalizing the role of the Protestant Reformation.

Over time the ritual wing of the Anglo-Catholic movement sought to re-interpret the life and worship of the church so as to bring it closer to an ide-alized image of medieval Catholicism. The 1662 or 1789 *Book of Common Prayer* was embellished with vestments, ornaments, architecture, and gesture from a pre-Reformation past. These movements proved enormously contro-versial on both sides of the Atlantic, but the energy of the competing strands in Anglicanism helped, paradoxically, to broaden the reach of its mission and to multiply congregations. Meanwhile vowed communities of celibate men or women, absent since 1540, came back into favor. Women's religious orders played an important role in the urban life of Episcopal churches in the late nineteenth century.[27] As the British Empire spread across the world, branches of the Church of England developed in the colonies. The question of how these were to be governed was initially not clear. The furor over the liberal biblical scholarship of John William Colenso (1814–1883), bishop of Natal, raised the question of who had jurisdiction over colonial bishops and revealed conflicting views. This debate directly provoked the calling of the First Lambeth Conference of the Anglican Churches in 1867, after which it gradually became clear that the Anglican churches of different parts of the world would subsist autonomously—but with regular meetings. The 1888 conference adopted the "Chicago-Lambeth Quadrilateral," partly inspired by the work of the "broad Church" American Episcopalian William Reed Hun-tington (1838–1909), a statement of the essential scriptural and traditional bases of shared Anglican self-definition.[28]

The twentieth century manifested one of the clearest markers of the dif-ference between the Church of England and the churches of the wider com-munion (as the Anglican family of churches has come to be known).[29] Once again the key issue was liturgical. The Anglican churches around the world

---

26. *Tracts for the Times: by members of the University of Oxford* [J. H. Newman, J. Keble, W. Palmer, R. H. Froude, E. B. Pusey, I. Williams and others], 6 vols. (London: J. G. F. & J. Riv-ington, 1834–1870).

27. A particularly moving instance of the sacrificial dedication of Anglican sisterhoods is afforded by "Constance and Her Companions" or the "Martyrs of Memphis" in 1878. See St. Mary's Episcopal Cathedral, https://www.stmarysmemphis.org/history.

28. For the quadrilateral and its adoption by the 1888 Lambeth Conference, see *The Book of Common Prayer of the Episcopal Church* (New York: Church Publishing, 1979), 876–78.

29. See the website of the Anglican Communion at https://www.anglicancommunion.org.

had authority to revise their own prayer books. The Episcopal Church in the United States revised its liturgy in 1892, 1928, and 1979. However, when the Church of England sought to revise the 1662 *Book of Common Prayer* in the 1920s, the approval of this revised version, extensively discussed and heavily supported by the church's representative bodies, was twice blocked in Parliament. Consequently the 1928 "proposed book" was never legally authorized, though elements of it, notably the marriage service, are widely used. Nevertheless, the drift toward encompassing in Anglican worship more of the scope of nineteenth-century diversity in its worship was irresistible. Whether through the introduction of "alternative services" in the Church of England or wholesale revision of the *Book of Common Prayer* in other churches, the second half of the twentieth century saw the influence of the Liturgical Movement. The instincts of the Liturgical Movement of the mid-twentieth century, with its desire to recover the worship forms of the early churches of late antiquity, coincided particularly well with the historic impulses of the Church of England going back to archbishops Thomas Cranmer and Matthew Parker (1504–1575). England consolidated its liturgical experiments into the *Alternative Service Book* of 1980, and then after twenty years of further experiment adopted *Common Worship* (2000) as the normal collection of services. Here the *Book of Common Prayer* became more of an idea or a concept than a single volume: the main texts are surrounded with an array of resources for special liturgies, and—even for the ordinary weekly worship of the church—a large range of variants are authorized.[30] Some parts of Church of England liturgy now consist of general guidance for the structuring of a service rather than prescribed forms.

## Theological Orientation of the Anglican and Episcopal Traditions

Churches established, or in the case of Roman Catholicism profoundly reshaped, in the century of the Reformation typically defined their teachings with detailed and lengthy statements of belief. Martin Luther produced his shorter and longer catechisms in 1529, the latter a substantial theological manual. John Calvin repeatedly revised his *Institutes* of 1536, originally intended as a work of catechesis, into its definitive form in 1559. The churches of the Swiss Confederation (by no means dependent on Calvin's authority) adopted the Second Helvetic Confession of 1566, drafted by Heinrich

---

30. For the 1980 Alternative Service book, see http://www.oremus.org/liturgy/asb/index .html; for *Common Worship*, see https://www.churchofengland.org/prayer-and-worship/wor ship-texts-and-resources/common-worship.

Bullinger (1504–1575) of Zurich. Most substantial and most long-lived of all was the Roman Catholic Church's *Roman Catechism* of 1566, sometimes slightly misleadingly referred to as the *Tridentine Catechism*. In this context of massive theological compilations, the Church of England was reticent. The catechism in the 1559 *Book of Common Prayer* was brief (under two thousand words) and intended to be learned by rote by children before confirmation. The Thirty-Nine Articles of Religion, edited in 1563 from an earlier draft by Cranmer and finally resolved in 1571, were likewise brief, though their Reformed character (despite the ingenuity of John Henry Newman in reinterpreting them in *Tract 90*) was inescapable.[31] They required belief in *sola scriptura* (article 6), justification by faith (articles 11–14), and predestination in a moderate and limited form (article 17). They rejected belief in purgatory (article 22), the use of unknown language in worship (article 24), the five "sacraments" renounced by the reformers (article 25), transubstantiation (article 28), and the celibacy of clergy (article 32). Despite innumerable attempts down the centuries to deny or minimize their Reformed character, the orientation of the articles is clear to any historian.

Notwithstanding, the Church of England was noteworthy for the reluctance displayed—often at the insistence of Queen Elizabeth I—to define its doctrine more fully, or allow development of the polemical implications of its teachings.[32] Still, Elizabethan bishops, among others, organized the translation of works of continental reformed theology. The *Decades* of sermons by Heinrich Bullinger of Zurich were translated and published in English in the 1570s, as were the sermons of Bullinger's colleague Rudolf Gwalther (1519–1586).[33] Thomas Norton (1532–1584), son-in-law of Thomas Cranmer, translated Calvin's *Institutes* into English in 1561, with a revised edition in 1574 that became standard for nearly two centuries.[34] Later in the sixteenth century, Henry Parry (1561–1616), later bishop of Worcester, translated the lectures of Zacharias Ursinus of Heidelberg (1534–1583) on the Heidelberg

31. The Thirty-Nine Articles may be read in *The Book of Common Prayer of the Episcopal Church* (as note 28), 867–76; see also B. J. Kidd, *The Thirty-Nine Articles: Their History and Explanation*, 2 vols. (London: Rivingtons, 1899).

32. See, e.g., the controversy over the Lambeth Articles of 1595, and most recently on this topic Debora Shuger, "The Mystery of the Lambeth Articles," *Journal of Ecclesiastical History* 68, no. 2 (April 2017): 306–25.

33. See [Heinrich Bullinger], *Fiftie Godlie and Learned Sermons: diuided into Fiue Decades conteyning the chiefe and principall pointes of Christian religion* (London: By Ralphe Newberrie [. . .], 1577); Rudolf Gwalther, *An hundred, threescore and fiftene homelyes or sermons, vppon the Actes of the Apostles* [. . .] (London: Henrie Denham, 1572).

34. [John Calvin], *The Institution of Christian religion, vvrytten in Latine by maister Ihon Caluin, and translated into Englysh according to the authors last edition* [. . .], [trans. Thomas Norton] (London: By Reinolde VVolfe & Richarde Harison, 1561).

Catechism into English, creating a textbook of moderate reformed Protestantism for English use. This translation, supplemented with the commentary of David Pareus (1548–1622), was published in multiple editions up to the 1640s.[35]

Some theologians, notably William Perkins (1558–1602) of Cambridge, went beyond the gentle reformed theology of Zurich and Heidelberg to teach the spikier points of predestination.[36] Yet what was taught in the universities of England (and preached in some parishes) was not quite "official" doctrine. That credibility gap allowed Richard Montagu, in his intentionally inflammatory pamphlet subtitled *a new gagg for an old goose* of 1624, to argue that contentious Calvinist doctrines were not, in fact, the teaching of the Church of England. Montagu was an outlier, but the political favor that he enjoyed from the Neile/Laud circle made his attempt to deny that the Church of England was aligned with the most radical Reformed churches extremely contentious and threatening to many. Nevertheless, the fear of Arminianism in England almost certainly exceeded its numerical significance. Regardless of their political or liturgical preferences, it is probable that most Church of England clergy and educated layfolk in the seventeenth century shared in a generic reformed Protestantism. When Gilbert Burnet (1643–1715), the Scottish Presbyterian turned Church of England cleric (later bishop) and political supporter of William III, issued the first volume of his *History of the Reformation of the Church of England* in 1679, Parliament passed a vote of thanks for the work.[37]

In the eighteenth century the major theological issues debated within the Church of England raised questions about the abstract relationship of the church to the Crown and the state, given that the state no longer accorded the Church of England a monopoly on legal worship. The essentially reformed character of the Church of England was not brought into direct question in a substantial, frontal fashion until the nineteenth century. The Tractarians, most notoriously John Henry Newman in *Tract 90*, argued that the heritage

35. Zacharias Ursinus, *The summe of Christian religion: deliuered by Zacharias Vrsinus in his lectures vpon the Catechism autorised by the noble Prince Frederick, throughout his dominions . . . translated into English by Henrie Parrie* (Oxford: Ioseph Barnes; London: T. Cooke, 1587); *The Summe of Christian religion: delivered by Zacharias Vrsinus in his lectures vpon the Catechisme, authorised by the noble Prince Fredericke throughout his dominions. . . . Translated into English first by D. Henrie Parry, and lately conferred with the last and best Latine edition of D. David Pareus Professor of Divinity in Heidelberge* (Oxford: Barnes; London: Broome, 1601).

36. See most famously William Perkins, *A Golden Chaine, or the Description of Theologie: Containing the order of the causes of saluation and damnation, according to Gods word*, trans. Robert Hill (London: John Legatte, printer to the Universitie of Cambridge, 1612).

37. Gilbert Burnet, *The History of the Reformation of the Church of England*, 3 vols. (London: Chiswell, 1679–1753).

documents of the Church of England could legitimately be interpreted in a way that was sympathetic to Roman Catholicism "properly understood"— that is, without the abuses and misconstructions of late medieval piety. Anglo-Catholic scholars strove to demonstrate that the Church of England's anteced-ents lay not with the continental reformers but with the ancient church and the early fathers: the church's relationship to its past was one of continuity, not of breach. (Protestant reformers since John Jewel in the 1560s had been arguing the same thing, that the reformed church simply returned Christianity to its ancient and patristic roots.)[38]

In the modern age there has rightly been diminishing enthusiasm for re-fighting the confessional battles of earlier centuries, but other signs of cracks or divergences of theological emphasis have arisen. Broadly speaking, the Church of England tends to fracture along the lines between those, on the one hand, who espouse liberal-critical approaches to Scripture and tradi-tional doctrine, often in conjunction with liberal approaches to cultural/ethi-cal liberation questions, and those, on the other hand, who take conservative stances on ethical and social questions in conjunction with either evangelical perspectives on Scripture or Anglo-Catholic perspectives on the sanctity of tradition. The historically puzzling alliance of evangelical and Anglo-Catholic conservatives was most obviously demonstrated in the controversies in En-gland over the ordination of women to the priesthood in the 1990s and over the roles of LGBT people in the church.

## Practical Implications for Worship

As is evident from the earlier part of this chapter, one cannot separate ques-tions of worship from the political history of the churches in this tradition, because so often the key political debates concerned worship and the status of the *Book of Common Prayer*. Nevertheless, some general observations about the character of Anglican worship—apart from the contentious history of particular documents—are called for here. First, one can hardly overstate the importance of the *Book of Common Prayer*, in its many variations, for the tradition. Far more than any other liturgical text in any other Christian tradition, the Anglican *Book of Common Prayer* defines who members of that

38. John Jewel (1522–1571), *Apologia Ecclesiæ Anglicanæ* (London: Reginald Wolf, 1562); translated as *An Apologie or answere in defence of the Churche of Englande, with a briefe and plaine declaration of the true Religion professed and used in the same* (London: Reginald Wolf, 1562). The work was republished as *The Works of John Jewel*, ed. John Ayre, 4 vols., Parker Society 23–26 (Cambridge: Cambridge University Press, 1845–1850), 3:1–48 (Latin) and 49–112 (English).

tradition are. Moreover, the *Book of Common Prayer* embodies a particular attitude toward tradition itself. It expresses respect for the inherited language of the ancient church, and even of the medieval church, with a determination to encapsulate the teachings of the Reformation, which the reformers regarded as being simply a restoration of the teachings and beliefs of the ancient church. Unlike nearly every liturgy from the churches issued from the Reformation, the Church of England aspired, at least until *Common Worship*, to set down in writing all that was said in the liturgical acts of priests and people. While certain things were left to the celebrant's discretion, from the sermon to the gestures used at the altar, in principle every Anglican was supposed to know what was being said in their church at any particular moment.

Second, Anglican worship is inherently responsory. While many Protestant churches have recently adopted responsory forms of liturgy, especially in the Communion, these were a key part of Church of England worship from the beginning. In the Middle Ages the responses were said in Latin by the clergy and their helpers within the chancel alone; in the *Book of Common Prayer*, the responses were said by the congregation in its entirety. Maybe the single most important contribution of Anglican worship was the expectation that the people would play a key part in the liturgical drama through their responses. That, in turn, was why it was so important that the service be entirely in English. This insistence that worship must follow precisely the forms set down by law was illustrated in a conference between Archbishop John Whitgift and two clergy objectors, Thomas Sparke and Walter Travers, in 1584. When Sparke attempted to begin the meeting with a prayer for guidance, Whitgift angrily retorted that "you shall make no prayers here: you shall not turn this place into a conventicle."[39] Prayer was to be according to the set forms, and those only.

As to the application of the principles of the *Book of Common Prayer*, the modern emphasis on Holy Communion as the standard pattern of Sunday morning worship is just that: modern. It dates from the last decades of the twentieth century. Since 1559 most Sunday worship consisted of Morning Prayer in the morning and Evening Prayer in the late afternoon. Technically, the liturgy for Morning Prayer does not make space for a sermon. According to Raphael Holinshed's report of the 1559 prayer book, the theoretical order of worship on Sunday mornings was Morning Prayer, the Great Litany, and then part of the Communion service, which was stopped short before the

---

39. The story is told in Benjamin Brook, *The Lives of the Puritans: Containing a Biographical Account of those divines who distinguished themselves in the cause of religious liberty, from the reformation under Queen Elizabeth, to the Act of uniformity in 1662*, 3 vols. (London: Black, 1813), 2:316.

beginning of the eucharistic prayer. Sermons were to be included within this ante-communion rite.[40] This order was probably followed in cathedrals, royal chapels, and other distinguished locations, but in many parish churches—and not just those led by advanced radical reforming clergy—Morning Prayer with sermon and Evening Prayer predominated. For the first generation after 1559, by no means were all parish clergy "licensed" to preach; those who could not were directed to read from one of the two *Books of Homilies* issued in 1547 and 1562.[41] However, vigorous Protestant objections to "dumb dogs," and the gradual shift to an all-graduate ministry by the mid-seventeenth century, ensured that preaching was the primary duty of the parish incumbent.[42]

Particular features of the *Book of Common Prayer* deserve brief mention. The most controversial element retained in the baptism rite was the signing of the recipient with the sign of the cross after baptism.[43] Only there was the sign of the cross prescribed, and more radical Protestants objected to it repeatedly. In other respects, the sign of the cross was a Catholic target of Protestant disdain, in England as elsewhere.[44] The use made of the Psalter varied from parish to parish. Officially, the prose translation of the Psalms, which figured largely in the orders for Morning and Evening Prayer, was that of Miles Coverdale made for the Henrician Great Bible of 1539/1540. However, translating the Psalms is a constantly challenging task: new English versions were offered in the Bishops' Bible in 1568 and the King James Version of 1611. Yet for many parishes the Psalms in meter, often according to the version by Sternhold and Hopkins, replaced the chanted Psalter from the prayer book for congregational singing.[45] Metrical hymns, which had been part of the life

40. Spinks, "Liturgy and Worship," 158–59 and references.

41. The modern edition of these works is *The Book of Homilies: A Critical Edition*, ed. Gerald Lewis Bray (Cambridge: James Clarke, 2015).

42. The Essex clergyman Ralph Josselin noted that his preaching was the essential criterion for his being appointed to the parish of Earls Colne: "The next day being the Lords day I preachd, upon their approbacion they desired mee I would come and live with them as their Minister." See *The Diary of Ralph Josselin, 1616–1683*, ed. Alan Macfarlane (Oxford: Oxford University and the British Academy, 2015), 10.

43. See "The Ministracion of Baptisme," in *Book of Common Prayer* (1559), http://justus .anglican.org/resources/bcp/1559/Baptism_1559.htm. "We receive this Childe into the congrega-cion of Christes flocke, and do sygne him with the signe of the crosse, in token that hereafter he shal not be ashamed to confesse the faith of Christ crucified."

44. An example of the fierce debates over the sign of the cross in Elizabethan England can be seen in James Calfhill, *An Answer to John Martiall's Treatise of the Cross*, ed. Richard Gib-bings, Parker Society (Cambridge: Cambridge University Press, 1846), first published in 1565.

45. For a typical early edition, see *The Whole Booke of Psalmes, collected into English meter by Thomas Sternhold, I. Hopkins and others . . . with apt notes to syng them withal* (London: John Day, 1565). Archbishop Matthew Parker also translated the Psalms into metrical verse in 1567, with tunes by Thomas Tallis.

of the Lutheran churches almost from the beginning, were slow to arrive in the Anglican traditions. Freely composed choral anthems formed a classic part of Evening Prayer "in Quires and Places where they sing," long before the rubric to that effect was inserted in the 1662 prayer book.[46] Only in the eighteenth century, under the influence of the nonconformist Isaac Watts (1674–1748) and of course Charles Wesley (1707–1788) did hymns in verse become a regular part of church music in the Church of England.

Despite enormous changes and frequently harsh divisions between conflicting movements or tendencies within the church or the communion, the liturgies of the churches descended from the Church of England continue to compel enormous loyalty and devotion. They have inspired poets, musicians, and devotional writers of all kinds during the centuries and continue to do so. There is little doubt that many of the manifestations of Anglican spirituality in the last two centuries would have bemused those who first shaped it in the sixteenth century. However, the cohesiveness and continuity of the Anglican tradition seems able to survive all the diversity and disagreement that from time to time appears within it.

## For Further Reading

Cummings, Brian. *The Book of Common Prayer: The Texts of 1549, 1559, and 1662.* Oxford: Oxford University Press, 2011.

Hefling, Charles, and Cynthia Shattuck, eds. *The Oxford Guide to the Book of Common Prayer: A Worldwide Survey.* Oxford: Oxford University Press, 2006.

Marshall, Peter. *Heretics and Believers: A History of the English Reformation.* New Haven: Yale University Press, 2017.

Prichard, Robert W. *A History of the Episcopal Church.* 3rd rev. ed. Harrisburg, PA: Morehouse, 2014.

Spinks, Bryan D. "The Book of Common Prayer, Liturgy, and Worship." In *The Oxford History of Anglicanism*, vol. 2, *Establishment and Empire, 1662–1829*, edited by Jeremy Gregory, 253–69. Oxford: Oxford University Press, 2017.

———. "Liturgy and Worship." In *The Oxford History of Anglicanism*, vol. 1, *Reformation and Identity, c.1520–1662*, edited by Anthony Milton, 148–67. Oxford: Oxford University Press, 2017.

46. "The Book of Common Prayer, as printed by John Baskerville," http://justus.anglican .org/resources/bcp/1662/ep.pdf.

— **14** —

# Methodist and Wesleyan Practices of Worship

*Matthew Sigler*

S ome of the best conversations about Christian worship have taken place in ministers' houses around the dinner table on Sundays. The worship service is often intricately reviewed; successes and foibles are carefully evaluated. If one were privy to such conversations, one would quickly pick up on some of the distinguishing traits of the ecclesial tradition represented in the parsonage. And if one were granted the ability to eavesdrop on such conversations within Methodist communities of the past, you might encounter dialogues along the following lines.

**Delmarva Peninsula, Maryland, 1801**
"My heart is so full, brother James. The work of God broke out mightily this morning, didn't it? Brother Jones professed his belief with such deep affection during our love feast. The fire of God's love began in the believers' hearts, but it soon reached the unconverted and caused them to cry aloud for mercy."

"Amen, brother Boehm. The power of God reached the hearts of many on the grounds. Believers praised Jesus with their tongues, hands, and feet. Sinners fell to the ground, and many found the love of God shed abroad in their hearts."

"Indeed, brother James, it was a melting time. Pass the peas, please."[1]

---

1. This account is based on Methodist itinerant preacher Henry Boehm's journal from July 5, 1801. See Lester Ruth, *Early Methodist Life and Spirituality* (Nashville: Abingdon, 2005), 194–95.

## Nashville, Tennessee, 1880

"Pass the roast beef, please, Thomas. . . . Eliza made it known to me again after the service how opposed she was to your reading the prayers. She said a Methodist minister need pray only from the heart."

"How ridiculous! Even those ministers who use no book nevertheless have their forms—and these are often most dreadful. I have heard 'heartfelt' public prayers that were so superficial and repetitious that I have heartily wished the minister had a prayer book and read his prayers."

"Indeed. Another roll?"[2]

## South Orange, New Jersey, 1940

"More tea, bishop?"

"No thank you, Nolan. . . . I visited one of our new ministers last week who was eager to point out the two dim, red lights hanging over the chancel."

"Does he know that the Roman Catholic Church uses one red light to signify the presence of the host?"

"Not at all. I asked him why he put two in his church, and he said that if one looked good, two would look even better."

"More young ministers cluttering up their services with pretty but petty nothings. Are you sure you wouldn't like more tea?"[3]

If our imaginative journey through these conversations reveals anything, it should be clear that Methodist worship exists somewhere in the tension between liturgical form and liturgical freedom.[4] Additionally, Methodism in the United States has also been deeply embedded in the peculiarities of the American religious landscape, meaning that it has both shaped and been shaped by broader currents in the religious piety of the States. Because of this, difficulties abound when trying to define what is distinct about Methodist liturgical practice. Nevertheless, a historical survey affords us a perspective that can help us observe some notable traits. In this chapter we will explore the roots of Methodism by looking at the Wesleyan revival of the eighteenth century. We will then turn our attention to American Methodist worship,

2. See Thomas O. Summers, "Forms of Prayer," *Methodist Quarterly Review* 4 (January 1882): 82.

3. See Nolan Harmon, "Are We Headed toward Formalism in Worship?," *The Pastor* 19 (March 1956): 4–5.

4. Karen Westerfield Tucker develops this argument more extensively in "Form and Freedom: John Wesley's Legacy for Methodist Worship," in *The Sunday Service of the Methodists: Twentieth-Century Worship in Worldwide Methodism*, ed. Karen B. Westerfield Tucker (Nashville: Kingswood, 1996), 17–30.

inevitably treating a complex history of two centuries with broad brush strokes.[5] After this overview, we will highlight some key attributes of worship within the Wesleyan/Methodist tradition and close with some thoughts on what the tradition can contribute to worship in the church today.

## Heartfelt Anglicanism Turned Outward

Methodism can trace its founding to two brothers, John and Charles Wesley, both of whom were Anglican priests. The brothers Wesley grew up in a pious family; their father was an ordained minister in the Church of England and their mother was a sometime reluctant Anglican with Puritan sensibilities. Along with their eight other brothers and sisters, John and Charles were formed in the rectory-turned-schoolhouse under their mother's academic and religious instruction. In addition to learning the Bible, Greek, and Latin, the children—including the girls—were trained in a regimen that would rival any boarding school. The three brothers who survived into early adulthood were trained at Oxford and ordained in the Church of England.

After a tumultuous missionary endeavor in North America, John and Charles returned to England, where shortly after both experienced a spiritual awakening. The evangelical revival that swept Britain in the first half of the eighteenth century had other notable leaders—George Whitefield, for example—but the Wesley brothers were soon at the helm of the movement. For the majority of their lives, John and Charles led the Methodists as a renewal group within the Church of England.[6] As the Methodist movement grew, many of its adherents pleaded for more ordained clergy sympathetic to the revival. This was especially the case in the newly established American republic, where ordained Methodists were few and far between. Eventually, John Wesley made the unorthodox decision to "ordain" his own clergy for ministry in the United States, signaling an inevitable break with the Church of England. Charles Wesley vehemently opposed this decision and remained a devout Anglican to his dying day.

5. The progeny of the Wesleyan movement are many. For this chapter I will focus primarily on the main branch of Methodism in America, the United Methodist Church, and its antecedents. For a fuller treatment of liturgical history within the pan-Wesleyan denominations, see Karen B. Westerfield Tucker, *American Methodist Worship* (Oxford: Oxford University Press, 2001).

6. This is, admittedly, an oversimplification of a complicated history. It could be argued that John Wesley made overtures toward greater independence from the established church well before his unorthodox measure of ordaining his own clergy. For certain, there were Methodist preachers not ordained in the Church of England but licensed to preach by John Wesley, who continually pushed for separation from the established church.

One cannot fully appreciate the dynamics of Wesleyan worship if one does not understand the soteriological aims of the movement. In the first place, the Wesleys were adamant that God's salvation in Jesus Christ was available to all. This stood in sharp contrast to the understanding of limited atonement that many held to in eighteenth-century England. Second, the Methodist movement emphasized that one could know that their sins had been forgiven. The question "Am I saved?" often dominated the thoughts of eighteenth-century pious Christians.[7] Not only did the Wesleys preach that all can be saved, they argued that one can know for certain that one has been saved through what they called "the witness of the Spirit." Drawing heavily from the eighth chapter of Romans, the Wesley brothers made clear that this was more than banal emotionalism; it was an objective reality of God's saving work, apprehended by faith and made real by the Spirit in a profoundly personal way. Another phrase that was used to describe the witness of the Spirit was "the love of God shed abroad in the heart" (Rom. 5:5 KJV, adapted).

Finally, the Wesleys preached that God had the power to "save to the uttermost" (Heb. 7:25 KJV, adapted), that God in Christ desires to save a person not only from the penalty of sin but from the root of sin itself. This claim was known as "Christian perfection." In his sermon on Christian perfection, John Wesley begins by detailing what he does *not* mean by the term. To be perfected in love does *not* mean that a person (1) is free from ignorance, (2) is free from mistakes, (3) is free from "bodily infirmities" (e.g., depression or anxiety), and (4) is entirely free from temptation. Wesley then defines what Christian perfection does mean: "Here it means perfect love. It is love excluding sin; love filling the heart, taking up the whole capacity of the soul."[8] Neither John nor Charles ever claimed to be fully perfected in love, but they maintained that Methodists were to continually seek after it.

These Wesleyan hallmarks—especially assurance and entire sanctification—found a readily available support system in the 1662 *Book of Common Prayer*. Where some saw the liturgical form of the prayer book as stifling to one's experience of God, the Methodist movement drew on the grammar and structure of the Anglican liturgy.[9] Consider, for example, the "Collect for Purity" prayed at the beginning of the service of the Lord's Supper: "Almighty God, unto

7. See, e.g., Olaudah Equiano, *The Interesting Narrative of the Life of Olaudah Equiano: Written by Himself with Related Documents*, 2nd ed., ed. Robert J. Allison (Boston: Bedford/St. Martin's, 2003), 170–79.

8. Sermon 43, "The Scripture Way of Salvation," ed. Anne-Elizabeth Powell, in *The Sermons of John Wesley*, The Wesley Center for Applied Theology, http://wesley.nnu.edu/john-wesley/the-sermons-of-john-wesley-1872-edition/sermon-43-the-scripture-way-of-salvation/.

9. Puritans, e.g., had long objected to certain facets of the prayer book, not only for what they saw as errant theology, but also because the forms themselves were seen as anathema to

whom all hearts be open, all desires known, and from whom no secrets are
hid: cleanse the thoughts of our hearts by the inspiration of thy Holy Spirit,
that we may perfectly love thee, and worthily magnify thy holy name: through
Christ our Lord. Amen." Early Methodists easily interpreted the collect as
directing the worshiper to God's ultimate aim for them, entire sanctification:
"that we may *perfectly* love thee."[10]

Accounts from the Wesleyan revival demonstrate the way in which the liturgy of the established church was seen by many as an ally in the movement.
Charles Wesley, for example, records that one Methodist in Manchester experienced assurance of salvation during the litany.[11] The Wesleys' own mother,
Susanna Wesley, sensed the witness of the Spirit during the Communion
liturgy. Not only could the liturgy of the Church of England assist in one's
experience of justification; it also provided a vital foundation for the person
as they sought to be perfected in love. Drawing from a term used generations
before, the Wesleys referred to the Lord's Supper as a "means of grace."[12] The
brothers encouraged the Methodists to participate in the sacrament of Holy
Communion as often as possible because, as Charles Wesley put it, the means
of grace "will keep [you] steady."[13] And both believed that these means were
given by God to form the believer into the image of Christ. Charles versified
this perspective in his 1740 hymn on the means of grace:

> Thou bidd'st me search the sacred leaves,
> And taste the hallowed bread:
> The kind commands my soul receives,
> And longs on thee to feed.
>
> Still for thy loving kindness, Lord,
> I in thy temple wait,
> I look to find thee in thy word,
> Or at thy table meet.

---

true worship. The Wesleys, in contrast, not only upheld much of the theology of the prayer
book but also promoted its use for growing in godliness.

10. See, e.g., Thomas O. Summers, *Commentary on the Ritual of the Methodist Episcopal
Church, South* (Nashville: A. H. Redford for the Methodist Episcopal Church, South, 1873),
21–22.

11. S. T. Kimbrough and Kenneth G. C. Newport, eds., *The Manuscript Journal of the
Reverend Charles Wesley, M.A.* (Nashville: Kingswood, 2007), 2:647.

12. The enumerated means of grace were not limited to sacraments, but John Wesley lists
the Lord's Supper among the "chief means" of grace. He does not include baptism among the
means of grace because it cannot be repeated in the life of a believer.

13. Letter to William Grimshaw dated October 29, 1756. See Kenneth G. C. Newport and
Gareth Lloyd, *The Letters of Charles Wesley: A Critical Edition, with Introduction and Notes*
(Oxford: Oxford University Press, 2013), 422.

Here, *in thine own appointed ways,*
I wait to learn thy will:
Silent I stand before thy face,
And hear thee say, *"Be still!"*

"Be still—and know that I am GOD!"
'Tis all I live to know,
To feel the virtue of thy blood,
And spread its praise below.

I wait my vigour to renew,
Thine image to retrieve,
The veil of outward things pass through,
And gasp in thee to live.[14]

For as much as the Methodist movement could value the established liturgy of the Church of England, the Wesleys also introduced a number of innovations in the way their societies worshiped. Perhaps the most notable was the introduction of hymn singing. While the Congregationalists benefited from the hymns and psalter of Isaac Watts, the Methodists were among the first to sing hymns within the Church of England. Not only did the Methodists sing hymns written by John and Charles Wesley at society gatherings, but they also introduced singing during the distribution of the Lord's Supper.[15] This was more than novel for Anglican parishes whose musical repertoire was typically limited to the clunky metrical psalter authorized by the church and, in some cases in the cathedral and university churches, service music.[16] The Wesley brothers also advocated for the use of extemporaneous praying alongside the written prayers of the *Book of Common Prayer*.[17] On multiple occasions John Wesley noted "not confining myself" to the written order and prayers of the established church.[18] At the same time, he was loathe to have Methodists reject written prayers altogether.

Another notable innovation was that of "field preaching," or giving a sermon in the open air. The brothers were initially hesitant to do so but were persuaded by George Whitfield that such unorthodox measures were needed to reach the working poor around Bristol. While these events were seen as

14. John and Charles Wesley, *Hymns and Sacred Poems* (London: Strahan, 1740), 37–38 (emphasis in original).

15. Tucker, *American Methodist Worship*, 119.

16. Paul Westermeyer, *Te Deum: The Church and Music* (Minneapolis: Augsburg Fortress, 1998), 168–72.

17. For a thorough discussion of this innovation, see Tucker, "Form and Freedom."

18. See J. Hamby Barton, "A Double Letter: John Wesley and Thomas Coke to Freeborn Garrettson," *Methodist History* 17 (1978): 61.

doxological in part, the Wesleys were clear that they did not serve as a substitute for attending parish worship. These were primarily evangelistic efforts to reach those who, for various reasons, might not be impacted by the church. Both brothers took great pains to encourage their followers to attend their local parish, although Methodists were not always welcome.[19] As the Wesleyan revival spread, John Wesley organized the movement into an interlocking array of groups ranging from the "bands" (composed of around five people) to the "classes" (a dozen) and the "society" (the largest grouping of all Methodists in a given area). Methodist leaders—some of whom were Anglican clergy—were mobilized as itinerant preachers who crisscrossed the British Isles on horseback.

Lastly, John Wesley incorporated a practice he learned from the Moravians and interpreted as a form of the early Christian *agapē* meal, the love feast. The service could vary because of the emphasis on testimony and extemporaneity, but it typically included prayer, hymn singing, and the sharing of bread and water (or, in some cases, coffee or tea). In 1737 John Wesley recorded his experience at a Moravian love feast this way: "After evening prayers, we joined with the Germans in one of their love-feasts. It was begun and ended with thanksgiving and prayer, and celebrated in so decent and solemn a manner as a Christian of the apostolic age would have allowed to be worthy of Christ."[20] In this case as in all the other innovations that the Wesleys initiated, a biblical warrant or the practice of what John Wesley called "the primitive church" set a precedent for what could be introduced in the worship life of the Methodists.

Worship in early Methodism can best be summed up as heartfelt Anglicanism turned outward. On the one hand, the Wesleyan revival valued the affective because of the movement's soteriological emphases. Hymn singing, extemporaneous prayer, field preaching, testimony at the love feast, and the like emerged out of a liturgical piety that placed a premium on the personal experience of God in worship.[21] On the other hand, the Wesley brothers promoted the revival as a renewal movement within the Church of England

19. Methodists were often blocked from the Table in their local parish. See Charles Wesley's journal entry on February 11, 1744: "Arthur Bates of Wakefield . . . informed me that his minister, Mr. Arnet, repelled him from the Sacrament and said he had orders from the Archbishop so to treat all that are called Methodists." Kimbrough and Newport, *Manuscript Journal*, 2:388.

20. John Wesley, journal entry, August 8, 1737, in *Journals and Diaries I*, ed. W. Reginald Ward and Richard P. Heitzenrater, vol. 18 of *The Bicentennial Edition of the Works of John Wesley* (Nashville: Abingdon, 1988), 537.

21. Here it might be helpful to indicate a difference between what I am calling "personal" in contrast to "individual." The former does not preclude the importance of others either in worship or outside the gathering; rather, it indicates that the entire person matters in worship— head and heart.

and, unlike dissenting congregations of their day, did not see the *Book of Common Prayer* as an obstacle to the Methodist awakening. Far from it, the language, rhythms of prayer, and sacramental piety were seen as an asset to the aims of the movement. It should be clear that Methodist worship has from the very beginning thrived in between liturgical form and liturgical freedom.

One final observation must be made as we conclude this look at the Wesleyan revival, namely that early Methodists understood the "fruit" of worship to be deeper love of God *and* love of neighbor. This is the impetus toward Christian perfection: to fulfill the greatest commandment in its entirety. Methodist worship, therefore, was turned outward, so to speak. Whether exemplified in the Wesleys' decision to preach outdoors or the Methodists' overt care for the poor, worship was never viewed as an escape from the world but as an act profoundly for the world that God so loves.

## A Denomination Made for America

The first Methodist societies in America began in the 1760s and, while representing a small portion of the population, quickly flourished in the years following the American Revolution. In 1775 Methodists accounted for 2 percent of the population. By the middle of the nineteenth century Methodists comprised 34 percent of the population.[22] Methodism's emphasis that God's salvation was available to anyone resonated with the optimism of the early republic.

As separation from the Church of England became inevitable, John Wesley prepared an edition of the 1662 *Book of Common Prayer* for the Methodists in North America.[23] Copies of his redacted version of the prayer book were sent alongside *A Collection of Psalms and Hymns for the Lord's Day* and were accompanied with a letter from Wesley conveying his expectations for how the American Methodists were to utilize the prayer book: "[I have] prepared a Liturgy little differing from that of the Church of England (I think, the best constituted national Church in the world), which I advise all the travelling preachers to use on the Lord's Day in all the congregations, reading the Litany only on Wednesdays and Fridays, and praying extempore on all other days. I also advise the elders to administer the Supper of the Lord, on every Lord's

22. John H. Wigger, *Taking Heaven by Storm* (Oxford: Oxford University Press, 1998), 3.
23. John Wesley edited nearly exclusively by redaction—the one key addition being the option for extempore prayer at the Communion service. For full treatment of the changes, see Karen B. Westerfield Tucker, "John Wesley's Prayer Book Revision: The Text in Context," *Methodist History* 34, no. 4 (July 1996): 230–47.

Day."[24] Given that the Lord's Supper would have been administered much less frequently in the Church of England at the time, Wesley's stipulation is notable. So too is his admonition for the use of extemporaneous prayer.

At least four editions of the *Sunday Service* were published between 1786 and 1792 for use in America as well as the British Empire. While some urban parishes continued to use Wesley's prayer book for a time, the majority of American Methodists quietly set aside "Wesley's last will and testament" following his death.[25] The sacramental services and other pastoral offices were parceled out into what would become known as "The Ritual" and were included in the *Book of Discipline*, but the *Sunday Service of the Methodists* would never be employed in the manner that Wesley envisioned. That fact was that most American Methodists were at least one step further removed from the Church of England than John Wesley. Bishop Nolan Harmon, writing in the mid-twentieth century, surmised that the fate of the *Sunday Service* was sealed in that the itinerant minister's saddle bag was simply too full for another book. Itinerant Methodist Jesse Lee concluded that Methodists would rather pray with their eyes shut than open.[26]

In spite of the tepid reception given to the *Sunday Service*, Methodists in America embraced the vibrant eucharistic piety bequeathed to them by the Wesleys even though most were limited in their frequency of reception owing to the scarcity of ordained clergy. For early American Methodists, the quarterly meeting became the primary opportunity to access the Lord's Supper. These venues—originally conceived as business meetings—were quickly eclipsed by the worship services that bracketed the gatherings. Quarterly meetings soon were punctuated by vibrant preaching services, complete with sometimes effusive expressions of emotion. The full spectrum of Wesleyan soteriology was enacted in these events with some people crying aloud for mercy, others singing for joy at having received the witness of the Spirit, still others groaning for sanctification. Early American Methodists often referred to these diverse, affective responses as "the work of God."

The climactic event at these multiday gatherings was often the Lord's Supper. New York Methodist Francis Ward recalled one Communion service in 1806 this way: "The Lord spread a table for his people in the wilderness, and

24. John Telford, ed., *The Letters of John Wesley* (London: Epworth, 1931), 239. An "elder" in this context referred to an ordained minister or "presbyter," as it might be called in other traditions.

25. James F. White, *John Wesley's Prayer Book: The Sunday Service of the Methodists in North America* (Cleveland: OSL, 1991), i.

26. Jesse Lee, *Short History of the Methodists in the United States* (Nashville: Southern Methodist Publishing House, 1810), 107.

hundreds partook of the sacramental bread and wine, the symbols of the Redeemer's passion. There they commemorated his dreadful sufferings, and covenanted with him anew, and there they received fresh effusions of his love."[27] Another Methodist from South Carolina described a vision that occurred during the consecratory prayer: "I had such a view of my savior hanging on the cross, that my flinty heart was broken in pieces, and my soul filled with joy unspeakable."[28] During the distribution of the elements at a 1789 quarterly meeting, "the work of God" broke out and forced a pause in the service.[29]

One in five Methodists were Black—including both free and enslaved—and in some areas of the country Black Methodists outnumbered the White members of the society.[30] Their presence in worship, nearly always segregated within the space, significantly influenced the liturgical piety of early American Methodism. Not only did Black Methodists participate in the extemporaneous prayers, singing, and testimony, but any worshiper—Black or White—was a viable candidate in which "the work of God" might occur. Many Black Americans were also licensed as Methodist preachers and led in the services. American Methodist worship of the late eighteenth and early nineteenth centuries occurred within the larger context of the Second Great Awakening. Methodists were at the vanguard of this revival of heartfelt religion that swept the early American republic.

## Becoming Respectable in Victorian America

As the number of Methodists proliferated, the ecclesial identity shifted to a more parish-centered base. In the growing cities of America, many Methodists built elaborate church buildings—a sharp contradiction to an earlier ethos that valued simplicity. While Methodist ministers continued to itinerate along the expanding borders of the country, American Methodism was becoming more gentrified in many places. Whereas exuberance and affective engagement in worship were once considered hallmarks of Methodist worship, many now viewed such practices with embarrassment.

Racial homogeneity only intensified this perspective. In the first two decades of the nineteenth century, many Black American Methodists formed their own denominations because of overt racism.[31] The exodus of Black

27. Ruth, *Early Methodist Life and Spirituality*, 214.
28. Lester Ruth, *A Little Heaven Below* (Nashville: Kingswood, 2000), 143.
29. Ruth, *A Little Heaven Below*, 139.
30. Wigger, *Taking Heaven by Storm*, 127.
31. Both the African Methodist Episcopal Church (AME) and the African Methodist Episcopal Church, Zion (AME, Zion) were formed in 1816 and 1821, respectively, because of persistent

Methodists from the church was merely the beginning in a series of splits that would parallel the divides within nineteenth-century America. Some left the denomination to form their own churches, such as the Wesleyan and Free Methodist churches. The main body of Methodists in America split in 1844 over the issue of slavery. For both the Methodist Episcopal Church (MEC) and the Methodist Episcopal Church, South (MECS), the fragmentation did not assuage the growing affluence and influence of the Methodists in America.

As Methodists in America found increasing privilege within the American religious, cultural, and political landscape, many began looking to their "liturgical cousins" in the Episcopal Church to adopt patterns of worship that were deemed more "respectable" for Victorian-era America.[32] In some congregations this was as seemingly innocuous as forming a choir or installing an organ in the sanctuary—both of which would have been suspect (or openly forbidden) within early American Methodism.[33] These liturgical changes were by no means monolithic or instantaneous. Many opined the loss of a more heartfelt piety. "The Church may have members, wealth, talent, and great worldly influence, but if the people have no confidence in its piety, it will be powerless as far as their spiritual benefit is concerned," wrote one Methodist minister in 1860.[34] Others sought to reclaim the importance of both form and freedom in worship. Thomas O. Summers was, arguably, the most important Methodist liturgist in the nineteenth century. A liturgical scholar, minister, and editor, Summers argued fervently that form and freedom were essential to Methodist liturgical practice. He oversaw the release and authorization of the *Sunday Service* for use in the MECS, but he also encouraged extemporaneous praying and heartfelt engagement of liturgical forms.[35]

Generally speaking, the trend in the latter half of the nineteenth century was toward a less affective or enthusiastic expression, undergirded by a more

---

racial discrimination. The story of Methodist worship within these two denominations is remarkable. See Tucker, *American Methodist Worship*, for a more thorough treatment.

32. The irony is that John Wesley's *Sunday Service* predates the Episcopal Church's prayer book by some ten years.

33. See Tucker, *American Methodist Worship*, 167–70, 246–47.

34. J. Anderson, *Our Church: A Manual for Members and Probationers of the Methodist Episcopal Church, South* (Nashville: Southern Methodist Publishing House, 1860), 191.

35. The *Sunday Service* was approved for use in the MECS in 1866 but does not appear to have had much popularity. To the end of his life, Thomas Summers advocated for the "admixture" of form and freedom in worship: "We may, indeed, attach so much importance to the form as to lose sight of the spirit; but then, on the other hand, we may use the form so as not abusing it, making it the means of keeping the spirit alive within us, fanning the flame of devotion, and causing our communion with God to be more intimate and delightful." *The Golden Censer: An Essay on Prayer, With a Selection of Forms of Prayer, Designed to Aid in the Devotions of the Sanctuary, Family and Closet* (Nashville: Southern Methodist Publishing House, 1859), 16.

formal pattern in worship. In 1905 the MEC and MECS jointly published a hymnal with an authorized order of worship for Sunday.[36] The order of worship included a number of elements that would have been considered too formal to Methodists of earlier generations, such as the *Gloria Patri*, Apostles' Creed, and numerous responsive readings. Such changes were not always embraced by rank-and-file Methodists, and because these forms were authorized but not mandated, some congregations simply ignored the order of service in favor of their own local pattern. For many, these liturgical additions were dismissed as "formalism of the worst sort."[37] One Methodist bishop recalled a parishioner, "Brother Cal," who quit singing in the choir because of his opposition to the "Amens" that were included at the end of anthems.[38] For others, the move to a more formal pattern of worship was necessary for a denomination coming of age. This development continued nearly unabated for much of the first half of the twentieth century with many Methodists, especially in urban areas, adopting an increasingly ornate style of worship. Divided chancels, the use of vestments, and the presence of acolytes became commonplace in such congregations. On the other hand, many who identified with the holiness branch of Methodism rejected these practices as being empty aestheticism.[39]

## Returning to Roots and Liturgical Renewal

The situation began to change after the Second World War. As Methodist liturgical historian James White put it, "[After World War II] we needed something stronger than aestheticism and found it in historicism."[40] Protestants of all stripes in postwar America were recovering liturgical rites of the Protestant Reformation. Simply put, liturgical aestheticism was woefully inadequate in dealing with the horrors of Buchenwald. Anxieties brought about by the Cold War only furthered the need to acknowledge humanity's brokenness. After decades of minimizing the doctrine of original sin, postwar rites reclaimed

36. For more details on how the joint order of service was developed, see Tucker, *American Methodist Worship*, 15–16.

37. Nolan B. Harmon, "Creating Official Methodist Hymnals," *Methodist History* 16, no. 4 (July 1978): 231.

38. Harmon, "Creating Official Methodist Hymnals," 231.

39. At the risk of oversimplifying, I am referring to those within the MEC and MECS who maintained John Wesley's emphasis on sanctification while many in the denomination moved away from this particular doctrine. This group tended to view the earlier period of Methodist worship in America as most normative while being highly suspicious of the trend toward formalized worship.

40. James F. White, "Does Our Liturgy Reflect Our Faith?," *Circuit Rider* 6 (March 1982): 4.

penitence and confession.[41] John Wesley's *Sunday Service* was brought out
from storage, so to speak. It was even arranged within a jazz setting for a
Methodist youth service. These developments were reflected in a new Communion order, authorized by the Methodist Church in 1964.[42]

Even greater changes were on the horizon, though, as the impact of the
Second Vatican Council began to reverberate into Protestant denominations.[43]
When the Methodist Church and Evangelical United Brethren merged to form
the United Methodist Church in 1968, the need for new worship resources
became paramount. For the next twenty years, Methodist liturgists drafted
numerous rites and resources that were authorized for use in the newly formed
denomination. Each of these reflected the influence of the Liturgical Renewal
Movement. James White, the principal author of what would become "Word
and Table I," spent a year in Rome observing the work of the Council for the
Implementation of the Constitution on the Sacred Liturgy.[44] White, along
with other Methodist liturgists Don Saliers, Hoyt Hickman, and Laurence
Hill Stookey, authored new rites for baptism, marriage, funerals, and a host
of other pastoral offices. They also oversaw the creation of new resources
for the liturgical year. These liturgies demonstrate (1) a greater emphasis on
Word and Table, (2) a recovery of the historic rites of Christian initiation,
(3) the essentiality of the community gathered for worship, (4) an accent
on the paschal nature of Christian worship, and (5) a greater fidelity to the
church universal with particular attention given to the first four centuries
of Christian worship. These liturgical emphases are most clearly seen in the
1989 *United Methodist Hymnal* and the 1992 *United Methodist Book of
Worship*.

As in the case of every other authorized Methodist worship resource, the
1989 hymnal and 1992 book of worship saw varying degrees of usage. For his
part, James White argued that the new service of Word and Table was "more
Wesleyan than Wesley's own service" because of its grounding in the early

41. See James F. White, "Protestant Public Worship in America: 1935–1995," in *Christian
Worship in North America* (Collegeville, MN: Liturgical Press, 1997), 118; and White, "Methodist Worship," in *Perspectives on American Methodism*, ed. Russel E. Richey, Kenneth E. Rowe,
and Jean Miller Schmidt (Nashville: Kingswood, 1993), 476.

42. In 1939 the MEC, MECS, and the Methodist Protestant Church merged to form the
Methodist Church.

43. Looking back on the 1964 rite, White notes that the service was obsolete the moment it
went to the printers because of the looming ecumenical impact of the Second Vatican Council,
which was already underway. See James F. White, "The New American Methodist Communion
Order," *Worship* 41 (November 1967): 559.

44. See James F. White, "The Development of the 1972 United Methodist Eucharistic Rite,"
in *Wesleyan Theology Today: A Bicentennial Theological Consultation*, ed. Theodore Runyon
(Nashville: Kingswood, 1985), 333.

centuries of Christian worship.[45] Wesley, after all, was a patristic scholar in his own right and held "the primitive church" in high esteem. Others were not so convinced. Some identified these changes with the aestheticism of the early twentieth century; others embraced a new style of "contemporary worship" that was often seen to be incompatible with the authorized rites.[46] Yet again, the tension between liturgical form and freedom was on display in these differing reactions.

## Key Attributes

This meandering history illustrates the challenge presented in offering definitive claims on the distinctive features of Methodist worship. Nevertheless, some key attributes can be discerned. In the first place, worship in the Wesleyan tradition is *rooted* in soil that goes deeper than the current moment. Another way to put this might be to say that Methodist worship has in its liturgical DNA a drive to be faithful. This, of course, begs the question "Faithful to what?" In short, worship in the Wesleyan tradition is rooted in the text and piety of the *Sunday Service*, the Wesleyan hymns, and the broader catholic tradition as it was received via Methodism's Anglican roots. The minister in 1850 using the marriage rite from the *Ritual*, the devout parishioner in 1950 singing "O for a Thousand Tongues to Sing," or the candidate reciting the renunciations from the baptismal service of 1989 are connected to the *Sunday Service*, the Wesleyan hymns, and the catholic tradition.

Second, Methodist worship is *inculturated* in its expression. John Wesley took to heart the thirty-fourth Article of Religion from the Church of England, which maintains that the rites and ceremonies of the church can be diverse.[47] In his use of extemporaneous prayer, field preaching, hymn singing, the love

45. James F. White, *OSL Convention 2000 Keynote Address* (Cleveland: Order of St. Luke, 2000).

46. This is, admittedly, an oversimplification of a complex term. For example, much of the Communion service was field-tested in a "contemporary" United Methodist worship service during the late 1960s and early 1970s. See my chapter "James F. White, Grady Hardin, and Methodist 'Contemporary' Worship in the 1970s: The 11:00 a.m. Cox Chapel Service at Highland Park," in *Essays on the History of Contemporary Praise and Worship*, ed. Lester Ruth (Eugene, OR: Wipf & Stock, 2020), 13–33.

47. John Wesley included this article in *The Sunday Service of the Methodists*, but it was renumbered as article twenty-two because of his abridgement of the original thirty-nine. It is worth noting that the full article goes on to say that "whosoever through his private judgement, willingly and purposely, doth openly break the traditions and ceremonies of the Church, which be not repugnant to the Word of God, and be ordained and approved by common authority, ought to be rebuked openly, (that others may fear to do the like,) as he that offendeth against the common order of the Church, and hurteth the authority of the Magistrate, and woundeth

feast, and so forth, Wesley exemplified a concern that worship practices both reflect and connect with the people gathered for worship. This emphasis only played out to greater extremes within American Methodism because of its unique position in the American religious landscape.

For as much as Methodist worship allows for inculturation of its practices, it is simultaneously *corporate or connected* in its orientation—the third attribute. This has served (to varying degrees of success) as a guardrail of sorts in how Methodists think about liturgical inculturation. Methodism is a connectional system, and the main branch of the tradition has also operated within an episcopal structure. For these reasons Methodists have always attempted to have some commonality in the way they worship. As noted in the history above, this has been realized to differing degrees owing to the valuing of both form and freedom, but it is nonetheless a key trait.

Fourth, Methodist worship has, from the beginning, been *personal* in its affect and content. The soteriological orientation of the Wesleys means that the entire person matters before God in worship and that the heart is the arena in which the saving work of God plays out. This must not be confused with emotionalism, as John Wesley makes clear in his writings. In this respect, the Wesleyan forms of worship as encapsulated in the *Sunday Service* serve as both a platform for and a healthy boundary to the emotions. Far from stifling the emotions, liturgical forms are an ally to affective engagement. By the same token, allowing for extemporaneity and heartfelt engagement within liturgical forms can prevent prayer from degenerating into empty formalism.

Lastly, Methodist worship has a clear telos: our sanctification. Worship ought to do something to the participant—namely, form us more clearly into the image of Christ. In the worship gathering we rehearse God's mighty acts in Christ Jesus, we intercede with Christ for the sake of the world, and we participate in the means of grace. For Methodists these acts of worship are inextricably linked to "going on to perfection." And, as mentioned above, Christian perfection is anything but self-serving holier-than-thou-ism, for it is the fulfillment of the Great Commandment, which is outward focused. If worship is truly *sanctifying*, it is profoundly for the sake of the world that God loves.

## Practical Implications for Worship

Methodists, of course, do not have a proprietary claim to these hallmarks, but the unique combination and enactment of these Wesleyan ways of worship have

---

the consciences of the weak brethren." John Wesley, *The Sunday Service of the Methodists in North America: With Other Occasional Services* (London: Strahan, 1784), 313–14.

enriched the church universal. In the first place, the Wesleyan liturgical heritage reminds us that one need not jettison the affective in worship. If, indeed, we are invited to bring our entire person before God, then worship should allow for the full gambit of human emotion. Whether weeping aloud, giving testimony to God's grace, or singing with resonant joy, the Wesleyan tradition reminds us that worship is not simply an intellectual exercise.[48] Relatedly, worship in the Methodist tradition illustrates that set patterns or liturgical forms can partner with dynamic freedom in worship. As demonstrated above, forms can nurture and guide the emotions instead of serving as a barrier to them. And liturgical forms are enlivened from this affective engagement as the worshiper participates fully in the liturgy—heart, mind, soul, and strength. With regard to the liturgical form itself, Methodists have gifted the entire church a treasury of poetic theology in the Wesley hymns. If one digs a bit deeper than well-known pieces such as "Hark! The Herald Angels Sing" and "O for a Thousand Tongues to Sing," one will discover invaluable compositions on a host of themes. For example, the Wesleys' *Hymns on the Lord's Supper*—a collection of 166 hymns on the Eucharist—has provided a framework for ecumenical dialogue between the United Methodist Church and the Roman Catholic Church.[49] Lastly, the Methodist liturgical heritage stands as a stalwart reminder that true worship is transformative. Sanctification is more than a trope in the Wesleyan tradition, but an audaciously optimistic claim that God in Christ is making all things new by "breaking the power of cancelled sin," as Charles Wesley versifies it in his hymn "O For a Thousand Tongues to Sing." Methodists gladly proclaim that in gathering together and participating in the full spectrum of liturgical practices, God is forming the worshiper into the image of Christ and sending them to bear this image to a broken and hurting world.

## For Further Reading

Ruth, Lester. *A Little Heaven Below: Worship at Early Methodist Quarterly Meetings*. Nashville: Kingswood, 2000.

Sigler, R. Matthew. *Methodist Worship: Mediating the Wesleyan Liturgical Heritage*. New York: Routledge, 2019.

48. In this respect, Methodist worship—especially in its earlier iterations—was a forerunner, of sorts, of Pentecostalism. The theological links between Wesleyanism and Pentecostalism have been well explored, but one should also note the liturgical connection. See Henry H. Knight, ed., *From Aldersgate to Azusa Street: Wesleyan, Holiness, and Pentecostal Visions of the New Creation* (Eugene, OR: Pickwick, 2010).

49. Geoffrey Wainwright, "Introduction," in Daniel Stevick, *The Altar's Fire* (Peterborough, UK: Epworth, 2004), xi.

Tucker, Karen B. Westerfield. *American Methodist Worship*. Oxford: Oxford University Press, 2001.

———, ed. *The Sunday Service of the Methodists: Twentieth-Century Worship in Worldwide Methodism*. Nashville: Abingdon, 1996.

White, James F., ed. *John Wesley's Prayer Book: The Sunday Service of the Methodists in North America*. Cleveland: OSL, 1991.

———. "Methodist Worship." In *Perspectives on American Methodism: Interpretive Essays*, edited by Russell E. Richey, Kenneth E. Rowe, and Jean Miller Schmidt, 460–79. Nashville: Abingdon, 1993.

# ← 15 →

# Anabaptist and Mennonite Practices of Worship

## *Valerie G. Rempel*

An act of baptism occurring outside the formal structures of the established church frequently serves as a handy marker for the beginning of a distinctly Anabaptist church tradition. While pockets of radical Protestants could be found throughout early sixteenth-century Europe, this baptism marked something new. Its participants helped shape a movement that now has a global presence of several million adherents.[1] Its insistence on the separation of church and state has shaped millions more.

The group of people gathered in a home in the Swiss canton of Zurich on January 21, 1525, were not your usual revolutionaries. They were, however, people frustrated by the slow pace of the Protestant Reformation in their city. Impatient and shaped by a different way of reading Scripture, they baptized each other. It was an act of faith that was punishable by death. To be rebaptized or "baptized again" (the literal meaning of the word "anabaptist") was

---

1. Mennonite World Conference (MWC), a global fellowship representing 58 countries and 107 national churches, reported 1.47 million members in its 2018 census data. The addition of other historic Anabaptist communities that are not part of MWC, such as the Amish, as well as other communal and denominational groups, likely raises that number to over two million. "Membership, Map, and Statistics," Mennonite World Conference, https://mwc-cmm.org/membership-map-and-statistics.

deemed heresy. Many of these first Anabaptists would be martyred for what they considered to be their first *true* baptism made upon their confession of faith in Jesus as Lord.[2]

## Ecclesiology

The life of any worshiping community is informed by its ecclesiology and shaped by its practices. The Anabaptist movement, which includes a wide variety of Mennonites, emerged in the context of the sixteenth-century Protestant Reformation and shares many of its distinct characteristics. Early Anabaptists affirmed the authority of Scripture over the tradition of the church. They agreed with other reformers that salvation is a gift of God's grace, freely given and made available solely through faith in Jesus as Lord. But the way they read Scripture and understood the nature of the church differed from many of their contemporaries in both the Roman Catholic and the emerging Protestant traditions. This frequently put them at odds with both the state and the state-supported church. It also shaped a distinct understanding of the church for Anabaptist-minded communities.

These communities are varied in their origins and later development. The direct descendants include many groups that take their particular names from early leaders. Mennonites make up the largest contingent and take their name from Menno Simons, a Dutch priest who converted and took on a significant pastoral role in the Low Countries and northern German region during the Reformation period. Communal groups such as the Hutterites, who take their name from a sixteenth-century leader named Jakob Hutter, and the Amish, a group that first emerged in the late seventeenth century under the leadership of Jakob Ammann, are also a part of the tradition, though specific beliefs and practices are often distinct from the center of the Anabaptist and Mennonite tradition. Later groups such as the Brethren in Christ (Be in Christ [Canada]), German Baptist Brethren, the Bruderhof Communities, and the Apostolic Christian Church are also included in the umbrella term "Anabaptist."

Early Anabaptists believed that the church should be a visible gathering of believers who entered into a voluntary relationship with each other upon their confession of faith. Water baptism served as the public witness to faith and initiation into the community. This "believers' church" model, familiar to

2. The stories of those martyred for their faith were gathered by T. J. Van Braght and published in 1660 as the *Martyrs Mirror* or *Bloody Theater*. The addition of woodprints by Jan Luyken helped boost its popularity. In some Anabaptist communities, the *Martyrs Mirror* was used for devotional purposes well into the twentieth century.

many today, challenged the power and privilege of what is sometimes called the magisterial church.

The magisterial church reflected the values of Christendom in the way that it linked the political power and protection of the state with the spiritual power of the church. When, during the early fourth century, the emperor Constantine began to privilege Christianity throughout the Roman Empire, he ushered in a way of relating that thoroughly shaped Western Christianity for more than a millennium. Vestiges of this way of understanding the church continue today. For example, when we refer to a country as a "Christian" country, we are drawing on an understanding of the church that is linked to a geographical area and a political context.

## Two Kingdom Theology

Early Anabaptists believed that the church should be distinct from the state and the state distinct from the church. This kind of "two kingdom" theology distinguished between the earthly secular realm governed by princes and magistrates, and the heavenly realm made visible by the church with Christ Jesus as Lord. Like many Christians, the Anabaptists affirmed the reality of both worlds. What distinguished Anabaptist communities was their emphasis on the visible nature of the church and the necessary separation between these kingdoms. Other leading reformers tended toward a positive view of the state's role in governing secular matters, viewing the state as ordered by God for the well-being of humankind. They looked to the state to support the established church in any given region. By contrast, Anabaptist leaders tended to align the earthly realm with the realm of the devil and to see it as corrupt.[3] They took the words from John's Gospel to heart, seeking to be, as Jesus described it, in the world but not of it (see John 17:14–17). This idea was further supported by 2 Corinthians 6:14–17 with its instructions to not be "yoked together" (NIV) with unbelievers but to "come out from them and be separate."[4]

Early Anabaptists critiqued other reformers for what they viewed as compromise in the way they continued to align themselves with local governing

3. See, e.g., the strong language of the early Schleitheim Confession, which presents the choice as between Christ and Belial. It urges separation from the world and even from other Christian bodies. John Christian Wenger, "The Schleitheim Confession of Faith," *Mennonite Quarterly Review* 19, no. 4 (October 1945): 249.

4. The importance of separation from those deemed ungodly has contributed to the splinter movements within Anabaptism. Communal groups such as the Hutterites and Amish broke off early, but other groups experiencing renewal or differing over points of theology have also separated, helping create multiple groups with varying organizational structures. There is no singular global Anabaptist or Mennonite church.

authorities. It's not that most Anabaptists wanted to do away with government.[5] They understood the practical necessity of some political order and took seriously the biblical injunction to pray for those in authority so that they might lead peaceful lives (1 Tim. 2:2). At the same time, they understood their true citizenship to be lodged in the kingdom of God and believed they were to be followers of Jesus in all things.

During the sixteenth century, it was hard for most people to imagine a Christian community existing outside a particular relationship with the state. The church even performed some civil function through the practice of infant baptism, which provided birth records, and the keeping of marriage and death records. Thus, when the group that gathered in Zurich baptized each other upon their confession of faith, they were doing more than challenging the theology of infant baptism as a means of salvation. They were challenging the very structure of the communities they were embedded in.

Challenges to the established Roman Catholic Church marked the entire Protestant Reformation. It was not limited to the Anabaptist movement. However, Anabaptists tended to take their ideas further than many other reformers. Indeed, the movement is sometimes referred to as the Radical Reformation or the left wing of the Reformation as a way to acknowledge that tendency.[6] As a result, early Anabaptists were often at odds with both religious and civil authorities, and their ideas were considered dangerous.

For example, the confession that Jesus is Lord is central to the Christian faith. However, when combined with a refusal to bear arms as unfitting for followers of Jesus and citizens of the kingdom of God, it can appear seditious. How could Anabaptists be trusted to help defeat enemies or protect their neighbors if they refused to bear arms?[7] This had a particular relevance in the sixteenth century as the Ottoman Empire sought to extend its reach into western Europe and helped increase public suspicion toward those joining the Anabaptist movement.

5. The most notable exception is the short-lived reign of Jan van Leiden, who, with a group of radical supporters, tried to establish sectarian rule in the German city of Münster. This event increased public suspicion of Anabaptists.

6. Or as C. Arnold Snyder notes, "Anabaptism was not so much 'Protestantism taken to its proper ends' as it was Radical Protestantism taken some ecclesiological steps further." *Anabaptist History and Theology: An Introduction* (Kitchener, ON: Pandora, 1995), 95.

7. Anabaptist groups continue to be a significant part of the Historic Peace Churches, which formally includes Mennonites, the Society of Friends (Quakers), and the Church of the Brethren. See Melvin Gingerich and Paul Peachey, "Historic Peace Churches," *Global Anabaptist Mennonite Encyclopedia Online*, 1989, https://gameo.org/index.php?title=Historic_peace_churches. The accusation of disloyalty to the state continues to be leveled at those who resist bearing arms.

By the end of the Reformation period, many of the early leaders and members had been martyred. While the exact number is uncertain, scholars estimate that several thousand men and women were put to death, many by fire or by drowning. This last was considered especially appropriate. Religious and civil authorities were agreed that since by the waters of baptism they had sinned, so by the water they would die.

## A Visible Church

In calling for a separation from the world, Anabaptists invariably turned toward each other as fellow believers, forming close-knit communities seeking to recapture the practices of the early church. They were not especially concerned with reforming the existing church but wanted to restore the church described in the New Testament. Because the Anabaptist movement was first considered heretical, many early communities worshiped in secret and supported each other through the sharing of goods and resources. The idea of "mutual aid" is not limited to Anabaptist communities but has continued to mark their approach to caring for one another.

Ministers were called out from among the congregation to teach and lead worship, even to mete out church discipline when needed. Their authority came not from their own sense of calling but from the membership who affirmed the gifts already visible in them. Their role was not a priestly role but a pastoral role that was focused on teaching and care for the members. Over time, various organizational structures of church councils or elders would emerge, but most communities resisted a professional clergy until the twentieth century. In theory, if not always in practice, the community was the locus of decision-making.

Viewing the church as the visible body of Christ placed a great deal of emphasis on the ethics of following Jesus. Believers were to live holy lives that gave witness to their new allegiance and the work of regeneration occurring through the Holy Spirit. Salvation meant a turning away from sin to experience rebirth into new life.

As a result, Anabaptist communities were concerned about the practical outworking of their faith. Whereas Martin Luther famously criticized the New Testament Epistle of James as placing too much emphasis on works rather than faith, Anabaptist communities resonated with the idea that faith without works was dead (James 2:26). Menno Simons, the former priest who emerged as a leader in the Low Countries and northern German regions, described what he called "true evangelical faith" as something that could not lay dormant "but manifests itself in all righteousness and works of love; it dies unto flesh and blood; destroys all forbidden lusts and desires; cordially seeks, serves and fears God; clothes the naked; feeds the hungry; consoles the afflicted; shelters the miserable; aids and consoles all the oppressed; returns good for evil; serves those that injure it; prays for those that persecute it; teaches, admonishes and reproves with the Word of the Lord; seeks that which is lost; binds up that which is wounded; heals that which is diseased and saves that which is sound."[8]

## Discipleship

To be a disciple of Jesus was no small matter, and it called for a radical reorienting of one's life. Early Anabaptists were sometimes criticized by other reformers for placing too much emphasis on right living. It is helpful to remember that one of the marks of the Protestant Reformation was the insistence that "works righteousness" was not the way of salvation. Protestant reformers were critical of the way the Roman Catholic Church seemed to place an emphasis on works as marked by the sacramental system that had emerged during the Middle Ages and that was later aggravated by the sale of indulgences.

Anabaptists agreed that works were not a means to salvation but insisted that becoming a disciple of Jesus should produce the fruit of righteousness. This has often been a tension within the Anabaptist and Mennonite tradition as "right living" was sometimes codified into particular behaviors or standards. Still, the intent has always been to take seriously the need to follow Jesus in one's daily life. This is understood to be true worship.

## Church Discipline

Preserving the unity and purity of the community took on special importance, as can be seen in the use of the ban for church discipline. Unlike Martin Luther, who spoke of the wheat and tares growing up together, to be separated at judgment day, Anabaptist communities were convinced of the need for a pure church. In practice, that meant the tares should be plucked from the field even now. Believers who fell away from faith or continued in sin were to be admonished and encouraged in their faith. If they refused, they were

8. Machiel van Zanten, ed., "Menno Simons on . . . the New Life," Menno Simons.net, http://www.mennosimons.net/newlife.html.

to be excluded from the community and especially from participating in the Lord's Supper. This exclusion was understood to be so painful that the offender would make every effort to repair the breach through the confession of sin and a renewed commitment to right living.

The practice of the ban could certainly be misused, but it is important to remember the context in which it arose and was first practiced. Banning someone from fellowship was a far milder punishment than imprisonment or even death, which Anabaptists knew all too well. Its goal was meant to be a restoration to fellowship.[9] Discipleship, meaning following Jesus, was best done in community.

## Reading the Bible

This emphasis on the ethics of the Christian life drew heavily from the Sermon on the Mount as recorded in Matthew's Gospel. Anabaptists tended to be radical Bible readers in the way they believed that Jesus's instructions to his followers were meant for the present age and were not simply a description of the age to come. Loving enemies, laying down the sword, sharing possessions, evangelizing—these were the marks of citizenship in the kingdom of God and arose in response to a reading of the Word.

Anabaptists have tended to read all of Scripture through the lens of the New Testament and especially the life of Jesus as recorded in the Gospel accounts. Salvation brought about regeneration, a new life lived in allegiance to Jesus and marked by a willingness to suffer even as Jesus did. A German word, *Gelassenheit*, usually translated as "yieldedness," described the posture of a true disciple. A follower of Jesus was expected to yield not only to the will of God but also to the decisions of the faith community and even to civil authorities in the face of persecution. Believers were not to pick up arms to defend themselves but to follow Jesus's example in all things, even if it meant imprisonment or death.[10]

Anabaptists looked to the Holy Spirit to guide their reading of Scripture and to be at work in their communities. The Spirit and the Letter (Scripture) were to be trusted and discerned together by the community of faith.

9. See, e.g., the language of the 1527 Schleitheim Confession, which describes the goal as breaking and eating one bread. Wenger, "Schleitheim Confession of Faith," 248.

10. In North America some Mennonite communities began using the technical language of "nonresistance" during the twentieth century. The language emerged in the context of negotiations for military exemptions based on objections of conscience. See Perry Bush, *Two Kingdoms, Two Loyalties: Mennonite Pacifism in Modern America* (Baltimore: Johns Hopkins University Press, 1998), 5–6.

Like other reformation-minded groups, Anabaptists insisted on putting Scripture into the hands of all believers. They were confident that the Holy Spirit could be trusted to guide the interpretation of Scripture and tended to be suspicious of authorities, whether civil or religious. Community discernment, enlivened by the Spirit, was understood to be far more trustworthy.

## Following Jesus Together

For Anabaptist communities, Jesus is understood to be at the center of one's faith and life. Following Jesus means becoming a disciple of Jesus, learning, through Scripture and the illumination of the Spirit, what it means to confess Jesus as Lord. It is Jesus who proclaimed the reign of God through his words and deeds, and who is the fulfillment of the Old Testament promise of a messiah. This is understood to be good news for the captive and those bound by sin.

Anabaptists have shared the historic Christian confession that, by his obedience, Jesus suffered, was crucified, and rose again. Death has been conquered and salvation made possible. It has been especially important for Anabaptists that in his death and resurrection Jesus made possible a reconciled relationship with God. It is this reconciliation that shaped expectations for the Christian community. Followers of Jesus are expected to live at peace with one another.

As noted earlier, the confession that Jesus is Lord gives witness to a shift in allegiance. While Anabaptist groups have sought to live peacefully with their neighbors and the governing bodies of the state, they have been quick to affirm that their primary allegiance is always to Jesus. They have resisted bearing arms for the state, for example, out of obedience to Jesus's words about laying down the sword and love of even enemies (Matt. 5:44; 26:52–54).

Discipleship called for a radical reorientation to the whole of one's life, but it was not expected to be an individual journey of faith. Rather, the community that formed shared this life together in lively anticipation of the second coming of Christ. Early Anabaptist worship services resisted formal liturgies, relying instead on the study of Scripture, listening to sermonic or other teaching material, singing and praying together to guide their fellowship. The community of faith was understood to be a place of shared participation and discernment.

Early services likely had a sense of informality that was helped by the kind of spaces they tended to occupy. Congregations met in houses, barns, forests, or caves and only gradually began to inhabit dedicated church buildings. In the Dutch regions, for example, the practice of hidden churches for groups that were outside the state church resulted in worship spaces that appeared to be homes or warehouses from the exterior but which allowed for large gathering spaces inside. When meeting houses were permitted in the Swiss and sourthern German regions, they tended to be plain spaces without much ornamentation. It was the people who were the church, and the space existed to facilitate the gathering of believers meeting for fellowship and instruction.

Early Anabaptists were also active hymn writers. Collections of spiritual songs circulated in the sixteenth century and appear to have been used for both private and corporate worship. Many of the early hymn texts were written by those who were facing martyrdom or by those recounting the witness of the early Anabaptist martyrs. These songs were meant to encourage believers in their own faith and persistence in the face of difficulties. A variety of Dutch and German hymnals were published by the end of the sixteenth century.[11] One of the most well-used collections of martyr hymns, the *Ausbund*, continues to be used by Amish communities to the present.

Apart from the *Ausbund*, few of these early hymns had a long life in Anabaptist communities. During the seventeenth and eighteenth centuries, Anabaptists increasingly borrowed from Lutheran and pietistic sources, even using the hymnals of the state church in any given region. Mennonite communities that migrated to North America eventually produced their own English-language hymnals, which included hymns from a variety of theological traditions as well as the gospel music that emerged in the wake of the First and Second Great Awakenings.

Anabaptist groups have varied in their adoption of musical instruments as aids to worship, with some groups using organs to accompany congregational singing as early as the late eighteenth century and other groups resisting musical accompaniment well into the twentieth century. Congregational singing has been important, however, in the way that it fosters wide participation in the worship service and gives visible witness to the community being formed by diverse voices and musical parts.

## Baptism, the Lord's Supper, and Footwashing

Like other Protestant groups, early Anabaptists rejected the sacramental system that had developed over the centuries of the Roman Catholic tradition. Here again, they took a more radical approach, influenced by the Swiss reformer Huldrych Zwingli.

11. Harold S. Bender, "Hymnology of the Anabaptists," *Global Anabaptist Encyclopedia Online*, https://gameo.org/index.php?title=Hymnology_of_the_Anabaptists.

Anabaptists rejected the idea that baptism was a literal washing away of sin. Rather, baptism symbolized the new birth that came about through faith in Jesus. A true baptism could happen only as people repented of sin and confessed faith in Jesus as Lord and Savior. This kind of decision required a level of maturity and intent that infants or even young children did not have. Since the water itself couldn't wash away sin, it was pointless to baptize infants.

Adult or believers' baptism also marked entry into the community of faith. Baptism was a kind of initiation that brought believers into fellowship with each other. It was never salvific but always an act of obedience that followed the witness of Jesus, who himself was baptized in the Jordan River, and his charge in the Great Commission to make disciples and baptize them in the name of the Father, the Son, and the Holy Spirit (Matt. 28:16–20).

Communion, or the practice of the Lord's Supper, also followed a Zwinglian perspective in the way it viewed the elements. The bread and wine were not changed into the literal body and blood of Jesus but were shared as symbols of Christ's broken body. This was a memorial meal, held as Jesus instructed, "in remembrance" (Luke 22:19).

The Lord's Supper was reserved for those who had been baptized into membership. Unlike the Mass, it did not have a sacramental function and thus did not need to occur every time the church gathered. Still, it remained a central element of fellowship and took on a kind of horizonal aspect in the way that it symbolized the community itself gathered around a shared commitment to be disciples of Jesus. The broken bread and shared cup united believers in their commitment to live as children of God and in right relationship with each other. Believers were expected to prepare for the service carefully, searching out unconfessed sin and reconciling any disputes with fellow members. The apostle's charge in 1 Corinthians 11:27 to not eat or drink unworthily was taken very seriously and members under discipline were excluded from participation. This was, at times, a painful outworking of the ban.

Until the mid-twentieth century, most Anabaptist groups practiced footwashing as a part of the celebration of the Lord's Supper. Footwashing followed the practice of Jesus, who washed his disciples' feet at the Last Supper. It called for humility and could function as a means of reconciliation as members who had been at odds with each other knelt to wash each other's feet. This kind of "yieldedness" was an embodied representation of Jesus's humility.

Anabaptist and Mennonite groups have preferred to call these central rites of the church ordinances rather than sacraments. They have also rejected the idea that believers need a set-apart priesthood to serve as a mediator between

God and humankind. Instead, believers are to serve as priests to one another, hearing each other's confession of sin, assuring each other of God's forgiveness, and sharing the Communion elements together.

## Establishing Communities of Faith

The early loss of key leaders and the threat of persecution shaped the way Anabaptist communities developed, contributing to a pattern of migration and isolation. Some Anabaptists, both Mennonites and Amish, primarily from the Swiss and southern German regions, settled in the American colonies early in the eighteenth century, with some moving north into present-day Canada to escape the American Revolution and the call to arms. Many Dutch and northern German Mennonites found a welcome in Poland as early as the sixteenth century. Later, at the invitation of Catherine the Great, many of them migrated into what is now Ukraine during the late eighteenth century, where they established Mennonite colonies.

Waves of migration brought their descendants to the United States and Canada as part of the westward expansion across the North American plains and prairies in the late nineteenth century. The devastation of World War I and the political climate of the new Soviet Union led to additional waves of migration again to Canada and from there to Mexico during the 1920s. During the 1930s and through the post–World War II period, migration shifted to South America, where Mennonite colonies were established especially in Paraguay and Brazil. Others were eventually able to move to present-day Germany.

In nearly every place they settled, Anabaptists sought to obtain the legal right to worship as they pleased and to not bear arms in military service. When these privileges were restricted, as sometimes happened over time and through political shifts, communities had to either accommodate the restrictions or seek new places to live. Economic opportunities were also a factor, especially when land restrictions were put into place.[12] In many places, Anabaptist groups formed ethnoreligious communities that found a theological basis in a commitment to live separated from the world but that hindered their ability to evangelize or recruit new members. As immigrants, they sought to preserve language and culture, encouraging marriage from within their own tradition. As a result, Anabaptist and Mennonite communities were sometimes slow to assimilate. The choice of some communities to adopt plain clothing, to limit

12. This happened in Poland and later in the Russian territories, helping prompt migration first to Russia and from there to the Americas.

the use of technology, or to express nonconformity in other ways also made boundaries less permeable.[13]

In some places, Mennonite colonies formed their own political structures in which the separation of church and state became blurred. As people who had experienced persecution, they were eager to find a place where they could thrive, even though that meant they were acquiring land that had previously been occupied by others. These are issues that Anabaptist and Mennonite communities are slowly beginning to acknowledge.[14]

## Missionary Activity

While the communal forms of Anabaptism such as the Amish or Hutterite communities remain fairly closed, most other Anabaptist communities are increasingly diverse in ethnicity and cultural expression. Periods of spiritual renewal and a commitment to evangelism helped spur the planting and growth of Anabaptist communities around the world. Evangelically minded Anabaptists joined in the worldwide Protestant missionary efforts of the nineteenth and twentieth centuries, so that Anabaptist expressions of faith are now found around the world. This, in turn, has reenergized Anabaptism as a global movement as new communities are formed and believers wrestle with what discipleship and love of enemy looks like in non-Western contexts.

More recently there has been the growth of what are sometimes called neo-Anabaptist communities. These new communities have rediscovered the theological emphases of sixteenth-century Anabaptism outside its historic rootedness in Eurocentric ethnoreligious communities. As a result, the Anabaptist movement is now a global one, though it does not share a common organizational center. Mennonite World Conference serves as a communion of Anabaptist and Mennonite groups from around the world that affirm a shared set of convictions, but it has no authority over any particular congregation or network of churches.[15] Through its initiatives and global assemblies, it has

13. For a concise description of "plain" groups and the way they have expressed nonconformity, see Cory Anderson, "Who Are the Plain Anabaptists? What Are the Plain Anabaptists?," *Journal of Amish and Plain Anabaptist Studies* 1 (2013): 26–56, https://doi.org/10.18061/1811/54897.

14. For example, Catherine the Great's invitation to Mennonites in Poland was part of a larger political agenda to remake the population of former Turkish regions. Mennonites moving into the high plains and prairies of the United States and Canada replaced the indigenous population that had lived off the land for centuries. Likewise, Mennonite colonists in Paraguay were surprised to find the land that had been promised to them already occupied by the Guarani people.

15. "Shared Convictions," Mennonite World Conference, https://mwc-cmm.org/shared -convictions.

especially nurtured a cross-fertilization of global relationships, theological reflection, and music and worship practices.

## Practical Implications for Worship

There is no common liturgy that unites Anabaptist and Mennonite communities of faith. While affirming the theological emphases of the historic Christian creeds, Anabaptists understand their communities to be noncreedal. Theological emphases are most often expressed in confessions of faith.

There are, however, some shared tendencies that have shaped worship services through the centuries, even as it is important to remember that groups vary in their cultural contexts and the degree of assimilation that has occurred. Amish house-church gatherings, for example, look very different from fellowships meeting in urban areas around the globe. Still, some common characteristics continue.

Anabaptist and Mennonite congregations often have a warm, family feel to them that grows out of an understanding of the church as a voluntary community of believers who share a common confession of faith and a relatively flat organizational structure. This emphasis on community encourages wide participation in decision-making and in the worship service itself. Scripture reading, the distribution of Communion elements, the sharing of testimonies, or leading in public prayer can all be done by the laity. This is the priesthood of all believers in action.

Preaching and teaching can also be shared by members of the community, though most congregations have moved to a dedicated clergy. Anabaptist preaching is expected to be rooted in Scripture and has often taken the form of exhortation. Preaching is meant to encourage believers in staying faithful to Jesus. This has often resulted in a strong ethical focus rooted in the teachings of Jesus. Themes of persistence in the face of suffering, the need to keep right relationships with each other, and the call to peace-making and separation from the world (often expressed as nonconformity) have been frequent emphases.

Congregational singing has been an important element of Anabaptist worship as it encourages wide participation in worship and allows for corporate expressions of faith. More recently, and especially through the collaborative relationships developed through the Mennonite World Conference and its assemblies, new songs with the rhythms of Africa, Asia, and Latin America have been collected. These contemporary songs continue in the tradition of stressing the joy of following Jesus and the call to peace-making in all areas of life.

Baptismal services are expected to be community events. This is in keeping with an understanding of baptism as a public witness to faith in Jesus. Groups vary in practice from pouring to immersion but share a commitment to the importance of adult or believers' baptism. In some places, child dedication services have developed as a way to signify a family's intent to raise their child in the Christian faith.[16]

The pattern of Communion services may vary in frequency, but they continue to be understood as memorial meals. Anabaptist meeting spaces do not have altars but Communion tables. The pattern of the service usually follows the description in 1 Corinthians 11:23–26. The elements are frequently passed one to another, which is another visible representation of the priesthood of all believers. Historically, the Lord's Table was reserved for those who had made a public confession of faith, had been baptized, and were in right relationship with the community of faith. In most settings, baptism and church membership have gone hand in hand. One is baptized into the church, which has a local expression in a gathered body of believers.

Over time, church buildings and meetinghouses have adopted the architectural patterns of various eras and locations. Nevertheless, they have tended to be plain spaces designed for good acoustics and emphasizing a pulpit or Communion table. Both represent central aspects of the community that gathers around the Lord's Table and the reading of Scripture.

It is rare to see a national flag in Anabaptist meeting spaces. The confession that Jesus is Lord is meant to be a confession of allegiance. While believers represent many nationalities, their primary citizenship is always understood to be in the kingdom of God.

## For Further Reading

Bush, Perry. *Two Kingdoms, Two Loyalties: Mennonite Pacifism in Modern America.* Baltimore: Johns Hopkins University Press, 1998.

Murray, Stuart. *The Naked Anabaptist: The Bare Essentials of a Radical Faith.* Scottdale, PA: Herald, 2010.

Oyer, John S., and Robert S. Kreider. *Mirror of the Martyrs: Stories of Courage, Inspiringly Retold, of 16th Century Anabaptists Who Gave Their Lives for Their Faith.* Intercourse, PA: Good Books, 2002.

16. Child dedication services may also serve as a kind of accommodation to the practice of infant baptism, especially for those more familiar with pedobaptism.

Roth, John D. *Practices: Mennonite Worship and Witness*. Scottdale, PA: Herald, 2009.

Snyder, C. Arnold. *Anabaptist History and Theology: An Introduction*. Kitchener, ON: Pandora, 1995.

Weaver, J. Denny. *Becoming Anabaptist: The Origin and Significance of Sixteenth-Century Anabaptism*. 2nd ed. Scottdale, PA: Herald, 2005.

# ─ 16 ─

# Baptist Practices of Worship

## Jennifer W. Davidson

As Baptist historian Walter Shurden says plainly, "Baptists do not agree on where they came from, who they are, or how they got that way."[1] Nonetheless, to understand Baptist worship's enduring characteristics today, it is crucial to recognize that the Baptist faith tradition emerged from the Radical Reformation's fiery furnace. Some of the earliest Baptists in England, including the early Baptist leader John Smyth, were heavily influenced by the Dutch Mennonites of sixteenth-century Holland. The earliest Baptists in North America came mostly from Britain (England, Wales, Scotland) and Ireland.[2] They tended to join with Congregationalists and Anglicans in New England. However, early Baptists in North America, particularly in the Massachusetts Bay Colony, "met with much opposition, especially because they refused to countenance the state church's control over them."[3] The radical Roger Williams was instrumental in founding the First Baptist Church in America in Providence, Rhode Island, in the early seventeenth century. Williams placed his most significant emphases on the separation of church and state and believers' baptism. Separatists and Independents were too impatient to wait for liturgical and theological changes to occur. Therefore, they separated themselves from a

---

1. Walter Shurden, "The Baptist Identity and the Baptist *Manifesto*," *Perspectives in Religious Studies* 25, no. 4 (1998): 321.
2. Robert G. Torbet, *A History of Baptists* (Valley Forge, PA: Judson, 1963), 201.
3. Torbet, *History of Baptists*, 202.

church that they believed had become burdened by ceremonial expression and too reliant on the *Book of Common Prayer* for their worship. Baptist theologian James McClendon identifies these theological traditions as "baptist with a small 'b' [which] refers not just to those who label themselves Baptist, but Christians of any sort . . . who see the radicals of the sixteenth century—the so-called Anabaptists—as their spiritual forbears, even if not progenitors."[4]

## Historical Influences on the Order of Worship

We learn about the order of early Baptist worship at John Smyth's Baptist Church in Amsterdam from a letter written by Hughe and Anne Bromheade circa 1609. Their description of worship reveals firm commitments to the centrality of prayer, Scripture reading, preaching, and the prominent role of laypeople:

> The order of the worshippe and goverment of oure church is .1. we begynne with A prayer, after reade some one or tow chapters of the bible gyve the sence therof, and conferr vpon the same; that done we lay aside oure bookes, and after a solemne prayer made by the .1. speaker, he propoundeth some text owt of the Scripture, and prophecieth owt of the same, by the space of one hower, or thre Quarters of an hower. After him standeth vp A .2. speaker and prophecieth owt of the said text the like tyme and space. some tyme more some tyme lesse. After him the .3. the .4. the .5. &c as the tyme will gve leave, Then the .1. speaker concludeth wth prayer as he began wth prayer, wth an exhortation to contribution to the poore, wth collection being made is also concluded wth prayer. This Morning exercise begynes at eight of the clocke and continueth vnto twelve of the clocke the like course of exercise is observed in the afternowne from .2. of the clocke vnto .5. or .6. of the Clocke. last of all the execution of the goverment of the church is handled.[5]

Thus, the order of worship is as follows: prayer, Scripture, prayer, sermon, additional speakers, prayer with exhortation, collection, prayer.

The Westminster *Directory* arguably had a significant influence on Baptist worship, the remnants of which we might still see today. *A Directory for the Public Worship of God* was developed by Presbyterian Puritans and a strongly vocal minority of Independents who were committed to a Separatist vision of the church and public worship. Because of the sturdy influence

---

4. Ched Myers, "Embodying the 'Great Story': An Interview with James Wm. McClendon," *The Witness* 83, no. 12 (December 2000): 14.

5. H. Leon McBeth, *A Sourcebook for Baptist Heritage* (Nashville: Broadman, 1990), 22.

of the Independents, the document was conceived as a manual or directory and not a liturgy or prayer book. The rubrics remained open-ended while the prayers served only as models for pastors to modify as they felt led. Ratified on January 3, 1645, the *Directory* established what remains as the order of worship for many Baptist churches today, outlined as follows: call to worship, prayer, Scripture, prayer of confession and intercession, sermon, prayer (Lord's Prayer—not recited, but as a guide and prayer for the needs of the day), psalm, and dismissal with blessing. The rubric regarding the prayer after the sermon likewise continues to be influential today. The *Directory* advises,

> Of Prayer after the Sermon—The Sermon being ended, the Minister is:
>     To give thanks for the great Love of God in sending his Sonne Jesus Christ unto us; For the communication of his Holy Spirit; For the light and liberty of the glorious Gospell, and the rich and heavenly Blessings revealed therein; . . . For the Covenant; and for many temporal blessings. . . . To turne the chiefe and most usefull heads of the Sermon into some few Petitions; and to pray that it may abide in the heart and bring forth fruit.[6]

Given the evidence cited above, it is possible to suggest that the long prayer that opened worship in Puritan and Separatist worship and the prayer after the sermon as described in the *Directory* represent the origins of the pastoral prayer as practiced in Baptist churches today.

Finally, we cannot underestimate the influences that revivalism and the frontier tradition have had on the structure of Baptist worship. With a strong focus on pragmatic concerns—namely, how many people converted to the Christian faith by the end of worship—the Sunday morning service was distilled into three units: the preliminaries (singing, prayer, and Scripture), the sermon, and the altar call (invitation to conversion).[7]

## Historical Influences on Extemporaneous Prayer

The practice of extemporaneous prayer has been characteristic of Baptist worship since its beginning. For Smyth and his Baptist followers, spiritual worship demanded that prayer be spontaneous and engaged without books. In *Differences of the Churches of the Separation* (1608), Smyth establishes a biblical foundation for banishing books from worship. He writes,

6. Bard Thompson, ed., *Liturgies of the Western Church* (New York: Meridian, 1961), 367.
7. See Melanie C. Ross, "Pragmatism versus Ecumenism? Rethinking Historical Origins," in *Evangelical versus Liturgical? Defying a Dichotomy* (Grand Rapids: Eerdmans, 2014), 10–31.

9. Because vpon the day of Pentecost fyerie cloven tongs did appeare, not fiery cloven bookes. Act. 2. 3. & always ther must be a proportion betwixt the type and the thing typed: vpon the day of Pentecost the fiery law was given in bookes Deut: 33. 2. Exo: 24. 4. 12 vpon the day of Pentecost the fiery gospel was given in tonges Act 2. 3. Mat: 3. 11. Act: 1. 5. the booke therefore was proper for them, the tong for vs.

10. Bicause as all the worship which Moses taught began in the letter out-wardly, & so proceeded inwardly to the spirit of the faithfull: so contrariwise all the worship of the new testament signified by that typicall worship of Moses must beginne at the Spirit, & not at the letter originally. 2. Cor. 3. 6. 8. 1. Cor: 12. 7. or els the heavenly thinge is not answerable to the similitude thereof.[8]

In the colonies of America, the Separatist Baptists and the Puritans mutually influenced each other by worshiping together until significant schism occurred on the issues of believer's baptism and the separation of church and state in the late seventeenth century. However, these traditions maintained an under-standing that extemporaneous prayer was a gift from Christ to his church.[9] In this regard, writes Horton Davies, prayer was conceived as "sincere, serious, spontaneous, heart-deep conversation with God."[10] Not only did the value placed on spontaneous, sincere prayer necessitate extemporaneous prayer in worship for the Separatists and the Puritans; it also required the repudiation of formalized responses by the people, including "congregational responses, with the single exception of the word *Amen*."[11]

## Worship under Threatening Conditions

Early Baptist identity was formed amid persecution and martyrdom at other Christians' hands (who, not inconsequentially, were associated with liturgical traditions). These experiences embedded into Baptists a deep and long-lasting suspicion of institutional churches. Church with a capital C, for Baptists, "is identified with the people who are worshipping, rather than an institution of which those worshippers form a part. In other words, the local congregation *is* the Church of Jesus Christ."[12]

8. McBeth, *Sourcebook for Baptist Heritage*, 17–18.
9. Horton Davies, *The Worship of the American Puritans, 1629–1730* (New York: Peter Lang, 1990), 134.
10. Davies, *Worship of the American Puritans*, 265.
11. Horton Davies, *The Worship of the English Puritans* (London: Dacre, 1948), 68.
12. Christopher J. Ellis, *Gathering: A Theology and Spirituality of Worship in Free Church Tradition* (London: SCM, 2004), 90 (emphasis added).

In colonial New England, arrest warrants were issued for some Separatist and Baptist worshipers, forcing them to meet secretly in one another's homes. These worship services were marked with great simplicity and did not rely on ordained clergy for leadership. Nathan E. Wood contends that this simplicity and agility of leadership and organization is what allowed the Baptist tradition to survive its persecutions. "It did not depend on any one man. Any one might expound the Scriptures to the others. Any one might pray in their assembly. Whoever of their number might be in prison, or absent for other cause, there was always some one present and ready to lead their service of worship. It was this fact which proved so baffling to the authorities in attempting to suppress the church."[13]

For different reasons, slaves were also compelled to worship in secret, away from the oppressive presence of slaveholders and the White gaze. These hidden and protected worship spaces came to be known as hush-harbor worship and allowed for a robust blending of African traditions with Christian worship. Among the key characteristics of hush-harbor worship, according to liturgical scholar Melva Wilson Costen, were uncomplicated worship, an emphasis on the "freedom of the Spirit to enable the preaching, singing, praying, shouting, and responsive listening," a commitment to "mutual community affinity," and communal support of one another.[14] Costen points out that while spontaneity and Spirit-led worship were necessary, "there is also evidence of 'liturgical form' and a sense of a rhythmic flow of the service."[15] The blending of African traditions, the emphasis on Spirit-inspired freedom and rhythmic flow, the opportunity to hear the gospel speak to the reality of oppression, and the ability to express both suffering and joy—all these elements of worship continue to shape Black Baptist worship to this day.

## Baptist Ecclesiology as Four Fragile Freedoms

Baptist ecclesiology tends to coalesce around the concept of freedom. Walter Shurden identifies "four fragile freedoms" that are all interrelated: Bible freedom, soul freedom, church freedom, and religious freedom.[16]

13. Nathan Eusebius Wood, *The History of the First Baptist Church of Boston 1665–1899* (Philadelphia: American Baptist Publication Society, 1899), 91.

14. Melva Wilson Costen, *African American Christian Worship*, 2nd ed. (Nashville: Abingdon, 2007), 25–26.

15. Costen, *African American Christian Worship*, 27.

16. See Walter B. Shurden, *The Baptist Identity: Four Fragile Freedoms* (Macon, GA: Smyth and Helwys, 1993); and Shurden, *The Life of Baptists in the Life of the World: Eighty Years of the Baptist World Alliance* (Nashville: Broadman, 1985).

### Bible Freedom

Bible freedom is the insistence on "freedom of access to the Bible and freedom of interpretation of the Bible."[17] Because Scripture is the primary means by which one comes to know the mind of Christ, the Bible is understood to be the final authority; however, "human understanding of the Bible is never final or complete or finished."[18] Therefore, Baptist engagement in biblical interpretation is (or ought to be) dynamic, open, and provisional.

Other Baptist scholars massage the concept of Bible freedom to emphasize reading communities' value in biblical interpretation. As a corrective to dangerously idiosyncratic interpretations, Baptists ought to discern the meaning of Scripture in community. "When all exercise their gifts and callings, when every voice is heard and weighed, when no one is silenced or privileged, the Spirit leads communities to read wisely and to practice faithfully the direction of the gospel."[19]

### Soul Freedom

Soul freedom, also referred to historically as soul competency, is the Baptist assertion that each individual, created in the image of God, "is competent under God to make moral, spiritual, and religious decisions. Not only is the individual privileged to make those decisions, but the individual alone is also *responsible* for making those decisions."[20] Often misunderstood by Baptists and non-Baptists alike, soul freedom does not originate in North American or post-Enlightenment notions of individualism; instead, its origins are before the Enlightenment and established in a theological rather than an anthropological standpoint. "God's freedom is the pattern for the gift of freedom in Jesus Christ."[21] Rather than the atomistic individualism that erodes communal life and faith, soul freedom is rooted in the "conviction that faith must not, indeed cannot, be coerced by any power or authority."[22]

17. Shurden, *Baptist Identity*, 11.
18. Shurden, *Baptist Identity*, 11.
19. The jointly drafted statement "Re-envisioning Baptist Identity: A Manifesto for Baptist Communities" (referred to later simply as the Manifesto) was composed by Baptist scholars Mikael Broadway, Curtis Freeman, Barry Harvey, James W. McClendon Jr., Elizabeth Newman, and Philip Thompson. The Manifesto was subsequently signed by a total of fifty-five Baptist scholars and theologians. The full text of the Manifesto appears online and is the one referenced here. See https://divinity.duke.edu/sites/divinity.duke.edu/files/documents/faculty-freeman/reenvisioning-baptist-identity.pdf. Citations will be by section (§) and paragraph (¶). Here, Broadway et al., "Manifesto," §I ¶1.
20. Shurden, *Baptist Identity*, 24.
21. Broadway et al., "Manifesto," Preamble, ¶2.
22. Broadway et al., "Manifesto," Preamble, ¶2.

Thus, Shurden defines soul freedom as "the historical Baptist affirmation of the inalienable right and responsibility of every person to deal with God without the imposition of creed, the interference of clergy, or the intervention of civil government."[23] For this reason, faith is conceived as personal, is characterized by the right to choose, and ultimately leads to the Baptist emphasis on believers' baptism.[24]

Baptist emphasis on the primacy of the person insists that "saving faith is personal, not impersonal. It is relational, not ritualistic. It is direct, not indirect."[25] Born from the Radical Reformation conflicts, the Baptist commitment to soul freedom subverts the authority of clergy, insists on the freedom of God to move in a person's life apart from the sacraments, and makes salvation a matter of the individual in relationship with God.[26]

Philip E. Thompson offers a compelling argument regarding the historical construction of soul freedom. He maintains that present-day Baptists "tend to retroject their own sensitivities and sensibilities onto their forebears," especially when it comes to our notions of soul freedom. North American Baptists have long conflated their understanding of soul freedom with the separation of church and state in such a way that they have lost its roots in the ultimate *freedom of God* to move in the world, apart from the ways ordained by the state church. The early Baptists were firm in their conviction that "God's prerogatives could not be usurped, yet precisely this was what happened in the rites, prescriptions, and theology of the state church. We need to be clear that the early Baptist believed the state church to be an affront not against individual conscience, but against God."[27]

Finally, Baptist belief in soul freedom informs the Baptist commitment that baptism is for believers. Through believers' baptism, Baptists formed an ecclesiology based on the concept of a believers' church—a gathering of individuals-in-community who have made a voluntary decision of faith through an experience of a personal encounter with God that led to conversion by conviction.[28]

---

23. Shurden, *Baptist Identity*, 23.
24. Shurden, *Baptist Identity*, 29.
25. Shurden, *Baptist Identity*, 25.
26. Shurden, *Baptist Identity*, 25.
27. See Philip E. Thompson, "Sacraments and Religious Liberty: From Critical Practice to Rejected Infringement," in *Baptist Sacramentalism*, ed. Anthony R. Cross and Philip E. Thompson (Waynesboro, GA: Paternoster, 2003), 44.
28. See Shurden, *Baptist Identity*, 29–31. The term "individuals-in-community" is recommended by the authors of the Manifesto to act as a corrective against the destructive, individualist ways that soul freedom has predominantly come to be understood since the mid-eighteenth century. See Broadway et al., "Manifesto," §II ¶1.

### Church Freedom

Just as individuals are free and responsible to choose a life of faith voluntarily before God, so the church, as a gathered assembly of individuals-in-community, is free under Christ to follow God's leading voluntarily. Baptist churches affirm the right of local churches "to determine their membership and leadership, to order their worship and work, to ordain whom they perceive as gifted for ministry, male or female, and to participate in the larger Body of Christ of whose unity and mission Baptists are proudly a part."[29] Church freedom is best expressed ecclesiastically in its local form: the church is located at a particular time and place and constituted of believers gathered by God.

Because of the Baptist commitment to church freedom and its concomitant affirmation of local churches' right to self-governance, there is tremendous diversity in Baptist churches' worship practices. As Shurden writes, "The Baptist freedom for worship aims at an authentic spiritual offering being presented to God. But Baptist worship does not dictate *how* worship is to be structured. Indeed, just as Bible Freedom offers individuals the right of private interpretation of the Bible and just as Soul Freedom issues into different types of personal conversion, Church Freedom results in different forms of worship, some of which are surprisingly formal and some exceedingly informal."[30] Worship at the local level is a communal event uniquely formed by the people who constitute a congregation. Worship often involves the active participation of ordained and unordained alike in the leadership of worship, from the call to worship, the reading of Scripture, preaching, and, in some congregations, presiding at the Lord's Table.

### Religious Freedom

Just as the Baptist church is free from centralized ecclesiastical control, it is also free from state control. "Religious Freedom is the historical Baptist affirmation of freedom *of* religion, freedom *for* religion, and freedom *from* religion, insisting that Caesar is not Christ and Christ is not Caesar."[31] Soul freedom and church freedom are rooted first in the freedom of God; so too is religious freedom. More than mere toleration, religious freedom is a right granted to all, not just Baptists. Inextricable from the freedom *of* religion is the attendant freedom *from* religion. "One's right not to believe is as sacred as

---

29. Shurden, *Baptist Identity*, 33. As with all the freedoms mentioned in this chapter, Baptist churches and denominations variously attain and fall short of living out their ideals.

30. Shurden, *Baptist Identity*, 40.

31. Shurden, *Baptist Identity*, 45.

one's right to believe."[32] Finally, religious freedom necessitates and manifests in the "separation of church and state and not accommodation of church with state."[33]

While many Baptist churches may understand themselves to be in a prophetic or even antagonistic relationship with state power, Robert P. Jones cautions that Baptists ought not to fool themselves into thinking that they are also *culturally* independent. Rather than seeing the church as distinct from the culture in which it finds itself, Jones urges that Baptists acknowledge how the church "historically has shared in *forming and deforming* the world as we know it."[34] Only then can the church "engage the world not only for the sake of itself but for the sake of all humans and indeed of all creation."[35]

Stemming from a firm theological belief in the sovereignty and freedom of God, these four fragile freedoms are the gift and the responsibility of every Baptist Christian. How then do these Baptist distinctives coalesce to shape Baptist approaches to worship?

## Ecclesiological Commitments Ordering Baptist Worship

While it is true that many Baptist congregations follow a similar order of worship from week to week, contemporary Baptists are not generally concerned about the order of worship in terms of its sequence. Instead, several liturgical principles stem from ecclesiological commitments that give shape to the design of worship. Christopher Ellis identifies five principles: (1) tradition alone need not structure worship, but worship must be open to spontaneity; (2) worship

32. Shurden, *Baptist Identity*, 50. Shurden goes on to quote John Leland's "The Rights of Conscience Inalienable" as a firm corrective to contemporary Baptists' abandonment of the idea of freedom from religion: "Let every man speak freely without fear, maintain the principles that he believes, worship according to his own faith, either one God, three Gods, no God, or twenty Gods; and let government protect him in so doing." See L. F. Greene, *The Writings of John Leland* (New York: Arno, 1969), reprinted from the 1845 edition.

33. Shurden, *Baptist Identity*, 50.

34. Robert P. Jones, "Revision-ing Baptist Identity from a Theocentric Perspective," *Perspectives in Religious Studies* 26, no. 1 (Spring 1999): 53.

35. Jones, "Revision-ing Baptist Identity," 53. Jones addresses the danger of Baptists talking out of both sides of their mouths when claiming political disestablishment. Writing in 1999, Jones is aware of a certain painful irony: "The call to cultural disestablishment from a denomination [in his case the Southern Baptist Convention] that currently counts as members seven of the eight top elected officials of arguably the most powerful country in the world, including the president and vice-president, would be laughable were it not for its dangerous implications. . . . We must not, as some of our own have done, attempt to assume simultaneously the role of persecuted religious communities and powerful political force, taking up the mantle of each as it suits our political advantage" (53).

practices are open to change; (3) simplicity and freedom allow for greater spontaneity (or, framed in the negative, there is a suspicion that ceremony and ritual are likely to interfere with the movement of the Holy Spirit); (4) robust communal worship will place an emphasis on congregational singing; and (5) Word-centered worship will also highly value preaching.[36] These principles give shape to four core liturgical values: Scripture, devotion, community, and eschatology (especially expressed in petitionary prayers on behalf of a heart-broken world).[37] In the following section I will highlight these values as they coalesce in key liturgical moments for Baptist worship.

### Devotion

Baptist worshipers place a high value on devotion and personal spirituality. Such piety is seen perhaps most clearly in Black Baptist worship that begins with a song service led by deacons. Baptists expect to experience God's presence in worship. Liturgical space is expansive when we consider the daily prayer practices of Baptist believers who regard the study of Scripture and personal prayer as essential components of faithful discipleship and worship.

### Scripture

For Baptists, the proclamation of Scripture and its interpretation through the sermon are climactic moments in weekly worship. Since the 1990s, it has become more common for Baptist churches to follow the Revised Common Lectionary. However, most of those churches will read only one of the suggested texts each week, likely retaining Calvin's preference in this regard. Many Baptist churches do not follow a predetermined lectionary; rather, a worship planning team or pastor will select the weekly Scripture. Some Baptist congregations, especially in Black Baptist worship traditions, heighten the congregation's ritual moment by standing to hear the Word. Scripture infuses other parts of worship, especially in prayers and congregational singing.

### Liturgical Time

Baptist churches that started following the Revised Common Lectionary also started to incorporate observance of the liturgical year. While previous generations may have decried Lent and Advent as "too Catholic," many Baptists today fully expect to mark these seasons in worship. However, congregations that do

---

36. Ellis, *Gathering*, 66–69.
37. Ellis, *Gathering*, 74, 89, 91, 95.

not follow a lectionary or plan worship around themes or sermon series still may
mark liturgical celebrations of Christmas, Palm Sunday, Good Friday, Easter
(or Resurrection Sunday), and Pentecost. Black Baptist churches also follow a
liturgical calendar that includes Watch Night, Emancipation Proclamation Day
(and Juneteenth), Beloved Community Day (Martin Luther King Jr.'s birthday),
Pastor's Anniversary, Women's Day, Revival, and other designated celebrations.[38] Despite historical commitments to the separation of church and state,
many Baptist congregations also incorporate civic holidays into their liturgical
celebrations, including Independence Day, Memorial Day, and Veteran's Day.

### Preaching

As already mentioned, the sermon tends to be the climactic event in Baptist
worship. Furthermore, because the Baptist tradition was influenced by revivalism, the sermon was often followed by an altar call. Many Baptist churches
continue to sequence worship in this way today. Others have abbreviated this
moment with a standard invitation to join the church during the closing hymn,
an invitation that may be spoken or printed in the bulletin.

Some Baptist congregations and conventions—the Southern Baptist Convention among them—forbid women from preaching. Some congregations
allow women to speak, but not from the pulpit. This distinction intends to
keep others from perceiving that the congregation condones women preachers. Other congregations and conventions—including most American Baptist
churches—affirm women preachers and women's ordination.

The preaching moment is rooted in the expectation that God has a word
for God's people today. Baptist worshipers expect that Scripture speaks to
our present needs, concerns, struggles, and joys.

### Prayer

The Baptist liturgical value placed on community has a direct influence
on the practice of prayer in worship. Congregational prayer practices such as
concerns and celebrations and altar prayer are integral to worship. Likewise,
the pastoral prayer, informed by the people's joys and heartaches, is intended
to draw the congregation into intimate relationship with one another and
with God.[39]

---

38. For a list of celebrations in the Black church calendar, see the African American Lectionary, a collaborative project of the African American Pulpit and American Baptist College of
Nashville, http://theafricanamericanlectionary.org/calender.asp.

39. For a thorough constructive theological exploration of concerns and celebrations, see Jennifer W. Davidson, "The Narrative Practice of Memory as Identity in Concerns & Celebrations

## Ordinances

Radical reformers rejected the term "sacrament" because they believed it was theologically misleading and conferred too much power to clergy. In their attempt to distance themselves from sacramentarianism, Baptists began to use the term "ordinance." Ordinances are *ordained* or commanded by Christ for his followers to do. They include the Lord's Supper and baptism (called the Gospel ordinances) and preaching, Scripture reading, prayer, and singing. Heavily influenced by Huldrych Zwingli, Baptists increasingly understood baptism and Communion as merely a proclamation of belief. They rejected any suggestion that human beings could enact a ritual that would trigger God to act on their behalf. These theological perspectives were later reinforced by Enlightenment sensibilities that were suspicious of mystery, favored rationalism, and bred individualism. An emphasis on obedience to Christ's commands led to an increasingly individualistic interpretation of baptism and Communion.

In more recent years, some Baptist theologians have advocated reclamation of the term "sacrament" so that they might embrace the ways God is mediated to us through embodied and material means. Because human beings come to know the world and the sacred through our bodies (both physical and spiritual senses), God would certainly come to us in concrete ways.[40] The incarnation assuredly affirms such a perspective.

## Practical Implications for Worship

Australian Baptist theologian Frank Rees uses conversation as a metaphor for worship: theology is a divine-human conversation, and worship is the unique context in which this conversation finds focus and expression.[41] Drawn into the divine-human conversation in worship, we "allow our lives to be gathered into such worship, to bring who and what we are into such worship, to affirm and celebrate, to lament and confess, to reach out in hope and missionary commitment."[42]

Free and robust participation of worshipers is rooted in the Baptist commitment that worship at the local level is a communal event uniquely formed

---

and the Pastoral Prayer: Constructing a Liturgical Theology of Prayer" (PhD diss., Graduate Theological Union, 2011).

40. Clark H. Pinnock, "The Physical Side of Being Spiritual: God's Sacramental Presence," in Cross and Thompson, *Baptist Sacramentalism*, 8.

41. See Frank Rees, "The Worship of All Believers," in *Baptist Faith and Witness Book 3: Papers of the Study and Research Division of the Baptist World Alliance, 2000–2005*, ed. L. A. (Tony) Cupit (Falls Church, VA: Baptist World Alliance, 2005), 32.

42. Rees, "Worship of All Believers," 33.

by the people who constitute a congregation. Providing the opportunity for diverse voices to speak in worship is a crucial way to preserve the diversity and plurality of religious experiences in Baptist congregations. In Baptist churches, every person ought to feel empowered to lead others in worship.

As the adage goes, with great freedom comes great responsibility. Baptist worshipers (clergy and lay alike) have the duty to learn their liturgical histories and engage in critical thinking about worship practices in their congregations today. It is not enough to assume that "this is the way we've always done it." What a deceptively authoritative phrase that can be, especially when it comes to worship. On the other hand, Baptists can affirm their worship traditions' unique gifts that have much to offer to our ecumenical sisters and brothers.

## For Further Reading

Abbington, James, ed. *Readings in African American Church Music and Worship*. Vol. 2. Chicago: GIA, 2014.

Cross, Anthony R., and Philip E. Thompson. *Baptist Sacramentalism*. Studies in Baptist History and Thought 5. Waynesboro, GA: Paternoster, 2003.

Davidson, Jennifer W. *River of Life, Feast of Grace: Baptism, Communion, and Discipleship*. Valley Forge, PA: Judson, 2019.

Ellis, Christopher J. *Gathering: A Theology and Spirituality of Worship in Free Church Tradition*. London: SCM, 2004.

Hall, Nancy E. *The New Manual of Worship*. Valley Forge, PA: Judson, 2018.

Holmes, Stephen R. *Baptist Theology*. London: T&T Clark, 2012.

Ross, Melanie C. *Evangelical versus Liturgical? Defying a Dichotomy*. Grand Rapids: Eerdmans, 2014.

Yee, Russell. *Worship on the Way: Exploring Asian North American Christian Experience*. Valley Forge, PA: Judson, 2012.

## — 17 —

# Evangelical Practices of Worship

## *Melanie C. Ross*

Ask any American religious historian to define the word "evangelical," and they will likely hedge a little before attempting an answer. This simple question stumped no less a luminary than Billy Graham, America's most famous evangelical preacher. When asked to define the term in the late 1980s, Graham turned the question back to his interviewer. "Actually, that's a question I'd like to ask somebody too," he replied. Evangelicals come in all shapes and sizes: liturgical, charismatic, denominational, nondenominational, and emergent, to cite a few possible varieties. Their worship is just as diverse. Sunday mornings across the evangelical spectrum can include everything from hellfire preaching and altar calls, to responsive readings and contemplative prayer, to upbeat praise music and speaking in tongues.

In this chapter, I use the term "evangelical" to refer to a group of self-identified Protestants who hold a high view of biblical authority, have a cross-centered theology that affirms the idea that Jesus suffered and died to atone for humans' sins, and stress the importance of individual conversion and evangelism.[1] Specifically, I am interested in the last part of that definition: the emphasis evangelicals have placed on evangelism and the questions they have raised about the role worship plays in the process of conversion. In what

1. D. W. Bebbington, *Evangelicalism in Modern Britain: A History from the 1730s to the 1980s* (London: Routledge, 1996), 1–19.

follows, I outline two historical case studies—Charles Finney's writings about revivalism in the nineteenth century and A. W. Tozer's critics of worship in the mid-twentieth century—to highlight shifts in evangelical worship over time and to press questions for further conversation.

## Charles G. Finney and the Anxious Bench

Charles G. Finney was born in 1792 in Warren, Connecticut, and early in his life moved to the "burned-over district" of upstate New York. On October 10, 1821, Finney had a conversion experience and gave up his career in law to pursue the life of an evangelist. The evangelistic campaigns that Finney led between 1824 and 1834 made his name synonymous with the final stage of the Second Great Awakening.[2]

### Finney's Context

To understand the controversies surrounding Finney, one must first understand the theological context of the First and Second Great Awakenings. The theology of the First Awakening of 1725–1750 was Calvinistic. Theologians of the time asserted, "Man had the natural ability to act rightly but he was morally unable to do so unless God, through the Holy Spirit, transformed or infused his soul with grace."[3] During the First Great Awakening, Jonathan Edwards wrote a famous treatise titled "A Faithful Narrative of the Surprising Work of God." By contrast, Finney's most famous sermon of the Second Great Awakening was "Sinners Bound to Change Their Own Hearts." The difference in titles illustrates the theological tension between the two awakenings well. Whereas Jonathan Edwards described revival in 1734 as "a marvelous work of God" and a "shower of divine blessing" that came to a parched land from the hand of God,[4] Finney asserted that the church should not sit back idly and wait for revival to mysteriously fall from the sky. Revival instead resulted from "the right use of appropriate means."[5]

---

2. Charles E. Hambrick-Stowe, *Charles G. Finney and the Spirit of American Evangelicalism* (Grand Rapids: Eerdmans, 1996), xi.

3. William G. McLoughlin, introduction to *Lectures on Revivals of Religion*, by Charles G. Finney (Cambridge, MA: Belknap, 1960), xiii.

4. Jonathan Edwards, *A Faithful Narrative of the SURPRISING Work of God: In the Conversion of Many Hundreds Souls in Northampton, and the Neighbouring Towns and Villages of New Hampshire in New-England in a Letter to the Rev. Dr. Colman, of Boston* (n.p.: C. Whittingham for W. Button, 1737), 348.

5. Finney, *Lectures*, 13.

## The Anxious Bench

Finney united traditional revival means such as preaching, prayer, and repentance with what came to be known as the "new measures," which included door-to-door visitations, allowing women to testify in mixed gatherings, and protracted meetings. Arguably the most controversial new measure, however, was Finney's employment of the anxious bench, a seat in which "the anxious may come and be addressed particularly and be made subjects of prayer."[6] Strictly speaking, the anxious bench was not a *new* measure, although its history is difficult to document. Revivalists prior to Finney sometimes used inquiry meetings—meetings separate from the revival services in which interested persons could seek further advice about their souls' welfare.[7] A similar practice was also employed at the famous revivals of 1801 in Cane Ridge, Kentucky, where as many as twenty-five thousand people gathered. A crowd of such density was difficult to control, and the "indiscriminate distribution of the participants" resulted in charges of immorality, which perhaps contained an element of truth.[8] One measure for controlling the mob was to collect the "mourners" (sinners) and seat them in the front of the crowd.

Scholars are uncertain as to how conscious Finney was of his borrowing, but in 1820 Finney combined the ideology of the inquiry meetings and the practice of bringing mourners to the front of the congregation into the form known as the anxious bench. The anxious bench rose to greater prominence than any of its precursors, in part because Finney placed it at the heart of his theology of revival.

The anxious bench proved highly controversial. Two of Finney's most outspoken critics were Albert Dod (1805–1845), an Old School Presbyterian and a professor at Princeton, and John Nevin (1803–1886), a theologian who taught at the German Reformed Church Seminary. Dod and Nevin charged that the anxious bench led to vulgarity, disorder, and, in Nevin's words, a "wildfire of fanaticism," which included "screaming, shouting, jumping, tumbling, and 'the holy grin.'"[9] They worried that the anxious bench was a gateway to other, more outlandish novelties in worship: gimmicks like phosphoric paintings on the walls of the church, or stationing a trumpeter in the belfry to illustrate the blowing of the archangel's trumpet. Dod feared that the house of God would

---

6. Finney, *Lectures*, 267.

7. Bill J. Leonard, "Getting Saved in America: Conversion Event in a Pluralistic Culture," *Review and Expositor* 82 (Winter 1995): 120.

8. Thomas H. Olbricht, "The Invitation: A Historical Survey," *Restoration Quarterly* 5, no. 1 (1961), https://digitalcommons.acu.edu/restorationquarterly/vol5/iss1/3.

9. John Nevin, *The Anxious Bench: The Mystical Presence*, American Religious Thought of the 18th and 19th Centuries (New York: Garland, 1987), 50.

be "transformed into a kind of religious laboratory,"[10] and Nevin insisted that "no satisfactory stopping place [could] be found."[11]

For Finney, however, the end justified the means. Methodology was not important so long as souls were being brought to Christ. Finney drew a parallel between an election campaign and a revival. In political spheres, the concern is not whether new or old measures are used but whether the candidate wins the election. Finney saw no reason why the spiritual realm should operate any differently.[12] In Finney's interpretation, Jesus himself was more concerned with results than with forms: "When Jesus Christ was on earth . . . he had nothing to do with forms or measures. . . . The Jews accused him of disregarding their forms. His object was to preach and teach mankind the true religion. . . . No person can pretend to get a set of forms or particular directions as to measures out of [the Great Commission]. Their goal was to make known the gospel in the *most effectual way*."[13] Proponents of the anxious bench enthused that if God had chosen to operate in a certain way, then they were in no position to find fault or condemn.

As is often the case in disagreements over liturgical matters, the roots of the controversy surrounding revival techniques were theological and went far deeper than matters of personal preference. In this case, the anxious bench challenged existing perceptions of Christianity on several levels.

### Novelty versus Tradition

Finney thought the church of his day had fallen soundly asleep. New measures were necessary for members of the collective church who "once in a while wake up, rub their eyes, bluster about and vociferate a little while, and then go off to sleep again."[14] Familiarity breeds apathy, and Finney believed that unless people were "greatly excited," they would not obey God. Sinners cling tightly to their vices and sins, and their grip is so tight that loosening it required dramatic means. In Finney's words, "[Some] persons will never give up their false shame, or relinquish their ambitious schemes, until they are so excited that they cannot contain themselves any longer."[15]

Although Finney readily admitted that it was more desirable for the church to engage in a steady course of obedience without excitements, he pointed to

10. McLoughlin, introduction to Finney, *Lectures*, xxxviii.
11. Nevin, *Anxious Bench*, 51.
12. Finney, *Lectures*, 465.
13. Finney, *Lectures*, 251 (emphasis in original).
14. Finney, *Lectures*, 11.
15. Finney, *Lectures*, 12.

Old Testament history to show that this had never been the case.[16] The nation of Israel experienced peaks and valleys; no sooner did God pour out his grace than did the people turn again to idols. The story of Israel followed a pattern of disobedience, punishment, repentance, and restoration: it was not a steadily upward climb to spiritual maturity. Thus, revival excitement was a necessary corrective to a church continually in danger of apathy.

Finney's critics vehemently protested the assertion that churches that relied on old measures and forms retained the form of religion while losing its substance. John Nevin was especially outspoken on this point. Nevin argued that Finney exchanged the stability of old forms for the tyranny of the ever-changing new, and that reliance on novelty was "the refuge of weakness."[17] Trusted measures such as creeds, catechisms, and ordinary pastoral ministrations had virtue, and if a minister had no power in a catechetical class, then he deceived himself if he thought he would gain power through the use of the anxious bench: "If it be true that the old forms are dead and powerless in a minister's hands, the fault is not in the forms, but in the minister himself; and it is the very impotence of quackery, to think of mending the case essentially by the introduction of new forms."[18] One of Nevin's most important claims was that the "inward must bear the outward." Nevin feared that sinners would rely on an intense outward experience that was incapable of sustaining a deep inward transformation. This is one reason Nevin advocated privacy over public displays of religion.

### Public versus Private

As noted, the theology of the First Great Awakening was Calvinistic. God bestowed blessings in his own time, and there was little humans could say, do, pray, or feel that would manipulate the process. Given this theological background, earlier revival preachers such as George Whitfield and Jonathan Edwards were not looking for public responses to their preaching. Conversion during the First Great Awakening was a private matter that one worked out alone with God. Persons seeking counsel about spiritual matters went to the minister's house, not the front of the revival tent. Indeed, Charles Finney's own conversion was a private one in which he sought the solitude of the woods in order to pray and be alone with God.

Nevin charged that the public nature of the anxious bench made it a hindrance to conversion as individuals become so consumed with the question

16. Finney, *Lectures*, 11.
17. Nevin, *Anxious Bench*, 23.
18. Nevin, *Anxious Bench*, 22.

of whether to leave their seats that they are distracted from the more pressing conviction of sin and repentance. Nevin said that this exchanged a higher question (repentance) for a lower one (action): "While the awakened person is balancing the question of going to the anxious bench, his mind is turned away from the contemplation of the immediate matter of a quarrel between himself and God. The higher question is merged, for the time, in one that is lower."[19] The soul passed from a state of conviction to one of excitement or agitation, and the "still small voice of the Spirit [was] drowned amid the tumult of conflicting thoughts."[20] Additionally, critics challenged that the anxious bench became a form of emotional manipulation, producing an adverse effect on both bold and meek personalities. On the one hand, public measures attracted hypocrites who sought attention and momentary stardom; on the other hand, the anxious bench manipulated the emotionally vulnerable into making a decision that they were ill-equipped to carry out. Bold and meek personalities alike associated the act of publicly going forward in a meeting with a deep, genuine conversion—a much more lengthy and difficult process. For this reason, many felt that private conviction was more desirable.

Finney was aware of the accusation that his revivals were charged with emotional manipulation, but in his view the public nature of the anxious bench made it a natural deterrent to those who would build their conversions on the unstable foundation of momentary religious fervor. Finney gave the example of a drunkard who was convicted by a passionate preacher to embrace total abstinence. Intellectually, the drunkard agreed with the preacher's words, and in his heart he fully resolved to give up his former life, but when it came time to sign a pledge, the drunkard was unwilling to do so. Finney knew well the deceitful power of the human imagination. The situation is not unlike the one in which we find ourselves every New Year's Eve. It is easy to make bold proclamations and resolutions when there is no cost involved, and it is another matter entirely to commit to the hard work and sacrifice that it takes to see the resolutions through. For Finney, the anxious bench was a necessary first step of commitment, a means of ensuring that religious fervor lasted long after the revival.

### Finney's Legacy

Charles Finney made a significant impression on the religious life of nineteenth-century America, and his influence is still evident today. Finney developed a three-part liturgical order that came to dominate the format of

19. Nevin, *Anxious Bench*, 30.
20. Nevin, *Anxious Bench*, 32.

American Protestant worship: preliminary songs that softened up the audience, a fervent sermon, and an altar call for new converts. Called the "father of modern evangelicalism" by some historians, Finney paved the way for later revivalists like Dwight L. Moody and Billy Sunday, who also employed invitations to come to the front of the preaching hall. Billy Graham issued the most famous invitations of all, telling people "your friends will wait for you" as the choir sang "Just as I Am."

Many evangelicals today praise Finney as an evangelistic hero: a giant of revivalism who seemed to "grab the Gospel from the dry stuffy practitioners of his day and take it to the common folk so they could scrape their boots, come in, and cast their own votes for heaven or hell."[21] Others are more skeptical about Finney's legacy. They worry that the threefold liturgical order he developed suffers from a series of theological deficiencies: the audience's attention is drawn from the glory of the risen Christ to the magnetic personality of the speaker; there is too much emphasis on an individual's "decision for Christ"; and worship is made the means to an evangelistic end, rather than an end in itself. To understand how these concerns further developed in the second half of the twentieth century, we turn to our second case study.

## A. W. Tozer and Celebrity Worship Culture

Less than a hundred years after Finney's death, pastor and author A. W. Tozer penned these famous words about the state of worship in 1961: "Worship is the missing jewel in modern evangelicalism. We're organized; we work; we have our agendas. We have almost everything, but there's one thing that the churches, even the gospel churches, do not have: that is the ability to worship. We are not cultivating the art of worship. It's the one shining gem that is lost to the modern church, and I believe that we ought to search for this until we find it."[22]

Aiden Wilson Tozer was born on April 21, 1897, in a tiny farming community in western Pennsylvania. He never liked his given name and for most of his adult life was known as "A. W." or simply "Tozer." In 1919, only five years after his conversion and with no formal theological training, Tozer began forty-four years of ministry with the Christian and Missionary Alliance denomination.

---

21. "From the Editor: Father of Modern Revivalism," *Christianity Today*, October 1, 1988, https://www.christianitytoday.com/history/issues/issue-20/from-editor-father-of-modern -revivalism.html.

22. A. W. Tozer, *Worship: The Missing Jewel in the Evangelical Church* (Camp Hill, PA: Christian Publications, 1961), 1.

For thirty-one of those years, Tozer served as pastor of Southside Alliance Church in Chicago. He wrote hundreds of articles for periodicals, conducted regular Saturday morning broadcasts over Chicago's WMBI for eight years, and published nine books during the last two decades of his life.

Tozer was a self-proclaimed "minor prophet" with a uniquely engaging style that was "half Jeremiah, half Mark Twain."[23] He loved the Bible and unflinchingly preached what he believed people needed to hear. Tozer attacked materialism, consumerism, and worldliness wherever he saw it infiltrating the church. In particular, he admonished Christian leaders for adopting leadership models from the business world and for allowing various forms of entertainment to take the place of biblical preaching and theocentric worship.

### Tozer's Context

During the 1800s, a process of secularization began to chip away at the influence church and home had previously exerted over young people. The 1859 publication of Darwin's *On the Origins of Species*, and the subsequent 1925 Scopes trial that allowed the teaching of evolution in public schools, caused fundamentalists great angst. Gradually, religious and moral influences, including the teaching of the Bible, were excluded from public schools. The Great Depression shook Americans' confidence in their economic system. Unemployment hit young people especially hard. As of 1936, an estimated 4.7 million Americans between the ages of sixteen and twenty-four were unemployed—a number that represented about one-third of all the unemployed in the country.[24] World War II brought not only international trauma but also a notable rise in teenage domestic crime. Street gangs emerged in most big cities, and bus and train stations were full of teenage "victory girls" who offered sexual favors to servicemen in exchange for a good time.

Since Hitler had risen to power with the help of a fanatical youth movement, American adults feared that their unemployed, idealistic youth could be just as easily manipulated by communists or fascists. Evangelicals began calling for the mass evangelization of young people as a means of saving the world from destruction. Tozer's tone in *Worship: The Missing Jewel* is characteristic of his time: the reason so many young people "go out and act like idiots," and the reason "gangsters and Communists and sinners of all kinds do what they do," is that they don't know what to do with their God-given

23. Glen G. Scorgie, *A Little Guide to Christian Spirituality: Three Dimensions of Life with God* (Grand Rapids: Zondervan, 2007), 52.

24. Thomas E. Bergler, *The Juvenilization of American Christianity* (Grand Rapids: Eerdmans, 2012), 20.

intellect and gifts. Tozer speculates that if these sinners "could by the Holy Ghost and the washing of the blood be made into worshiping saints [then] things would be so different."[25]

A generation of evangelical leaders rose to meet the challenge with a new organization called Youth for Christ (YFC), which rose to national prominence through wildly popular Saturday night youth rallies. The peak years of the YFC rallies came at the end of World War II, between 1944 and 1950, and continued strongly in many places through the 1950s. In historian Joel Carpenter's description, these meetings "featured carefully orchestrated visions of innocence, heroism, and loyalty to a global cause, all wrapped in a contemporary idiom borrowed from radio variety shows and patriotic musical reviews."[26] For example, a 1945 YFC Memorial Day rally in Chicago drew seventy thousand people to Soldier Field. The musical program featured a three-hundred-piece brass band, a choir of five thousand, and several well-known gospel singers, including George Beverly Shea. On the field, high school cadets performed a flag ceremony, and four hundred nurses marched in the form of a cross. War heroes and athletic stars attested to their faith, a preacher delivered the gospel message, and hundreds in the audience signed decision cards during the invitation. At the conclusion of the meeting, a spotlight circled the darkened stadium while a huge neon sign blazed "Jesus Saves" and the choir sang "We Shall Shine as Stars in the Morning."[27]

The Chicago rally was not an isolated occurrence. YFC rallies across the country followed a similar pattern of youth-tailored revivalism: "Saturday night in a big auditorium, lively gospel music, personal testimonies from athletes, civil leaders or military heroes, and a brief sermon, climaxing with a gospel invitation to receive Jesus Christ as personal Savoir."[28] Of course, in the quest for novelty and entertainment, many rallies got caught in a "one-upsman trap" of "magicians, gospel whistling, musical saws, single-string oil cans." The most outlandish attraction was a gospel horse that "moved his jaws to show 'how the girls in the choir chew gum' and demonstrated his knowledge of the Bible by tapping his hoof three times when asked 'how many Persons are in the Trinity?'"[29]

25. Tozer, *Worship*, 9.

26. Joel A. Carpenter, "Youth for Christ and the New Evangelicals' Place in the Life of the Nation," in *American Recoveries: Religion in the Life of the Nation*, ed. Sherrill Rowland (Urbana: University of Illinois Press, 1989), 135.

27. Carpenter, "Youth for Christ," 128.

28. Bruce Shelley, "The Young and the Zealous," Christian History Institute, https://christian historyinstitute.org/magazine/article/the-young-and-the-zealous.

29. Shelley, "The Young and the Zealous."

Since the fate of the world depended on winning youthful converts, YFC leaders went to great lengths to paint Christianity as the most attractive way of life available. In the early days, YFC rallies could compete with some of the best that the entertainment world had to offer. Indeed, for fundamentalist teenagers who were forbidden to attend movies, listen to "worldly" music, or otherwise indulge in questionable entertainment, YFC was "quite literally the best show in town."[30] Evangelical youth leaders demanded that teenagers abstain from drinking, smoking, petting, dancing, Hollywood movies, and rock and roll. They also urged teenagers to stand up for Jesus at school and witness to their friends. In return, teenagers demanded a "sanctified youth culture," complete with fun, popularity, movies, music, and celebrities.

Tozer strongly opposed YFC-style evangelism efforts. He complained that evangelicals had taken "inexcusable liberties with both the message and the method." His observations in 1944, during the peak of YFC rally popularity, re worth quoting at length:

> It is now common practice in most evangelical churches to offer the people, especially the young people, a maximum of entertainment and a minimum of serious instruction. It is scarcely possible in most places to get anyone to attend a meeting where the only attraction is God. One can only conclude that God's professed children are bored with Him, for they must be wooed to meeting with a stick of striped candy in the form of religious movies, games and refreshments. . . . Any objection to the carryings on of our present gold-calf Christianity is met with the triumphant reply, "But we are winning them!"[31]

"Winning them to what?": this was Tozer's nagging question. "To true discipleship? To cross-carrying? To self-denial? To separation from the world?" Tozer concluded that the answer to all these questions was a resounding no.[32]

### Music Debates

During the course of Tozer's life, worship music would become a particularly contentious subject for evangelicals. In the second half of the 1950s, performers and record companies began to cash in on popular religious sentiments. For example, in 1955 "Angels in the Sky" by the Crew Cuts and "The Bible Tells Me So" by Don Cornell reached the top fifteen on *Billboard*'s

---

30. Bergler, *Juvenilization of American Christianity*, 52.
31. A. W. Tozer, *Man—the Dwelling Place of God* (n.p.: Bibliotech, 2020), 136.
32. Tozer, *Man—the Dwelling Place of God*, 136.

pop charts. Elvis Presley's "Peace in the Valley" and Pat Boone's "There's a Gold Mine in the Sky" charted in 1957, and Fats Domino's "When the Saints Go Marching In" charted in 1959.[33] Christian teenagers embraced the new music, and some YFC leaders either got local hangouts to include some sacred platters in their jukeboxes or created their own teen centers complete with "sacred" jukeboxes.[34] Proponents argued that the songs could witness to unbelievers. However, Tozer joined his voice to a chorus of critics who expressed strong misgivings: "Movie stars now write our hymns; the holy name of Christ sounds out from the gaudy jukebox at the corner pool hall, and in all-night stomp sessions hysterical young people rock and roll to the glory of the Lord."[35]

Evangelical critics especially denounced the eroticism they perceived in the new music. Gunnar Urang, head of the music department of Trinity Seminary in Chicago and former Youth for Christ music director, complained that some gospel singers tried to imitate "torchy croners" by "making a song about the love of Christ sound like an expression of fleshly love." In Urang's evaluation, "the use of musical 'gimmicks' like 'slides and slurs, meaningless high notes, or a crooning style' all but proved that the artist was not singing under the control and inspiration of the Holy Spirit, and might not even be a true Christian."[36] Tozer voiced similar concerns: "The influence of the erotic spirit is felt almost everywhere in evangelical circles. Much of the singing in certain types of meetings has in it more of romance than it has of the Holy Ghost. Both words and music are designed to rouse the libidinous. Christ is courted with a familiarity that reveals a total ignorance of who He is. It is not the reverent intimacy of the adoring saint but the impudent familiarity of the carnal lover."[37] More often than not, these critiques fell on deaf ears, as evangelical teens demanded that Christian music reflect the emotionally intense, romantic spirituality they were creating in their youth groups. Teenagers who grew up in Youth for Christ during the 1950s and early 1960s were primed to accept the Jesus People movement, Christian rock music, and small groups that would be needed to reach later generations.

33. Don Cusic, *The Sound of Light: A History of Gospel Music* (Bowling Green, OH: Bowling Green State University Popular Press, 1990), 112.

34. Thomas E. Bergler, "I Found My Thrill: The Youth for Christ Movement and American Congregational Singing, 1940–1970," in *Wonderful Words of Life*, ed. Richard J. Mouw and Mark A. Noll (Grand Rapids: Eerdmans, 2004), 137.

35. A. W. Tozer and Harry Verploegh, *The Size of the Soul* (Camp Hill, PA: WingSpread, 2010), 116.

36. Quoted in Bergler, "I Found My Thrill," 139.

37. A. W. Tozer, *Born After Midnight* (Camp Hill, PA: Christian Publications, 1989), 38.

### Juvenilization of Evangelical Worship

Leaders justified youth culture Christianity by asserting that Youth for Christ was not a church and its rallies were not church services. But one of the most pressing questions the evangelical movement would eventually face was how the activities of "parachurch" movements like Youth for Christ related to Sunday-morning worship. Periodically, youth led services in traditional congregational settings, but these occasional efforts were not frequent enough for many youth ministers and their charges. Youth groups obtained permission to conduct services away from the sanctuary, in a youth building or the basement. It was here that the local church youth ministry could try to match the parachurch events. Teens were segregated from the rest of the congregation, and while this move seemed regrettable, many believed it was the only way for the church to hold on to the younger generation.[38] The problem, of course, was that youths inevitably grew into adults. Although the teenagers of the church outgrew youth worship services, they did not outgrow their love of the musical styles, freshness, and freedom they had encountered in these events. It seemed that the "youth group" would have to be continued into adulthood. American evangelicals had created what Thomas Bergler aptly calls a "juvenilized" Christianity.

By the time of Tozer's death in 1963, YFC youth rallies had run their course. Teens had many other options for social activities, and as a growing alienation between generations culminated in the late sixties, the idea of spending Saturday night with their parents and other adults became unappealing.[39] In the early 1970s, however, two young men reinvented the rally and placed it squarely in the local church: David Holmbo, youth minister and associate music minister at South Park Church in Park Ridge, Illinois, and his friend Bill Hybels. Youth ministry historian Mark Senter reports that instead of organizing a rally, Holmbo and Hybels created the same dynamics within their church on Tuesday night.[40] Son City, as their program came to be called, used virtually every method previously associated with rallies, including contemporary music, drama, testimonies, media, and preaching that was highly relevant to students' lives. Son City became everything that the Youth for Christ rallies had ever been, except that it was now based in a church and had a distinctly seventies flair. When attendance grew to approximately one thousand young people, the leadership of Son City decided to implement these same principles

38. Terry W. York, *America's Worship Wars* (Peabody, MA: Hendrickson, 2003), 27.
39. Mark H. Senter III, *When God Shows Up: A History of Protestant Youth Ministry in America* (Grand Rapids: Baker Academic, 2010), 271.
40. Senter, *When God Shows Up*, 268–69.

on an adult level by starting a church. Willow Creek Community Church was born, and within two years of its founding, services grew from 125 to 2,000 people. For the next thirty-plus years, evangelical churches around the country would imitate Willow Creek's marketing strategies and entertaining worship style. American evangelicals recreated old-time religion in the trappings of youth counterculture and in so doing inaugurated a new "juvenilized" version of Christianity.

## Practical Implications for Worship

What "new measures" have helped or hindered American worship in the twenty-first century? What are the risks and the benefits in promoting special worship styles for a specific age group? The case studies we have just examined illustrate how difficult it can be to balance novelty and tradition in worship.

Tozer once asked his readers to imagine a newspaper advertisement that one of the "snappy gospeleers" of his day might write to announce an upcoming revival meeting by Charles Finney. Tozer worried that it might sound something like this:

> Here's what you've been waiting for!
> Presenting Chas. G. (Chuck) Finney
> Amazing revival star
> Sharp at 8:00
> "Chuck" will give out with some thrilling talk.
> He preaches—but good.[41]

"A thing like that is too horrible to contemplate without pain," Tozer declared, opining that the great revivalist of the Second Great Awakening himself "would have blasted such tawdry boasting out of the world."[42] By contrast, Tozer worried that many of his contemporaries not only allowed such talk about themselves but actually seemed to delight in it. Finney himself worried about the long-term consequences of some of his innovations. Writing a decade after the introduction of the anxious bench, Finney observed, "Efforts to promote revivals of religion have become so mechanical, there is so much policy and machinery, so much dependence upon means and measures, so much of man and so little of God, that the character of revivals has greatly

---

41. Quoted in Lyle Dorsett, *A Passion for God: The Spiritual Journey of A. W. Tozer* (Chicago: Moody, 2008), 182.

42. Dorsett, *A Passion for God*, 182.

changed within the last few years."[43] While the complex relationship between worship and evangelism needs to be renegotiated in every generation, perhaps the lesson to be learned from Finney and Tozer is this: God is as capable of using new ways of spreading the gospel as he is of using the old. However, we limit the Spirit, splinter the church, and are guilty of idolatry if we insist that novelty is the only means God has chosen to bless.

## For Further Reading

Bebbington, David W. *Evangelicalism in Modern Britain: A History from the 1730s to the 1980s*. London: Routledge, 1996.

Bergler, Thomas E. *The Juvenilization of American Christianity*. Grand Rapids: Eerdmans, 2012.

Lim, Swee-Hong, and Lester Ruth. *Lovin' on Jesus: A Concise History of Contemporary Worship*. Nashville: Abingdon, 2017.

Ross, Melanie C. *Evangelical Worship: An American Mosaic*. New York: Oxford University Press, 2021.

43. Charles G. Finney and William Gerald MacLoughlin, *Lectures on Revivals of Religion* (Cambridge, MA: Belknap Press 1960), 1.

# — 18 —

# Pentecostal and Charismatic Practices of Worship

## J. Kwabena Asamoah-Gyadu

In this chapter we look at worship practices within Pentecostal and charismatic streams of Christianity. The theological core of the Pentecostal faith is the experience of the Holy Spirit and the manifestation of his gifts and graces in the church. The analogous expressions "Pentecostal" and "charismatic" thus refer to Christian movements in which the experience of the Holy Spirit is affirmed, valued, and consciously promoted as normative to Christian life and worship in keeping with developments in the early church.[1] The religious activities of Pentecostal/charismatic churches and movements have influenced expressions of other forms of Christianity in many ways. A visible expression of this impact is the way in which Pentecostal/charismatic worship practices have been adopted by or have indirectly influenced those of non-Pentecostal denominations. The embrace of charismatic renewal movements within historic mission denominations, for example, has become an important means through which these older churches are becoming "pentecostal-ized." Developments in media technology within the past half century have opened up the world, and with religious activity now very much a mediatized

---

1. J. Kwabena Asamoah-Gyadu, *African Charismatics: A Study of Independent Indigenous Pentecostal and Charismatic Movements in Ghana* (Leiden: Brill, 2005).

phenomenon, faith institutions tend to influence each other through media access.

Pentecostal worship practices have influenced non-Pentecostals through a variety of means. Pentecostal gospel music is now widely available on the internet and through televised services. These services also circulate through portable recording devices, making access to them easy and convenient. Additionally, Pentecostal-style gospel-life prerecorded music, with every conceivable musical instrument at play, makes possible the use of technology-driven music without musical experts being physically present. Pentecostal-style "praise and worship" segments—consisting of the singing of choruses, mass extemporaneous praying, and prophetic declarations—have found their way into hitherto formal liturgical mainline church services to enliven them. These diffused innovations in worship, consisting of the incorporation of charismatic phenomena into historic mission denominations, help accommodate the desire of the youth for contemporary, spontaneous, and entertaining forms of religious expression.

## Pentecostal Worship

Worship as a theological idea refers to the total human response to God's salvific agenda as revealed in Jesus Christ. Worship is essentially the celebration of the acts of God in history as articulated in the Christ event.[2] It is supposed to be a holistic lifestyle activity that is an outflow of the relationship that believers have with the living God. However, worship is also used to describe what Christian congregations do when they gather as believers. Paul outlines in Colossians 3:16 that, when they come together, believers are supposed to "admonish one another" and sing psalms and hymns to God (NIV). This means the expression "worship" could also be used as a verb with reference to engagement in specific activities that affirm belief in God. All those actions—whether verbal or nonverbal, public or private, ordered or spontaneous, symbolic or imaginative—through which Christians respond to God in Christ therefore constitute worship.

In 1 Corinthians 14, Paul places these activities within the context of the assembly of the church for worship. He takes it for granted that the ingredients of worship will emanate spontaneously from the church's experience of the Spirit of God in the worshiping community. We deal here in this chapter with worship as a liturgical activity in which Pentecostals engage in specific practices meant to express faith and belief in the God of salvation. As a stream

2. Franklin M. Segler, *Worship: Its Theology and Practice* (Nashville: Broadman, 1967), 8.

of religion that believes in the experience of the Holy Spirit, Pentecostalism's most significant features include the normalization of speaking in tongues, revelations, prophecies, healing, exorcism or deliverance, and other pneumatic phenomena in Christian life and worship. Unlike, say, in the historic mission denominations where belief in the Holy Spirit may only be confessed as a creedal formula, in Pentecostal/charismatic Christianity belief and experience are always held together. The experiences in question relate to those pneumatic manifestations that for Pentecostals are a sign of the presence of the Spirit either upon a person or within worship gatherings.

Pentecostals believe the Spirit of God is in action in such manifestations as speaking in tongues, prophesying, seeing visions and receiving revelations, and other inspired utterances such as declarations of words of knowledge. It is precisely because of the experiences of the manifestations of the Spirit that Pentecostals usually describe particular worship services as powerful or full of the anointing. The anointing refers to God's power in action. Pentecostal/charismatic worship practices, we noted earlier, have led to the "pentecostalization" or "charismatization" of the church, and the incorporation of Pentecostal/charismatic practices of worship into non-Pentecostal liturgical services accounts for these developments. In 1995 Harvey Cox, writing about Pentecostalism, spoke highly of its innovative worship practices.[3] Indeed the subtitle of his book, *The Rise of Pentecostal Spirituality and the Reshaping of Religion in the Twenty-First Century*, adequately captures the thrust of the global religious renaissance led by the Pentecostals and their historically younger progenies, the various charismatic movements. Cox's subtitle speaks volumes not only for the significance of Pentecostal Christianity but also for the effects of worship practices on other churches and denominations.

## Experiential, Participatory, and Interventionist

It is instructive that most of the cover pictures of books on Pentecostalism—both academic and popular—tend to feature pictures of crowds in emotional worship scenes. These scenes, without exception, show large groups of people with mouths wide open to indicate singing. Some may be shedding tears to indicate they have been touched emotionally by the Spirit, with hands raised to show kinetic movements. These pictures make the point that Pentecostal/charismatic worship services tend to be very expressive and participatory, and most of the time people meet in expectation that the presence of God

3. Harvey Cox, *Fire from Heaven: The Rise of Pentecostal Spirituality and the Reshaping of Religion in the Twenty-First Century* (Reading, MA: Addison-Wesley, 1995).

will fall powerfully on those gathered. The worship services are cathartic and interventionist in terms of expectations of divine-human encounters.

On what constitutes Pentecostal/charismatic worship practices, consider this historical development from the life of the church in the West African country of Ghana. In the mid-1960s the Synod of the Presbyterian Church of Ghana (PCG) appointed a committee to look into why large numbers of their members were leaving the PCG to join Pentecostal churches or attend their meetings. The committee came to the conclusion that many Presbyterians who joined the meetings of the Pentecostals did so because of disappointments with the religious culture and spirituality of their own denominations. The general complaint was that Presbyterian worship services were dull and they lacked spiritual power and sufficient prayer.[4] What is important here is the distinction drawn by the PCG committee between worship in their denomination and that of the Pentecostals.

The observations point firstly to what constitutes Pentecostal worship practices and secondly to why these practices appealed better to mainline church members even then: "The worship is appealing, and people take an active part in it and obviously enjoy it. Sermons are usually interrupted by hymns and hallelujah or Amen shouts. The service is enriched by dancing, clapping of hands and the use of rhythmic instruments like hand drum, banjo and cymbals. The quality of their church-music and preaching may be poorer than in our church but is much more appreciated by people who can enjoy it for hours."[5] In other words, the committee acknowledged that Pentecostal worship services were expressive, exuberant, and spontaneous with the extensive use of musical instruments helping to enliven the atmosphere. In addition to the observations above, the PCG committee referred to Bible teaching, healing, and miracles that were present at indigenous Pentecostal worship services, also contributing to their attractiveness to people. In indigenous Pentecostal worship, the report noted, a number of signs were shown in order to prove to everybody that the Holy Spirit was present and working. The PCG, on the basis of these observations, subsequently encouraged the formation of renewal groups within its congregations and also allowed for innovations in its liturgical practices that have continued until today.

What exactly constitutes the worship practices that had become so attractive to African Presbyterians with their Western Reformation heritage? While the beliefs of historic mission churches may be embodied in codified creeds,

4. Presbyterian Church of Ghana, Minutes of the 37th Synod Report, August 29–31, 1966, 42 (hereafter, PCG Synod Report).

5. PCG Synod Report, 42.

formal theological systems, icons, and ordered liturgical structures and colors, as noted earlier, those of Pentecostalism are usually "embedded in testimonies, ecstatic speech, and bodily movement."[6] When Christian G. Baëta studied the African spiritual churches in Ghana in the early 1960s, he described their worship as consisting of certain activities that are explained in terms of the experience of the Holy Spirit. He then noted the following: "These activities and 'signs' include rhythmic swaying of the body, usually with stamping, to repetitive music . . . , hand-clappings, ejaculations, poignant cries and prayers, dancing, leaping, and various motor reactions expressive of intense religious emotion; prophesyings, 'speaking with tongues,' falling into trances, relating dreams and visions, and 'witnessing,' i.e. recounting publicly one's own experience of miraculous redemption."[7]

These are the practices that had proven attractive to Presbyterians and that the various denominations now incorporate into their worship services too. Pentecostal worship practices are based on the nature of Pentecostal spirituality, which is seen in the experiential and interventionist approach of Pentecostals to religion. Pentecost, Cox writes, is about the experience of God, not about abstract religious ideas. Thus, Pentecostal spirituality depicts a God who does not remain aloof but reaches down through the power of the Spirit to touch human hearts in the midst of life's turmoil.[8] For Pentecostals, worship offers an auspicious context to encounter a living and transforming God.

### Pentecostal Worship as Experiential

Earlier I noted that at the heart of Pentecostal practices of worship is the experience of the Holy Spirit. The most fundamental religious experience that defines this experiential character of Pentecostalism is what is described as the baptism of the Holy Spirit with the evidence of speaking in tongues. Glossolalia, as it is called, is the Spirit-inspired utterance that Pentecostals believe must accompany the baptism in the Holy Spirit following conversion. Speaking in tongues plays a very democratizing role in worship. It is used in public prayer, in prophetic utterances, and also in singing, what is known as "singing in the Spirit." The gift of tongues allows people to pray in nonrational, meditative language that is not mediated.[9] Indeed, the public usage of tongues is one phenomenon that still distinguishes Pentecostal worship

6. Cox, *Fire from Heaven*, 15.
7. Christian G. Baëta, *Prophetism in Ghana: A Study of Some Spiritual Churches* (London: SCM, 1962), 1.
8. Cox, *Fire from Heaven*, 5.
9. Walter J. Hollenweger, *The Pentecostals* (London: SCM, 1972), 272.

services clearly from non-Pentecostal ones. Whereas the use of tongues in Pentecostal/charismatic worship contexts could be uninhibited, its use in non-Pentecostal churches, even when allowed, is still a bit limited and cautious.

The praying and singing in tongues that we talk about here are important to Pentecostal worship practices. This is true first of all because tongues is unintelligible speech that is basically directed toward God (1 Cor. 14:2, 14–15, 28). Second, Pentecostals argue that Paul does not forbid the use of tongues in the assembly, and therefore its use in public prayer is encouraged. It is also clear from Paul's teaching that spontaneous prophecy could be delivered in tongues and interpreted in the context of corporate worship. Third, Paul held tongues-speaking in the highest esteem as a means of communicating with God. To that end, Paul's reference to prayer as inarticulate groanings too deep for words in Romans 8:26–27 must be understood as referring primarily to glossolalia.[10] Cox captures the relevance of glossolalia as a distinctive mode of religious expression for Pentecostal worship in the following observation:

> Not only is the ultimate mystery indescribable and its ways unsearchable. Not only is the infinite God unapproachable in mere human language. The even deeper insight of ecstatic utterance is that, despite all this, human beings can nonetheless speak to God because God makes such speech possible. Prayer itself is an act of grace. We are unable to pray, but the Spirit "maketh intercession." Our corrupt and inadequate language is transformed by God's love into the tongues of angels . . . the "excruciating pain" of linguistic atrophy, desiccation, and banality is transfigured, if only momentarily and episodically, into free-flowing praise. No wonder the people one sees and hears "praying in the Spirit" in Pentecostal congregations and elsewhere frequently appear so joyful.[11]

In my experience in witnessing Pentecostal services, "singing in the Spirit" during worship, which invariably means "singing in tongues," can lift both the singer and the listeners to a higher level of spiritual experience. It is an overwhelming and edifying experience that makes the presence of God palpable during corporate worship. The phenomenon of singing in the Spirit, Pentecostals would say, changes the atmosphere of worship to the extent that the very presence of the living God becomes real. In the following quotation, Tom Smail describes the phenomenon of "singing in the Spirit" in the context of worship as a form of collective religious experience:

10. Frank D. Macchia, "Sighs Too Deep for Words: Toward a Theology of Glossolalia," *Journal of Pentecostal Theology* 1 (1992): 47–73.
11. Cox, *Fire from Heaven*, 96.

Singing in the Spirit by-passes the rational faculties; it reminds us that alongside the praise of the renewed mind there is the praise of the renewed heart that, when it is being evoked by the Spirit, expresses not simply our superficial feelings, but engages the deep primal emotions at the hidden center of our being in our self-offering to the living God. Such praise is direct, spontaneous and simple. It escapes from a complicated conceptuality and a second dependence on such liturgical resources as prayer-books and hymn-books and responds in immediacy and freedom to the contact with the living Lord that the Spirit makes possible and, in joyous serenity, rejoices and mediates upon his poured-out grace and his revealed glory.[12]

Smail's description of speaking in tongues in fact reiterates Paul in 1 Corinthians 14:14: "For if I pray in a tongue, my spirit prays, but my understanding is unfruitful" (NIV). The expression "unfruitful" implies that the human intellect in this kind of ecstatic praying lies dormant, contributing little to the process of articulating thoughts in words. It suggests what Ralph Martin describes as an enraptured fellowship with God when the human spirit is in such deep, hidden communion with the divine Spirit that words—at best broken utterances of our secret selves—are formed by a spiritual upsurge requiring no mental effort.[13]

Speaking in tongues or glossolalia therefore retains a very strong place in Pentecostal/charismatic worship. It enables individuals so empowered with that grace to "speak mysteries" to God. When it occurs as a means of relating prophecy during worship, it also allows God to communicate with his people. In the Pentecostal/charismatic worship context, the fact that God can grant to people the ability to prophesy in tongues and grant some others in the congregation the grace to interpret is a profound testament to the community of faith that God is really immanent when it comes to Christian worship. This immanence of God is further testimony to worship as the context for experiencing the signs of the Spirit. It is a fairly common occurrence in Pentecostal worship to find leaders and members praying and prophesying in tongues especially in dire and desperate situations in which answers are needed to make tough choices or God's intervention is needed in the solution to crises.

Closely related to the significance of tongues in Christian worship is the use of what Paul describes as *charismata pneumatika*, or gifts of the spiritual. These refer to those gifts of grace that, as we have noted, Pentecostals

12. Tom Smail, "In Spirit and in Truth: Reflections on Charismatic Worship," in *Charismatic Renewal*, by Tom Smail, Andrew Walker, and Nigel Wright (London: SPCK, 1995), 109–10.

13. Ralph P. Martin, "Aspects of Worship in I Corinthians 14:1–25," in *Charismatic Experiences in History*, ed. Cecil M. Robeck Jr. (Peabody, MA: Hendrickson, 1985), 74.

expect would be used to enrich times of worship. The activities of worship described by Paul in 1 Corinthians 14:1–12, according to Gordon D. Fee, are bidirectional—toward God on the one hand and toward the community on the other. Prayer in tongues represents speech that is directed toward God, and prophecy represents speech directed toward the community.[14] Participation in worship is a participation in ministry because the essence of ministry is to be open to the Holy Spirit. Those who are open to the Spirit become mediums of his grace to others. When worship as ministry touches others, they are always edified and the purpose of gathering as God's people is also fulfilled. In Pentecostal/charismatic practices, then, when the church meets for worship, the Spirit is expected to manifest his presence through the phenomena that I cast as signs of the Spirit.

One of the things that makes worship in Pentecostal/charismatic services distinctive is that participants worship in expectation. This distinctiveness of Pentecostal worship is explicable in terms of the integration of charismatic experiences into Christian gatherings. The hallmark of "excellent gifts" according to Paul is to edify the congregation. The creation of space for the use of spiritual gifts enables spontaneity in worship and encourages people to freely function in their gifts of grace to bless and edify fellow worshipers. This integration of spiritual gifts in worship raises the issue of participation. In the description that Paul gives of worship in 1 Corinthians 14:26, there appears to have been a great deal of Spirit-led spontaneity on the part of the whole community.[15]

### Pentecostal Worship as Participatory

That Pentecostalism is an experiential religion par excellence is argued by James D. G. Dunn, who points out that the challenge Pentecostalism poses to traditional church spirituality, liturgy, and ecclesiology can be summed up in two words: experience and ministry.[16] According to Dunn, experience within the context of Pentecostal worship refers to "the rediscovery that when we talk of the Spirit in Biblical terms we are talking also about the inspiring, transforming, and empowering *experience* of the grace of God in the life of the believer and of the church." Pentecostal/charismatic renewal, Dunn explains, "has challenged us to recognize the importance of the emotional and non-rational in a fully integrated faith and life [and] to give place to

14. Gordon D. Fee, *Listening to the Spirit in the Text* (Grand Rapids: Eerdmans, 2000), 96.
15. Fee, *Listening to the Spirit*, 95.
16. James D. G. Dunn, "Ministry and the Ministry: The Charismatic Renewal's Challenge to Traditional Ecclesiology," in Robeck, *Charismatic Experiences in History*, 81.

these less structured and less predictable elements in our worship."[17] Cox submits that Pentecostalism is the most experiential branch of Christianity. It is, he writes, "a protest against 'man-made creeds' and the 'coldness' of traditional worship."[18]

The participatory nature of Pentecostal worship is based on its experiential orientation. Such worship involves the use of high-amperage music, voluble praise, bodily movement including clapping and swaying, personal testimonies, sometimes prayers in the Spirit, and periods of intense prayers for healing.[19] The inclusion of prayers for healing is the reason for the use of the word "ministration" in Pentecostal worship. At corporate worship, there is space for people to be prayed for according to their physical and spiritual needs. Worship services start characteristically with mass spontaneous prayers, with many taking a cue from the leader as people pray loudly in tongues. This may move quickly into the segment referred to as "praise and worship," which normally involves singing choruses, accompanied by high-amperage keyboard music with jazz instruments, clapping of hands, and vigorous youthful dancing. When the worship hits fever pitch, the tempo of the music may be reduced. With appropriate kinetic gestures—hand raising, prostration, kneeling, weeping, and other symbolic and emotional expressions—worshipers literally abandon themselves in submission before God.

It is not unusual for worshipers to get ecstatic with screams and uncontrollable weeping. Some may be "slain in the Spirit"—especially when hands are laid on them—and fall to the floor under the "intoxicating" influence of the anointing Spirit. In one case I witnessed, many members of the choir, overwhelmed by the palpable anointing at the meeting, simply cried and cried. These worship practices are highly infectious. Worshipers praised the Lord in any way and language they felt led to do, but mostly in tongues. There was singing in the Spirit—that is, singing in tongues—from several locations in the room. When the commotion ended, the pastor mounted the podium and declared that the Lord's visitation had been great and wonderful. Members shouted in approval. The experience, he continued, must be considered enough blessing from the Spirit of the Lord. That meant there was no need to preach, at least on that occasion. The pastor went on to conduct ministration—that is, pray for those who wanted to be healed of various ailments or needed God's grace in any area of their lives. The blessing was pronounced after ministration, and members departed.

17. Dunn, "Ministry and the Ministry," 81.
18. Cox, *Fire from Heaven*, 14.
19. Cox, *Fire from Heaven*, xvi.

Pastor Eric Kwapong is widely acknowledged in Ghana as a leading expo-
nent of Pentecostal/charismatic worship. Kwapong's ministry as a leader of
worship is described on the blurb of his book *True Worship Experience* as one
that is often characterized by "a strong manifestation of God's tangible presence resulting in spiritual, emotional, physical healing and transformation."[20]
Kwapong writes that any time true worship takes place, something significant
happens. That is because, as he explains, "worship touches the very heart of
God."[21] "Significant things" in this context simply means manifestations of
signs of the Spirit—prophecy, words of knowledge, visions, revelations, and
experiences of general release from bondages—for those who need it and
the edification of God's people. This sort of Pentecostal worship practice is
what Walter J. Hollenweger refers to as "oral" in nature. On the relationship
between orality and participatory worship, Hollenweger notes that "[the]
most important element of an oral worship is the active participation of
every member in the congregation, even if this amounts to several thousand
people dancing, singing, praying individually and collectively, playing all
kinds of instruments . . . and appreciating or judging the sermon with inspiring shouts or critical remarks and questions. . . . The Pentecostals thus
demonstrate that the alternative to a written liturgy is not chaos, but a flexible oral tradition, which allows for variations with the framework of the
whole liturgical structure."[22]

Similarly, the key aims of such worship, as outlined in the Pauline Epistles,
are to ensure a participatory celebration that strengthens, builds up, and edi-
fies God's people. The pneumatic manifestations of Pentecostal worship are
popularly referred to as "performances" of the Spirit. For Pentecostals, not
only does the Holy Spirit possess people during worship—whether personal
or communal—but the Spirit also saturates the atmosphere with his presence.
In Pentecostal worship it is characteristic to have a certain democratization
of charisma because, under the influence of the Spirit, people can enjoy full
participation. Russel Spittler writes that Pentecostal/charismatic movements
have democratized access to the sacred; this democratization is done by holding out as valuable that "intensely personal religious experience called baptism
of the Holy Spirit."[23]

20. Eric Kwapong, *True Worship Experience: Entering into the Presence of God* (Lanham,
MD: Pneuma Life, 2001).
21. Kwapong, *True Worship*, xiv.
22. Walter J. Hollenweger, *Pentecostalism: Origins and Developments Worldwide* (Peabody,
MA: Hendrickson, 1997), 271.
23. Russel P. Spittler, "Corinthian Spirituality: How a Flawed Anthropology Imperils Authentic Christian Existence," in *Pentecostal Currents in American Protestantism*, ed. Edith L.
Blumhofer, Russel Spittler, and Grant A. Wacker (Urbana: University of Illinois Press, 1999), 6.

### Pentecostal Worship as Interventionist

Worship as a function of religion takes place within the context of salvation/liberation, which bespeaks of "the transformation of our human situation from a state of alienation from the true structure of reality to a radically better state in harmony with reality."[24] The primary religious experience in the Pentecostal tradition is to be born again or regenerated in Christ. In this experience, God intervenes in lives that may be headed for destruction in order to restore them to proper functioning order, and therefore testimonies of conversion tend to be central in Pentecostal worship contexts. Hollenweger notes that, for the Pentecostal believer, the fundamental experience necessary for salvation is conversion or regeneration.[25] In effect, true worship in the Pentecostal sense has its foundation in the experience of the individual whose life, it is expected, would be presented to God as a daily "living sacrifice" (Rom. 12:1–2). Those who gather for worship, it is assumed, will be people with a shared experience in terms of their encounters with Jesus Christ and the transforming power of the Holy Spirit.

Paul Tillich indicts Protestantism for replacing ecstatic experiences in religion with doctrinal and moral structure.[26] Even before Tillich, Rudolf Otto in his classic work *The Idea of the Holy* had bemoaned the fact that orthodox Christianity had not been able to keep the nonrational element in religion alive. Orthodox Christianity had failed to recognize the value of the nonrational dimensions of religion, and by this failure, he said, it "gave to the idea of God a one-sidedly intellectualistic and rationalistic interpretation."[27] Pentecostal/charismatic worship, because of its orientation toward experiencing the immediacy of God's presence and manifestations of pneumatic phenomena, is very therapeutic. Pentecostals have experienced Jesus as Savior not just from sin but also from sicknesses, diseases, and other negative situations in life. Pentecostal worship services therefore incorporate moments in their informal liturgies devoted to praying for the sick and afflicted.[28] Through its process of ministration, experiences of conversion and healing, for example, are mediated to worshipers through the laying on of hands. Usually this will follow the message of the day, in order to emphasize that the message that is preached works.

---

24. John Hick, *An Interpretation of Religion: Human Responses to the Transcendent* (New Haven: Yale University Press, 1989), 10.

25. Hollenweger, *Pentecostalism*, 247.

26. Paul Tillich, *Systematic Theology* (Chicago: University of Chicago Press, 1963), 3:117.

27. Rudolf Otto, *The Idea of the Holy* (Oxford: Oxford University Press, 1923), 3.

28. Amos Yong, *In the Days of Caesar: Pentecostalism and Political Theology* (Grand Rapids: Eerdmans, 2010), 123.

Music plays a critical role in this therapeutic and edifying process of Pentecostal/charismatic worship. Pentecostals worship in expectation that, in the midst of the singing and prayer, the presence of the Holy Spirit will be felt and that people will encounter this power. Pentecostal worship, because of its experiential and therapeutic nature, is constituted by modes of religious expression that greatly appeal to African religious sensibilities. In the words of Hollenweger, "It should be clear to the theologian that the place where wholeness and healing may be expected . . . is the Christian community. Health and sickness are not private; they belong to the realm of public liturgy and for those who need help."[29] Pentecostal interventionist worship practices make room for those touched by the Spirit to confess not just their sins but also their engagements in occultic and other negative practices that may be interpreted as holding them back from enjoying God's graceful blessings. Pentecostals worship in expectation that the power of God will intervene in healing and restoration from affliction. To worship as a Pentecostal/charismatic practice, then, is to respond to the Holy Spirit as God's inspiring, transforming, assuring, healing, and empowering presence.

## Pentecostalism, Worship, and Spirituality

Walter J. Hollenweger observes that Pentecostalism has its roots in Black religion and that this stream of Christianity has been doing well in non-Western societies because the oral nature of Pentecostal theology is consistent with primal piety.[30] Harvey Cox also takes up the matter of the affinity between Pentecostalism and primal piety in his work *Fire from Heaven*. Primal piety, according to Cox, "touches on the resurgence in Pentecostalism of trance, vision, healing, dreams, dance, and other archetypal religious expressions."[31] Kwame Bediako also demonstrates how African charismatic figures develop their theological ideas on healing, exorcism, and pastoral care "consciously in relation to the thought-patterns, perceptions of reality and the concepts of identity and community which prevail within the primal worldview of African societies."[32] These primal modes of religious expressions are more pronounced in nonliterate traditional cultures, such as those of Africa. In these cultures, theology is located in the everyday activities of life because there are no distinctions between sacred and secular realities.

29. Hollenweger, *Pentecostalism*, 229.
30. Hollenweger, *Pentecostalism*, 18.
31. Cox, *Fire from Heaven*, 82.
32. Kwame Bediako, "The Primal Imagination and the Opportunity for a New Theological Idiom," in *Jesus in Africa: The Christian Gospel in Africa History and Experience* (Yaoundé, Cameroon: Editions Clé; Akropong-Akwapim, Ghana: Regnum Africa, 2000), 86.

The Pentecostal worship practices we have discussed resonate quite forcefully with notions of religion in non-Western societies such as Africa. The Spirit-driven elements of Pentecostal worship are not alien to the primal imagination. I am not suggesting that African Pentecostals deliberately seek to entertain elements from traditional piety in their styles and forms of worship. However, the specific African religious contexts within which these churches function and their innovative approaches to worship reveal deep affinities between them and a primal way of being religious. As Kwesi Dickson points out with particular reference to music in traditional religion, "Worship would have much less meaning if it did not center round a significant amount of the kind of stirring music that generates religious emotion."[33] In traditional religion, as in Pentecostalism today, the drums, music, and dance work together to invoke the presence of the supernatural realm into the natural. Thus drumming, dancing, speaking in strange tongues, prophesying, and other such manifestations and exuberance in worship are all critical features that are as much a part of Pentecostalism as they have always been of traditional African religious festivals.

Worship in the African traditional religious context is built on an ardent desire for communicating with and experiencing the felt presence of the supernatural. Its key emphases are spirit possession, spontaneity, and prophetic utterances. African religions pay a great deal of attention to the search for divine intervention in a precarious environment of perilous spirits and witches. Through the acts of possession and consultation, the needs of the people are presented to the deity for action. The popularity enjoyed by religions in non-Western societies depends very often on the particular religion's ability to deal with the evil forces and powers with which people believe they contend on a daily basis. On that score, Pentecostalism has proven popular in Africa because, by integrating healing and exorcism into worship through ministration, it provides ritual contexts within which people may experience God's presence and power in forceful and demonstrable ways.

## Practical Implications for Worship

In his book *Ecstatic Religion*, I. M. Lewis writes that "belief, ritual, and spiritual experience are the cornerstones of religion" and the greatest of them is spiritual experience.[34] The distinctive style of Pentecostal/charismatic worship

---

33. Kwesi A. Dickson, *Theology in Africa* (London: Darton, Longman & Todd, 1984), 111.
34. I. M. Lewis, *Ecstatic Religion: A Study of Shamanism and Spirit Possession* (London: Routledge, 2003), 1.

with its emphasis on experience therefore introduces a nonnegotiable element in Christian worship. Thus, as I have argued, it is precisely because of its charismatic nature that Pentecostal worship has proven attractive, especially in the lives of those who find the non-interventionist character of historic mission Christianity inconsistent with the biblical material.

What we learn from the worship practices of Pentecostal/charismatic churches is that they avoid making worship impersonal and routine. It does not all depend on the priest or worship leader, and it affords worshipers the opportunity to experience the presence of God. Indeed, Pentecostal/charismatic renewal movements and churches constitute a critique to the staid and overformalized liturgical forms of worship found in historic mission denominations. In Pentecostal/charismatic Christianity, we find a breed of churches that are pointing the way to the recovery of worship as the context for encountering a living God who truly inhabits the praise of his people.

## For Further Reading

Albrecht, Daniel E. *Rites in the Spirit: A Ritual Approach to Pentecostal/Charismatic Spirituality*. Sheffield: Sheffield Academic, 1999.

Asamoah-Gyadu, Kwabena J. *Sighs and Signs of the Spirit: Ghanaian Perspectives on Pentecostalism and Renewal in Africa*. Oxford: Regnum International, 2015.

Fee, Gordon D. *Paul, the Spirit, and the People of God*. Grand Rapids: Baker Academic, 2011.

Packer, J. I. *Keep in Step with the Spirit: Finding Fullness in Our Walk with God*. Rev. ed. Grand Rapids: Baker Books, 2005.

Robert, Cecil M., and Amos Yong, eds. *The Cambridge Companion to Pentecostalism*. Cambridge: Cambridge University Press, 2014.

Vondey, Wolfgang. *Pentecostal Theology: The Living Gospel*. London: T&T Clark, 2017.

# Acknowledgments

We would like to thank the following individuals who reviewed early drafts of our publishing proposal and offered sage advice: Lester Ruth, David Music, Michael Hawn, Paul Westermeyer, Robin Leaver, Byard Bennett, Bridget Nichols, Martin Tel, Corneliu Simut, Dan Sharp, Chris Bounds, Jim Samra, Jelle Creemers, Klaus Issler, Frank Senn, Dan Sharp, and Earl Waggoner.

The brainstorming with our editorial advisory board not only produced a rich conceptual framework for the series but also corralled leading academic practitioners to write these chapters. See the names of the board members in the front of this book.

Special appreciation goes to John Witvliet and Nicholas Wolterstorff for endorsing the project by writing insightful and original introductions—Nick for the series, John for this book.

Finally, we credit Robert Hosack and the editorial board at Baker Academic for partnering with us to bring the series to fruition. Bob's careful shepherding and the fabulous work of Brandy Scritchfield, a top-notch production manager, helped shape our efforts into an even more coherent product. Many thanks to Philip Bustrum and Mel Wilhoit for superb indexing work.

# Contributors

**J. Kwabena Asamoah-Gyadu** (PhD, University of Birmingham) is Baëta-Grau Professor of Contemporary African Christianity and Pentecostal Theology of the Trinity Theological Seminary, Accra, Ghana. He has served as visiting scholar to several international universities and is a member of the Lausanne Theology Working Group.

**John F. Baldovin**, SJ (PhD, Yale University; MDiv, Weston School of Theology) is professor of historical and liturgical theology at the Boston College School of Theology and Ministry. He is a Jesuit priest who has also taught at Fordham University and the Jesuit School of Theology at Berkeley.

**Paul F. Bradshaw** (PhD, London; DD, Oxford; MA, Cambridge) is emeritus professor of liturgy, University of Notre Dame, specializing in early Christian worship, and the author or editor of over 30 books and 130 essays or articles.

**Euan Cameron** (DPhil, University of Oxford) is Henry Luce III Professor of Reformation Church History at Union Theological Seminary in New York. He is a priest in the Episcopal Church.

**Jennifer W. Davidson** (PhD, Graduate Theological Union; MDiv, Lutheran Theological Seminary at Philadelphia) is professor of theology and worship at Berkeley School of Theology and a member of the Core Doctoral Faculty at the Graduate Theological Union.

**Nicholas Denysenko** (PhD, The Catholic University of America; MDiv, St. Vladimir's Orthodox Theological Seminary) serves as Emil and Elfriede Jochum Professor and Chair at Valparaiso University. He is a deacon of the Orthodox Church in America.

**Joris Geldhof** (PhD/STD, Katholieke Universiteit, Leuven, Belgium) is professor of liturgy and sacramental theology at the Faculty of Theology and Religious Studies at KU Leuven. He chairs the Liturgical Institute in Leuven and is a past president of Societas Liturgica.

**Nina Glibetić** (PhD, Eastern Christian Studies/Liturgy, Pontifical Oriental Institute, Rome) is assistant professor of liturgical studies at the University of Notre Dame.

**Maxwell E. Johnson** (PhD, University of Notre Dame) is professor of theology at the University of Notre Dame and a presbyter in the Evangelical Lutheran Church in America. He is the author, coauthor, or editor of over twenty-five books and more than ninety articles and book chapters and is also a past president of the North American Academy of Liturgy and a member of the scientific advisory board of *Ecclesia Orans*.

**Mark A. Lamport** (PhD, Michigan State University; ThM, Princeton Theological Seminary) is professor of practical theology at graduate schools in Arizona, Colorado, Indiana, and Virginia and in Belgium, the Netherlands, and Portugal.

**Andrew McGowan** (PhD, Notre Dame; BD, Melbourne College of Divinity) is dean of the Berkeley Divinity School and McFaddin Professor of Anglican Studies at Yale.

**L. Edward Phillips** (PhD, University of Notre Dame) is associate professor of theology and Christian worship at Candler School of Theology, Emory University.

**Joanne M. Pierce** (PhD, Theology, University of Notre Dame) is professor emerita of religious studies at the College of the Holy Cross (Worcester, Massachusetts). She retired from teaching after thirty-three years, both there and at Barry University (Miami, FL). She continues to write and specializes in medieval liturgy and ritual.

**Valerie G. Rempel** (PhD, Vanderbilt University) is director of accreditation at the Association of Theological Schools. She was previously the vice president and dean of the seminary at Fresno Pacific University, where she held the J. B. Toews Chair of History and Theology. She has been an active churchwoman with service on local and international boards.

**Melanie C. Ross** (PhD, University of Notre Dame; MA, Yale University) is associate professor of liturgical studies at Yale Divinity School and Yale Institute of Sacred Music.

**Craig A. Satterlee** (PhD/MA, University of Notre Dame; MDiv/STM, Trinity Lutheran Seminary) is bishop of the Evangelical Lutheran Church in America's North/West Lower Michigan Synod. He is distinguished affiliated professor at the Lutheran School of Theology at Chicago and the John S. Marten fellow at the University of Notre Dame.

**Matthew Sigler** (PhD, Liturgical Studies, Boston University) is associate professor of worship and historical theology at Seattle Pacific University and Seminary. He is an ordained elder in the United Methodist Church, and his research focuses on Wesleyan liturgical praxis.

**Bryan D. Spinks** (DD, University of Durham) is the Bishop F. Percy Goddard Professor of Liturgical Studies and Pastoral Theology at Yale Institute of Sacred Music/Yale Divinity School.

**Martin Tel** (DMA, Church Music, University of Kansas; MA, Calvin Theological Seminary; MMus, Organ Performance and Literature, University of Notre Dame) is the C. F. Seabrook Director of Music at Princeton Theological Seminary.

**John Witvliet** (PhD, Liturgical Studies, University of Notre Dame) is director of the Calvin Institute of Christian Worship and professor of worship, theology, and congregational and ministry studies at Calvin University and Calvin Theological Seminary.

**Nicholas Wolterstorff** (PhD, Harvard University) is retired from teaching philosophy for thirty years at Calvin College and for fifteen years at Yale University. He has been a visiting professor at Harvard, Princeton, Oxford, Notre Dame, Texas, Michigan, Temple, the Free University of Amsterdam, and Virginia.

# Index